HSIN HSING, TAIWAN:
A CHINESE VILLAGE IN CHANGE

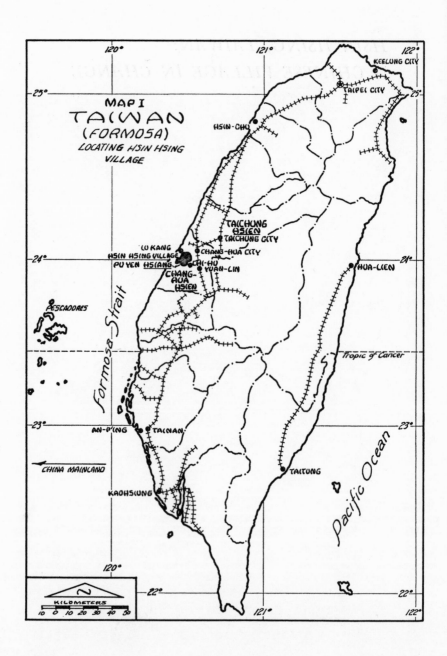

MAP I
TAIWAN
(FORMOSA)
LOCATING HSIN HSING
VILLAGE

KEELUNG CITY

TAIPEI CITY

HSIN-CHU

TAICHUNG
HSIEN
TAICHUNG CITY

LU KANG
HSIN HSING VILLAGE
CHANG-HUA CITY
PU YEN HSIANG
CHI-HU
YUAN-LIN
CHANG-
HUA
HSIEN

HUA-LIEN

PESCADORES

Formosa Strait

Tropic of Cancer

AN-P'ING
TAINAN

CHINA MAINLAND

TAITUNG

Pacific Ocean

KAOHSIUNG

N
KILOMETERS
10 0 10 20 30 40 50

HSIN HSING,

TAIWAN:

A CHINESE VILLAGE
IN CHANGE

Bernard Gallin

UNIVERSITY OF CALIFORNIA PRESS

BERKELEY AND LOS ANGELES

1966

University of California Press
Berkeley and Los Angeles, California

Cambridge University Press
London, England

Library of Congress Catalog Card Number: 66-14734

Printed in the United States of America

To Rita,
who has shared so much

Preface

The ethnographic research which is the basis for this community study was conducted in Taiwan over a period of sixteen months during 1957–1958. Except for some demographic data for the village which were gathered from 1959 records, all the data are from not later than the end of 1958. This book, then, will present a picture of the village community as it was up to and through the period of 1957–1958, although the village has undoubtedly changed in some respects in the intervening years.

All Chinese words used throughout the book are in the Mandarin, rather than in the local Taiwanese (Min-nan) language, and are romanized in the Wade-Giles system. Most Chinese terms used can be found in the glossary. If a Chinese word appears in the text only once and is immediately explained there, it does not appear in the glossary of Chinese Words.

My field research was first reported as a Ph.D. dissertation at Cornell University in September, 1961. I wish to express my sincere appreciation to Professors Robert J. Smith, Knight Biggerstaff, Lauriston Sharp, Harold Shadick, and Morris E. Opler for their constant stimulation, guidance, support, and encouragement throughout my graduate training and fieldwork. Additional thanks are due Professor Smith, who so generously gave of his time and energy in the supervision of the dissertation, and to Joyce Lewis Kornbluh for her valuable editorial assistance.

The Ford Foundation, through its Foreign Area Training Fellowship Program, provided the funds which made possible the generous period of research and some additional time for analysis of the data. For this I am extremely grateful.

I am appreciative of assistance in locating a village from the Joint Commission on Rural Reconstruction (JCRR) in Taiwan and especially Messrs. Y. T. Chen, Leonard L. C. Chang, and Stephen Tsai, members of that organization. Thanks are also due Professor Chen

Shao-hsing, a sociologist at National Taiwan University who was so helpful in his comments on my demographic data, but who more importantly, provided me with help and deepened my understanding of Taiwanese life. My wife and I owe thanks to our good friends Wang Chung-lu and his wife Nieh Hua-ling, who were so helpful in orienting us to life in Taiwan, to Mr. and Mrs. Lu Kuo-hwa of Taipei, and to Dr. Howard S. Levy, then of the American Embassy Chinese Language School in Taichung, and Virginia Warick Levy, who through their friendship and kindness did so much to make our stay in Taiwan a pleasant one.

My sincere appreciation goes to Mr. Lai Chin-tun (Jerry Lai), my Taiwanese language interpreter and friend whose warmth of personality, patience, understanding, and loyalty did so much to make the village research a success.

Much of the analysis, additional library research, and the writing and preparation of the book was made possible by a grant from the Asian Studies Center, Office of International Programs, Michigan State University. I am indebted to the center for its support and to its director, Dr. William T. Ross. Also, during the final period of the writing of this book, a number of people provided me with the benefit of their helpful comments and suggestions; for this I owe thanks to Professors Charles C. Hughes, John Donoghue, Ralph Nicholas, Joseph Spielberg, Warren I. Cohen, all of Michigan State University, and Herbert P. Phillips of the University of California at Berkeley. I also wish to express my thanks to Mrs. Hilda Jaffe of Michigan State University for her dedicated editorial assistance on the final manuscript.

The book could never have been written without the full cooperation of the people of Hsin Hsing village who so willingly took us into their midst and shared their lives with us. To them go my warmest respect, appreciation, and indebtedness.

Finally, I owe much to my family. To my parents and brothers for their years of understanding and support of my desire to follow my own interests, I am very grateful. Most important, my deepest gratitude goes to my wife, Rita Schlesinger Gallin, for her fullest participation in the fieldwork, her immeasurable efforts and help in the preparation of the dissertation, and finally of this book, and for her never-ending patience, understanding, and encouragement.

Michigan State University
June, 1965

B. G.

Contents

TABLES

MAPS AND ILLUSTRATIONS

[1

Introduction

This book, primarily a study of a Hokkien Chinese agricultural community on the west-central coastal plain of Taiwan, is based on a field study carried on during sixteen months of actual residence in Hsin Hsing village. It is more than simply an ethnographic description, however, since it also provides a picture of the changing life of the Chinese peasant, at least in one area of the island.

Taiwan provides an especially unique opportunity for the study of the nature of Chinese culture change and its dynamics. In a relatively brief span of years it has evolved from a traditional, premodern society to an emerging urban-industrial society. As more and more scholars have come to realize, the essential material for the study of this dynamic process is available there for analysis.

At the same time, until fieldwork can be carried on again on the Chinese mainland, research in Taiwan is perhaps the closest one can come to studying a Chinese cultural group living in a Chinese context. This has unfortunately been the case since Western scholars were virtually halted in their firsthand ethnographic research on the mainland of China when the Communists assumed power in 1949. The several studies published before and since then, ranging in type from J. L. Buck's (1930, 1937) detailed land-utilization and farm family surveys to the anthropological and sociological community study type (see bibliography), are of scattered areas dotting the great Chinese land mass. For the extremely important area of southeastern China, Fukien and Kwangtung, where most of the Taiwanese came from, only three published Western language studies exist—those of Kulp (1925), Lin (1947), and C. K. Yang (1959). Other than some scattered general studies (discussed briefly in Chapter 2) and a number of brief works dealing with highly specific subjects, this book, which combines ethnography with detailed analysis, is the first of its kind to be made available for Taiwan.

Culturally, Taiwan has been and still is a part of China. Before the influx of Chinese between 1945 and 1949, immigration from the southeastern part of the mainland to Taiwan had been going on for several hundred years, beginning in the 1600's and virtually ending about 1900 when it was almost completely stopped by the Japanese regime. Throughout the early period and even after the Japanese occupation and administration of the island, the traditional Chinese culture brought over from southeastern China was maintained with little major change.

During the Japanese occupation of Taiwan, except for the period just before and during World War II when they attempted to Japanize the island, the government tried deliberately to inhibit fundamental changes in the Chinese culture.[1] As George Barclay (1954b:52) has pointed out, during most of their occupation it was advantageous to Japanese colonialism to maintain the Chinese social and economic order which already existed in Taiwan. It was by means of the traditional Chinese system, which facilitated the maintenance of social control, that Japan was best able to function as a colonial power and to derive the greatest advantage from this area, which soon became an integral economic part of the Japanese empire. Because of this policy of maintaining and utilizing the existing Chinese social and economic system, the fifty years of Japanese rule had limited direct effect on much of the traditional social life of the Taiwanese. This was especially true of the rural agricultural areas of Taiwan, where direct contact with the Japanese was infrequent and where the Japanese had, therefore, limited influence on the cultural level of life. Some superficial changes—religious forms, for example—were in later years forced on the Taiwanese rural people by the Japanese, but they were quickly dropped when Chinese rule was restored at the end of World War II. Today, unlike the situation in the urban centers of Taiwan where Japanese cultural influence was much stronger and is still evident, only few Japanese-introduced traits can be observed in rural Taiwan, and the people attach little importance to them.

However, during the later years of the Japanese period and especially during most of these past two decades under the Nationalist Chinese, the socioeconomic impact on the whole Taiwanese population has been significant. The combination of relatively efficient government, orderliness of life, and public health measures, together with an extensive system of communications on a relatively small island has greatly facilitated rapid population increase on a stable land base and a rapidly increasing growth of urban centers.

Out of these developments, the most significant changes for the rural population have been the extension of village contacts and involvement with urban centers far beyond the immediate village area, and, with this an increased spread of urban influences or at least their effects into the rural villages. These increasingly significant extensions have taken the form of the villagers' increased involvement in the greater market economy, the necessary migration of more and more villagers to the expanding cities with their newly developing economic opportunities, and, of course, the increased impingement of the government on the rural areas.

In this study of a peasant community, I will describe and analyze the manner in which the Taiwanese agricultural villager is being transformed from a peasant primarily involved in a basically subsistence type of agriculture to one who is becoming more and more involved in the market economy of the country and who has widespread contacts with an urban way of life. I will show how such developments are interrelated with and have increasingly effected certain changes in village social organization, community and kinship solidarity, and some of the general patterns of village life. However, we will also see that the cultural and social changes have been weighty in some areas of life and scant in others.

These changes in the Taiwanese village are perhaps far less dramatic and less drastic than those which the Chinese Communists are now attempting to institute among the Chinese peasants on the mainland, where in the past social change was relatively slow due to its massive size, poor system of communications, and lack of an effective centralized government organization. In order to achieve a strong Communist state, the Chinese Communists are consciously attempting to accelerate the process of urbanization, breaking down the traditional large kinship-group oriented rural society and the provincialism of the entire Chinese population. They hold that a single-class Communist society can be achieved only through the total transformation of the agrarian population, dominated by a peasant mentality, into an agrarian proletariat with a national and social consciousness. The commune system has perhaps been one technique used to speed the urbanization process and to develop an "urban mentality" by transforming the thought processes of a large agrarian segment of the population through education, mass organizations, and group cooperation as well as by changing its standard of living. It is unfortunate that we are unable to observe this changing phenomenon on the mainland today, because we are undoubtedly missing much which would greatly contribute to our understanding of the process of change in such a complex society. There are, of course, qualitative and quantitative differences between the mainland and Taiwan, much as there are differences between various areas of the mainland. Nevertheless, by observing and analyzing the nature of culture change in Taiwan, we may not only be able to understand the changing Taiwanese situation but may also gain insights into the nature and development of Chinese culture and society generally and, perhaps also, by analogy derive some insights into what is now taking place on the Chinese mainland. For many of the changes now taking place both in Taiwan and on the mainland are primarily due to the same cause—the encroachment of urbanization on a traditionally agrarian culture, whether enforced by the Japanese, the Nationalist Chinese, or the Chinese Communists.

FIELD METHODS AND PROBLEMS

In the selection of a research site, I looked for a Taiwanese village with several attributes. These were that the inhabitants be of mainland origin, preferably descendants of early emigrants from the province of Fukien; that the village have agriculture as its primary means of livelihood; that it have a moderate-sized population, preferably between five hundred and one thousand inhabitants, to facilitate the achievement of familiarity with most of the people and with all aspects of village cultural life; that it be fairly traditional both culturally and socially and as typical as possible of the general villages in that area; and that housing be available inside the village for me, my wife, and our interpreter. It was also important that the village not be too near a major city, and yet not be geographically or culturally isolated from the main flow of Taiwanese life; it had to be identifiable as a definite community.

And, of course, it was important that the villagers be receptive to having a foreign observer move into the village.

It is no easy task to search for a village in which to carry on research in an unfamiliar country. The island of Taiwan, which on the map appears to be minute, is actually 250 miles long from north to south and 90 miles wide; it has an area of 13.8 thousand square miles.

At the start of my search, I talked with the staff of the Joint Commission on Rural Reconstruction (JCRR), a Chinese and American agency which plays an important role in rural development in Taiwan. They briefed me on the cultural and geographic areas of rural Taiwan, and we decided that the *hsien* (counties) of Chang-hua, Taichung, and Yun Lin (all on the west-central coastal plain of Taiwan) offered the best possibilities for a suitable village. The next step was to travel by jeep within this area with JCRR field agents to visit many different kinds of villages and make a final choice. The interpreter, whom I hired at that time to live and work with my wife and me in the village, was a companion on these excursions. (For a discussion of translation methods and the use of the interpreter in the field see Appendix 1.)

During the time we were investigating the many villages, we also visited local Farmers' Associations and *hsiang* (district) public offices. We held many long discussions with local officials to get additional information about particular villages to determine their suitability. Finally, we chose Hsin Hsing village, in Pu Yen Hsiang, Chang-hua Hsien, since of the villages being given final consideration, it was the only one in which housing was available.

At the outset it was difficult to determine the typicality of the village chosen, but Hsin Hsing does not appear to differ significantly from other villages in the area. Like any other village it has its own characteristics, but as far as I could determine, aside from a somewhat smaller average landholding per family compared to other villages of the district, few cultural or social differences of major consequence existed.

For more than sixteen months, during 1957–1958, my wife and I lived in Hsin Hsing, conducting both formal and informal interviews. As residents of the village living in one wing of the home of a former village landlord, we were invited to almost all village functions. By living in the village, we became semiparticipant observers and could observe the daily interaction among people, recognize and identify individuals, and better understand relationships between families and between their members. We actually established reciprocal visiting relationships, much like those the villagers had amongst themselves, with a great many people of Hsin Hsing and some from neighboring villages.

When we moved into the village we were formally introduced to the entire population at a regular village meeting. At that time the village elected leaders, and I told the villagers that I was interested in the customs of the Taiwanese village people. Soon after getting settled, we began the actual study by mapping the village and surveying all the village households to determine the composition of the families. During this survey, we became acquainted with a large number of villagers with whom we talked about village life and some of its problems, gaining some initial insights into the village's economic situation and the similarities and differences among village families.

Although a number of especially articulate villagers were developed as key informants over a period of time, in actuality almost the entire population served as informants. During the early part of the study in Hsin Hsing, interviews were carried on through conversations; most of the data were recorded out of sight of the informants after the interviews were completed. When the informants were fully at ease with us during the later phase of the research period, interviews were recorded on the spot. In order to obtain quantifying data to supplement the unstructured interviews, a limited number of additional surveys and questionnaires were also conducted during this time.

From the very beginning of our stay in Hsin Hsing, the villagers showed great interest in our presence. In a sense, many of them seemed to be quite pleased that we had decided to live in their village. A number of them actually pointed out that life was now much more interesting and exciting for them. For one thing, our presence in Hsin Hsing (we were the only Westerners ever to have lived anywhere in that area) resulted in an increased number of visits from outside relatives and friends. Many of these people came to visit in the village with the idea of at least getting a view of the foreigners. Not long after our arrival we learned that some Hsin Hsing villagers, upon meeting or visiting relatives or friends from other villages, would actually extend an invitation to them to "come visit and I'll take you in to have tea with the Americans." While some villagers or their guests would be too embarrassed to actually come into our house, they were not too embarrassed to stand at the windows or doors and peer in at us for a length of time. When this occurred, we would frequently issue a personal invitation to come in and sit awhile. This kind of entertaining proved to be quite fruitful in that early in our stay we got a very good idea of the extent, the nature, and the kind of relationships that Hsin Hsing villagers have beyond their own village. It also gave me some opportunities for entree into the other villages from which these people came and therefore served as an important means for gathering information and pictures of the area villages. On the basis of such contacts and others we were then frequently invited to visit neighboring villages and even some not so near.

During the early part of our stay in Hsin Hsing, the villagers generally tried to keep us from witnessing or even hearing about the various and frequent magical rituals which most often took place late in the night. Gradually, as we began to make several friends in the village who took an interest in us and our work, we were quietly informed of the performance of these rituals. Once we had managed to be present at one or two of these rituals, our presence became an accepted matter-of-fact occurrence. After a brief time I was even able to take photographs of the various magical activities which are described in some detail in later chapters.

Within a month after we had taken up residence in the village, apparently as a matter of courtesy we were invited to a wedding festival in Hsin Hsing. Our presence seemed to make a big hit with the villagers and especially with their guests, who soon happily engaged me in various kinds of drinking games. With this initial contact experience over, there was scarcely a single festival or a happy occasion or even a funeral ceremonial to which we were not invited. It was not at all unusual for me to be asked to make a brief public talk to congratulate the newlyweds or to take part in a funeral by wearing a mourning band for the deceased. When village festivals were being planned and money collected from each village family to finance the occasion, after several months in the village we were asked to pay the head tax for all members in our household in much the same way as the villagers paid it. We were considered by the Hsin Hsing villagers as part of the population.

In the later part of the fieldwork, I was at times actually asked by villagers, including the village mayor, to advise them on the settlement of a conflict in which at least part of the village was engaged with another village. However, our virtually complete acceptance by the villagers did not come until we had been in the village nearly a year, when I was unavoidably involved in a conflict in which at least part of the Hsin Hsing villagers were engaged with a neighboring village. In the situation, which concerned the Li Fan case discussed in Chapter 6 (and which has been described in detail in an article I wrote in 1959), I did find it necessary and perhaps even desirable to render some advice and assistance. Once this had been done successfully, I found that what formerly had been a good situation for fieldwork had now turned into an excellent relationship with almost the entire village. Thus, whereas until that time I was still recording interview notes in private, I could now record interviews as they were carried on. Most villagers who would usually spend time talking with me only when they had nothing else of importance to do now willingly made themselves available for interviews whenever it was at all possible. What I had earlier recognized as a good field situation, and it was, had now turned into an ideal one.

Relations with the local officials in the district Public Office (similar to our town hall), the district police, the district Farmers' Association, and the local land records office were of course also extremely important. Access to public and private records such as demographic data, maps and surveys, and land tenure data records depended upon my relationships with these people. For the most part, I was able to secure all the necessary available official records, though this always entailed the utmost patience.

However, the availability of written historical records, documents, and statistics for the period prior to about 1950 was unfortunately rather limited. While a great deal of literature written during the eighteenth and nineteenth centuries of the Ch'ing dynasty, e.g., *Chang-hua Hsien Chih*, about Taiwan in general is available, such writings seldom deal with specific local areas. This seems true also of Japanese material. In addition, it has been a frequent Chinese historical practice to copy the material for such books from older chronicles. Therefore, books about Taiwan do not adequately describe the particular area during the period prior to 1950. (This problem is further discussed in a note for Chapter 2.)

The absence of family records in Hsin Hsing village makes it difficult to establish even as simple a fact as the date of the founding of the village. Much historical and statistical data pertaining to the Hsin Hsing area and maintained by the Japanese have been lost. Only a few documents recording the history of the immediate area still remain; these are generally scattered here and there in local government offices and libraries. Therefore, it was necessary to obtain information from ancestral tablets and interviews with villagers, especially the older people.

On the other hand, a good many official records, documents, and statistics relating to the Hsin Hsing area are available for the period after 1950. These fairly detailed records, usually filed village by village in the district Public Office, include such material as population records and data on land tenure, irrigation, and taxes.

These records, when available, were used extensively to supplement the material gathered through interviews. Often, although material collected on the basis of such interviews represents more attitude than fact, I attempted to compensate for this weakness by using many informants and checking their information with whatever recorded material was available. Thus, by constant comparison and contrast of verbal interviews and recorded material I was able to reconstruct some of the more recent historical events that are important in understanding the development of Hsin Hsing village as a community and as part of the rural structure of Taiwan.

THE STUDY OF A COMMUNITY

In the course of the fieldwork we managed to visit other villages in the area frequently in order to compare them with what we had found in Hsin Hsing. During such visits and other intervillage contacts it was clearly observable that the villagers of Hsin Hsing have many reciprocal relationships with residents of these other villages which they depend upon very much in one way or another—whether for marriage partners, for cooperation in religious activities or irrigation, or for farm labor and the like. On this basis, then, Hsin Hsing village is not unique but is typical of the villages in the general area with which it shares a common cultural and social life.

Nevertheless, we must remain aware of the necessary limitations on generalizing from a single peasant community, or even a whole area, which shares in a Great Tradition or major civilization. It cannot be fully representative of the many cultural and social levels of life of that tradition or civilization. No one village or area can typify Chinese culture or society as a whole. The community study per se cannot be used as a basis for generalizations about all of Chinese culture or even about some specific value or condition in that culture. Its value lies elsewhere.

The community study provides firsthand data essential to gaining a better perspective of the culture. It suggests that for some areas of life our image of traditional culture, on which any analysis of the dynamics of contemporary China must be based, may not be accurate. Eventually it can stimulate us to reassess some of our most basic conceptions of Chinese culture.

Thus, for example, while examining the interplay of the many aspects of village life, this book, like some before it, explores in detail some of the traditional truisms and assumptions usually made about Chinese culture and society. In some instances it validates some traditionally based assumptions, as when it reports the continued significance of family and patrilineal kinship groupings even in present-day changing rural life. At the same time, much as Fried (1953) has enlightened us on the importance of non-kin interpersonal relations (*kan-ch'ing*), so this book presents subjects previously neglected, such as the significance of kinship relationships which are not based on the patrilineal kin tie and the nature of some traditional attitudes and ways of life.

The community study technique enables us to apprise significant cultural facts as they may have actually existed in the past and now exist for the masses of Chinese peasantry. It provides the data necessary for a perceptive inquiry into the dynamics of Chinese culture. Through it one becomes aware of facts which may yield insights into the larger society. It is this which I hope to provide in this book.

[2
The Setting

In any community study there is always the question of where to begin outlining the picture of village life; on what does one focus first? While the question is perhaps just as urgent during the actual field-work, in the field it is possible to observe and ask questions on many subjects at the same time and to move from one subject to another in the course of an interview. But in attempting to put the ethnography down on paper, the decision must be made where to begin.

I have chosen to begin this book as I began my fieldwork—with a general picture of village life that will provide a context which can give meaning to particular aspects of village life. This picture will be followed in Chapters 3 and 4 by a description of the village livelihood, although it has perhaps been more common to begin Chinese ethnographies with a discussion of family and kinship (here Chapters 5 and 6). The importance of the economic sphere in Hsin Hsing is explicit in the very purposes of this book as noted in Chapter 1 and the conclusions of Chapter 9; its importance was implicit throughout the fieldwork as it will be throughout this book. We now turn then to the setting of the village so that specific topical chapters which follow will have some contextual meaning.

Travel to Hsin Hsing village from the capital city, Taipei, is neither easy nor brief. The approximately one hundred and seventeen-mile trip to Chang-hua, the closest major city, must be made mostly by train via the seacoast or by the interior route through Taichung City. This takes about three hours by diesel express or six hours or more by a local train. It is generally possible to find a seat on the diesel express, but on the local trains one must almost always stand a good part of the way.

Once out of Taipei the countryside is almost all rice paddies and farmland. Even in the mountain area between Taipei and Taichung, terraced rice paddies form a part of the green and lush vegetation typical of Taiwan. The train goes through a series of tunnels in these rugged mountains, and if one happens to be traveling with a Taiwanese companion, he will probably point out that these tunnels,

10

like the railroad lines, were all built during the Japanese occupation.

The mountain ranges serve as a kind of climatic divide. The area north of the mountains, which includes the Taipei region, is known for its long rainy season and cold raw winters. In the area south of the divide, and especially around Taichung and the interior mountain region, the weather tends to be milder, with far less rain and many days of bright sunshine.

On the trip south from Taipei to Chang-hua City the train crosses several large rivers which originate in the interior mountains and flow west to the Strait of Formosa. The rushing torrents of water during and immediately after the rainy season dwindle to a trickle during the dry season, meandering through wide, sandy, and rocky river beds.

At Chang-hua City the traveler must leave the train for a bus headed southwest to the old port city of Lukang. Although the buses leave every fifteen minutes during the day, they are invariably crowded with people and their bundles of produce, fish, a chicken or two, or even building materials.

The thirty-minute trip in an old wooden Japanese bus is made entirely on dirt roads. The ride may be dusty or wet according to the season, but it is always bumpy and noisy. In the dry season strangling dust pours into the bus from all sides. During the wet season, there is always a possibility that the passengers will have to leave the bus and wade while the bus creeps slowly along over the flooded roadbed. Many menthol-distilling factories, brickworks, and small rice mills line the way. The bus must cross many small irrigation canals and maneuver around oxcarts. As the bus moves further away from Chang-hua City and approaches the seacoast area of Lukang, a change in the agricultural landscape, resulting from differences in irrigation systems, becomes more and more noticeable. In those places where there is still no irrigation system, there are large areas of dry fields.

After a half-hour wait in Lukang, the traveler boards another, similar bus for the trip to the village, which lies about three miles inland or southeast of Lukang. The uncomfortable fifteen-minute ride ends when the bus comes to a halt in front of the Hsin Hsing village store.

The houses in the village are constructed of bamboo, mud or fired brick, and plaster. The foundations and structural uprights are usually brick; the walls are a latticework of bamboo strips, filled in with plaster which is a mixture of mud and cow dung. The plaster filling is usually whitewashed. Sometimes the main supports are not brick but heavy bamboo poles. Newer houses, and the older houses of the wealthy, generally have roofs of cement tile, while the oldest and poorest houses have thatched roofs. Houses made of mud bricks are always thatched.

Taiwanese villages are laid out in three basic patterns. Probably the most common is the nucleated or compact type; the dwellings form a compact cluster which is surrounded by the arable land of the village. The second is linear, laid out along a riverbank or road, and the third, the least common, is the scattered settlement whose houses are spaced out over a larger area, which sometimes makes it difficult to determine the exact boundary of the village. Hsin Hsing, like most of the villages in the area, is a compact cluster of dwellings surrounded by farmlands. One can walk completely around the central cluster in about fifteen minutes.

The dwelling cluster is bounded on the southwest by the *hsien* dirt road which connects Lukang with the market town of Chi Hu (all of the villages in this immediate area lie on one or the other or both sides of this road) and on the northeast by an irrigation drainage stream which flows into the sea near Lukang. There are two villages quite close to Hsin Hsing. Lo Ts'e (now incorporated into Yung P'ing village) is along the road about three hundred yards to the northwest, and Ta Yu lies along the same road about eight hundred yards to the southwest. Like all the neighboring settlements, both are separated from Hsin Hsing by fields.

There are a few fields lying within the dwelling area itself. These are small, mainly garden plots, and are mostly on the outskirts rather than within the village. Hsin Hsing villagers own the fields across the road from the village as well as those between Hsin Hsing and the neighboring villages of Ta Yu and Lo Ts'e, but most of the fields operated by the villagers—either as owners or tenants—are usually not so conveniently located. Many lie to the west on the other side of the road and as much as two or three miles away. Some can be reached only by dirt roads and by narrow paths between the fields. The villagers ride their bicycles as far as they can and walk the rest of the way, often carrying heavy farm implements. A boy might go along leading or riding a water buffalo.

Village agriculture is focused primarily on wet-rice cultivation. Hsin Hsing village is located in one of the principal agricultural areas of the island, the long flat west-central coastal plain. With the Strait of Formosa to the west and the interior mountains to the east of the area, there is a natural flow of water from the mountains to the lower lands and finally to the sea. The usually plentiful water supply is harnessed by an intricate network of irrigation systems which consist of rivers, dams, pumping stations—both publicly and privately operated—and artificial waterways and ditches which eventually carry water into the maze of fields.

The area is subject to great seasonal variation in both temperature and precipitation. Although it lies in the semitropical zone—being just north of the Tropic of Cancer—the winters of this coastal area, unlike the interior, are cold and raw while the summers are extremely hot and humid. Winter temperatures seldom fall below the middle forties, but icy winds frequently blow with almost gale force across from the mainland and the Strait of Formosa. Although the area itself never has snow, on a clear January or February day snow-capped peaks of the high interior mountains to the east can be seen from the village.

As in most of Asia, rain is seasonal. Between 80 and 85 percent of the annual rainfall comes during the late spring and summer months (April to September) (Chen, 1950:5).[1] During the heaviest rains and the late summer typhoon season, roads as well as paddy fields are often flooded. In this particular area, frequently the rain alone makes it possible to transplant the rice seedlings, for the irrigation water is often late in reaching the Hsin Hsing area, lying as it does so far from the mountain headwaters. With the passing of the rainy season the weather is relatively dry for the remainder of the year, and all crops depend almost entirely on water from the elaborate irrigation system.

For two decades or more this area has been able to harvest three crops annually. In the irrigated areas two crops of rice are grown; sometimes a vegetable or some other crop is substituted. The third dry crop is usually wheat or sweet potatoes. On dry land, two or possibly three crops a year are grown as well. Such intensive cultivation has been made possible through a favorable climate, irrigation facilities, and an increased availability of chemical fertilizer. It has also come about partially as a result of the population increase, which has provided additional labor to work the available land and to exploit previously undeveloped lands.

Although most of the original inhabitants from the mainland settled on the relatively fertile coastal plain where Hsin Hsing is located, the land resources could not be fully exploited because of their small number. Today, this situation is reversed, and in spite of large-scale irrigation, land scarcity makes it necessary for parts of expanding families, and even whole households, to move to urban centers to find work. Land scarcity in the whole Hsin Hsing area is so severe that even villagers who remain there must go outside the village to earn a livelihood for their families or to supplement the family income. Although the problem may be unusually acute in Hsin Hsing village and in some neighboring villages, it must nevertheless be recognized that it is characteristic of a large part of Taiwan. If the population of the rural areas of the island continues to grow at its present rate, the land scarcity which is now so severe in the Hsin Hsing area will undoubtedly become a major problem for the greater part of the Taiwan countryside.

THE HISTORY OF THE VILLAGE AND AREA

The village seems to have been founded about 1785. This estimate is based on the five generations of ancestors listed on the ancestral tablets of the family considered by other villagers to be the oldest
in Hsin Hsing. The first generation recorded on the master tablet, in
each case, is said to be the founder of that particular descent line in
the village.

The ancestors of the village, like much of the Taiwanese population, originally came from the Amoy area of Fukien. While the exact
origin for the ancestors of most Taiwanese is either the Ch'uan Chou
area north of Amoy or the Chang Chou area south of Amoy, almost all
the ancestors of the people in the Hsin Hsing village area came from
Ch'uan Chou.[2] Some informants believe that their ancestors came
from the mainland directly to this village. Others think they might
have first lived nearby and then moved into the village. There is
almost complete agreement, however, that all the ancestors entered
Taiwan through the port city of Lukang, only about three miles from
Hsin Hsing, which has long played an important role in the life of the
area.

Early in the Chinese history of Taiwan—beginning in the middle
1660's—Lukang was an important port city, second only to Tainan to
the south. In fact, up to the time of the Japanese occupation of the
island, Lukang was a major Taiwanese culture center. It reached its
peak of activity from about 1786 to 1851, when it was the chief port of
entry for many of the immigrants from the mainland and was of major
importance to Taiwan's trade.

In this early period Lukang was a highly urban settlement. The
city's prosperity was at its height during the Ch'ing dynasty in the late
eighteenth century, when its population reached one hundred thousand. At that time a hundred ships (each ship under forty-seven tons)
went in and out of the port every day, and the city's many narrow,
cobblestoned streets were flanked by rows of shops selling such commodities as salted and dried fish, cloth, and other products.

In addition to its prominence as a port, Lukang also served as an
important labor center and general marketplace for the surrounding
area. Men from nearby villages who found that the low yield of the
dry, non-irrigated land could not furnish an adequate income found
ample opportunity for work in Lukang in the shops or as coolie
laborers in the city's port facilities. The livelihood of many of the
villagers of the area therefore depended in large part upon their labor
in Lukang, and thus the city, only about three miles from Hsin Hsing,
very early served as a source of urban influence.

With the advent of the Japanese in 1895, Lukang very soon lost its importance as a port, for Japan's plans for the colonization of Taiwan did not include maintaining Lukang as a trade and immigration center. The Japanese set about cutting off the movement of people and goods between Taiwan and the mainland, and, to divert the colony's trade from China to Japan, they built the port of Keelung in northern Taiwan (Barclay, 1954b:12, 18–42). The demise of Lukang both as a port and as a major urban center was hastened by the silting up of the harbor, which had begun even before the coming of the Japanese. As a result of Japanese indifference to Lukang as a port, the harbor soon became unusable.

The final blow by which the Japanese doomed Lukang's importance was the routing of the extensive west coast railroad system far from Lukang. The city could then neither be maintained as a major market town nor as a point of trans-shipment for the area's produce. Its decline as an urban center and as an influence on the surrounding area was reflected in an accompanying population decrease from one hundred thousand in the late eighteenth century to fifty-one thousand in 1954 (*Women te Lukang Chen*, 1954). The decrease took place despite the high rate of population growth in the rest of Taiwan.

Today, Lukang stands several miles from the sea, a city much diminished in size and importance. It offers little economic opportunity for its inhabitants, and despite some light industry, few village people are employed there. Nevertheless, although it is now a small, out-of-the-way city, it offers nearby villagers a convenient local marketplace and a center for some entertainment. Most important, it still functions as a religious center. From the earliest times the Chinese immigrants brought their gods with them from the mainland to Taiwan. These gods and goddesses, such as Matsu, became firmly established as important deities in Taiwan; the Matsu temple in Lukang is believed by the people of the area to be the oldest or second oldest Matsu temple on the island. For this reason Lukang is still one of the most important focal points for the religious pilgrimages of those who maintain loyalty to the Goddess Matsu.

The historical picture of this area at the time of the late Ch'ing dynasty comes from data furnished by older or better educated residents of the area and several local Chinese and Japanese gazetteers.[3] These various sources were used, wherever possible, to corroborate one another. The sources note that in the late nineteenth century the area was sparsely populated and that its inhabitants lived in constant fear of bandits. Up to the early part of the twentieth century dry farming produced most of the staples grown, since there was only a very limited system of irrigation. Crops like wheat, soybeans, sorghum, sweet potatoes, peanuts, a plant used to make dye for cloth, and broom grass were the main products. Rice growing played little part in the economy. The almost total lack of irrigation, presumably combined with a high mortality rate, prevented any rapid increase in population. There were not even enough people to exploit the land fully.

The present area of Hsin Hsing was at that time the site of only a few scattered households. The inhabitants were so few and so weak, and the bandits so many and so strong, that Hsin Hsing and eleven nearby villages formed a mutual protection association. When a village was attacked by bandits, it sounded large gongs as an alarm signal; the signal was relayed from village to village, and the able-bodied men rushed to the aid of the community under attack. The associated villages still maintain an informal organization today, though its function is now the production of a joint annual religious procession (which will be discussed in Chapter 8).

The coming of the Japanese to Taiwan had major repercussions not only for Lukang but for the Hsin Hsing village area generally. Once their rule was established on the island, the Japanese moved quickly to bring about law and order by suppressing the bandits. They eliminated the lawless element from the countryside and brought new security to the village people.

The Japanese also took in hand the extreme complexities of a tri-level land tenure system of landlords, tenants, and subtenants. (See details in Chapter 4.) In order to establish clear property rights and increase the efficiency of tax assessment and collection, the Japanese carried out extensive land surveys from about 1898. In 1905 the "Land Investigation Regulations" were promulgated; they resulted in a greatly simplified land tenure structure which included only landlords and tenants. This basic system is still in force today. Even in more recent years, although the Land Reform Program of the Chinese Nationalist government modified the internal content of the land tenure structure, its form has remained roughly the same.

At the same time, the Japanese gradually extended the irrigation system to serve much larger areas (see *Pu Yen Chuang Yen Ke Chih*)[4] as part of their effort to integrate the colonial area of Taiwan into the Japanese economy. The development of a major irrigation system enabled the agricultural population to expand its rice production greatly, and this rice ultimately became its major export to the Japanese homeland (Barclay, 1954b:18–42).[5]

The expansion of the irrigation system, accompanied by a greater emphasis on agriculture in the area, occurred at about the time that the main impact of the closing of the port of Lukang began to affect the villagers, who thus lost the opportunity to supplement their livelihood by working in the port. The increased irrigation meant that wet-rice could be planted profitably. Wet-rice production demands a greater labor force, and this absorbed the men who had formerly worked in Lukang.

The expanded area of land under cultivation increased the food supply and generally improved the standard of living. In addition, the Japanese introduced some Western public health ideas and new means for controlling disease. Apparently, these factors are closely related to the extensive population growth which then began to take place in Taiwan. The Japanese also improved the primitive communication systems of the area. A major program of electrification and improvement of rail and bus lines was instituted throughout the heavily populated areas of the island.

The material influence of the Japanese occupation and administration of Taiwan was enormous. Not only did Japan create in Taiwan an important element of its colonial empire but in so doing it indirectly began to produce important economic changes which had implications for the development of the rural areas and the island itself. While agriculture provided the major portion of Taiwan's exports to the home country, new, imported commodities also became readily available to the Taiwanese villager at low prices; many inexpensive canned foods became common in the village household. In spite of these changes, the world depression had apparently little effect in the Hsin Hsing area. In fact, few villagers were even aware that there was a world depression in 1929 and in the 1930's, which may be due to the almost total lack of industry in rural Taiwan or in Taiwan generally at that time.

The advent of the Japanese brought a higher standard of living for the Taiwanese people, but the improvements were offset by the war with China in 1937 and, more notably, by the entrance of the United States into the war in 1941. Japan had to muster all its own resources and those of its colonies, and good times soon turned into hard times for the Taiwanese farmer. At first, village men were lured off the land to work at high pay on Japanese construction projects, and others were conscripted to work in Japanese army labor gangs in both Taiwan and in Southeast Asia. Often families were left with only the women, children, and old men to work the land. The supply of artificial fertilizer which had been so important in developing intensive rice cultivation was almost completely cut off. The little food that could be produced under these difficult conditions was usually confiscated by the Japanese authorities to supplement the food supplies in Japan, and villagers were frequently reduced to a diet consisting mostly of sweet potatoes. The gratitude they had felt for the prewar accomplishments of the Japanese was offset by the severity of Japanese rule during the hard war years.

The defeat of the Japanese and the coming of the Chinese National-

ists brought a change in regime to Taiwan. This is known as the
"Restoration." At the outset the Taiwanese people welcomed the
change, feeling that the coming of the Chinese represented a reunion
with their own "race." With the advent of peace, there was a general
return of men to the land. Only one Hsin Hsing villager had been
killed in the war in Southeast Asia. The other villagers from Hsin
Hsing who had surrendered or been taken as prisoners while working
in Japanese labor groups were returned to Taiwan in ships. The return of these men to the land was followed by a general population
increase, and in the Hsin Hsing area this quickly aggravated the problem of land scarcity; tenancy became a greater problem than ever
before. Families could neither buy nor rent enough land to support
themselves adequately, and, in addition, the war period had brought
about a significant alteration in local patterns of division of labor. In
the absence of the men the women had assumed new roles and responsibilities and had begun to take an active part in the operation of the
land. This change was so well established that from about 1948 on it
became possible for the men to work elsewhere for periods of varying
length to supplement the family's farm income. This was the beginning of a new and ever-increasing trend of mobility to Taipei, a trend
not confined to the Hsin Hsing area, although it may have begun
there earlier than in most other parts of Taiwan. Some men hired out
as farm laborers or worked as itinerant merchants in the area. But it is
significant that local industrial development has been so slight that it
has offered no economic alternatives to the villagers.

After 1949, when the movement of the remnants of the Chinese
Nationalist forces from the mainland to Taiwan was halted, the
regime instituted a new policy of government rule and reform. The
Land Reform Acts between 1949 and 1953 were the most important
aspect of this policy. The Land Reform, the increased availability of
fertilizer, the infusion of great quantities of economic aid from the
United States, and the great increase of supplementary income from
villagers working in Taipei have all contributed to an apparent rise in
the Taiwanese farmer's standard of living. But the basic problem of
population pressure and land scarcity continues to worsen, affecting
both economic and social aspects of village life.

LANGUAGE AS AN INDICATION OF HISTORICAL SEQUENCE

In 1958 there were four main languages spoken in Taiwan: Japanese, Taiwanese, Mandarin, and Hakka. The latter three are usually
referred to as dialects of Chinese, but since they are not mutually
intelligible, they are actually different languages, and will be referred

to as such. Taiwanese, also called Min-nan *hua,* is a Fukienese language like Amoy. It is spoken by the majority of the people of Taiwan, and, although it is spoken with different accents, the speakers of the different variants can understand each other. The accents vary according to the place of origin of the speaker's ancestors. Regional differences have developed in Taiwan as well, so that the accent of the coastal area where Hsin Hsing is located differs from the accents of Taichung or the mountains.

Hakka, another Chinese language, is spoken by the Hakka people (*k'o jen,* "guest people") who originated in Kwangtung province on the mainland. Because of the minority position of the Hakka in Taiwan, they have often had to learn Taiwanese, although Min-nan speakers seldom learn Hakka. The Hsin Hsing village area has no Hakka speakers, and there has been little or no reason for the people of the region to learn Hakka. They are, however, well aware of the Hakka people and of the differences between their languages.

Mandarin, the third Chinese language, is now the official language of the government, replacing Japanese. Japanese first became important in Taiwan through the school system developed by the former rulers. In the 1920's the Japanese government began to augment Taiwan's school system, and "by 1943, 70 percent of Taiwanese children of legal school age were attending some sort of school" (Barclay, 1954b:68n). A limited number of Taiwanese children, usually those whose parents had some status, attended a special primary school system set up by the colonial government for the Japanese children on the island. Classes in these schools were conducted in Japanese. Most children, however, attended the public primary schools whose classes were "conducted in the local dialect" although the children "were required to learn to read in Japanese" (Riggs, 1952:138). All secondary schools and colleges conducted classes "exclusively in Japanese" (Riggs, 1952:138).

In the rural area some children from wealthy landed families attended school beyond the primary level. Because of their education, they were given official jobs under the Japanese regime and mainly spoke Japanese. Today, these men, like a great many urbanites educated under the Japanese, still speak fluent Japanese. The same men now are working for the Mandarin-speaking Nationalist regime and so usually speak Mandarin. They have rarely had the opportunity to use their native Taiwanese and are often chided for speaking their own language very badly.

Most of the rural people though, who did attend public school, usually did not go beyond the primary school level. Many villagers, and almost all rural women, attended school irregularly or not at all. Among all these villagers then, many learned no more than a few words in Japanese, such as expressions to be used when entering the predominantly Japanese-manned police stations and other official places. Some uneducated men, however, learned a modicum of Japanese when they served in the Japanese army labor corps during the war period.

Under the Japanese the teaching of the Chinese written language as well as the traditional Chinese classical literature in the schools was illegal. However, village men tell about a Chinese school "secretly" conducted in a temple in Lukang even through the late 1930's. There children and teenagers were taught to read and write Chinese and to study the Chinese classics. Only a very limited number of people from Hsin Hsing and the neighboring villages attended such schools, and there were few who attended the Chinese school who did not attend the Japanese primary schools as well.

In the Hsin Hsing area, then, except for the few Taiwanese who managed to attend secondary schools or colleges or who were laborers during the war, the number of persons able to read and speak Japanese (or read Chinese) was small. Grajdanzev, mostly on the basis of Japanese sources, noted that "after 1937 five and one half million Chinese (in Taiwan) could not read a newspaper in their own language, though most of them do not know Japanese" (1942:170). The effectiveness of the Japanese educational system for much of the population of the rural area has perhaps been exaggerated. Although the Japanese school system was greatly expanded between 1937 and 1943, it appears that it did not have time to develop any depth in its effect on the peasant.

Under the Nationalist government's theoretically "compulsory" education, almost all students and former students of the present school system can now speak some Mandarin, which is the only language used in the school after the first or second year. Some of the younger middle-aged men have developed a functional knowledge of simple Mandarin as a result of recent work contacts in Taipei or service in the Chinese army.

The language situation in Hsin Hsing and the surrounding rural area is as follows (for 1958): Very young children speak only Taiwanese (Min-nan) up through the first few years of school. Children in higher grades and young people up to the age of about twenty-six speak Mandarin with varying degrees of fluency in addition to their native Taiwanese. Their fluency depends upon the amount of schooling they have had, how long they have been out of school, and the amount of contact they have had with the language at work or in other special situations after leaving school.

Some men and a few women between twenty-four and forty-five speak some Japanese in addition to Taiwanese. The men learned it either in the Japanese schools or in the Japanese army labor gangs. The caliber of Japanese spoken by this group depends usually on the amount of schooling they had or the amount of their contact with the Japanese. A few men in this age group speak some Mandarin, learned from contact with mainlanders or while working in Taipei or local government offices. They do not speak it fluently in most cases, since they only learned it recently. Very few women in this age group speak Mandarin at all. The age group also contains a small number of Mandarin-speaking mainland Chinese who work in the area in some official capacity.

Few villagers above the age of forty-five speak Japanese or Mandarin unless they learned either language through a government job or contact with the Japanese or mainland Chinese group. Villagers over forty-five usually speak only Min-nan.

ADMINISTRATIVE SETTING

The village is the smallest political unit in Taiwan. Several villages make up a *hsiang,* and several *hsiang*—plus several *chen* (township)—comprise a *hsien.* Sixteen *hsien,* including the Pescadores, now make up the province of Taiwan. Hsin Hsing village is one of twenty-two villages in Pu Yen Hsiang in Chang-hua Hsien.

The *hsien* is the highest level of government in which the residents of Hsin Hsing and other Taiwanese villages participate, which they do through the elections of *hsien* assemblymen. On the lower level, the villagers vote for their own village officials—*lin* (neighborhood) leaders, mayor, and village representative to the *hsiang* council. The latter council elects the *hsiang* mayor. The present election system, except for the village mayorality "elections" established during Japanese times, was instituted in the postwar period after the arrival of the Chinese Nationalists.

Under the Japanese colonial regime the population had no way to express itself politically on the district, county, or national level. Today, under the Chinese Nationalist government, although the rural population does have a voice in local and district political affairs, the people have little direct influence at the provincial level and no opportunity—either directly or indirectly—to participate in national governmental affairs. Even their influence on *hsien* politics (although assemblymen are elected directly by the people) is very slight.

The Kuomintang, the National People's Party, is considered and referred to as the "Ruling Party" in Taiwan. The party participates in elections for *hsien* assemblymen and for *hsien chang* (magistrate of the county) by running its own candidates who are usually heavy contributors to the party. In Chang-hua Hsien, these candidates are most often local Taiwanese. They are usually opposed by independent candidates, some of whom are elected, at least as *hsien* assemblymen; thus far, all of the *hsien* magistrates have been Kuomintang members.

On the *hsiang* (district) level, at least in Pu Yen Hsiang, all candidates who have been elected *hsiang chang* (district mayor) have been members of the Kuomintang. They have also been leading members of the local political factions which include in their membership only limited numbers of Kuomintang people. In all elections of the *hsiang chang* by the *hsiang* council, the Party, through the efforts of its small but effective local membership, has always successfully supported the candidacies of its own members. (The Kuomintang, apparently in an attempt to build its local prestige and strength in the rural areas of Taiwan, also involves itself in district affairs by maintaining an office in each district seat. In Pu Yen, the Kuomintang office is virtually next door to the district Public Office. The Party office, staffed by several full-time people, serves as an unofficial mediating agent in local disputes, including domestic quarrels such as divorce cases, and also offers its services free of charge to villagers who need assistance in the writing of formal letters of petition to the courts or some government office.)

The local factions in Pu Yen Hsiang are not dedicated to any special principles or objectives, but for the most part are organized around particular personalities. While village candidates for representatives to the *hsiang* council, or village mayors, may have some relationship with *hsiang* level factions, their allegiance is usually to village kinship groups rather than political factions. The activities of the *hsiang* level factions do not extend down to the village level, except as they include individual villagers.

In general, the villagers consider elections unimportant, and candidates on all levels often buy votes. A few packs of cigarettes or some bath towels and soap may be all that is needed to secure someone's vote. One villager said, "you can only accept a gift from one candidate, and then you are obligated to vote for him." In addition, it is not unusual to read in the newspapers or hear of election irregularities which have caused whole elections to be declared invalid and taken to court for prosecution. On occasion, the *hsien* Kuomintang party committees have been deeply involved in such cases. For example, in Chang-hua Hsien in 1958, seven of the nine candidates running for eight seats in the *hsien* assembly tried to bribe one candidate to withdraw his candidacy so that there would be no real contest and the rest would win automatically. In this case, it was discovered that a leading Kuomintang committeeman was responsible for the attempted bribery.

However, the direct influence of the Kuomintang in the rural villages themselves is rather insignificant, even though the party does claim some members in the local area. For example, many of the mainlanders who work in the area in some official capacity are Kuomintang members. Taiwanese involved in *hsiang* and *hsien* politics often belong to the party. In addition, some better educated Taiwanese who hold local civil service jobs in the Public Office or in the school system are members. There are even a few ordinary and uneducated village men who have been drawn into party membership, possibly from ambition. Thus, the village storekeeper and the twenty-one-year-old son of one of the poorer families of the village are party members. As far as can be determined, though, these men play an insignificant and relatively inactive part even in local party affairs. A perhaps typical attitude toward membership in the Kuomintang was "such things are not for honest working people."

VILLAGE SOCIAL ORGANIZATION AND LEADERSHIP

Hsin Hsing village itself has several elected officials which include a mayor, a village representative to the *hsiang* council, and the heads of each of the seven *lin* into which the village is divided. Of these offices, those of the mayor and the village representative are most important, since these individuals actually have a formal function within the village as well as in its outside relations. The mayor organizes and conducts the village meetings which are usually held once every two months, organizes the village for its annual work session on local public projects, and stands as the direct intermediary between the village and the police and local government. In a lesser way, the village representative who meets regularly with the district council serves the important function of maintaining the village's relationship with the other villages of the *hsiang* and with the *hsiang* officials.

The role of the *lin chang* (neighborhood chief) is relatively simple; he aids the mayor and village representative in communicating with the villagers. He summons the people to village meetings, work sessions, and any other official functions which require the participation of the whole village or a specific part of it. (Nonofficial village functions such as religious rituals are usually led by other men.)

As in traditional China, the village officials, i.e., the mayor and the village representative, who are now elected, in almost all instances are men of some means (usually large landholders or, most likely, landlords). They usually have many outside contacts through large family networks. Ideally, they are educated and generally respected, and preferably they are men with some local prestige who are willing to use that prestige for the benefit of the village. Again, as will be seen later, the villagers who fit this description—wealthy, educated, with many outside contacts through family—have usually been members of the landlord class.

While in most instances these village officials are among the recognized leaders of the community, there are usually in addition informal, nonelected local leaders who are influential in the village and area. Such informal leaders are very often also wealthy landlords, important in their kinship group, and many times wield a great deal of power from behind the scenes. Informal leaders also may be drawn from the ranks of less wealthy men who, by virtue of their education and perhaps age as well as past displays of community responsibility, have gained the respect of the community.

Each village household has a single vote in the selection of any village official. The job of *lin chang* is relatively insignificant, and although a formal election is held, the *lin chang* is usually selected in advance by consensus of the families in the *lin*. But this is not usually the case with the mayor and village representative. Both positions have a rather high prestige in both the village and area, and as a result there may be competition for these offices. If there is competition, it is usually between men who represent the natural cleavages in the village. These cleavages for the most part follow kinship lines.

Many relationships within the village are greatly affected by kinship. Often, especially during elections or in times of conflict, there tend to be alignments between socially integrated exogamous family groupings on the basis of their relationship through patrilineal descent and patrilocal residence. Because of their demonstrated common descent, such village kinship groupings interact in various activities so that they exert considerable sociopolitical influence in the village and at times, to some minor degree, in the immediate area. While one localized grouping has a population of about one hundred and thirty-five, and another slightly below one hundred, other groupings have fewer people and member families, and also lesser influence in the village. Each of the groupings, however, is similarly organized with a main group head and subheads of smaller descent lines or groupings, and each attempts to compete in village affairs for the benefit of its members. The villagers refer to the above groupings as *tsu* (lineages), even though they are far from being the equivalent in size and organization of the *tsu* described and discussed by Hu (1948) or even Freedman (1958). (This and other such matters on family and kinship organization will be discussed in detail in Chapter 5.) Thus, Hsin Hsing, like so many other villages in Taiwan as well as in Fukien, is a multi-*tsu* village. (Within each village *tsu*, collateral relatives refer to each other as *ch'in tsu,* meaning relatives of the same *tsu*.) But since the *tsu* in Hsin Hsing village are not large in population, all members also use appropriate kinship reference terminology for each other.)

Hsin Hsing also has a number of very small family groupings; some are composed of several recently divided families and several are unrelated family units. Most of these have been unable to expand significantly and so have little effective organization or influence in village affairs. Some of these try to ally with a *tsu* organization whenever possible. This is especially true if they happen to bear the same surname as a village *tsu* but do not trace a common ancestor with it; under such circumstances they may even attempt to identify with and participate in some of the *tsu's* secular activities.

The latter means of attempting to relate to others forms the basis for still another kind of relationship found in Taiwan as well as on much of mainland China—a relationship formed by people who bear the same surname and with whom an original ancestor, often mythical, can be assumed but not actually demonstrated. In the Hsin Hsing area the relationships between such people do not carry any specific kinship terminology, except in so far as one might use a fictive kinship term to address another person who is older or of higher status. (But this would be strictly out of courtesy, and such kinship courtesy terms can be and often are used to show respect for any older villager.) All the people who bear the same surname but are not members of the same *tsu* are, however, lumped together under the heading *ch'in t'ang* (meaning relatives of the ancestral hall). All of these people therefore can be said to comprise what can be considered the largest exogamous unilateral group, which gives all of them at least the potential basis for the formation of a clan organization.

Still another kind of grouping of relatives are matrilateral, affinal relatives, or other people who recognize a relationship as a result of the adoption of a girl between their families. All of these people refer to each other as *ch'in ch'i*, literally meaning "relatives." Matrilateral and affinal relatives also have kinship terminology applied to them, but such words are always prefixed by a term indicating that the relationship is through a mother or wife and thus applied to an outside relative. However, the use of kinship terms for these relatives, especially for affinal female descendants, is not extended either vertically or horizontally as far as it is with patrilineal relatives. Therefore, neither mother's sister's children nor wife's sister's children have kinship terms applied to them; they are simply *ch'in ch'i*.

Of all the Hsin Hsing families, most of which are the conjugal type, about 81 percent bear one of four surnames—Huang, Shih, K'ang, or Shen—which in one way or another make up the several significant village *tsu*. The other 19 percent carry eight other surnames. Generally speaking, all family groupings which have the same surname and trace some degree of kinship through a common ancestor tend to live close

together—in a compound or in several houses in close proximity; they
are also usually in the same *lin*. (See Chapter 5 for a complete discussion of kinship patterns in the village.) For example, most of the
Huangs live in a single very large house, the Shens occupy several
separate houses which form a sort of compound, and the Shihs live in
adjacent houses. However, not all of the village's K'ang families came
into the village at the same time or trace their descent through a
common ancestor, nor do all of the Shih families, nor all of the
Huangs. The lack of a common demonstrated ancestor and therefore
of a *tsu* relationship on the part of some families with the same surname is also evidenced by their separate locations in the village as can
be seen with the several K'ang family groups and the two Shih family
lines. The village map shows the tendency of related families to cluster
together as closely as possible.

The houses of the villagers, at least the original sections built, are of
one basic type; they vary mainly in size. The basic structure is a single
length of rooms, with the ancestral-worship room in the center, flanked
by one or two rooms on either end which are used for sleeping and
cooking. Many houses in the village have been enlarged by the addition of wings which give the dwelling an L or U shape, but most of
them were originally built according to the basic plan.

When a family increases, as when it is extended through the marriage of sons, the house is usually enlarged. As the family continues to
increase, more and more wings are added when finances permit. Sometimes these wings are added in a fairly orderly way, and sometimes
they are added in such a random fashion as to make the house a kind
of maze. Each household or nuclear family then has its own apartment
in the large house. However, there are only three houses in Hsin Hsing
which have been enlarged in this manner. (See Figures 1 and 2 for
diagrams of enlarged houses.)

Other families tend to build new houses near the original family
house rather than add wings. Over the years, each of these individual
houses is expanded to fit the new housing needs of the growing family.
Interspersed throughout the village are the smaller houses of families
which are either made up of very small groups or are completely
unrelated to any other family in the village.

However, relationships between village families cross kinship and
even village lines. For example, several kinds of associations draw
unrelated village families together: a Mother-Father Association which
aids member families at the time of a death; sworn brother groups;
moneylending societies; a Farmers' Association village membership
unit; small local cooperative pumping station associations and an area
Water Conservation Association for maintaining irrigation systems;
and a Mother-Sister Association (somewhat similar to a Parent-

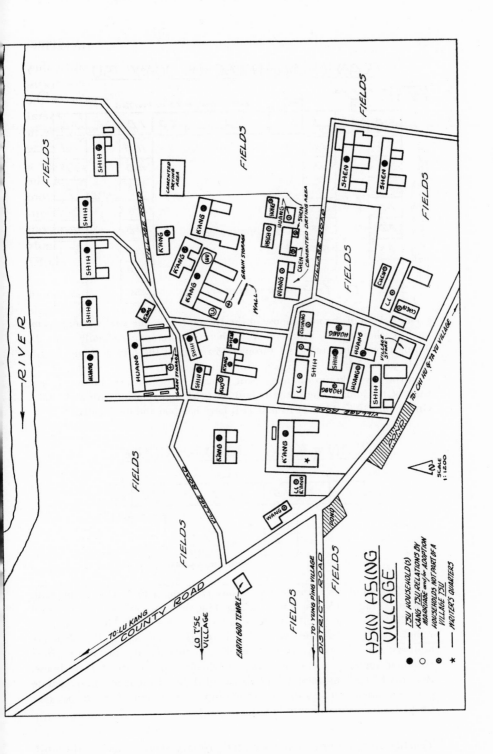

Map 2. Hsin Hsing village.

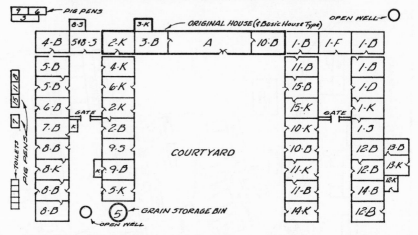

FIG. 1. Plan of the main house of the Huang *tsu*. *A*, ancestral worship room, used by whole *tsu*; *B*, bedroom; *K*, kitchen; *S*, storeroom; *F*, family room; *D*, dining room. The numbers 1 through 15 represent the fifteen Huang households which inhabit the Huang *tsu* main house. It will be noted that the rooms which make up the apartment of each household may be in different parts of the house. The house is built of brick and cement, with a tile roof. Only rooms 10-K, 10-B, 11-K, and 11-B have bamboo and mud walls.

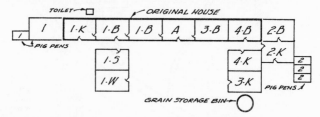

FIG. 2. Plan of the K'ang brothers' house. *1*, K'ang T'u; *2*, K'ang Ting-shan; *3*, K'ang Ting-shan's first son; *4*, K'ang Ting-shan's second son. *A*, ancestral worship room, used by all four households; *B*, bedroom; *K*, kitchen; *S*, storeroom, and *W*, water buffalo shelter. K'ang T'u and K'ang Ting-shan are brothers. A number of years ago they divided their family into two separate economic units; at the same time they divided ownership of their house. Recently K'ang Ting-shan and his sons divided their large family into separate economic units and also divided ownership of their half of the house. (See Chapter 5 for a discussion of family division.)

Teacher Association) at the district primary school serving the children from Hsin Hsing and other nearby villages. Villagers also have relationships beyond the village through economic, educational, and religious activities, and especially through matrilateral and affinal relatives.

THE POPULATION AND ITS ECONOMIC BASE

In 1958, the population of Hsin Hsing village was listed in the census records of the Pu Yen Hsiang office as 657 persons in 115 households.[6] A look at the available population records for Hsin Hsing and the twenty-two villages of Pu Yen Hsiang indicates a rapid but steady population growth for the area, which is in line with the trend in the rest of Taiwan. Population statistics for the village are available only for the period after 1953. Nevertheless, interviews with older people and reference to national statistics indicate that the population of Hsin Hsing village and the surrounding area was sparse in the early part of the twentieth century. There seems to have been a substantial population increase in the relatively prosperous late 1920's and 1930's, and especially in the postwar period after social order had been reestablished. But, apparently starting in the late 1940's and especially in the 1950's, village population growth leveled out as the continuing increase was siphoned off by out-migration.

With regard to the national population growth figures, Barclay notes that "over the entire census period (1905–1943) growth averaged 1.76 percent per year" (1954b:13). In the first two decades of the century the natural increase of the population was about one percent. "By 1940 Taiwanese were increasing at close to the rate of 2.5 percent per annum" (Barclay, 1954b:13).[7] For more recent years the average annual rate of population increase in Taiwan (1953–1956) was 3.8 percent per annum (United Nations, 1957:114–115).[8] The average annual rate of population increase for mainland China for this same period (1953–1956) was 2.2 percent per annum (United Nations, 1957:114–115). Of Taiwan, Barclay writes that "Natural increase of such dimensions is exceptional. Such growth in itself implies that some change has taken place in the organization of human activities" (1954b:13).

This steady rise in rate of population increase cannot be the result of a rise in the Taiwanese birthrate. Over these years the Taiwanese birthrate shows a decline. The prewar birthrates in the 1930's were in the middle forties per thousand persons. In the immediate postwar period, apparently as a result of a continuing high degree of economic and political dislocation, the birthrates dropped to the high thirties. For the first half of the 1950's the rates were again up almost to the middle forties per thousand, but with a falling trend so that the 1957 and 1958 figures show less than forty-one births per thousand persons.

This most recent decline may well be a result of marriages delayed because of such things as military conscription.[9] (See Table 1.)

The basis for the rapid population growth in Taiwan has been the dramatic decline in mortality rates. These dropped from an average of 33.4 deaths per thousand in the years 1906–1910 (Barclay, 1954b:146), to an average of 25.8 deaths per thousand in 1920–1924 (United Nations, 1954:36–41), to 9.5 deaths per thousand in 1953 (United

TABLE 1

FERTILITY INDICES FOR TAIWANESE ONLY [a]

Year	Births per 1000 persons
1915	41.4
1920	40.6
1925	41.5
1930	45.9
1935	46.1
1940	44.2
1947	37.1
1948	38.8
1949	40.7
1950	42.8
1951	49.0
1952	45.9
1953	44.4
1954	43.8
1955	44.5
1956	44.1
1957	40.8
1958	40.9

[a] Figures provided by Professor Chen Shao-hsing, sociologist and demographer of the National Taiwan University in May, 1959. The birthrate here is based on end-of-the-year figures instead of mid-year figures which are usually used in the United Nations Yearbook.

Nations, 1954:36–41), and to 8.0 deaths per thousand in 1956 (United Nations, 1957:192–193). These changing mortality figures may be attributed primarily to better public health facilities and improved sanitation, both of which made diseases of epidemic proportions such as plague and cholera, and endemic diseases such as malaria, almost unknown in Taiwan starting in the latter half of the Japanese period (the 1920's).

The acceleration in the rate of national population growth in Taiwan is reflected in Hsin Hsing village and the surrounding area. Although there are no early statistical data available for this region, some of the older people maintain that when they were children the

village area was sparsely populated. At that time, what are now the
large family groups in the village were only small family units living
in much smaller houses than they now do. Villagers also recall that in
the late 1920's, and especially in the 1930's, the local irrigation system
was expanded so that water was brought to new lands. This permitted
an increase in agricultural production, particularly in rice, so that the
land could support a larger population. Older villagers also speak of
the introduction of new health measures by the Japanese.

Apparently, then, Hsin Hsing village and Pu Yen Hsiang follow
very closely the natural demographic trends, and in this respect closely
typify Taiwan as a whole. (Those differences that do exist, e.g., the sex

TABLE 2

BIRTHS, DEATHS, NATURAL INCREASE FOR HSIN HSING VILLAGE, PU YEN HSIANG, 1956–1957

		Population			Births			Deaths			Natural population increase
		Male	Female	Total	Male	Female	Total	Male	Female	Total	Births minus deaths
Hsin	1956	302	339	641	17	13	30	2	3	5	25
Hsing	1957	312	332	644	16	11	27	2	2	4	23
Pu Yen	1956	13,239	13,466	26,705	654	594	1,248	125	121	246	1,002
	1957	13,441	13,784	27,225	542	548	1,090	127	138	265	825

ratio for the area [discussed below], point up the peculiar problem of
land scarcity in the Hsin Hsing area.) For the years 1956 and 1957, the
average rates of natural increase for Hsin Hsing village and for all of
Pu Yen Hsiang respectively were 37.4 per thousand persons or 3.74
percent, and 33.9 per thousand or 3.39 percent.[10] (The breakdown of
this in births and deaths for these two years can be seen in Tables 2
and 3.) These rates are not too different from the figures available for
all of Taiwan for the years 1953–1956. The averages for these years
show a natural population increase of thirty-eight per thousand or 3.8
percent (United Nations, 1957:114–115, 192–193).[11] (See Table 4.)

The population data for Hsin Hsing village and Pu Yen Hsiang for
the five years between 1953 and 1958 show that females outnumber
males. In Hsin Hsing the average ratio of females to males was about
100:94.2 during those years. In Pu Yen Hsiang it was about 100:98.5.
The figures indicating this can be seen in Tables 5 and 6.

In 1954 there were 105 males to every 100 females for all of Taiwan.
This latter large excess of males over females includes those males

(only civilians) who came from the mainland in the postwar period (HRAF, Taiwan, 1956:75). But even in 1940, when the Taiwanese population was more settled and the mainlanders had not yet arrived, the ratio was still 102:100. However, in a discussion Professor Chen Shao-hsing has noted that the latter ratio includes Japanese and that

TABLE 3

CRUDE RATES OF BIRTHS, DEATHS, NATURAL
INCREASE FOR HSIN HSING VILLAGE,
PU YEN HSIANG, 1956–1957

		Number of births per 1000	Number of deaths per 1000	Natural rate increase per 1000	Percent of natural increase
Hsin Hsing	1956	46.80	7.80	39.00	3.90
	1957	41.93	6.21	35.72	3.57
Pu Yen	1956	46.73	9.21	37.52	3.75
	1957	40.04	9.74	30.30	3.03

TABLE 4

CRUDE RATES OF BIRTHS, DEATHS, NATURAL INCREASE
FOR TAIWAN, HSIN HSING VILLAGE,
PU YEN HSIANG, 1953–1957

	Average number of births per 1000 persons	Average number of deaths per 1000 persons	Average natural increase per 1000 persons	Average percent of natural increase
Taiwan 1953–1956	46.5	8.5	38.0	3.80
Hsin Hsing 1956–1957	44.4	7.0	37.4	3.74
Pu Yen 1956–1957	43.4	9.5	33.9	3.39

for Taiwanese only it would be closer to 101:100. But in the rural area of Pu Yen Hsiang, and especially in Hsin Hsing village, there are many more females than males registered with the Hsiang Public Office. This apparently is an indication of the increasingly greater mobility of men to urban areas to find work. (This increasing mobility will be discussed in detail in later sections.)

As noted earlier, the 1958 population figures for Hsin Hsing village list 657 persons living in 115 households (*hu*) or an average of 5.71 persons per household. For all of Pu Yen Hsiang in 1958 the average number of persons per household was 5.83. These figures can be seen in Tables 7 and 8. The size of the average household for all of Taiwan was 5.5 persons (Statistical Abstract of Republic of China, 1955:27).

In Hsin Hsing village households have practically no outsiders, either relatives outside the immediate family or servants of any kind.

TABLE 5

SEX RATIO, HSIN HSING VILLAGE
(Females = 100.0)

	1953	1954	1956	1957	1958	Average
Male	289	303	302	312	320	
Female	305	309	339	332	337	
Sex Ratio	94.8	98.1	89.1 [a]	94.0	95.0	94.2

[a] There is no apparent reason for this drop in 1956. It may possibly be a result of a statistical error in the Pu Yen Hsiang Public Office records.

TABLE 6

SEX RATIO, PU YEN HSIANG
(Females = 100.0)

	1953	1954	1956	1957	1958	Average
Male	12,508	12,946	13,239	13,441	13,572	
Female	12,581	13,014	13,466	13,784	13,909	
Sex Ratio	99.4	99.5	98.3	97.5	97.6	98.5

TABLE 7

AVERAGE NUMBER OF PERSONS PER HOUSEHOLD,
HSIN HSING VILLAGE, 1953–1958

	1953	1954	1956	1957	1958
Total population	594	612	641	644	657
Number of households	109	112	115	115	115
Average number of persons per household	5.45	5.46	5.57	5.60	5.71

There are relatively few families of what is commonly called the joint type, composed of parents, unmarried children, and more than one married son with his wife and children. There are a number of the so-called stem type, generally composed of a parent or parents, the unmarried children, and only one married son with his wife and children. Most households in Hsin Hsing are the nuclear type, composed of parents and their unmarried children. (This material will be discussed in more detail under family and kinship in Chapter 5.)

As Tables 7 and 8 show, there has been a gradual increase in the number of persons in the average household in both Hsin Hsing and Pu Yen Hsiang. This is not, however, an indication of an increase in the number or size of joint families or a decrease in family division. Family division has, in fact, increased as a result of land scarcity and other related factors. The increase in household size is probably the reflection of increase in the size of nuclear families as a result of a decrease in infant mortality and a general decrease in the death rate. For example, in the sixteen-month period during which this research

TABLE 8

AVERAGE NUMBER OF PERSONS PER HOUSEHOLD, PU YEN HSIANG, 1953–1958

	1953	1954	1956	1957	1958
Total population	25,089	25,960	26,705	27,225	27,481
Number of households	4,476	4,523	4,665	4,705	4,715
Average number of persons per household	5.61	5.74	5.72	5.79	5.83

TABLE 9

AGE GROUPS BY PERCENTAGE OF POPULATION IN TAIWAN
(from Barclay, 1954a)

Ages	Percentages for			
	1930	1940	1950	1953
0–14	41.0	44.2	41.3	42.2
15–39	39.0	37.3	40.8	39.8
40–64	17.5	15.8	15.4	15.5
65 and over	2.5	2.7	2.5	2.5

was carried on, Hsin Hsing village had twenty-two births and only five deaths. Of the latter, four were very old people in their eighties, and only one was an infant.

In Hsin Hsing village in 1956, 82.8 percent of the population was below the age of forty. This is quite similar to what Barclay (1954a:48) notes for the whole Taiwanese population. (See Tables 9 and 10.) [12] Such figures indicate that the population of Taiwan and Hsin Hsing is comparatively young, but they represent villagers who were registered as having their residence in Hsin Hsing. Many villagers, especially young adult males, actually live, though temporarily, in Taipei where they work to supplement the family income. While a number of them have made the move permanent and are actually registered as having their residence in Taipei—which is reflected in the reverse sex ratio in the village, that is, more females than males—many other villagers, both male and female, who work in Taipei continue to register their residence in Hsin Hsing.

This means that the number of registered villagers who actually live permanently in the village is well below the census figure. In fact, during the agricultural slack seasons in recent years, the actual proportion of villagers working in the city may come close to 15 percent of the total registered population. Many of them, especially the males, return to the village for the planting and harvesting. At these times they may cultivate their own fields, or at harvesttime join with groups

TABLE 10

AGE GROUPS BY PERCENTAGE OF POPULATION
IN HSIN HSING VILLAGE, 1956

Ages	Number	Percent
0–10	206	32.1
11–20	159	24.8
21–30	88	13.7
31–40	78	12.2
41–50	45	7.0
51–60	34	5.3
61–70	19	3.0
70 and over	12	1.9
Total	641	100.0

of fellow villagers in exchanging labor, or hire out as members of village labor teams. (Farm labor will be discussed in detail in the chapter on agriculture.)

If we were to deduct the registered villagers who have actually lived and worked in Taipei in the past several years, we would see that the village population apparently reached its optimum size during the early 1950's. Its growth has more or less leveled off despite the continuing high rate of natural increase. This is clearly indicated in the most recent village population figures (not used in this section) which give 609 inhabitants as the village total. This figure is thus more like the village population figures for 1953–1954.

The reason so many Hsin Hsing villagers must supplement their family income in Taipei is clear when one notes that the main livelihood of the local people is intensive agriculture, which furnishes only about 65 percent of the village income; the rest comes from nonagricultural sources, especially work in Taipei. There is not enough land available to the villagers to support the growing population.

According to the April, 1957, official records, ninety Hsin Hsing

village farm families cultivated 61.74 *chia* (147.6 acres) of arable land
as owners and/or tenants.[13] Of this total, 16.29 *chia* (38.9 acres) were
still held by thirty-eight families as tenant land. The average amount
of arable land cultivated per household was 0.68 *chia* (1.6 acres).[14]

Because of the limited amount of land available, most villagers who
want to buy or rent land for cultivation cannot be too particular
about its location. They are usually willing to acquire any piece of
land, so long as it is in the general area and can be conveniently
reached by bicycle. Thus a villager's land usually consists of several
tiny plots scattered throughout the surrounding countryside. On the
average, the size of the separate plot is well under 0.3 *chia* (0.7 acres),
which means that villagers must spend much of their time shuttling
back and forth among their scattered small fields. If the fieldwork
demands only a few light tools, the trip by bicycle is fast enough, but if
it requires a water buffalo and heavy equipment like a plow, the trip
from field to field takes a great deal of time. However, having the plots
scattered this way can also be an advantage; all the land cultivated by
one villager is not necessarily dependent upon the same irrigation
ditch or even perhaps the same irrigation network. Thus a shortage of
water in one waterway need not effect all of a farmer's holdings.

Many of the fields cultivated by Hsin Hsing villagers are almost two
miles away, on the far side of the two neighboring villages Ta Yu and
Yung P'ing. For example, in the Yung P'ing area where Hsin Hsing
villagers rent or own much land, the fields are cultivated by farmers
from at least three different villages. One field may be adjoined on
three sides by fields owned or held by farmers from Ta Yu, Yung P'ing,
or Hsin Hsing. This, of course, means these villagers will have some
relationship with each other, especially if the fields are irrigated. (See
Land Tenure Map, Chapter 4, for details.) The proximity of fields
held by men from different villages is especially common in the area
around Hsin Hsing, since the villages here are so close together that
there is not very much open land between them. There are also a
number of Hsin Hsing-owned wet fields beyond the two-mile range of
the village, which are therefore not shown on the land map. In fact, a
few villagers cultivate relatively large plots of dry land almost six miles
from the village, since these crops do not usually need constant attention. In these cases the land is either tenant land still owned by public
enterprises or is formerly land publicly or privately owned sold to the
tenant under the Land Reform Acts of 1951–1952. The Hsin Hsing
villagers originally rented these lands after the last war, when the
competition for land was at its height.

These fragmented and scattered landholdings result from several
factors. The insufficiency of land caused villagers to buy or rent land
wherever it was available. In addition, the system of inheritance of

landownership rights as well as the types of ownership patterns in
Taiwan tend to foster such fragmentation and scattering of landholdings. The ownership of land is for the most part inherited in equal
shares by the family's sons, including any son or sons by adoption.
Although by law daughters may also inherit land, since they are usually married out of the family they do not participate in the inheritance.

All of the land owned by villagers comes under the official heading
of privately owned land. Land can be owned by individuals or families
under individual or joint ownership. Individual-ownership land is a
piece of surveyed land which is owned and registered in the name of a
single owner. Joint-ownership land is land surveyed as a single field
and recorded in the name of one representative owner which is actually owned jointly by a number of people; each of the joint owners
owns a portion of the surveyed field and cultivates his plot separately.
The third kind of private-ownership land is corporate land. There are
only a few relatively insignificant instances in Hsin Hsing of village
patrilineal kinship groups (tsu) owning corporate land. In each case
the landholding is small and is recorded in the name of the eldest tsu
male—who in some instances has long since died. Most often tsu land
is leased—usually on a rotation basis—to tsu family members. The
rent paid is used to finance tsu functions such as the upkeep of the
tsu's main ancestral-worship room (no Hsin Hsing village tsu has an
ancestral temple) and sometimes the expenses of ancestral worship.
The land reform law has technically eliminated the category of such
tsu or corporate landholdings.

Neither the earlier Japanese nor the present land tenure system
permits subtenants in Taiwan; there is no such concept of ownership
or tenancy of "subsoil" or "land surface" as was found to exist in many
instances on the mainland (as discussed in Fei, 1939:174–196). According to both the law or official records and the villagers' concept of
land tenure, a family—usually under the name of its senior male
member—owns land. The land may be cultivated by that family itself
or, for various reasons, leased to a tenant. The tenant cultivates the
land and pays a predetermined rent—usually in kind—to the landlord. Until the 1949–1953 Land Reform Acts, tenants had no rights on
the land except those granted by the landlord. Land reform has radically changed this. Today tenants and their families have certain
rights on the land they cultivate and therefore a greater degree of
security.

In spite of the pressures of the constantly increasing population on
the land, there has been little development of any kind of important
local industry. Except in some scattered brickworks and menthol-
distilling factories in the area, there is little demand for the labor of

villagers who hold too little land to support their families.[15] Some
village men peddle vegetables during the slack agricultural seasons or
find some other seasonal work, but there is no real solution to the
economic problem. Since Lukang offers few job opportunities for village people, the only alternative is for the village's labor surplus to
move on to Taipei to find work. While the move to Taipei for most
village men is merely a temporary migration to supplement family
income, some establish themselves in the city and move their entire
families there. Those who still have a small piece of land in the village
area then usually rent it out, or ask someone else to cultivate it for
them. The owner thus gains some economic security by retaining title
to the land; very few people will sell their land outright.

DIET AND NUTRITION

The Hsin Hsing villager is far from self-sufficient, either for food
or other needs. After the harvest the villager consumes his own vegetables, rice, and sweet potatoes, but during the course of the year, he
must buy a great part of his staple food. Vegetables, additional rice,
pork, fish, salt, tea, sugar, sesame seed oil, peanut oil, lard, and any
number of other items are purchased either in Lukang or from itinerant merchants. Additional necessary annual purchases like clothing,
tools, and other necessities, almost none of which are produced by the
villagers themselves, show how dependent the villager is on the outside
world.

The diet of the Hsin Hsing villager, except perhaps for the most
poverty-stricken, depends more on occasion than perhaps anything
else. The foods eaten at daily mealtimes are usually quite simple and
inexpensive, and thrift dominates these ordinary meals. However, on
special religious or other festive occasions when it is necessary to feed
guests, thrifty regard for the kinds and quantities of food served becomes the least important factor. A villager invites criticism from his
fellows if he is not thrifty in his everyday eating and living habits, but
the man who exercises thrift on a festive occasion when outside guests
are present usually earns the reputation of being "stingy."

An additional determinant of diet is the phase of the agricultural
cycle. During the harvest season, for example, it is customary for everyone engaged in the heavy work to eat five meals a day. The meal at
the end of the day's work is particularly elaborate and nutritious. A
man may also earn himself the reputation of being stingy if, for example, he is frugal with respect to the food he serves his field laborers at
harvesttime. Word of his stinginess spreads quickly, and such a farmer
may find it difficult to obtain field labor at future harvesttimes. The

villager's diet is greatly affected by factors other than his financial condition or even his own personal likes and dislikes in food. Social pressure is a determining force.

Although the financial condition of the family does play a part in determining the differences in exact details of meals, most villagers' meals are very much alike. Rice is always preferred as the center or focus of each meal. Various items such as dried fish and some steamed, dried, or fresh vegetables may be added to the rice. Pickled items may also be included for variety and flavor.

Many village families, however, because of poverty or, sometimes, for reasons of thrift, substitute sweet potatoes for rice. If fresh, the sweet potatoes are steamed; otherwise, shredded dry sweet potatoes will usually be steamed together with the rice with which they are mixed. Sweet potatoes are much less expensive than rice, since they are grown on the less desirable nonirrigated dry land. Generally speaking, the villagers do not like sweet potatoes, and the adults complain that when children eat sweet potatoes they soon become hungry again and that they have stomach pains. On the other hand, rice is universally enjoyed and is held to be satisfactorily filling.

FOOD AND RITUAL ENTERTAINMENT

The villagers' best opportunities for good eating as well as entertainment come mainly on religious, magical, and other occasions which are usually marked by festivity. These festive occasions are fairly frequent and have widely diverse origins; the religion of the villagers is Taoist, with an admixture of Buddhist and animistic beliefs and, of course, ancestor worship. In addition, the people frequently take part in magical rituals requiring the offices of shamans and various forms of divination in the case of illness, when demons are thought to be involved. Ample food of relatively high quality is served at almost all of these frequently performed religious and magical rituals, especially when outside guests are present. The amounts and kinds of food vary with the occasion. At one of the ordinary pai-pai (any ritual in which food or other items are sacrificed to gods or ancestors), which in the Hsin Hsing village area occur at least four times a month and at which there are usually no guests, the additional food may be some cooked pork or fresh fish and soup. This food is used for the ceremonial sacrifices and eaten later. There are elaborate food preparations for larger pai-pai dinners such as those for the village god, or at marriage festivals to which outside guests are always invited, or to a lesser degree at dinners for laborers at harvesttime. Sometimes at weddings, funerals, or other such occasions there are as many as eighteen courses, served with wine. Chickens, ducks, and geese are slaughtered, and on some of these occasions the villager will even slaughter one of his pigs to feed his many guests.

Other than these large festive occasions, the simple monthly *pai-pai* are the sole occasions when a family which can afford it may eat more and better food without incurring criticism from neighbors. Therefore, although it may not be necessary to include pork in the minimum sacrifice at the particular ritual, these occasions have become socially sanctioned opportunities for eating better foods than usual. This is one reason why the villagers look forward to and continue to observe even the least important *pai-pai* ceremonies.

At the same time, there is a certain amount of ambivalence among some adults toward the larger *pai-pai*. They realize that they can scarcely afford the high cost of such festive occasions which often saddle them with debts. However, in addition to the pleasurable anticipation with which the villagers look forward to these occasions, social pressure also makes it necessary for each family to take part in these ritual affairs. Each guest who attends such a large dinner is expected to reciprocate and invite his host to some similar occasion in the future.

This kind of socially necessary variation in the eating habits of the Hsin Hsing villagers means that the diet and general nutrition of the villagers is not at all constant in either quantity or quality.

Besides the feasting the ritualistic events occasion, they are the villager's main source of entertainment as well. For in addition to the festive dinners served on such occasions as the village god's birthday, a funeral, or the going-away party for village boys going off to the army, usually there is also entertainment. This may be formal, such as a travelling professional puppet show, or informal, such as drinking and finger games. Such events attract neighbors as well as friends and relatives from surrounding villages. Therefore villagers enjoy these entertaining ritualistic events, not only in their own village, but in neighboring villages with which they have ties of kinship, friendship, and the like.

For entertainment outside their own village or neighboring villages, the people sometimes go to Lukang to see a movie at the local theatre. The movies may be of Chinese, Japanese, or American origin. There are usually two showings a day, one in the original language with Chinese titles and the other with Taiwanese (Min-nan) dubbed in for the convenience of the many illiterate village people.

More often the villagers go to the local Taiwanese opera house in Lukang, where travelling companies perform regularly to large crowds. Although the movies and the opera are relatively inexpensive, villagers do not often indulge in these forms of entertainment. This is mainly because of the amount of time involved in going to Lukang and seeing the show, and only partially because of the cost. When the villagers do attend, they generally go in small groups of young boys, or young girls, or a group of older women.

CLOTHING

The villagers' clothing, like their food, is marked by simplicity and a show of thrift. It is not at all uncommon to see a villager wearing work clothes which have been patched several times. Even for special occasions such as a marriage or a large *pai-pai* festival most villagers still dress very simply.

The style of clothing usually varies with age. Older villagers generally wear the traditional Chinese clothing of pantaloons and jacket, although in very hot weather men of all ages wear shorts and a T-shirt when working. In colder weather boys and men (other than the older and more traditionally dressed men) wear ordinary khaki wash pants and several shirts, and a sweater or jacket if they happen to own one. For protection against the cold, a villager depends on a number of layers of clothing, usually cotton, rather than a few layers of woolen items. The cotton padded jacket is worn more by older men and women than by young people.

While older women wear the more traditional clothing, younger women and girls prefer and usually wear the Western-style dresses, skirts, and blouses which have become very popular since the war. Such clothes are usually made to order either by village seamstresses or in Lukang. Young girls and women wear the Chinese tunic dress (*ch'i p'ao*) on the occasion of their marriage, on special outings to Lukang or Taipei, and during important village festivals. Many of the older villagers tell of the old days when "everyone, including the rich, wore coarse cloth, since in those days people were thrifty." But today, these old people complain, "people are no longer satisfied with coarse cloth and want to wear the better cloth."

Still, few villagers remember ever having made their own cloth. "Cloth has practically always been purchased in Lukang or from itinerant merchants." Before the Japanese period, inexpensive undyed cloth was apparently imported from the mainland, and during the Japanese period, cloth manufactured in Japan was used. Since the end of the war, the Taiwanese textile industry has grown rapidly, mainly in the vicinity of Chang-hua City and Ho-mei, and today all the cloth used by villagers is Taiwanese-made.

Nowadays there is a great deal of specialization, and it is both uneconomical and difficult for villagers to make their own clothing unless a member of the household, usually one of the daughters, has studied sewing. A family's clothing is usually made to order by locally trained seamstresses in Hsin Hsing or neighboring villages, or by tailors in Lukang, at relatively little expense. For example, if one supplies the cloth, a village seamstress charges NT $8 (US $0.22) and a Lukang seamstress NT $15 (US $0.42) to tailor a Western-style dress.[16] Most of the villagers consider homemade clothing rather crude and neither as well made nor as stylish as clothes made outside the home. Items such as men's khaki wash pants, all kinds of sweaters, and windbreakers are usually bought ready-made in Lukang or in Taipei by those villagers who work there.

Wooden clogs are the most common footwear in the village, and it is interesting to note the development in the last few years of a great variety of design and color in the plastic band which goes over the instep. In addition, the flat top surface of the wooden clog may now also display designs. Thus, buying a pair of clogs in Lukang is very much like buying a pair of leather shoes in the United States. There are numerous styles and colors from which to choose, all on display in the shops in the market or the sidewalk stands on the street.

Unless he has worked in Taipei and worn shoes there, a village man's first pair of leather shoes is usually bought at the time of his marriage. Girls sometimes own a pair of very inexpensive leather flat-heeled shoes. In addition, the younger people usually own a pair of sneakers which they wear to school and on trips outside the village area.

In the village area people usually go barefoot while working during the day, and then at night, after washing their feet, they wear wooden clogs. The people are thrifty with their footgear, and one frequently sees men or women carrying their wooden clogs, or a young girl her leather shoes, as they walk along the road on the way home from some affair. The affair has ended, and with it the reason for wearing shoes.

HEALTH, SANITATION, AND
MEDICAL FACILITIES

The health situation in Hsin Hsing village has changed considerably for the better in recent years. Before the Japanese began their public health program, diseases of epidemic proportions were common. Cholera and malaria, which are now almost nonexistent, were great killers, and the mortality rate for infants and children was extremely high. Native medicines were of limited value. However, first under the Japanese and now the Chinese, Western medical technology, medicines, and public health techniques have greatly reduced the high mortality rate.

Through the use of Western medicines, especially penicillin, the many diseases still common in the countryside are fairly easy to control

and are seldom fatal. Intestinal disorders and skin and eye infections
and diseases are common and troublesome in the villages because of
poor sanitary facilities and practices. These result, of course, from a
general ignorance of the principles of sanitation and the causes of
disease. Since the villagers know that these diseases are not usually
fatal, they tend to avoid the expense and bother of consulting a doctor
or going to a clinic, and the nonfatal illnesses often go untreated. Only
the more educated villagers realize the importance of sanitation in
preventing illness and are willing to take the trouble to maintain some
semblance of sanitary practices.

The village water is commonly drawn from open wells. While the
villager knows that drinking water is supposed to be boiled, he is
usually satisfied if it comes close to the boiling point, or at best has just
begun to boil. In visits to town he will frequently buy a drink from a
street stand, and seldom consider whether the water used in the drink
has been boiled. Intestinal illnesses are common, although the villagers frequently know enough to avoid serious difficulty.

Clothing is usually washed in the pond across the road which
borders the village. The same pond is used by water buffalo for bathing and elimination, and the village storekeeper uses water from it to
wash off ice before putting it in drinks or making a flavored shaved-ice
refreshment. The village women wash their cooking and eating utensils in this same pond, and no one ever uses hot water and soap for
these purposes.

Most villagers' houses are extremely cluttered and, in most cases,
quite dirty. Major housecleaning and general cleaning of the village
grounds are usually done only twice a year, immediately before the
Chinese New Year and before the annual inspection of every house by
police and public officials. This inspection was instituted by the Japanese, and has been continued by the local government under the
mainlanders. Each house is examined for cleanliness and general neat-
ness and receives a grade of excellent, pass, or fail. If a house fails the
inspection, the family is liable to a fine and must remedy the condition.

The village has no running water. Water for household use is drawn
from the open wells which are scattered around the village. Although
open wells would seem to be a potential hazard for small children, few
accidents occur, perhaps because young children are seldom allowed to
crawl around on the ground and are usually in the care of an older
child or an adult.

The only form of toilet facilities are outhouses, the small outside
shelter with a hole in the floor formerly so common in rural America.
The cleanliness of these facilities varies with the household. The contents are regularly collected and used to fertilize vegetable crops. This

practice makes it dangerous to eat raw vegetables, and most vegetables are cooked before eating.

VILLAGE COMMUNICATION FACILITIES

The Hsin Hsing area has had electricity since the early 1930's. When electricity first came to Hsin Hsing village, almost all of the villagers immediately took advantage of the opportunity. According to the older villagers, the electric company paid for the installation of poles and other parts, but many villagers found the cost of the electricity itself prohibitive and were forced to discontinue service. Later, some of the electric poles not in use were removed from parts of the village.

Today, well over half of the village households again have electricity, although in most cases there is a bare minimum of one or sometimes two lights to a household. The majority pay a small amount each month to the electric company, for which they are allowed one electric outlet or light; the electricity only comes on at night. But many of the villagers, by doing a little electrical work themselves, are able to manage more than one outlet. They are especially active during times of festivities when lights are needed in more than one room at a time. When most of the villagers engage in this kind of improvisation, the fuses for the whole village's electric supply often burn out, and the village may be left in darkness for a day or two or sometimes for as long as a week until the electric company is notified or until some young man replaces the fuses. At other times only a minimum of light is needed, and usually a single light is strung in the doorway between two rooms, for example, between the ancestral-worship room (*kung t'ing*) and the bedroom or kitchen, or wherever the family happens to be at the time.

There are four radios in the village, but not all of them are in working order at any one time. Two of them were obtained through public or government agencies; the village mayor was given one by the Hsiang Public Office, and the elected head of the Farmers' Association village unit received one from the association. Small groups of villagers often listen to these radios in the evening. The other two instruments in Hsin Hsing are privately owned. The villagers' favorite programs are the frequent broadcasts of the Taiwanese opera.

The mail system in Taiwan is quick and efficient, and the village has a daily mail delivery by a regular postman. Most of the mail coming into the village is from family members who have gone to such places as Taipei to work or from village men who are away on military service. A few newspapers come into the village each day through the mail. Like the radios, two newspapers are sent free of charge by the government to the village officials. Copies of *Harvest Magazine,* an agricultural magazine published by the JCRR, are received monthly by several village subscribers.

A bus runs past the village almost every hour during the daytime. The bus travels between Lukang and Chi Hu, and at both places connections can be made with buses going to various cities where there are trains to other parts of Taiwan. Most of these transportation facilities have been available since Japanese times, although they were not then used as frequently as they are today. Now that so many villagers work and live in Taipei, individuals and their families move rather regularly between the village and this city. Villagers in the area have increased their mobility a great deal during the last decade, and today, most villagers, including older people and adolescents, have travelled at least once to Taipei.

Within the general village area the most important means of transportation is the bicycle. Almost every village family owns at least one bicycle and a few are two-bicycle families. For the villagers the bicycle is an extremely practical machine. It can transport several people at a time to the fields and can also carry small animals and produce to market. The people in the Hsin Hsing area had some bicycles during Japanese times, but they were expensive and thus fell into the luxury class. At that time most things were still carried by hand. Since the restoration of Chinese rule, and especially since the growth of the bicycle industry in Taiwan, the bicycle has become less expensive and is now practically indispensable in village life.

CONNECTIONS WITH THE OUTSIDE WORLD

The steadily increasing impingement of the outside world on the village, as well as the concomitant development of extensions beyond the village, make it evident that Hsin Hsing and the other villages of the immediate area are far from being small, isolated units.

Not only are transportation facilities and general means of communication available but they are used regularly by most of the villagers. The general economic and social connections of Hsin Hsing extend far beyond the limits of the village and even the district. Contact with people from other places is quite frequent. The general store in the village has a limited stock of merchandise which is usually overpriced, so the villagers buy only a few necessary items there. On the other hand, men and boys frequently congregate there, especially during the agricultural slack season, to talk and to play chess and other small gambling games. As the site of the village bus stop along the Lukang--Chi Hu road, the store also serves as an important vantage point for the dissemination of news and gossip of the area, since so many people regularly go past by bus or bicycle. Itinerant merchants and artisans frequently stop in the village to sell their wares and services and are patronized by many villagers; some residents, however, go regularly to Lukang to shop. Villagers who supplement their farm income by peddling vegetables in season travel around the area, thus coming into contact with the people of nearby villages. Other outside contacts are made in Taipei by village people who go there to work and thus move regularly back and forth between city and village.

In addition to the economic factor which provides these extended intervillage relations and more outside contact in general, there are many other factors operative (some which we have already had an indication of and others which will be explored in later sections). Factors such as the expanded school attendance by villagers do much to bring young villagers into regular contact with students from other villages and even other areas, especially if the school is above the primary level. Contacts between the villagers and outside are also increased by the Farmers' Associations and the general expansion of the irrigation system, and, of course, the factor of social organization and the Chinese kinship system, which is basically patrilineal and patrilocal, is extremely important. As a result of this kinship system and its rules of marriage, as well as the villagers' preference for marrying nonrelatives from outside the village, there is an extension of kinship relationships beyond the village area. The matrilateral and affinal relationships furnish important social, economic, and sometimes political links between Hsin Hsing villagers and people in other villages. All these relationships have combined to extend the villager's orientation well beyond his own community. However, it is primarily the economic sphere that forms the basis for this newly emphasized orientation, and it is to this that we will first turn.

[3
The Land and the Agricultural Process

To understand present-day life in Hsin Hsing, it seems fruitful to look first at the nature of village livelihood and recent changes in it. By examining the nature of the economic change and especially its consequences—for example, the ways in which the villager, in order to improve or at least maintain his livelihood, has become increasingly involved in complex relationships beyond the village limits—we will be better able to understand the changes in other areas of life, such as social organization, village leadership and cooperation, family and kinship, and life history and religion. It will be seen in the following chapters that the changes produced in these other aspects tend to reinforce the processes of change in the economy, and hence in the village generally.

Agriculture and the land-man relationship have always been the basis of the livelihood of Hsin Hsing villagers. The major part of village income, in fact, still comes from sources related to the land. But the land resources, both in quantity and productive capacity (as already briefly noted in Chapter 2 in the section on population and its economic base), have not kept pace with the natural population increase. And yet, from all available evidence, in spite of the imbalance between agricultural income and productivity and natural population growth, the village income and standard of living have risen.

While this is important, our main concerns in Chapters 3 and 4 will be the nature of the economic organization in Hsin Hsing village, the developments which have brought about changes in the area, and how these have enabled the villagers to deal with the imbalance of land productivity to population.

Two major developments have affected Hsin Hsing and many surrounding villages as well: one is the effort, by government and villagers, to improve agricultural methods and the land tenure system so as to increase productivity and support more people; the other is the

47

apparently ever-increasing tendency of the villagers to turn from their traditional land-based economic pattern to other sources of income. This has mainly taken the form of migration from the village to urban centers. We shall see that these developments have affected both liveli-hood and standard of living in Hsin Hsing. But we shall also see, especially later, that they have produced changes in social and politi-cal patterns as well and that all the developments have, by mutual reinforcement, affected village life by weakening community organiza-tion and solidarity, thus broadening the emphasis of village relation-ships beyond village, area, and kinship group.

In Chapter 2 we saw that in the nineteenth and early twentieth centuries the local population was relatively small. Dry cultivation was practiced in the area until the present expanded irrigation system was created. Agricultural production per unit of dry land had been low, and required so many man-hours that villagers preferred to supple-ment their family income with other forms of labor if available. In that period the port city of Lukang was an important outlet for local village labor. Fortunately, soon after the demise of the port, irrigation facilities in the area expanded rapidly, and thus agriculture—mainly wet-rice—successfully absorbed much of the village labor as produc-tion increased. Middle-aged villagers report that thirty-five years ago, when they were boys, most of the villagers grew rice in wet fields.

For more than twenty years in the Hsin Hsing area, farmers have cultivated three crops a year on their irrigated and dry land. The irrigated crops are the more important, since irrigated land comprises 93.3 percent of the cultivable acreage. Depending on the amount of water available for irrigation at the appropriate time, the farmers devote the first two of the annual crops to rice; if the water supply is insufficient, they plant other crops instead. The third is a winter crop, when there is no water for irrigation. The farmers may use all the cultivable land for it.

The first two crops of the year are usually wet-rice which is grown, naturally, on the irrigated land. The growing season for the two rice crops covers the period from early February to early November. Since the villagers' land is scattered throughout the area and irrigation schedules vary from one place to another, there is a resulting difference in rice-planting times for the Hsin Hsing farmers. The yield of the first crop may exceed that of the second by as much as 25 percent, because of the difference in season and available irrigation water be-tween the two growing periods.

There are two major types of rice grown in Taiwan; their periods of maturation are slightly different. One type is the native *tsai lai* rice, and the other is *p'eng lai* rice, introduced into Taiwan by the Japa-nese. *P'eng lai* rice generally brings a better market price, but the type grown depends mainly on the type of soil in the field. In the Hsin Hsing village area, most of the farmers grow the native *tsai lai* rice because it best withstands the weather, disease, and insects.

Within each major type of rice there are also sub-types, each of which has a slightly different growing season. A farmer may plant different types or sub-types in different plots, so that he will not have to plant and harvest all his rice fields at the same time.

The entire rice-growing operation is performed by hand labor. The farmer germinates his best rice from an earlier crop and then broadcasts it in a small, muddy, well-fertilized seedbed. While the seedlings grow—a period of thirty to fifty days for the first crop and fifteen to twenty days for the second—the paddy field is prepared for the transfer of the seedlings. The field is prepared in several operations; a water buffalo draws a wooden plow with a steel blade of adjustable depth and two different kinds of harrows. The preparation of one *chia* (= 2.39 acres) of land takes about seven days for one water buffalo and one laborer. Since many villagers do not own a buffalo (and even a landlord usually does not own one since he would not do his own heavy work), the animal and its owner—usually a fellow villager—must be hired to do the fieldwork. In 1958, the cost of hiring a water buffalo and a laborer was about NT $60–70 per day.

After the rice paddy is flooded the seedlings are removed from the seedbed by hand and transferred in rows by a small group of hired specialists. Such a man can transplant about 0.15 *chia* (0.36 acres) of land in one day. In 1958 he was paid over NT $20 a day, and at night he was given a large dinner, wine, and cigarettes. In the Hsin Hsing area this is considered a fairly high wage for a day's work. On the day the rice seedlings are transplanted, the wives of many farmers go to the village Earth God Temple to worship and pray for a good crop. Such food as whole fish, meat, and fowl are sacrificed and later served to the laborers.

Three times during the growing season the rice paddies are allowed to become relatively dry, to make weeding possible. This is done by the farmer's family or by hired village women who receive about NT $6 per day and no food. Also, during the growing period (about eighty-five to one hundred days after transplanting for the first crop, but a shorter time for the second), the fields are fertilized twice and sprayed with insecticide if necessary.

Rice harvesting is done by men and women in groups of ten; they are either hired or exchange labor. Usually a group of all men is preferred. Such a group can harvest an average of a little over 0.5 *chia* (1.2 acres) per day. The amount of land harvested depends upon the distance of the field from the house, and thus the distance the rice must be carried after threshing.

A group of ten laborers works in the field as a unit, usually taking turns at the different tasks. Four laborers will cut the rice while four others collect it and thresh it in the rotary foot-pedal threshing machine. (This machine was introduced by the Japanese in the 1930's, and is now found throughout the area.) The machine is sometimes owned by the land operator but is often either borrowed or rented. While the eight laborers are cutting and threshing, another laborer binds up the threshed rice straw, leaving it in bundles across the field. Still another laborer separates the rice from the straw in the box of the machine and puts the threshed rice into baskets, which are later carried to the farmer's house for drying, winnowing, and storing. The straw bundles are later collected and put in big stacks near the farmer's house. The straw is gradually used for fuel, compost, and animal bedding.

The harvested rice is then used to pay taxes and rent and for fertilizer or for human and animal (fowl) consumption. The surplus may be sold either to an itinerant broker or one in Lukang. The rice which is eaten or sold to brokers is milled locally. One *chia* of land in the first crop produces about 7,000 to 8,000 *chin* of *tsai lai* rice, or about 10,000 *chin* of *p'eng lai* rice. (One *chin* is equivalent to one and one-third pounds.)

However, the landholdings in Hsin Hsing are small, and it is fairly common for more than 50 percent of the village farmers not to realize any cash for the crop. The greater part of the rice crop in general, even in areas with larger landholdings, is used by the farmer to feed his family and to pay various operating expenses. These operating expenses include, beyond labor costs, the payment of taxes, land payments either to the government—if the land was purchased under the Land Reform Acts—or rent to a private landlord, and payment for fertilizer. (The payment of these expenses in kind creates a problem which will be discussed in some detail later in this chapter.)

If the third crop is wheat, it is planted immediately after the second crop, anytime from late October to early or even mid-December. Wheat in Hsin Hsing is harvested from mid-February to mid-March, depending on when it was planted. It is harvested by hand, the plant being pulled up root and all. It is threshed in the same machine used for rice and then completely dried in the sun. Usually, a broker comes to the village soon after the harvest to buy the farmers' wheat. Although the price for a *chin* of wheat is higher than for a *chin* of rice, one *chia* of land can produce less than half the amount of wheat than it can of rice. (One *chia* of land produces about 3,000–4,000 *chin* of wheat.) In the past the crops have often been plagued by a wheat disease, and for this reason many farmers still do not like to grow wheat.

In the Hsin Hsing area sweet potatoes are the principal dry-land crop. Sweet potatoes can be grown in either cold or hot weather and on either wet or dry land, although somewhat wet, sandy soil grows the best and largest potatoes. Too much rain during the growing season will ruin the plant. For this crop a seedbed is prepared, and the seedlings are transferred into mounds in a large field, where the potatoes mature until they are harvested. In Hsin Hsing sweet potatoes are grown in two different seasons. The early crop is planted around mid-May and harvested between mid-November and mid-January, the late crop is planted around late October and harvested from mid-January through mid-March.

In the Hsin Hsing village area as in much of rural Taiwan, the sweet potato is a standard part of the diet. And although it is an important food for human consumption, it is probably even more important as a food for animals. A large part of the sweet potato crop is sliced or shredded, dried in the farmer's courtyard by women and children, and then stored for later consumption by humans and livestock. Villagers who harvest a large sweet potato crop on portions of their dry land usually save only part of it for their own future use; they sell the remainder for cash to other farmers in the surrounding area.

In dry-land cultivation two crops, such as the sweet potato and the soybean, are often planted side by side in alternate rows and allowed to mature in this way for the entire growing season. This system of planting is a variation of the *hutze* or interplanting system and is commonly employed for the third crop in Hsin Hsing and the surrounding area. The system "involves planting a crop in the field a few weeks before the harvest of the previous crop, [and] makes more intensive use of the land" (Chang, 1954:4). It extends the growing season and also gives the young plants a good start while the weather is still mild. For example, a few weeks before the mature second crop is harvested, the third crop is planted between its rows. This can be done even when the second crop is wet-rice, since water is not needed in the paddy fields in the last few weeks of growth.

Because operating expenses are high, as is the general cost of living today, and because the villagers do not have enough land to till, many find it increasingly difficult to make ends meet by growing only the standard rice crops. In such cases they have two alternatives; they can go to Taipei to work and earn extra income, or they can use their small amount of land in such a way as to obtain the largest possible income from it. The latter alternative is preferred by many who have found the best possible answer in the cultivation of vegetables for market sale.

It is common for farmers cultivating irrigated land to substitute other crops for rice on a portion of their land. Such substitute crops, especially various kinds of vegetables, require more attention and labor than rice but have the greater advantage of yielding a larger and quicker cash profit. However, the farmer who grows these crops must use part of the cash he makes to buy rice, which must be used in exchange for fertilizer (obtainable only through government agents), for payment of taxes and/or rent, and for his family's consumption. Perhaps for these reasons, and also because one must be willing to take a chance with a new crop which may sometimes become diseased or fail completely, other farmers prefer to grow rice on their small landhold-ings and earn the necessary supplementary income by finding employ-ment in Taipei, returning home to work the land during the busy seasons.

Sometimes, however, the decision to switch to another crop is forced upon even the most conservative rice grower. A shortage of irrigation water or a delay in its arrival may make it impossible to grow rice at all. If the last possible calendar date for transferring the rice into the paddy fields passes before the irrigation water arrives, the farmer is forced to substitute a crop which does not depend upon large quanti-ties of water at special times.

To date farmers who have chosen or been forced to grow vegetables have found it both interesting and exciting, perhaps because it is still relatively novel. And although the new crop does require a great deal more work than rice, the vegetable growers seem to find great pleasure in comparing and discussing the progress of their vegetable crops. This apparent trend toward the cultivation of vegetables began about four or five years after the restoration of Chinese rule, at about the same time Hsin Hsing villagers began to go to Taipei in search of supple-mentary income. The trend was apparently created by the villagers' need for additional income, but at the same time it was made possible by significant changes in the procedure for growing vegetables.

In the early years before and just after the restoration, farmers planted vegetables mainly for their own use. A very few planted some cucumbers, peanuts, and maize as cash crops. Insects, a major problem, deterred many farmers from large-scale cultivation of vegetables for market sale. The vegetables had to be planted and harvested by cer-tain dates for fear of the coming of insects. Because there were no insecticides, the villagers sometimes used ritual practices such as charms, the action of shamans, or village worship to get rid of the insects. Recently, however, the increased availability of insecticides has all but eliminated the insect threat, and most vegetables can now be grown almost anytime. The only limitations are those of temperature and water. Today some vegetables can be found in the market throughout the year, thus offering the population a greater variety of vegetables.

In Hsin Hsing village, intensive cultivation of vegetables for market sale began with the onion, the red pepper, and then the green pepper. Often, too many farmers planted the same vegetable, its market price dropped, and most of them then switched to another vegetable that promised a good market. Today many farmers carefully watch the market situation and through the radio, or more usually by word of mouth, observe the fluctuations in the price of various vegetables.

A progressive farmer who hears about a new vegetable crop being grown in the area or reads about a new crop in an agricultural magazine like *Harvest Magazine* may then try to learn how to grow the same vegetable by setting aside a small portion of his land for the experiment. Such was the case with the green pepper. It was first planted in Hsin Hsing for market about 1955. By 1958 there were more than eleven farmers marketing it.

In recent years more and more land surface in Hsin Hsing, as well as in the area generally, has been given over to the cultivation of vegetables. One estimate holds that today the Hsin Hsing land devoted to market vegetables is twice what it was eight or nine years ago and still increasing. In fact, a reliable informant estimates that, exclusive of income from labor outside the area, approximately 10 percent of the village income is now derived from marketing vegetables, 70 percent from rice, 10 percent from the mint plant, 5 percent from farm labor, and 5 percent from miscellaneous sources. Such an increase in vegetable cultivation certainly represents a trend toward crop diversification, with the result that now the area is becoming much less the one-crop area (rice) for which it was formerly known.

In addition to farmers who substitute vegetable growing for partial or total rice cultivation on their land, there are a few farmers who grow mint or sugarcane. While the vegetable farmers are men who were forced by climatic or economic necessity to grow alternate crops, the mint and cane growers are men who, by virtue of sufficient land and money, can afford to gamble on reaping a greater profit from the cultivation of an alternate crop. Such men chose to grow mint or sugarcane because they are long-term crops demanding much less labor, time, and energy than is required for vegetable cultivation.

The man who grows mint instead of rice usually has contacts outside of the village. He must be familiar with the menthol oil market, and especially with the local menthol-distilling factories which can distill his mint crop for sale to the dealers. At the same time, he must have enough time to tend to all the details of arranging for the distillation and sale of the menthol. Two of the few villagers in Hsin Hsing who frequently grow mint are former landlords who have many contacts outside the village through politics and business dealings.

The mint plant, planted only once a year, yields four harvests during the course of that year. It can be planted anytime after the cold in mid-February and throughout March. The harvest then starts with the first cutting, about mid-May and throughout June. Once cut the crop grows again; in forty days it is ready for cutting. The third crop matures in about fifty days and the fourth in about sixty days. The last crop is harvested toward the end of November, before the cold weather and winds again set in.

Since sugarcane requires eighteen months to cultivate, the man who plants it instead of rice is usually one who has land enough—probably over one *chia*—to allow him to put a decent acreage into cane and still have enough left for crops which bring more immediate returns. And he must have enough capital or other means to finance his family during the long growing season of the cane.

Before the war, when the price of sugarcane was higher than it is today, many farmers in Hsin Hsing and the surrounding area grew this crop. Now, however, few farmers are willing to tie up their land for one crop of cane when the fields, over the same period of time, could otherwise produce four different crops. Those few farmers in the area who have recently cultivated sugarcane have done so in the belief that it would bring a greater profit than they could get from rice. However, in 1958 they were disappointed when the low market price of sugar brought them even smaller profits than they would have realized from rice. Today, despite the coaxing and cajolery of agents of the Taiwan Sugar Corporation, even these few farmers are loath to plant sugarcane, and the acreage devoted to cane in the area is steadily decreasing.

The third annual crop is grown during the winter when there is no irrigation water available. In Hsin Hsing village and the area generally, the crops cultivated are wheat, sweet potatoes, soybeans, or vegetables such as the green bean. All are crops which do not require much moisture and can tolerate the cold and the strong winter winds. In fact, wheat cannot withstand the hot and often wet weather of the spring, summer, and early fall of the first and second crop periods, but needs rather cooler weather.

THE VILLAGERS' VIEW OF THE CALENDAR AND THE AGRICULTURAL CYCLE

The basic traditional calendar in Taiwan is lunar, and lunar months are referred to here by numbers just as they are by the villagers. The more recent solar calendar is used when villagers refer to recently introduced legal functions such as school activities, tax collection, military conscription, and so on. Farmers almost always use lunar references when they discuss calendar dates for various agricultural events, like the months in which crops are planted and harvested. However, for the dates of the equinoctial or seasonal changes which determine the earliest and latest times for planting a crop if it is to be harvested at the proper time, the villagers usually use Chinese "solar terms" (*chieh ch'i*).[1] These, unlike the lunar calendar dates, "indicate the position of the earth with reference to the sun and consequently the seasonal climatic changes" (Fei, 1939:145). The villagers, in using these solar terms, equate them with dates in the lunar calendar which vary from year to year. The use of such a solar term, Ta Shu ("Great Heat") is an example of this. Its approximate date in the solar calendar is July 23; in 1958 this solar date corresponded to the seventh day of the sixth moon of the lunar calendar. The villagers feel that the rice seedlings of the second crop should be transferred one week before to one week after Ta Shu. The villagers do not like to transplant at other times, although occasionally a lack of water will force a delay. Some, rather than delay beyond these limits, will give up and replace the rice with something else, such as a vegetable.

The agricultural cycle marks which months are busy and which ones are slack for the villagers. Below is a list of the months of the year and how the villager relates them to the agricultural cycle. Some of the events may actually encroach a good deal into other months, but the villager still associates certain months with certain agricultural processes. The months here are given first in the lunar calendar since, in speaking of actual dates, these are what the villager uses; their approximate solar equivalents follow in parentheses. Descriptions of activities are quoted from interviews with the farmers.

First month (mid-February to mid-March)
"This is a moderately busy month with many farmers harvesting their sweet potatoes and harvesting their third crop."

Second month (mid-March to mid-April)
"This is a busy month. The farmers plow their fields and prepare the fields for the transplanting of the first crop of rice which is done during this month."

Third month (mid-April to mid-May)
"This is a slack month. There is only weeding to be done in the fields."

Fourth month (mid-May to mid-June)
"This is one of the slackest months. There is no work in the fields, but only the checking of the irrigation water and the checking of the fields themselves."

Fifth and sixth months (mid-June to mid-August)

"These are two of the busiest months of the year. The farmers harvest their first crop of rice and prepare the fields for the second crop of rice."

Seventh month (mid-August to mid-September)

"This is a moderately slack month with only weeding to be done in the fields."

Eighth month (mid-September to mid-October)

"This is a very slack month. There is no work in the fields other than checking irrigation water and the fields themselves."

Ninth to mid-tenth month (mid-October to late November)

"These again are two of the busiest months of the year. The farmers harvest their second crop of rice and some prepare to plant their third crop."

Eleventh and twelfth months (mid-December to mid-February)

"These are slack months. There is no work to be done in the fields. The farmers usually repair their houses, agricultural implements, and irrigation ditches during this time."

We note that what the farmer considers important enough to list on this monthly schedule are not only operations which consume a great deal of time and effort but also, and perhaps more important, the farming operations which harass him with deadlines and time limitations, like the planting and harvesting of the rice crops. Other operations are omitted from the farmer's listing. Thus, although he may actually be busier when cultivating certain vegetables, since he does the planting, harvesting, and marketing of vegetables without any hired or exchange laborers, he usually omits these operations from the monthly listing. There is usually no definite scheduling of vegetable crops and therefore no deadlines to meet.

FARM IMPLEMENTS, OWNERSHIP AND EXCHANGE

The farmer does not need a great variety of implements and tools for his work. This was evident in a survey of the tools owned by eighty-seven village farm households in August, 1958. (See Table 11.) As might be expected, small and inexpensive tools which are used frequently are quite plentiful in the village. In fact, there is sometimes at least one such implement in each household, like the steel hoe, sickle, and bamboo baskets. Tools which have a limited use, even an inexpensive tool like the hand thresher, are found only infrequently in a farming household.

Large and expensive tools and work animals are also found in relatively small numbers. The oxcart, water buffalo, threshing machine, water wheel, and winnower are quite important to the farmer, but he rarely owns them. A villager may either rent a threshing machine from another villager or borrow it from a good friend or kinsman. However, a water buffalo for plowing or a buffalo and cart are more likely to be hired on a daily basis, its owner being hired to work the animal.

The villager who does not own a water buffalo or a threshing ma-

TABLE 11

SURVEY OF TOOLS AND IMPLEMENTS OWNED BY
87 HSIN HSING VILLAGE FARM FAMILIES,
AUGUST, 1958

Tools and implements	Good condition	Poor condition	Unusable
Water buffalo	17		
Oxcart	12		1
Foot thresher	10		
Hand thresher	2		1
Water wheel	10	4	4
Plow	28	2	5
Hand harrow	27		1
Foot harrow	10	1	
Hoe	87	1	
Sickle	136		1
Bamboo basket	144		2
Outside granary	15	4	2
Stone rice grinder	6		5
Hatchet	7		2
Leveler	7		
Pitchfork	17		
Insecticide sprayer	4		1
Winnower	8	1	
One-bar bicycle	39	2	2
Two-bar bicycle	22		
Sewing machine	23	1	2

chine must adjust his own schedule in advance of the plowing or harvesting in order that it will not conflict with the schedules of people from whom he might borrow or rent the item. This can be troublesome if threat of a typhoon makes it imperative that he, like everyone else, harvest the rice crop immediately. Such an individual must take his chances and wait for the first available thresher. Luckily, such emergencies do not occur often. Even within the same village, farmers usually have slightly varied plowing or harvesting schedules.

Borrowing of small tools as well as many household items is both common and frequent in the village. When there is need for a tool, people prefer to borrow it from another villager with whom they have the closest relationship. Thus, a villager might have a relationship of frequent mutual borrowing with family members, neighbors, or friends. Sometimes a villager borrows a farm implement from a *ch'in ch'i* (a matrilateral or affinal relative), and in that case no money is paid nor a feeling of obligation incurred. But usually, unless a *ch'in ch'i* lives nearby, it is not likely that a large piece of equipment can be borrowed.

However, the decision to borrow a tool from another depends upon how good the *kan-ch'ing* [2] is between the two people. This is true even for *ch'in tsu* relatives—such as patrilateral parallel cousins—whose *kan-ch'ing* may not necessarily be very good. If the *kan-ch'ing* between two people is not good and one lends the other a tool, then the borrower will feel an obligation toward the lender and worry about it and will later send a gift of something to the lender in order to cancel the obligation. Until this is done, the borrower feels uncomfortable. Therefore, rather than become involved in an uncomfortable situation, a villager often prefers to pay the NT $20 rent for a threshing machine to someone with whom his *kan-ch'ing* is not necessarily good. The payment makes it a simple commercial transaction, and there is no obligation.

Many villagers do not like to borrow an implement which seems to be in bad condition, since if it breaks down the borrower will be expected to repair it. Therefore, to avoid possible trouble, many villagers prefer to rent the implement so that they have no such responsibility.

But no matter whom the villager approaches for the loan of a tool, it is quite unusual to get an outright refusal. If the owner of the implement does not wish to lend it at all, or at least not to that particular person—perhaps because he has a reputation for not returning things promptly—he will offer some excuse. But since the villagers generally know quite well who is likely to be willing to lend them things, they limit their requests accordingly, and embarrassing situations do not often arise.

Certain implements, such as insecticide sprayers, which few farmers own, can be rented at a nominal charge from the local Farmers' Association. The government and the Farmers' Association are fostering the use of insecticides and thus make sprayers available.

Most really expensive farm implements are owned jointly by several villagers. The families which join together to buy a threshing machine, winnower, stone rice grinder, insecticide sprayer, or water wheel do so for various reasons. Entering into a joint-purchase arrangement, however, is dependent upon the existence of good *kan-ch'ing* between them. Some households which are related, such as brothers or even patrilateral parallel cousins, may have inherited a threshing machine or winnower jointly from their fathers or have recently purchased the item together. There are neighboring households which, for the sake of convenience, purchase some implement which none of the participants could or would have purchased independently. Finally, there are men in the village who are friends and join together to buy an expensive implement like an insecticide sprayer which they can all take turns using. Villagers who are friends usually influence one another. For example, several good friends in the village all grow the same vegetables for market sale. Village men who are good friends and share economic interests have many economic and social ties between them.

ANIMAL HUSBANDRY

Most of the village families raise some livestock. They may include pigs, fowl, some rabbits and goats, and a few water buffalo for work purposes. (See Table 12.) Livestock is generally not considered

TABLE 12

SURVEY OF NUMBER OF LIVESTOCK OWNED BY
87 HSIN HSING VILLAGE FARM FAMILIES,
AUGUST, 1958

Livestock	Number
Water buffalo	17
Pigs	241
Chickens	361
Ducks	372
Geese	131
Rabbits	52
Goats	11

an important source of household cash income. Even the many pigs raised in the village (241 in August, 1958) are not considered a source of real income, since the villagers feel that raising pigs is more "like putting money in the bank." The reasoning behind this commonly made statement is that the price the butcher pays just about covers the money and time it costs to raise the pigs. Thus, when a farmer raises pigs he knows that as soon as the animals are sold he will have a sum of money at his disposal; it is, therefore, a sort of enforced saving. Usually the money has long since been earmarked for some special project—to build an extension to the family's house, to pay the expenses of an engagement or marriage, or to pay off a loan. However, if there is an impending marriage in the family, it is usual to slaughter one or more pigs for use in the marriage feast. Thus, when a village woman was asked when her twenty-two-year-old son would be married, she answered, "when the pigs are big enough." In explanation she continued, "Do you think that a poor family like ours could afford to *buy* two pigs in order to give our son a proper wedding?"

Almost every family in the village raises at least a few pigs. They are of three types: the native Taiwanese, the Berkshire, or a crossbreed of the two. These pigs are kept in sties which are typically constructed with mud floors, bamboo sidewalls and straw roofs; they are either attached directly to the side of the house or situated several yards away. Some rather recently constructed sties in the village, however, are more modern; they are specially designed with cement or brick floors and walls and cement tile roofs. The local Pu Yen Hsiang Farmers' Association usually subsidizes the construction of a few such sties in each village every year, paying about one-quarter of the total cost of construction.

For the most part, the care and feeding of pigs is the responsibility of the village women and older children. Much time is spent preparing pig food. This consists of sweet potatoes and certain green vegetables grown especially by the farmer for his pigs and other livestock. This is all cooked in a starchy water called "rice soup," which is the water in which the family's rice is washed before it is cooked. According to the Farmers' Association and government agricultural agencies, it is not necessary to cook pig food, but their word has not been very effective in the village. Most villagers, despite the great amount of time it takes, still continue to follow the traditional way of preparation in the belief that pigs will not grow fat on raw sweet potatoes.

Every few days the pig sty is cleaned out. This is usually done for the important purpose of collecting the excrement and the rice straw, which partially covers the floor, for use as fertilizer. Compost is made from the dung and used for various crops. Uncovered compost heaps are usually found alongside the pig houses, and it is not unusual for some garbage to be added to the heap. Children as well as fowl can often be seen climbing on the open compost heap.

When a pig becomes ill it is common to call a local veterinarian. Sometimes the farmer himself will give the sick pig a shot of the penicillin which can now be readily purchased in Lukang.

Possibly as a result of a lack of selective breeding, a somewhat inadequate diet and inadequate use of antibiotics, unsanitary living conditions and the climate, pigs in Hsin Hsing usually take from nine to fifteen months to reach full size, a good deal longer than similar breeds take in America. When a pig does reach full growth, a tax must be paid by the farmer to the government at the Public Office before it is slaughtered. The tax must be paid whether the farmer is selling the pig or using it for his own purposes. Pigs are usually sold to a butcher from a village in the area or from Lukang. The price brought by the pig varies according to the market rate. If the farmer takes the pig to the butcher himself, he receives extra payment for his trouble.

When a villager sells his pigs he holds a *pai-pai* to pay homage to the god of the pig house. The worship is held near the pig house and consists of "vegetables and rice" (cut-up meats and fish in a soup), "sacrifices" (a whole fish and a whole piece of meat), incense, and paper imitation money. The food is usually then served to invited village friends and *ch'in tsu*. Since the occasion is not considered really festive, no *ch'in ch'i* from outside the village are invited for the dinner.

There is hardly a village household which does not raise some chickens, ducks, and geese. Few villagers sell either the fowl or the eggs but use both for village festive—usually religious—occasions. These are practically the only times that most village families will eat what they consider such a fine and expensive food as fowl. Of the three, chicken is the most highly prized and is considered the most nutritious and delicious of all meats.

There are farmers in other villages in the area who specialize in raising ducks and chickens. They sell their fowl and eggs to the markets in Lukang or other towns. On rare occasions a Hsin Hsing villager may go to such a farm to buy eggs for some special festival when more eggs are needed than his own flock can supply. Hsin Hsing villagers, like most villagers in the area, do not hatch their own eggs. Itinerant merchants on bicycles come through the villages and sell baby chicks and ducks. Although all fowl roam freely about the village and there are no fences to keep them from straying, if a chicken or duck disappears and is later found dead, the villagers can usually identify their own. They seldom lose a fowl or confuse another farmer's with their own. Some villagers do, however, cut a special mark in the web between the duck's toes or apply a dab of colored paint to their geese.

At night the fowl are usually kept under bamboo cages, since few villagers have anything which resembles a chicken house. The area is plagued by large rats which frequently kill chickens and ducks at night; a villager often loses several birds in one week. Disease also takes its toll of the village stock. The villagers do not know what these diseases are, and they watch helplessly while sometimes as many as a quarter of all the fowl in the village die within two weeks. No veterinarian is called.

Women and girl children care for the household's fowl, which involves little more than feeding them twice a day. Chickens, geese, and ducks are mainly fed white rice and specially grown green vegetables. Geese are fed sweet potatoes as well. The women also slaughter the fowl, although some of them, especially young girls, prefer not to kill fowl. When the throat is cut the blood is collected in a bowl of uncooked rice and later made into a kind of soup.

A few villagers also keep some rabbits and goats. Rabbits are used for food on festive occasions and are also sold in the market. Goats are kept in preparation for a marriage, when they, as well as a pig or two, are slaughted, used in the religious ceremonial, and later fed to the guests.

As shown in Table 12, in 1958 there were seventeen water buffalo in Hsin Hsing village. These are kept strictly as work animals and are not considered as food by most of the villagers. This is perhaps related to the feeling built up over the years toward this useful, hardworking, and tame animal. Villagers say that they have no such feeling for pigs, which do nothing all their lives but prepare for the day when they will be eaten, but some of the village women actually become ill at the thought of eating beef. On the other hand, many village men, especially those who have worked or served in the army outside the village area, boast of how they have often eaten beef.

In the village, young boys and sometimes old men take care of the water buffalo when the animal is not working in the field. The young boy is in fact referred to as the "cow boy" and can often be seen riding on the animal's back or leading it along the narrow paths between the fields where the buffalos can graze. In the market town of Chi Hu, five miles southeast of Hsin Hsing, there is a special market where water buffalos are bought and sold on two fixed days each month.

AGRICULTURAL LINKS BEYOND THE VILLAGE

Most crops are not kept in the village very long after they are harvested. The bulk of them is used to pay the farmers' operating expenses or is sold. Some vegetables are preserved for future use as food for the family and for livestock. For example, sweet potatoes, radishes, and cabbages are cut up, dried in the sun, and then stored in sacks. In addition, a small quantity of fresh sweet potatoes is frequently stored in the house, also to be used as food for family and livestock. The potatoes are piled on the floor in the corner of one room of the house. It is common to use a corner of the main room of the house—the kung t'ing, the ancestral-worship room—for this purpose. Thus, besides the religious altar in the rear, one frequently finds in this room all kinds of stored valuables such as rice, fertilizer, and some of the farm implements. The rats, which frequently destroy part of the crop while it is growing in the field, also take their toll of the food stored in the house.

Those villagers who grow cash vegetable crops usually market them in three market towns or cities: Yuan Lin, almost fifteen miles from the village; Chang-hua, about ten miles; and Taichung, about twenty-five miles. Often some of the men in Hsin Hsing who grow the same vegetables cooperate in the marketing operation. Since the market price is usually about the same in each one of the three markets, the men agree in advance where each will go to sell his vegetables. This prevents any one market from being flooded with a vegetable and thus lowering the price. The choice of market is arbitrary, and if one man happens to get a better price for his vegetables, he is considered lucky, and no more is thought about it. Perhaps the next time the men will change markets.

If the villager has a large enough load to take to the wholesale market, it may take him several days to sell his vegetables. In that event he usually sleeps in the market unless he happens to have some relative such as a *ch'in ch'i* in the town with whom he can stay; a hotel is considered too expensive. A few villagers ship vegetables like peppers or cabbages by truck freight to more distant markets in the cities of Kaohsiung or Taipei. This is done with the aid of a vegetable broker with whom they have made contact; he also takes care of the sale of the vegetables in the market for a percentage of the profit. The villager and the broker use the mails to maintain contact about prices and shipping arrangements. Although only a few villagers now work with a broker, it seems likely that more will adopt the method, for it permits the farmer to sell to the best advantage in different parts of the island.

After a farmer harvests his rice crop he dries it in the sun and stores it either in bamboo-and-mud bins in the house or else in very large, round, white-plastered bamboo or wooden storage bins in front of the house. This latter method is mostly used by those farmers who produce a large amount of rice. The rice is held in these storage places until it is time to make payment in kind for land rent, land taxes, or for fertilizer. The number of these large rice bins that now go unused and unrepaired is evidence that the villagers are right when they say they were able to keep and store much more rice for later sale on the market under the Japanese.

After the operating expenses are paid and any surplus is sold, the remaining rice is stored unmilled for the family's use. As it is needed, the villagers have their rice milled, usually in the next village, at a cost of about NT $2 for every one hundred *chin* of rice. Of one hundred *chin* of unmilled rice, approximately twenty *chin* is lost when the rice is husked and polished. The husks then belong to the mill, but the farmer can take home the product of the polishing, the ground rice powder, to feed to pigs and other livestock. The farmers usually purchase the husks from the mills to use as fuel for cooking stoves.

Village farmers who grow wheat usually sell their whole crop to brokers who come regularly with their carts and haul away the sacks of wheat which they have purchased after a good deal of haggling with the farmer over the price. Although the final price is usually only slightly more or less than the general market price, both sides seem to enjoy the whole bargaining procedure. The few farmers who have a surplus of rice also sell it to these brokers; the process of the sale is as long and lively as that for wheat. In fact, bargaining seems to occur in all transactions concerning the sale of goods, though it is rather unusual when services are being arranged for.

FARM LABOR

Except for the landlord who hires labor to do almost all the daily heavy work on his land, the members of the farmer's family usually do most of the work in the fields. A good deal of this everyday work is now done indiscriminately by men, women, and older children. However, besides these daily tasks there are special farming operations which regularly demand additional labor, often highly skilled or specialized. Thus, laborers are either hired and paid in cash, or labor is exchanged for such tasks as plowing, transplanting seedlings, weeding, and harvesting. Rice, sweet potatoes, mint and sugarcane are the main crops which require additional labor at various times. Securing the necessary labor becomes a special problem at rice-harvesting time, since the harvesting in the whole area must be completed in a limited period.

The additional labor is usually found in the farmer's own village or the surrounding area and on rarer occasions outside the area. Such labor often includes small land cultivators who are not at the time working on their own land and landless villagers. The landless or nearly landless villagers who work as laborers do so in addition to some other kind of work locally or in Taipei. Members of the families of larger land-operators may not necessarily have to hire out as laborers during the agricultural busy seasons, but they nevertheless frequently do so. How often they do this may depend on the amount of land and the kind of crops they are cultivating, how many available hands there are in the family and how old they are, and how busy they happen to be on their own land at the times when extra farm labor is in demand. Self-cultivators above middle-age do not usually hire out as laborers, but their children frequently do. In addition, a man who is planting a crop like sweet potatoes, which is harvested at a different time, may have free time during the rice harvesting season and hire out as a farm laborer.

The presence of women working on the farm has been quite accepted in the rural areas since World War II, when manpower was in such short supply. Village women whose husbands spend a good deal of time working in Taipei are especially active on their own land. However, the heavier fieldwork such as plowing, harrowing, and transplanting is not considered women's work. Therefore, if the male of the household is away at the time, the woman must hire the necessary labor. Frequently, men who work in Taipei and still retain a small piece of land in the village come home for the busier farm seasons to take care of their own land if their Taipei job permits. Generally, these men hire or exchange labor for the harvest. They usually remain in the village area for the entire harvest period and work on other people's land in order to make their return to the village more profitable.

Hiring labor for plowing a field, planting hills of sweet potatoes, transplanting rice seedlings, or even harvesting a mint field is rather simple; the farmer merely hires the few individuals necessary to do the job, usually from his own village. They may be specialists in plowing or transplanting rice seedlings, or they may be just ordinary villagers who are hired to weed the rice paddies or harvest a mint crop and are pleased to get the extra work when they are not busy with their own fields. On the other hand, hiring labor groups for the harvesting of rice and sugarcane is quite a different matter and quite complex.

One very important type of labor group hired to harvest rice is a group of ten people. This group is most frequently all male, although women may be included and sometimes make up as much as half of the group. The male laborers usually prefer not to have women in the group; women cannot handle the heaviest jobs such as carrying the baskets of rice to the farmer's house, which makes it necessary for only the men in the group to do this exhausting work. Men over the age of seventeen or eighteen and below fifty-five are preferred for the harvest work. On the other hand, since women laborers are easier and cheaper to hire, many landholders prefer to have some women in the labor team to cut down on harvesting costs. However, if it is imperative to complete a harvest quickly, then even the landholder prefers not to hire women; it is felt that they tend to slow up the work. In the latter case, it is not unusual to hire more than ten people in order to complete the harvest in the shortest possible time.

Frequently, the hired labor teams have the same small core of men each year. The core group is usually composed of men from the same village who have little land of their own. Such a group often hires out in villages throughout the immediate area and may even go to other areas whose harvest is earlier than the Hsin Hsing area. A single Hsin Hsing villager who does not belong to such a group can sometimes find work in a labor group outside his own village, but then only if he has

a *ch'in ch'i* or friend elsewhere who can tell him about a labor group
which is short a man or two.

The land-cultivator must usually make arrangements a week or two
before the harvest in order to obtain the services of a labor team. In
spite of the large population of the area, at harvesttime it is not easy to
hire labor at the last moment, not only because many farmers harvest
at about the same time, but also because so many local men are off
working in Taipei. It is also for this reason that a labor team is often
forced to complete its number with women.

There are several ways to go about hiring a labor team. If the group
happens to be from the farmer's village there is no problem, since he
knows about the team and has ample opportunity to make the necessary advance arrangements. Usually, however, there are not enough
labor teams in one village, which makes it necessary for him to contact
outside groups. The contact is perhaps most often made through someone who acts as a broker, who himself may be a member of a labor
group. The broker is given a deposit of NT $1 for each of the team's
ten members. The acceptance of this money has the force of a contractual obligation; the money itself is then kept by the laborers as a
bonus.

Another method of contacting outside labor groups is accomplished
through the arrangements of *ch'in ch'i* or friends who live in other
villages and therefore know of labor teams. This source of contacts is
especially fruitful, because Hsin Hsing villagers have many *ch'in ch'i*
living in populous villages in the area. One large village about two
miles from Hsin Hsing is a particularly good source of labor; its rice
harvest is a good deal earlier than that of Hsin Hsing because the
earlier arrival of the irrigation water there lets its farmers plant
sooner.

Infrequently, labor groups come from a greater distance to work in
the Hsin Hsing area if they can be assured of work for several successive days. Several farmers may get together and hire the same labor
crew for different days. In such instances the group sleeps in the village
and receives all its meals from the farmers. And in this case, even the
women who happen to be part of the labor group are fed all their
meals.

More commonly, however, the labor groups are recruited from the
immediate area; they therefore arrive for work early in the morning
and go home in the evening. The members of such a group are fed
"five meals a day." Two of these are mid-morning and mid-afternoon
snacks eaten in the field as is the third meal, lunch. The other two
meals are eaten at the farmer's house, but only the evening meal is
elaborate. The women members of the labor group are fed only the
two snacks and lunch in the field.

The pay scale for the members of the labor groups varies annually with the price of rice. The exact rate paid by the small landholders of Hsin Hsing usually follows that paid by large landlords. The wages may either be paid individually to each member of the labor crew or else paid in a lump sum to the group according to the amount of land harvested. In the former system the men are paid from NT $22 to NT $25 per day, the women about NT $10 per day. Where payment is based on amount of land harvested, the lump sum to the group is divided equally among the men after they have paid the wages of any women among them. The latter wage system is more commonly used in the second rice crop of the year and the individual payment method usually for the first rice crop, since it is larger than the second and requires more work.

In Hsin Hsing there are about fifteen families which hire labor groups simply because they have no labor to exchange. This is usually the case when the head of the household is working in Taipei or is an older man. Others who hire laborers rather than exchange labor are somewhat wealthier people who can afford to pay in cash rather than in their own labor to get their land harvested.

A pure exchange labor group usually is more of an ideal than an actuality. Such a group is composed preferably of ten persons for rice harvesting. Ideally, they must be ten people who all cultivate approximately the same amount of rice paddy; thus, they can move from one piece of land to another until all their land is harvested, without having to calculate the labor hours devoted to each individual's land. If the need for a quick harvest is urgent, as it sometimes is in the first rice crop, the group decides which land to harvest first by inspecting each member's crop to determine which is the ripest, and it then proceeds in that order. If there is good reason to hurry the harvesting of the first crop, the farmers prefer not to rely on exchange labor, but hire a labor team. Therefore, there is less labor exchanged in the first crop than in the second.

This type of exchange labor harvesting group is not often found in Hsin Hsing, simply because it is not easy to find ten people with approximately the same amount of land to harvest. But there are some such groups in Hsin Hsing made up of individuals such as *tsu* members, neighbors, or sworn brothers who are intimate. The people in such a group, because of their relationship, are not concerned if some people in the group have more land to harvest than others. There is, for example, in Hsin Hsing a group consisting of several households with the same family name who are all descended from the same grandfather; they all live in apartments in the same large house and form a pure exchange labor group. These families for the most part have very good relations and enough men to exchange labor in this

way. While the men and boys of these households do the actual harvesting, the women work together to dry the rice in the courtyard,
keeping each family's rice separate.

Probably the most common kind of labor group in Hsin Hsing and
the area is a mixed group of ten people, some hired and others exchange laborers. Such a group is composed mainly of people who
cultivate different amounts of rice land and usually includes some who
are the equivalent of hired laborers and cultivate no rice land at all.
Such groups generally have no fixed membership, though it is common
for the same group of men, often *tsu* relatives or friends, to form the
core of the group and to include additional villagers each year to
complete the team. Preferably, these additional farmers till at least a
moderate amount of rice land. Farmers with a very small amount of
land usually hire laborers, as do those with such large amounts of rice
land that it takes too long to exchange labor.

Because of the composition of this mixed labor group a special
system of accounting has been worked out which is based on the
knowledge that the team will harvest more of some members' land
than others and probably no land at all for a few. The group therefore
manages itself almost like a hired labor group. When the group harvests the land of one of its members, the owner pays into the group's
fund wages for each member based on the amount of land harvested.
The owner of the land harvested furnishes all the food to the group
just as if it were a hired team. When all the land of its members has
been harvested, all the money which has been paid is equally divided.
Once this is done, if there is still a demand for farm labor, the group
may decide to hire out as a labor team; if some of the members do not
care to hire out they are replaced at random.

The farmer attempts to plan the harvest so that it can be completed
in one day, since he must supply food for the laborers. If necessary, the
labor team may be increased by one or two members, either by hiring
a few additional people or by recruiting members of the farmer's own
family to help.

There are also some special cases of exchange labor in Hsin Hsing
village. One farmer does field labor in exchange for free medical service for the family from the local doctor, one of the former large landlords of the village. In this case there is no way to calculate the equivalence of the services exchanged, but the families of the two men have
been very close for many years, and they appear to be satisfied with the
arrangement.

There are also instances of exchange labor between villagers who
have some special work to be done, such as building a house. Although
the labor exchanged may not be for the same kind of job, the men
simply calculate the exchange on the basis of a day of work for a day of

work. Sometimes, however, a man who is building an addition to his house may just hire a few village men during the agricultural slack season and pay them a fixed wage for the day's work, about NT $15–20 a day.

Today only a few villagers grow sugarcane. The period of harvesting for cane varies according to the time of planting, but usually it comes during what is normally a slack farm season. The sugar company, which contracts with the farmer to have him grow sugarcane on his land, regularly sends specialists to the fields to determine when the sugarcane is at its peak of readiness for harvesting. Usually, a field planted in sugarcane is relatively large, and may require a group of as many as thirty or forty people to harvest just under one *chia* of land. The group is generally hired from one of the very large villages in the area that is populous enough to supply the entire team. This labor team works as a single group of men, women, and young people, which is broken up into smaller crews according to function, such as cutting the cane, gathering it and tying it in bundles, or putting it on the oxcarts which take it to the railway line for shipment to the sugar company factory. The whole group is paid a lump sum for division among the members and is fed only refreshments in the field, not a whole meal. Hsin Hsing villagers are very seldom members of a sugar-harvesting labor gang.

THE FARMERS' ASSOCIATION: AN "EXTERNAL" FORCE

The Farmers' Association has been important in the Taiwanese rural area since Japanese times. Under the Japanese regime the local farmers owned stocks or shares in the local district associations, and Hsin Hsing villagers feel that the association was run partly by the Japanese government and partly by the farmers. In those days the government attempted to introduce new farm techniques and crops to the farmers through the association.

Today, the work of the local district Farmers' Association has become more important than ever. The Pu Yen Hsiang Farmers' Association has several large buildings which are used for offices, meeting rooms, classrooms, and warehouses for the storage of rice and farm equipment. The provincial Food Bureau lends some financial support to the association for the building of the warehouses where the large amounts of grain collected from the farmers as tax are stored for the bureau by the association. Almost all the villagers who cultivate land and are therefore classed primarily as farmers belong to the Farmers' Association. In order to become a member, the farmer must purchase at least one share of association stock at a price of NT $5, a low fee which virtually guarantees that all farmers will become members. On the basis of the profits of the Farmers' Association, dividends in the form of towels, soap, or tea sets are regularly given to members.

The members of each village unit of the Farmers' Association elect a "small unit head" who is the Farmers' Association's agent in the village. It is his job to distribute association literature and to notify the members of meetings and classes. It is also his job to record the amount of land for which each farmer wishes to obtain fertilizer from the Food Bureau through the auspices of the Farmers' Association in exchange for rice. Although the unit head used to receive NT $50 a month to cover his expenses, in 1958 the arrangement was changed so that now he receives only the actual office supplies necessary for his job. In each village in Pu Yen Hsiang, the unit head is given a radio by the Farmers' Association for his use as long as he holds the position. He also regularly receives a newspaper, which is an organ of the provincial government, and *Harvest Magazine.*

The members in each village elect one representative for every fifty members to the association's governing body. These representatives in turn elect a supervisor, who then appoints the General Secretary who actually runs the *hsiang* Farmers' Association. The General Secretary is the highest paid employee of the organization and is in charge of the many other paid employees. The main duty of the representatives is to attend the annual meeting of representatives to vote on the yearly program and budget which has been worked out by the General Secretary and his staff.

Today, most of the villagers and employees of the Pu Yen Hsiang Farmers' Association feel that the local units are relatively independent. However, there are Farmers' Associations on the *hsien* and provincial level which are supposed to "teach" and to lead the operation of the local organizations. The local units in turn pay fees to the higher level units. In addition, there is a section in both the *hsien* and provincial government's agricultural departments which deals with farmers' organizations and supervises the operations of the Farmers' Associations. Thus, there is control of the operations of the local Farmers' Associations by these three higher levels. The monthly program, budget, and proposed special programs of the local associations are first discussed in local committee, and then the proposals and budget are sent to the Hsien Farmers' Association for suggestions and to the government agency for approval, changes, or rejection.

Both farmers and staff members of the association generally seem to agree that such guidance and supervision by upper levels of the government is a good thing. It is felt that the supervision of the *hsien* government is grounded in the law and assures the farmer that the programs and large amounts of money handled by the Farmers' Association will be properly administered. However, since the organization, as the official agent in the rural area for the provincial Food Bureau, must perform a number of unpleasant tasks such as the collection of rice and loans, this leads to some distrust of the Farmers' Association by the farmer.

The Farmers' Association has three basic functions. The first, and perhaps the most important, of its functions is its extension services. Many of these are performed with the financial and advisory cooperation of the JCRR. The second function is moneylending, which is of two kinds: loans to farmers by the association itself and loans to farmers by the provincial Food Bureau under the management of the association. The third function is performing, for a fee, some of the work of the provincial Food Bureau. The association sells fertilizer to the farmer and collects (handles and/or stores) rice from the farmer to pay for it. It collects rice for the land tax, for the required rice sale to the government, and for the semiannual payments in kind on land purchased from the government under the Land Reform Program.

Extension Services

The extension services offered by local Farmers' Associations vary a great deal from district to district. Because of the extension services it offers, the association in Pu Yen Hsiang is known to be one of the very best on the island. These services include educational instruction, sponsoring of 4-H Clubs, provision of rental farm implements, providing cash subsidies and loans to members to encourage farm improvements and modernization, and sale to members of such items as seed, bean cake, and bicycles below the market price.

The forms of instruction sponsored by the Pu Yen Hsiang Farmers' Association have been varied and apparently successful. Regular sewing classes are held for the daughters of members, and since the classes are free, many village families wish to take advantage of the opportunity. However, the facilities are so limited that when classes are held, each village may send only a small quota based on the number of association members in the village. In Hsin Hsing large numbers of girls wish to attend the classes, and it is the responsibility of the formal village leaders—the mayor, the village representative, and the village Farmers' Association unit head—to select the students. However, usually the village leaders wish to avoid any possible conflict or criticism over their choices, and, although some girls may meet the qualifications set up by the association better than others, straws are drawn to determine which girls will attend. The method all too often sends less qualified girls to the classes, and these often drop out before the course is over. Several Hsin Hsing villagers have complained of the wastefulness of this method of choice, and claim that the village leaders are refusing to assume their full responsibility.

Other classes are held for training boys in agricultural techniques. There are also occasional adult classes on the proper use and application of fertilizer and planting techniques for some crops. The experts on various subjects who are brought in to speak to these classes are sometimes too technical for their audience, are not trained in practical application, and are strangers who know little of the immediate agricultural problems of the area. When this happens, the farmers tend to lose respect for and interest in such sessions. The Farmers' Association also sends trained women into the villages to teach women and girls how to prepare powdered milk for children and introduces new farm tools, new types of seeds and crops, fertilizer, and insecticides to the local area.

Under the auspices of the Farmers' Association the 4-H movement has been introduced in some villages in Pu Yen Hsiang. The movement is relatively new in Taiwan, having been introduced with the help of JCRR in the early 1950's. The movement has been in existence in Pu Yen Hsiang only during the past few years; so far it has met with only moderate success. The 4-H groups are for boys and girls between the ages of fourteen and twenty-two. The program attempts to teach them the proper care of fields and livestock, home economics, and general record-keeping for income and expenses. Another purpose, set forth when the goals of 4-H are presented to the villagers, is to keep the young people busy and out of trouble.

There is no 4-H group in Hsin Hsing village since there is no one qualified and willing to lead the program. Such a position demands an educated man who has free time and a knowledge and an interest in modern farm techniques. The person best suited to lead the program in Hsin Hsing is a relatively poor man who does not have enough free time and who is not particularly respected by many villagers because of his poor financial condition. "If a poor man should tell people something sensible about what to do, no one would pay any attention. After all, no one wants to listen to the words of a poor man. But let the poor man suddenly become famous and rich, and people will listen to his most ridiculous ideas."

In addition to these many educational programs, the Farmers' Association also often subsidizes a farmer who is willing to attempt something new, such as buying an insecticide sprayer, building a new type of pig sty, or cementing a courtyard in front of his home for the drying of rice or vegetables. The association can give a partial subsidy to only a few farmers in the many villages each year. Usually, villages in which there are farmers interested in using the subsidy draw lots. However, the subsidies are so small that a great deal of money must be added to finance the building of a pig sty or a cement drying area, so only a few villages take part. Once the village receives the subsidy, there is likely to be only one, or possibly two, farmers with enough extra cash to take advantage of it. A cement drying area built with the help of this public money quickly becomes a semipublic area. The actual owner has first claim on its use, but if he is not using it, any other villager may do so without asking his permission. On the other hand, a drying area which is not cemented is definitely considered private property, and before a villager may use it he must gain the permission of the owner.

Moneylending (Rural Credit)

A major problem which still confronts the Taiwanese farmer, just as it did the mainland farmers under the Nationalists, is the difficulty in obtaining low-interest loans. The little progress made thus far in easing this problem in the Hsin Hsing area has been through the efforts of the local Farmers' Association. The association in Pu Yen has used its own available funds, together with the financial and organizational help of JCRR, to offer low-interest loans to small farmers. Other loans which have been made available by the provincial Food Bureau and the Land Bank have been of little help in easing the credit situation of the small farmer, since such loans require too much security or else are mainly for business purposes. The result is that most farmers still resort to high-interest private moneylenders or to moneylending clubs.

The Farmers' Association, under the Shih Fan Tai K'uan, "Model Money Lending" system, makes cash loans which are to be repaid in cash, to small farmers. The rules for the granting of these loans are made by each district Farmers' Association, but they must be approved by JCRR. The loans can be made only to regular members of the Farmers' Association, to help them purchase farm implements necessary to increase their production. The maximum loan made by the Pu Yen Farmers' Association in 1958 was NT $3,000. This was lent for a maximum period of two years, and payments on the loan were due every six months. The actual time permitted for repayment of the loan depends upon the amount of money borrowed. The interest rate charged by the Farmers' Association is 1.5 percent per month.

The only security demanded of the borrower is the guarantee of two other members of the Farmers' Association. A committee of the association decides if the borrower is a good risk by examining the amount of land he operates (owned and rented). According to the Extension Head of the Farmers' Association, the most important consideration is that the man can be trusted and also that he have good guarantors. Thus, if his reasons for wanting the loan are accepted, even a man who owns only a small piece of land may be able to borrow the maximum amount of money for the full two-year term. At the Pu Yen association

probably more than one-half of these loans are made to tenant farmers
and to people who are both landowners and tenants. However, the
funds available for such loans are limited, and can therefore play only
a small part in alleviating the rural credit situation.

In 1958 there were also two types of loan systems sponsored by the
provincial Food Bureau and administered by the Pu Yen Farmers'
Association. One system, called Sheng Ch'an Tai K'uan, "Money
Lending for Production," makes available through loans small
amounts of cash directly proportional to the amount of land the borrower operates (owns or rents). For each *chia* of land he operates a
farmer can borrow NT $600. Farmers who operate small amounts of
land, like the majority of Hsin Hsing farmers, therefore do not like to
borrow money under this plan since the amounts are too small and
involve too much red tape. An additional, and perhaps greater, disadvantage of this system is that the money borrowed, plus the interest,
must be paid back in rice rather than in cash. The rice to be repaid is
not calculated at the market price but at the rather lower official price.
Consequently, the farmer must pay back much more rice than he
could have bought with the money he borrowed plus the interest.

The other Food Bureau loan plan is to aid poor people who do not
have enough rice to eat. These people may borrow brown husked rice
(unpolished) at a low interest rate. This rice loan must then be repaid
in new unhusked rice. According to an employee of the Farmers' Association, the brown husked rice loaned out by the Food Bureau under
the administration of the Farmers' Association is rice stored in the
association warehouses which the Food Bureau wishes to get rid of
before it spoils. The only people who are eligible for such a loan are
poor people who grow rice.

The government Land Bank also offers loans, but these are usually
made to large landholders who want the money to engage in business,
offering their land as security. Thus, in times of financial need most
small farmers must still resort to private moneylenders who require
little security but charge interest rates of about 3.6 percent per month.
Such loans are frequently for short terms because the interest rate is so
very high. The moneylenders are usually landlords or former landlords and businessmen who have cash on hand and engage in such
business as an investment. However, there are also small farmers who
happen to have some cash on hand and lend it for a short time at the
same high interest rates. These men will also sometimes lend small
sums of money for a short time without interest to someone with whom
they are intimate—some *ch'in tsu* or *ch'in ch'i*, or even some very close
friends who are not related to them in any way.

Another common means of borrowing money in the Hsin Hsing
area, and in urban centers, is through a moneylending club. These

clubs, which are very popular in Hsin Hsing, are similar to the clubs formerly found in many parts of mainland China (Fei, 1939:267–274) and in Japan (Embree, 1939:138–147). Loan clubs, usually with ten to fifteen members, are organized by a man or woman who is considered reliable and trustworthy and who needs a large sum of money for some special purpose such as building a new house, buying some land, or paying for engagement gifts or dowry. The members, enlisted by the organizer, are usually his relatives, friends, or neighbors or sometimes even acquaintances of any of the others. The members are generally people who are interested in being of help to the organizer in his financial need, but there are others who participate only because they hope to make a profit.

The operation of such a moneylending club is quite complex. By means of such a system a person in financial need is often able to obtain an interest-free loan which is to be paid off over a fairly long time—usually more than a year—in equal monthly installments.[3] If the amount involved is very large, such a club may use rice instead of money for the initial loan and for all payments. Under this system, all the payments are made twice a year, that is, after each rice harvest, over a period of years. For the most part, only rice growers participate in this latter transaction.

Generally speaking, then, the problem of farm credit has not yet been solved in the Hsin Hsing village area. A very large proportion of small farmers in financial need must still borrow money under the traditional high-interest systems. The problems of poor credit facilities, along with other financial burdens of the land, seem to be a factor in the increase in the number of families which are forced to find ways of supplementing farm income.

Agent for the Provincial Government's Food Bureau

It is only through the increased use of fertilizer that it is possible for the Taiwanese farmer to cultivate the land so much more intensively than before. In the middle and late 1930's Japanese chemical fertilizer and bean cake imported from Manchuria was used in Taiwan. Then, as now, the fertilizer was distributed for the government by the local Farmers' Associations. Under the Japanese, however, the villagers report, the system of distribution and payment for the fertilizer was quite different. Then, the farmer could easily obtain as much fertilizer and bean cake as he needed and desired so long as it was available. The cost of the fertilizer could be paid in cash (as could the land tax) after the sale of the rice harvest to a merchant. Now, payment for the fertilizer is only made in rice, partly before and partly after the harvest. Today, the government, operating through the provincial government's Food Bureau, has a monopoly on the importa-

tion of the chemicals from Japan which make up the greater part of all
the artificial fertilizer used in Taiwan. Only a relatively small amount
of chemical fertilizer is manufactured in Taiwan itself and sold on
the open market.

Although the provincial government's Food Bureau still distributes
the imported fertilizer through the local Farmers' Associations, the
farmer today cannot purchase the kinds and amounts of fertilizer he
wants. Instead, the fertilizer is only available to farmers who agree to
grow crops specified by the Food Bureau. In 1958, chemical fertilizer
could be obtained by the farmer only if he grew rice or jute as his first
two crops and wheat or vegetables as his third crop. Payment for
fertilizer to be used on rice was made in rice at the rate of one *chin* of
rice for one *chin* of fertilizer. Only the fertilizer for jute, wheat, or
vegetables could be bought for cash. The amount of fertilizer the
farmer was allowed to purchase was determined by the size of area to
be planted.

The fertilizer to be used for each crop is paid for in two installments: 40 percent at about the time of delivery and the remaining 60
percent after the harvest. Thus, in February or March, for example,
the farmer must pay, in rice, 40 percent of the cost of the fertilizer used
for the first rice crop. Then, sometime between the end of June and
the beginning of August, he must pay the 60 percent still due for the
first crop plus 40 percent of the cost of the fertilizer used for the second
rice crop. The farmer must deliver the rice to the Farmers' Association.
This sort of exchange system creates a number of problems for the
farmer and is responsible for a good deal of his bitterness towards the
government.

As a direct result of the government's monopoly, most of the better
fertilizers tend to be cheaper when purchased at the Farmers' Association than they would be at the shops of local merchants which have
only limited amounts for sale. (The merchants acquire the more desirable imported Japanese fertilizer through devious means which will
be discussed later.) Thus the farmer prefers to buy his fertilizer
through the Farmers' Association at the favorable price. However,
many farmers in the Hsin Hsing area now grow vegetables or some
other crop instead of rice, especially as the second crop, and the association does not allocate fertilizer for such purposes. These farmers, of
course, still need fertilizer, and therefore many declare to the Farmers'
Association that they will plant so much acreage in rice when they
have no such intention. As a result, when payment for the fertilizer
thus obtained is due, these farmers must buy rice on the local market
or from a villager with a surplus in order to meet their obligation.

Even the villager who does grow the rice he has declared to the

Farmers' Association has problems. The farmer who grows rice as his second crop must save some of his rice from the November harvest in order to make the 40 percent payment for the fertilizer for the first rice crop in February or March. If this rice is stored it is in constant danger from rodents, but if the farmer eats or sells his rice, he must then buy rice in the spring at the higher off-season price, in order to make the 40 percent payment for the fertilizer needed in February or March.

A larger problem concerns the association's role in collecting the farmers' rice for the Food Bureau. (This same problem arises when the farmer makes payment in rice after the harvest for land tax, land reform land, and the enforced rice sale to the government. This will be discussed later.) In order to deliver his rice to the Farmers' Association almost three miles from Hsin Hsing, the farmer must either use an oxcart or make several trips by bicycle. To save time and energy, he may hire an oxcart if he does not own one. The rice will not be accepted by the Farmers' Association (acting for the Food Bureau) if it is not dry enough. If this happens, the farmer must take his rice home again and dry it further.

Today, some people in the area who own oxcarts and who have enough capital to maintain large stores of dry rice make it a business to take over the full responsibility of delivering the farmers' rice to the Farmers' Association in acceptable condition. These people obtain the names of farmers and the amount of rice they owe to the government from the Farmers' Association. They then pick up the rice of the willing farmer and give him a guarantee, in the form of a receipt, specifying that the businessman agrees to take over the farmer's responsibility for the rice payment. If the farmer's rice is not dry enough, the agent can then use his own rice stores to make payment. The charge to the farmer for this service is 5 percent in kind of the rice delivered. Many farmers use this service in order to relieve their anxiety over the possible refusal of their rice and also to eliminate the problem of finding a means of delivery.

Still other problems face the farmer under the government's system of fertilizer distribution. When the farmer acquires his fertilizer through the Farmers' Association, he must take the kinds and amounts of fertilizer being sold, regardless of what he would like or thinks he needs. And, in order to buy the ammonium sulphate fertilizer which is necessary for the rice crops, the Hsin Hsing area farmer must also buy a good deal of nitrogen calcium (known as "black fertilizer") which is used mainly for sugarcane and sweet potatoes. The farmers in southern Taiwan, who grow more sugarcane, must take the ammonium sulphate as well as the nitrogen calcium fertilizer. The result is that many farmers in each area sell the fertilizer they do not need to fertilizer merchants at a loss. The merchants then transport it to the area in which that type of fertilizer is in demand; there it is sold in local feed and fertilizer shops at a slightly higher price than at the Farmers' Association.

Large numbers of farmers are affected by the results of their false claims that they will grow rice in their fields in order to be allowed to purchase fertilizer at the Farmers' Association. These false reports also affect government economic statistics. The reports made to the Farmers' Association on the amount of land surface to be planted in rice are one of the important bases used by the provincial government's Food Bureau in estimating the annual Taiwanese rice production. The official rice price mentioned earlier is determined annually by the Food Bureau according to this estimate and then is approved by the Provincial Assembly. However, since so many farmers report an intention to plant more rice than they actually intend to, the estimate regularly tends to be greater than the actual production, and as a consequence the official rice price is usually considerably lower than the market price, which is dependent upon the actual rice supply.

The difference between the official and the market prices of rice has a definite and detrimental effect on the farmers. The landowner pays a land tax for paddy land in rice which must be delivered to the Farmers' Association. In addition, the provincial government's Food Bureau requires each farmer to sell a certain amount of rice to the government at the official rice price. The additional amount of rice due is added to the land tax bill, and the farmer receives a cash payment for it at a later date. This amount of rice is directly proportional to the amount of the land tax paid in rice. Thus, for every "14.16 kilograms" (about 23.4 *chin*) of rice paid in land tax, the farmer must sell "12 kilograms" (about 19.8 *chin*) of rice to the government at the official rice price, which may be as low as 70 percent of the market price.

A number of illiterate farmers in the Hsin Hsing area do not realize that they are selling rice to the government at this lower official price. Some of them are under the impression that the money they later receive from the Food Bureau is a rebate due them because they sent in too much rice for their land tax. Apparently, no one has explained the procedure to them.

Regarding this procedure, Ko Kuo-chi, a Provincial Assemblyman, in the January 1, 1958, issue of *Tzu Chih Tsa Chih, Self-Government Magazine,* sharply criticized the government's Food Bureau for the price it had decided to pay the farmers for their rice. He noted that the government was paying the farmer only NT $97.80 per 100 *chin* of rice, while on the market the farmer could obtain NT $130 for the same 100 *chin*.

The government policy has the effect of a virtual attempt to force the farmer who owns paddy land to grow rice. If the farmer substitutes vegetables or some other cash crop, he must nevertheless pay his land tax in rice and sell rice to the government at the official price as well. Therefore, in order to have the rice to sell to the government at the official price, the farmer who does not grow rice is forced to buy it on the market at a much higher price than he will get from the government.

IRRIGATION: ANOTHER EXTERNAL FORCE

The basic economy of the Hsin Hsing area is directly dependent upon the irrigation system. If the land did not receive water through this system, the present sizable agricultural production would not be possible and certainly could not support the large population in the area. The yearly rains usually come in one short season in late May, June, and July, and would be of little value if the water were not stored and channeled to the land at the proper time through elaborate irrigation works. The irrigation water is so important that it frequently causes social conflict between individuals and even between whole villages.

The Hsin Hsing area, and much of Taiwan, is served by two different types of irrigation systems. By far the most important is the public system, which is organized and operated by the Water Conservation Bureau through the Water Conservation Association. Under their administration water is distributed to the major portion of the land in the area. The second system is private and is administered by privately organized cooperative water-pumping associations. The pumping stations of these associations have recently extended the distribution of water to many formerly nonirrigated fields. The cooperatives build their own pumping stations, which draw water from rivers such as the drainage river behind Hsin Hsing, and then use private, and sometimes public, irrigation ditches to transport the water to the fields of its members. (See map 3, showing Pu Yen Hsiang villages and irrigation system.)

The Public Irrigation System

The public irrigation system is organized and operated under the direction of the government. The agency in control, the Water Conservation Bureau, is subordinate to the provincial government's Department of Civil Administration and under the official guidance of the Water Conservation Bureau is the Water Conservation Association, which is made up of a membership of the many farmers who use irrigation water. Theoretically, this association operates and controls the irrigation system, but actually, it is under the authority and direc-

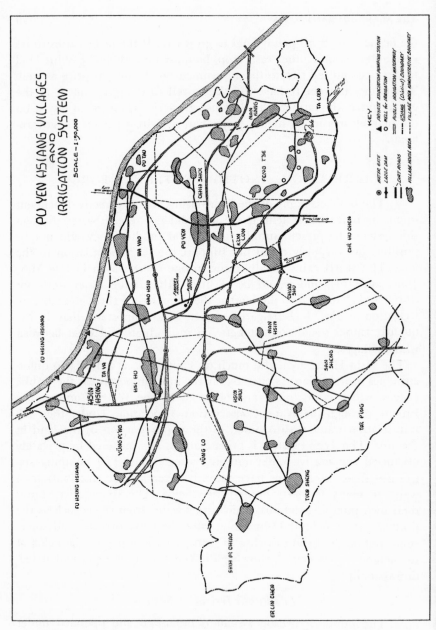

Map 3. Pu Yen Hsiang villages and irrigation system. Source: Pu Yen Water Conservation Working Office.

tion of the government bureau. The association, like the Farmers' Association, is supposed to work for the benefit of its members.

The Hsin Hsing area is a member of the Chang-hua Water Conservation Association. The association is broken up into four district associations, which are further subdivided into smaller working units, each unit having its own area office. Every district association elects representatives which in turn elect an executive body to determine policy. Each working unit elects a man to be its "small water unit chief." It is the job of this individual to see that the distribution of the irrigation water goes smoothly in his area and to report any problems to the Water Conservation Association. These men, like the representatives and the members of the executive committee, receive no pay for their work. However, the association does employ a number of people in the various offices in each area who are responsible for the actual operation of the irrigation works.

In the Hsin Hsing area, the elected representatives and small water unit chiefs of the Water Conservation Association are all relatively wealthy men and for the most part belong to the landlord class. The villagers consider these people "local gentlemen" because "they work for the local area," and therefore the villagers like to vote for them. The economic position of these local gentlemen is secure, and they have enough education to be in a position to contribute to the local area and work for the benefit of the people. "If a man's family does not have enough to eat, how can that man contribute anything to the area?"

The farmer membership of the association pays the expenses for the operation of the irrigation system by the association. Although the money they pay is called "membership dues," the farmers refer to it and consider it to be a "water tax." The money goes to the Water Conservation Association and is used to pay the salaries of the hired workers and to maintain the irrigation system. Part of this money goes to the Water Conservation Bureau as a "kind of water rights tax, just as the bus company pays a tax for road rights."

The irrigation water supplied to the Hsin Hsing area is carried by many rivers from the interior mountain area of Taiwan. Once in the plains area, a series of dams on the rivers divert some of the water into long canals which run alongside the rivers. These canals then turn inland at a point just before the site of the next dam, so that the canals are not continuous. Along each of these canals is a series of smaller water gates, each of which feeds the water into narrower irrigation ditches which go off for long distances between the fields and become narrower as the water supply lessens. If the water level in the irrigation ditch is higher than the field surface, a small opening made in the ditch wall allows the water to flow into the fields. If, however, the water level is low and/or the field surface high, the water must be pumped into the field with a foot treadle waterwheel, usually operated by one to three people at a time.

The irrigation water is fed into the many fields which receive it on a rotation system. The fields nearest to the water source receive the water earliest. Thus, when the first water gate in the irrigation canal is closed, the water is diverted into the irrigation ditches and flows into the adjacent area; the flow of water below this water gate is practically stopped. The water in these irrigation ditches is received first by the land closest to the water gate. In each small area the narrow irrigation ditch is blocked with an earth dam which diverts the water into the fields. When the fields are sufficiently flooded, the dam is opened and the water proceeds through the irrigation ditch to the next small dam, where it is again diverted into the fields. When all the fields in the area have been flooded, the first water gate on the canal is opened, and the water flows on through the canal until it reaches the next closed water gate, which again diverts it into the ditches and to the fields. So the rotation system continues down the line, with the land furthest from the water gates and irrigation ditches receiving the water last.

Under such a system, if there is a water shortage the areas nearest the water gates and dams have the best chance of receiving an adequate water supply. The farmers call this area the "water head." The area most distant from the water gates and dams is known as the "water tail." Farmers whose fields must wait until the last for water usually suffer from an insufficient water supply for their crops, especially for rice.

Even if there is not a water shortage, the farmers who cultivate fields in the water tail normally plant their rice later than the farmers in the water head, which creates a natural staggering of the planting and harvesting in the area. However, when there is a water shortage, it is often necessary, especially for the farmers in the water tail, to delay the transplanting of the rice seedlings and sometimes even to substitute another crop. Most of the land tilled by the Hsin Hsing villagers is in the water tail, and during the course of the research period it was common to see plowed fields waiting for weeks to be flooded or to see rice withering in the dry and cracking soil. As a result frequently the rice production of the area is disappointingly small, and the water problem is a constant concern of the villagers, even the young children. Water and the coming of water is often the main topic of conversation for weeks on end.

Sometimes the water problem becomes so grave that farmers may resort to "stealing water," secretly opening a water gate or an earthen dam in an irrigation ditch so that they can obtain their water out of turn and ahead of time. Frequently, when this or some other form of stealing water occurs, there is physical violence. Since a concentration of fields in a small area is likely to be cultivated by farmers from several villages, violence between individuals often causes animosity between villages.

Sometimes when the water supply is short, it is very late in coming through the irrigation canals to the Hsin Hsing area because it is being held up at a gate in the water head area. If this creates an emergency, equipment is brought in to pump the water directly from the river into the canal and then into the ditches of the area. The operation of this pumping equipment is almost entirely paid for by the Water Conservation Association, but at the same time, part of the expense of maintaining the pumps must usually be borne by the farmers of that area.

When a serious water shortage occurred in 1958, it was after many requests by the farmers of the area and through the efforts and influence of their small water unit chief, a rich landlord, that pumps were finally brought in. However, instead of the pumps being installed immediately, problems developed which delayed their use for several days. Those farmers who were mainly from one village with land in the water head declared that they would not participate in paying the extra costs of operating the pumps. This unusual noncooperative attitude was the result of bad *kan-ch'ing* between themselves and the farmers from other villages over the election of the small water unit chief.

The farmers with fields in the water head were receiving what little water was coming through the system. In addition, when the pumps brought in more water, these farmers felt free to continue to use the water since it ran through public ditches. Therefore, the farmers with fields toward the water tail decided that they too would refuse to pay for the pumping so long as the people in the water head were taking the water without paying for it. They also felt that by the time the water reached the water tail under the normal rotation system it would be too late to be of use. Therefore, they insisted that everyone, including the farmers of the water head area, share in the costs of pumping and also that the normal rotation order under which the water tail received the water last be changed. Since most of the water coming through the irrigation system would be pumped into it, they insisted that all the farmers draw lots to determine the order of rotation. Because the villages of the water head refused to participate in any such arrangement, the Water Conservation Bureau office and the local police were asked to settle the dispute. These officials agreed in this instance that the rotation order should be determined by drawing lots. However, the farmers of the water head area still refused to take part, and the Water Conservation Bureau and the police who had been requested to intervene then told the farmers to mediate the dispute themselves.

Dependence upon mediation as a primary solution to all disputes seems to be as common in rural Taiwan today as it has traditionally been. The reason for this is that rural people usually do not wish to become involved with the authorities and so seek to mediate most problems among themselves. The person who immediately takes a dispute to the authorities is considered unreasonable. If the problem is recognized as being severe, and it does become necessary to take it to the authorities, too often they—including the police, courts, and local civil officials—do not wish to become involved in local problems. Involvement costs them time and trouble and may mean making enemies. Therefore, wherever it is at all possible, the authorities insist that the disputants mediate their own problem.

However, in the mediation of disputes, one of the disputants not uncommonly has an advantage, simply because he is more powerful, that is, has more prestige, money, and influence. Although the idea of reasonableness of disputants' demands is inherent in the concept of mediation, such a powerful disputant is not likely to be particularly reasonable in his demands for settlement.

This was the case in the above mentioned irrigation problem. Obviously, in order to change the rotation order successfully, all farmers concerned had to be in unanimous agreement. However, the farmers in the water tail area could do little to force the issue, since the farmers in the water head area had nothing to gain by cooperation. Finally, as the situation became critical, the pumps were put into operation by the small water unit chief and his assistants in order to try to save the rice crops. The allocation of the excess expenses for operating the pumps was left for a later decision.

While for the most part the public irrigation system runs smoothly as long as there is enough water, there are occasions where a lack of cooperation upsets the operation of the system and the fair distribution of water to all. There have been a few occasions when several men from a large village in the water head area opened the dam on the river so that little water flowed into the canal and down to the water tail. They did it simply to make it easier to catch fish. This demonstration of complete lack of social responsibility toward their fellows was condemned by all the villagers whose fields were affected by the cutoff of the water supply. However, the villagers of the water head area, who were not affected, did not actively censure their fellows even though they did not condone the act. The apparent lack of concern for the welfare of people of another area is not unusual. In this case the police did intervene, but because of red tape the case dragged on, and had still not been settled by the time my field research was concluded in September, 1958.

Private and Cooperative Pumping Station Associations

In the Hsin Hsing area there is still much dry land to which the public irrigation system has not yet been extended. In the last six to seven years much of this dry land has been transformed into more productive wet land with the building of privately operated pumping stations. Sometimes such pumping stations are very small and are built by one or two people as an investment. However, they are more often built as cooperative ventures and use large pumps to irrigate relatively large areas.

A small private pumping station was built by a Hsin Hsing villager to irrigate the land immediately behind the village and the land which lies between Hsin Hsing and the neighboring village of Ta Yu. It irrigates about eight *chia* of land, most of which is owned and cultivated by Hsin Hsing villagers, although about one *chia* of land is operated by people from Ta Yu village. When the owner found that the operation of the pumps was not profitable, he turned the station into a cooperative by selling shares to most of the farmers who had previously paid him for the water they used. In 1958 there were sixteen shares in the cooperative, each valued at about NT $1,200. This was calculated on the current price of rice; the capital of the cooperative is maintained in rice. This cooperative also sells water to non-shareholders with small fields in the area. The price for irrigating 0.1 *chia* of land per crop is one hundred *chin* of rice. Farmers who have very small portions of land in the area do not usually join the cooperative, preferring to buy the water when they need it.

Since it is a small one, this cooperative has no elected officers. One Hsin Hsing villager who is also a shareholder is hired by the cooperative to tend the pumps and see to the distribution of water to the members and purchasers. If a minor repair or decision must be made, this caretaker may take it upon himself to resolve it. However, if any major decision or large repair must be made, then a meeting of the shareholders is called, and the decision is made by general agreement.

A large cooperative pumping station operates in Ta Yu village and irrigates almost forty *chia* of land. The membership is large and the organization formal. Officers are elected and decisions are made at meetings by a vote of the membership. Two landlords who own large portions of the land irrigated by this cooperative are the elected leaders and exert considerable influence on all decisions which are made. It is to the advantage of the cooperative to have such wealthy men as their leaders, since they know many public officials in the Water Conservation Bureau and Association and can therefore exert a great deal of influence if any problems should arise in dealing with these agencies.

The farmers who receive water from private irrigation systems must also be members of the area Water Conservation Association, and therefore pay for the use of the water which is considered public. Water is usually distributed among members of the pumping station cooperatives on the basis of rotation, the order of which is determined by drawing lots. The land of some farmers served by the pumping station was formerly nonirrigated, so these men had to dig their own irrigation ditches. However, some members of the cooperative also cultivate paddy land which is in the water tail area of the public irrigation system. In these cases, when the farmers joined the cooperative, the public irrigation ditches were frequently used to carry the privately pumped water to their land, usually at times when there was no public irrigation water coming through the ditch. The use of these public irrigation ditches for the water pumped by the cooperative is sometimes responsible for disputes and even violence, as will be seen in the case of a Hsin Hsing farmer who was not a member of the large cooperative. Li Fan took water for his field from the public ditch. Two members of the cooperative accused him of stealing the cooperative's water, claiming that there was little public water coming through at the time, and beat him severely. This incident caused controversy and antagonism between Hsin Hsing and Ta Yu, the village in which most of the members of the cooperative lived. When mediation yielded no solution to the conflict, the villagers finally resorted to the courts. (This case is described in detail in Chapter 6.)

The building of these pumping station cooperatives has greatly increased agricultural production for the lands they serve. Much of the land they irrigate was formerly dry land producing only such crops as sweet potatoes, special broom grasses, cucumbers, and peanuts. Today, these same lands are good rice producers. In addition, the lands benefiting from the private irrigation systems can usually receive water earlier than the surrounding water tail land which gets water from the public irrigation system. Consequently, while the water tail land frequently receives too little water too late, the land privately irrigated by the pumping stations usually receives ample water much earlier. This means that farmers benefiting from the private irrigation systems rarely have any difficulty in planting and harvesting according to the dates specified by the agricultural calendar.

Thus, the expansion of the irrigation network, both public and private, has required villagers to involve themselves with people and government in places where they previously had few, if any, relations. Irrigation networks cross village and even area boundaries. Although villagers in premodern Taiwan also had relationships with other villages and areas, it is evident that the recent expansion of agriculture has made the increase in their outside relations both possible and necessary. During a period of drought while I was in the village, I found the villagers both aware and concerned with whether the provincial government would hold the large mountain water resources back in order to generate electric power or would release the water earlier to be used for irrigation.

The effect that irrigation has had on the villagers' outside concerns is no different from the effect on their lives of the recently expanded operations of the Farmers' Association through its facilities and, especially, its improved extension services.

But perhaps one of the most striking changes in the village has been in land utilization—the important switch to vegetable growing, a cash crop, which necessitates a development of interest in marketing. This change in land utilization is very closely related to land tenure problems such as land scarcity and the recent important development of out-migration of villagers to the city. These will be discussed in the next chapter.

[4

Changing Land Tenure and
Its Effect on
Community Organization

The traditional (Ch'ing) land tenure system in Taiwan has undergone a number of modifications over the years. Each was instituted with the advent of a new regime, and marked the inception of major changes in other aspects of rural life. As we have seen, the colonial administration policies of the Japanese were instrumental in producing the first significant involvement of the Taiwanese peasant in the market economy. Nevertheless, it was not until the restoration of Chinese rule, when the population growth began to exert noticeable pressures and the Nationalist Chinese sponsored the Land Reform Program, that major changes took place in the economy which reached directly into most of the areas of Taiwanese rural life.

The system of land tenure in Taiwan has always been a controlling factor in the lives of the agricultural population, and to understand Taiwanese life fully it is necessary to understand the land tenure system and its history. From the late nineteenth century onwards the rural villagers suffered the results of the concentration of landownership into too few hands. This situation culminated finally in the Land Reform Program of 1949–1953, which, for the first time, secured the Taiwanese tenants' rights to the land they tilled through firm rental contracts, reductions in rent, and the Land-to-the-Tiller Program.

Putting untilled land under cultivation became a great concern of the government at the time of the Manchu conquest of Taiwan in 1683, according to T'ang (1954:23–27). Under the Manchu (Ch'ing) dynasty, any person applying for rights to occupy uncultivated land was considered the owner as long as he kept his acres under proper cultivation. Not surprisingly, this program led to a situation in which people with enough capital, "a relatively small number of great families" (Ginsburg, 1953:32), obtained rights to large amounts of land

88

and then hired other people, usually immigrants from the mainland, to cultivate the land for them as their tenants.

As the population increased in the later years of the Ch'ing administration there was increasing pressure on the land, and many tenants began to sublease part of the land to others. These subtenants became the lowest rank in a three-stage hierarchal structure of land tenure (Ginsburg, 1953:26–27, 32–33; Grajdanzev, 1942:72–84; T'ang, 1954: 23–27).

In 1904, nine years after taking control of Taiwan, the Japanese government altered this hierarchal system of land tenure by buying out the original landowner and conferring the rights of ownership on the tenant. When, in 1923, the Japanese applied the Japanese Civil Code to Taiwan, full legal rights were given to the new owner (the former tenant), who was now officially known as "landlord."

This move benefited the original tenant who was given full ownership rights, but it did nothing to improve the lot of the mass of actual cultivators (now tenants instead of subtenants) whose land rent was no lower than before. As a result, "tenancy disputes" became more numerous beginning in 1927. In that year the Japanese authorities encouraged the formation of local associations of landowners and tenants which were charged with the responsibilities of promoting better relations between landlord and tenant, preventing tenancy disputes, and fostering agricultural production (T'ang, 1954:26). Although many such associations were formed, "the question of farm rents was entirely outside of the jurisdiction of these associations. It [the rent question] was not only left unsolved, but there was even a marked tendency for farm rents to keep on increasing" (T'ang, 1954:26).

In 1939, in the midst of the Sino-Japanese war, the Japanese government issued a rent control law which was applicable to Taiwan and Japan alike. This law had little effect in Taiwan because it did nothing to reduce rents; it only stabilized the situation. (See Grajdanzev, 1942:72–84, especially p. 82 for a discussion of the Japanese attempts to deal with Taiwanese land tenure problems.)

Although the farm tenancy system continued, after 1945 the Japanese rent control law of 1939 was no longer enforced when Taiwan reverted to Chinese rule. With the increase in the rural population and the general upset of the island's economy, farm rents began to rise, and demands increasing security and rent deposits were made. Worst of all, in many cases tenants were arbitrarily evicted (T'ang, 1954:25–28).

Tenancy had been a great problem in Taiwan under both the Japanese and the Chinese since landownership was concentrated in the hands of relatively few owners (Klein, 1958:53; see also his Tables 17 and 18). "The high rate of tenancy reflects the great scarcity of cultivable land in Taiwan in relation to the demand for it. Landownership became even more concentrated in the postwar period than in the pre-war period" (Klein, 1958:53). Large numbers of tenants and would-be tenants were in continuing competition for the land they needed to support their families. The competition, unfortunately, tended to put the tenants at the landlords' mercy and helped perpetuate the already unsatisfactory land tenure system.

Klein also points out that the "increased demand for food by urban dwellers and for rural land by farmers, resulted in the many abuses practiced by rural landowners becoming qualitatively worse and quantitatively more numerous than before. One of the notorious abuses was that of charging oppressively heavy rents" (1958:53). From "1945 through 1947, rents of 60 per cent and 70 per cent (of the annual main crop) became not uncommon in the more fertile and densely populated areas. In some areas the rent was 'ironclad' which meant that in the event of crop disaster or failure, the rent, determined as a percentage of the normal or expected yield was to be paid in full anyway" (Klein, 1958:53–54).

The high rental rates in the moderately fertile Hsin Hsing village area seem to have been standardized according to the type and quality (grade) of the land being rented, and were, in addition, influenced by the relationship between the particular landlord and tenant. Hsin Hsing villagers imply that land rents before the Land Reform Reduction Law were no higher than they are today. Their most vivid memory is one of insecurity on the land rather than excessive rents. Many seem to have forgotten how bad the rent situation really was. Former landlords, however, admit almost nostalgically that land rents in this area were as high as 60 percent of the annual main crop. But the landlord paid all the taxes, and he and the tenant shared the expense of the fertilizer. The tenant paid all the labor costs.

Everyone agrees that rent was generally paid in kind, seldom in money, and "the landlord, as a rule, charged the tenant a fixed amount of rice for paddy land regardless of how small a crop the tenant might raise or what crop he planted" (Chang, 1954:10–11). Nevertheless, if the tenant, through his own efforts, increased the production of his rented land, he usually had to pay a larger rent. There is no question that this greatly stifled the tenants' incentive to increase production. The payment of rent in kind—in rice for paddy land— meant that "In case the tenant planted crops other than rice, he had to sell his crops and buy rice from [the] market to meet the charge. The buying and selling of crops meant extra losses to the tenant" (Chang, 1954:11).

There is no indication before 1949 in the Hsin Hsing area that the landlord collected rent in advance. Usually, he took 60 percent of the rent immediately after the first crop was harvested and the remaining

40 percent following the harvest of the second crop. This system of
rent collection continued in Hsin Hsing village until the Land Reform Program. However, villagers say that some landlords in other
places collected rents on a 70 percent–30 percent basis, and a few even
insisted on the rent being paid in full immediately after the first
crop.

The only thing which gave the tenant any security in his tenancy
was a good personal relationship or good *kan-ch'ing* with the landlord.
This, of course, was only possible if the two lived close enough together to have some sort of contact. Although there certainly were
large economic, social, and usually educational differences, so that in
extreme cases tenants scarcely dared to approach the house of the
landlord except on business, a definite personal relationship often did
develop. A landlord generally had a paternalistic feeling toward his
tenant, and the tenant in turn felt an obligation to him.

In those earlier days, the tenant always helped the landlord who
lived in the immediate area, and especially one who lived in Hsin
Hsing, with certain jobs. He was available to assist the landlord to
build a house or to help at funerals, weddings, and other ritual occasions. Sometimes the tenant would send a birthday present or a duck
or a chicken to the "good landlord in thanks" and in order "to keep
good *kan-ch'ing* between them." In case of a death in the landlord's
family, the tenant would send a sacrifice to show his respect. But such
behavior from tenant to landlord depended strictly on their actual
relationship so that not all tenants sent gifts or provided help for their
landlords. Some landlords were considered "tight"—a term the villagers often use to refer to a man who is "close-fisted" with money, or
to a man who, if he is a landlord, does not concern himself with his
tenant or other people if it is going to cost him anything. Such a
landlord would not be too likely to receive "favors" from his tenants.

If there was a crop failure, the "good" landlord usually gave the
tenant some sort of rent reduction. Although there were in those days
no special regulations covering rent reductions in emergencies, the
tenant and landlord would discuss the problem if a crop failed because
of a typhoon or a water shortage. The tenant might be asked to pay 70
to 80 percent of the normal rent, according to the seriousness of the
crop damage. Once one landlord gave a tenant such a rent reduction,
it was not uncommon for other landlords to follow suit.

However, there were inflexible landlords who would not reduce the
rent under any circumstances. In such cases any good *kan-ch'ing* that
had ever existed between landlord and tenant would certainly deteri-
orate. Then, since tenants had no lease or written contract, the landlord might ask for a higher rent on the land for the next year, which
might be a first step toward taking the land away from the tenant

entirely and finding a new tenant. Thus, while a tenant felt he would have some security on the land, if he could cement his relationship with his landlord or landlords, even such security was of questionable duration. And the tenants' problem was worsened by the small size of the fields, which meant that it was not uncommon for a man to have more than one landlord.

A good many landlords who rented land in the area to Hsin Hsing villagers did not live there. A number lived (as some still do) in relatively distant villages, and a few, usually businessmen, lived in Lukang or Taichung City. Since absentee landlords usually did not rely exclusively upon their land rents for a livelihood, they were often not very strict with their tenants. In the event of a crop failure, the villagers recall that most of these absentee landlords were willing to allow a rent reduction, perhaps even more so than the landlord who lived in the village area. It was not, of course, easy for the absentee landlords to operate their land by themselves or to find a new tenant or hired laborer to take care of the land for them. The landlord who lived in the village area could operate the land himself with hired laborers or else easily find a new tenant.

The tenant whose landlord lived in the immediate area considered the maintenance of good *kan-ch'ing* an important factor in determining his tenure. He apparently realized, nevertheless, what a slender reed it was, since he admitted that absentee landlords were easier to deal with. Keen competition for land, especially in the postwar period, resulted in a constant danger that other would-be tenants might approach the landlord and offer him a higher rent or other concessions. Under such circumstances the tenant could only try to fulfill all of his obligations to the landlord with the hope of maintaining a precarious goodwill.

I heard of several landlords in Hsin Hsing village and the immediate area who switched tenants every year, with hardly a word of explanation, as they received better rental offers. Although such landlords were extremely unpopular in the countryside, there was little that tenants could do. These landlords were well known in the area for such practices, and when labor was in short supply during the extremely busy part of the agricultural season, many local farm laborers refused to work for them. This technique of getting back at unpleasant landlords is still used today. One landlord family in Hsin Hsing was greatly disliked by the villagers in the postwar period and to this day often has difficulty in obtaining labor at harvesttime.

The case of this family is an excellent example of the landlord-tenant problem in Hsin Hsing. Good feeling and mutual aid had existed between the old landlord, who was head of his family, and many of his tenants. After the death of the old man—which was prior to land reform—his wife and sons were not concerned with continuing these good relations. Whenever the opportunity arose for securing higher rents from a new tenant, the wife and sons threw the former tenant off the land. Most of the villagers felt hostile towards this family for its greediness and betrayal of the formerly good *kan-ch'ing*.

Ironically, in the postwar period, it was the constant fear and uncertainty which prevented the active growth of any movement or demand among the tenant farmers in this area for some kind of land reform. Such activity would immediately endanger a tenant's relationship with the landlord, especially the local ones, and his tenure on the land would be jeopardized. Even to complain about the situation was dangerous. Other farmers, desperately in need of additional land, might inform the landlord that the tenant was criticizing his treatment or perhaps abusing or neglecting the land. Then, after planting the seed of distrust, the informer might offer to rent the land himself. The tenant's fear of such competitive tactics and his insecure relations with his landlord ensured his continued submission to the system.

LAND REFORM PROGRAM

In mainland China, land reform in the form of a rent reduction program had been attempted as early as 1929 by the Chekiang provincial government (Chang, 1954:16). The program and others, which were intended eventually to transfer landownership from landlord to tenant, were attempted by other provincial governments also, as well as by the Nationalist government in various provinces such as Fukien, Szechwan, and Kwangsi up to the time of the Communist take-over in 1949 (Chang, 1954:16–19; T'ang, 1954:89–95). However, while some of the programs were successful, they were all very limited and at best effective only in localized areas of the mainland.

After the Nationalist government took over in Taiwan, a large-scale Land Reform Program was successfully carried out on the island. This was a "Three Step Program" instituted officially by the National government in 1951 and completed in 1953. Chang (1954:20) wrote: "The first phase, also the mildest reform, seeks improvement of the tenant's living without overthrowing the tenancy system or changing the tenant's status. The second phase, the converting of a fraction of tenants into owner-farmers by selling public land to them, may be taken as a trial or transitional stage. The third phase, Land-to-the-Tiller, aims at turning all tenants into owner-farmers . . . the last and final goal of land reform."

The program was based on a law known as the "Regulations Governing the Lease of Private Farm Lands in Taiwan Province," promulgated by the provincial government of Taiwan on April 10, 1949.

The law provided for a ceiling on farm rental of 37.5 percent of a predetermined estimated yield, regardless of any production above that figure. In the event of a crop failure, the law stipulated that "the lessee and the lessor may make arrangements between themselves for the reduction of rent in accordance with local custom. . . . If the total yield is less than 20 per cent of the normal yield, the entire rent payment shall be remitted" (T'ang, 1954:222). It guaranteed, through landlord-tenant contracts, that the rights and welfare of the tenant farmer would be safeguarded. However, there was still "no adequate provision for the protection of tenant's rights owing to the restrictions imposed by certain articles of the Land Law and the Civil Code. Hence there occurred, after the enforcement of farm rent reductions, many cases in which some landlords tried to take back their leased land from their tenants by resorting either to compulsion or promises of material benefit" (T'ang, 1954:32).

Loopholes in the law made it possible for landlords to make up for having to reduce the land rent by charging house rent and other new charges. In 1949 there were several cases of landlords who successfully convinced their gullible, or perhaps trusting, Hsin Hsing village tenants that there was no reason to draw up a land contract, since their verbal agreement had always been adequate in the past. On this basis, the landlord promised, the tenant "could consider that his family would be able to work the land forever on the same basis of mutual trust and good *kan-ch'ing* which had always existed between them." The rent would, of course, be the legal 37.5 percent paid by other tenants.

In several instances in Hsin Hsing and in other villages—according to an informant who works in the Public Office and used to have a position in the Land Office—uneducated tenants were persuaded not to report themselves as tenants. In these cases, since there was no one claiming tenancy rights, the landlord would say that he himself tilled this land. If later the rightful tenant should dispute the matter (and there have been a number of such cases), the landlord would officially claim that the tenant was not a tenant at all but only a hired laborer. In this way, the landlord, who realized there was to be a transfer of land to the tenants, felt he had a better chance to retain ownership of his land. In Hsin Hsing village, there are still a few small plots of land covered by such a verbal agreement between a landlord and his tenant.

Farm Rent Reduction Act of 1951

The many instances of landlords' abuses of tenants plus the weak enforcement of the 1949 provincial law led to a need for the "Farm Rent Reduction to 37.5 Percent Act." This national act was passed by the Legislative Yuan on May 25, 1951, and promulgated by the President of the Republic of China on June 7, 1951. Although it did not eliminate all abuses of tenants, it went a long way toward this end in the Hsin Hsing area as in all of Taiwan.

The act strictly enforced the rent reduction policy, holding land rent to 37.5 percent of the main annual crop. Production was predetermined on the basis of two crops a year in the Hsin Hsing area. Under its provisions any increase in production brought about through the tenant's own efforts benefited the tenant only, not the landlord. The rent was still to be paid in kind and in two installments, one after each harvest. The act also contained rules for rent reductions in cases of crop failure, specifying that the "Farm Tenancy Committees" of the area should investigate each case, determine the extent of the crop failure, and stipulate the amount by which the rent should be reduced. "If, owing to crop failure, the total yield is less than 30 per cent of the normal yield, the entire rent payment shall be remitted" (T'ang, 1954:225).

More important, the 1951 act provided security never before known by the Taiwanese tenant farmer. The tenant's right to work the rented land without fear of being evicted by the landlord was secured by a minimum six-year contract. The law even provided that when the six-year lease expired, the landlord could not take back the land for self-cultivation if he could not cultivate it himself, if his income was already sufficient to support his family, or if the tenant and his family, by loss of the leased land, would lose their means of livelihood (Chang, 1954:22–23).

With the tenant's security on the land protected, he no longer had to kowtow to his landlord or attempt to maintain good kan-ch'ing. Today, it is common to hear a tenant, formerly courteous to his landlord whether he liked him or not, actually curse him when he comes in his own wagon to collect and load the tenant's land rent. (The tenant formerly delivered the rent to the landlord.) On one such occasion in Hsin Hsing, K'ang, a landlord from another village, came to pick up his rice rent. In Mandarin, the name is pronounced K'ang, but in the local Taiwanese dialect, it is pronounced K'ung. But K'ung in Taiwanese also means stupid. The Hsin Hsing tenant, while watching the landlord load the rice in his wagon, laughingly repeated over and over for all to hear, "K'ung K'ung is here for the rent." It was obvious to everyone including the landlord that the tenant was punning on his name. While the others stood around and laughed, the landlord continued his work without a word.

The 1951 act also eliminated many other abuses of tenants by landlords. The landlord could be imprisoned if he forced the tenant by duress or force to give up the land. Collecting farm rent or deposit money in advance was also illegal, and the landlords' penalties were just as severe for any other infringement of the law.

At this point some landlords chose to sell much of their land, simply because the rent reduction cut too deeply into their profits. Many others, aware that there was ultimately to be a land expropriation law, felt it was wiser to sell large portions of their land before the expropriating act became effective. Consequently, in many cases the landlord threatened that if the tenant did not buy the land he would sell it to someone else. Even tenants who could scarcely afford it were virtually forced to purchase. Under the 1951 act, Article 15 (T'ang, 1954:226), a landlord wishing to sell his land was required to give first preference to his tenant. "If the lessee makes no written reply to the said offer within fifteen days, he shall be deemed to have waived his preferential right." However, the prices of land under such circumstances were usually rather low, since many of the landlords were eager to sell quickly. Many of these same landlords later expressed regret that they had been so hasty.

On the whole, these early sales by landlords proved to be very much to the advantage of the tenants, who got the land at a price often much lower than the price later set by the government in the 1953 Land-to-the-Tiller Act. If the tenant had not purchased the land after the 1951 act, he might never have obtained the land at all. In many cases the tenant could not gain ownership through the Land Reform of 1953 because the piece of land he leased fell within the three *chia* maximum limit of medium-grade paddy land which the law allowed a landlord to retain.

The 1951 act also established a land commission known in Taiwan as the Farm Tenancy Committees, a reorganized form of the Rent Reduction Committees established under the 1949 law. These committees generally assumed responsibility on the local level to supervise the rent reduction and to render assistance in carrying out the final reform—the Land-to-the-Tiller Program (Chang, 1954:32–37). (For further details see T'ang, 1954:224–228, translation of the "Farm Rent Reduction to 37.5 Percent Act" of 1951.)

Regulations Governing the Sale of Public Farm Lands Act of 1951

In July, 1951, the government began the first of two major sales of nonirrigated public land. The first was the sale of national and provincial public land; the second, which began in January, 1952, was mainly a sale of the expropriated holdings of the Taiwan Sugar Corporation (Chang, 1954:54). Before the sales, tenants on the public land were paying 25 percent of the annual crop production as rent. After buying the land, the new owner's financial burden was much greater. The purchase price was paid in twenty semiannual installments to the government; the amount of these payments did not exceed the 25 percent of the crop paid in rent, but as an owner, the farmer was responsible for taxes and other charges. The financial benefits of ownership would thus not accrue to the new owner until the entire purchase price was paid off in ten years. The sale was important and contributed to the landownership of a few former tenant families in Hsin Hsing. However, it was far less important and attracted less interest than the Land-to-the-Tiller Act which went into effect in 1953 (Chang, 1954: 60–61).

The Land-to-the-Tiller Act of 1953

Under the act, the government was given authority to expropriate the land of landlords and to create owner-farmers. Basically, it provided for government purchase of certain tenant-cultivated lands for the purpose of resale to the tenant-cultivators. In the Hsin Hsing village area, where most of the land is of medium grade, most landlords could retain a maximum of three *chia* (7.2 acres) of paddy land or six *chia* (14.4 acres) of dry (nonirrigated) land. The purchase price of the expropriated land was "fixed at 250 per cent of the total annual main crop yield (the standard volume of main crop as stated in the earlier 37.5 per cent rent contract). Of the purchase price, 70 per cent paid to the landlord is in land bonds and 30 per cent in government enterprise stockshares" (Chang, 1954:65).

The government's "resale price" of the land to the former tenant "is the same as the purchase price, plus a 4 per cent interest per annum and is to be amortized by the purchaser in ten equal annual installments" (Chang, 1954:65–66). Former tenants make a total of twenty semiannual payments, one after each harvest. The payments can be in rice for paddy land, or in cash for dry land, based on the current value of sweet potatoes. According to the law, "the average annual burden to be borne by the purchaser shall not exceed the burden on the same grade of land presently borne by the tenant farmer under the 37.5 per cent rent reduction program" (T'ang, 1954:190).

There was a general restriction written into the Land-to-the-Tiller Act to prevent the reaccumulation of land by large landholders or the manipulation and shifting of ownership of land reform land. It stipulates that "any purchaser who has acquired land under this Act shall not transfer the land to any other person before the purchase price is fully paid; transfer of land, after its purchase price is fully paid, shall be permitted only when the transferee can till the land himself or can use it for industrial purposes" (T'ang, 1954:191, translation of the Law, Chapter IV, Article 28). This means that technically there is no limitation on the amount of land that may be purchased and accumulated, except that the purchaser must have the ability to cultivate it.

However, there is always the possibility that there might again be an expropriation of land in excess of three *chia* of paddy. Under this same section, there is a provision that "In the event that the purchaser cannot till the land himself before its purchase price is fully paid, he may request the Government to purchase the land for resale to other farmers. The Government shall, in such case, reimburse to the purchaser in one lump sum the purchase price already paid" (T'ang, 1954: 191; the Law, Chapter IV, Article 29).

According to Article 8, tenant-cultivated land to be purchased by the government for resale to the present tiller or tillers falls into seven categories: (1) land owned by landlord in excess of the permitted retention acreage; (2) land under joint ownership (no matter how small the amount); (3) the private portion of any land owned jointly by private individuals and the government; (4) land under government trusteeship; (5) land owned by private individuals or family clans for purposes of ancestral worship and land owned by religious institutions; (6) land owned by the Shenming Hui (a popular religious association in Taiwan) and land owned by other juristic persons and corporate bodies; and (7) land which the landlord does not wish to retain and requests the government to purchase (T'ang, 1954:186; "the Law" Chapter II, Article 8).

LAND TENURE STATISTICAL DATA
FOR HSIN HSING VILLAGE

Analysis of the land tenure records covering the present period for Hsin Hsing and other villages of the area provides a fairly complete picture of the land tenure situation of the post-land reform period.[1] However, to obtain a similar picture of land tenure immediately before the inception of the Land Reform Program, it is necessary to work backwards, using the records of the post-reform period as a basis, plus those few pre-reform records which are available. One such pre-land reform record is the 1949 list of landlord-tenant contracts for Hsin Hsing village. Land tenure figures can be calculated from this list of contracts; these, not entirely accurate, still present a picture of the pre-1953 situation, which is valuable for comparative purposes.

Prior to the Land Reform Program (see Table 13) there were 92 farming families in over 100 households in Hsin Hsing village. These cultivated about 61.5580 *chia* of land (148 acres). Of this amount, 25.8204 *chia* (63 acres) was privately owned by Hsin Hsing villagers and 35.7376 *chia* (85 acres) was leased. House lands and roads, then as today, made up an additional 2.9909 *chia* (7 acres) of uncultivated land owned by Hsin Hsing residents. (In the following pages this uncultivated land will not be considered, since we are concerned only with productive land.)

Neither the total amount of land cultivated by Hsin Hsing villagers nor the actual number of farming families changed significantly as a result of the land reform. Nevertheless, there were striking internal

TABLE 13

BREAKDOWN OF TOTAL LAND CULTIVATED (OWNED AND OPERATED) AND
NUMBER OF FAMILIES IN EACH CATEGORY IN HSIN HSING VILLAGE FOR
PRE-LAND REFORM (1949–1951) AND POST-LAND REFORM (1957)

Land classification	1949–1951		1957	
	Area *chia*	Number of families	Area *chia*	Number of families
Privately owned (individual, joint, corporate)	25.8204	62	29.5567	62
Land reform land	—	—	15.3716	36
Tenanted land	35.7376	58	16.2925	38
Total number of farming families	—	92	—	90
Total land surface cultivated	61.5580	—	61.2208	—
House and other uncultivated lands	2.9909	—	2.9909	—
Total land surface owned and operated, cultivated and uncultivated	64.5489	—	64.2117	—

changes in the land tenure situation in the village, especially after the Land-to-the-Tiller Act of 1953, which greatly affected the figures on landownership and tenancy. Privately owned land rose to 29.5567 *chia* (71 acres), and an additional 15.3716 *chia* (37 acres) of leased land sold to the former tenants under the 1953 act caused tenancy to decline to 16.2925 *chia* (39 acres).[2]

EFFECTS OF THE LAND REFORM PROGRAM

The 61.5580 *chia* of land cultivated by Hsin Hsing villagers at the time of the 1949 "Regulations Governing the Lease of Private Farm Lands in Taiwan Province" was of two types: leased land and privately owned land. (See Tables 13 and 14.) Of this, 35.7376 *chia*, or 58.1 percent of the total, was rented by fifty-eight Hsin Hsing village households. Actually, there were a few more tenants, working a few very small plots of land, who were not recorded or given contracts in 1949. These few had been persuaded by their landlords to allow themselves to be classed as laborers instead of tenants. The remaining

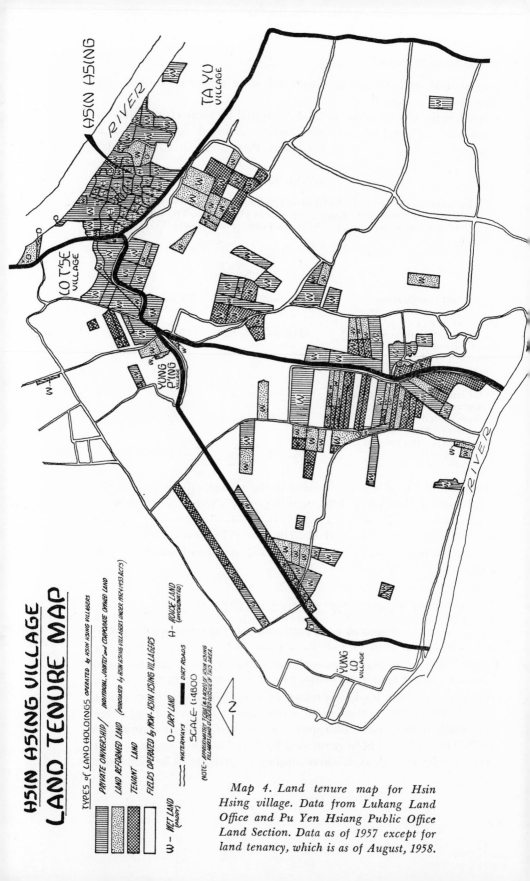

HSIN HSING VILLAGE
LAND TENURE MAP

TYPES of LAND HOLDINGS OPERATED by HSIN HSING VILLAGERS

PRIVATE OWNERSHIP/ INDIVIDUAL, JOINTLY and CORPORATE OWNED LAND

LAND REFORMED LAND (PURCHASED by HSIN HSING VILLAGERS UNDER 1952 & 1953 ACTS)

TENANT LAND

FIELDS OPERATED by NON-HSIN HSING VILLAGERS

H – HOUSE LAND (UNCULTIVATED)

O – DRY LAND

W – WET LAND (PADDY)

— — WATERWAYS   ===== DIRT ROADS

SCALE (:4800)

NOTE: APPROXIMATELY 75% (6.4 ACRES) of HSIN HSING VILLAGERS LAND IS LOCATED OUTSIDE OF THIS AREA.

HSIN HSING

RIVER

TA YU VILLAGE

LO T'SE VILLAGE

YUNG P'ING VILLAGE

YUNG LO VILLAGE

RIVER

N

Map 4. Land tenure map for Hsin Hsing village. Data from Lukang Land Office and Pu Yen Hsiang Public Office Land Section. Data as of 1957 except for land tenancy, which is as of August, 1958.

25.8204 *chia* of cultivated land was privately owned by Hsin Hsing villagers under individual, joint, or corporate ownership. The largest part of all cultivated land was paddy land. (See Table 14.)

Most of the leased land in 1949 was owned by 25 different private landlords. A small part belonged to publicly owned enterprises. Of these twenty-five private landlords, only two were Hsin Hsing villagers; they owned about 5.2 *chia* of land or about 14.6 percent of the total leased land—almost all of which they rented out to fellow villagers. (See Table 15.) Of the remaining leaseholds, 28.5

TABLE 14

AREA AND TYPES OF LAND CULTIVATED BY 92 HSIN HSING HOUSEHOLDS
BEFORE LAND REFORM, 1951

Land type	Paddy field	Dry field	Total (*chia*)	Percentage (*chia*)
Owner-cultivated	25.4867	0.3337	25.8204	41.9
Tenanted	31.9950	3.7426	35.7376	58.1
Totals	57.4817	4.0763	61.5580	100.0

TABLE 15

OWNERSHIP OF HSIN HSING VILLAGE TENANTED LAND, 1949–1951

	Total number of *chia* Hsin Hsing tenanted land	Hsin Hsing tenanted land owned by Hsin Hsing landlords	Hsin Hsing tenanted land owned by private outside landlords [a]	Hsin Hsing tenanted land owned by public enterprises
Amount of tenant land	35.7	5.2	28.5	2.0
Percent of tenant land	100.0	14.6	79.8	5.6
Number of private landlords	25.0	2.0	23.0	—

[a] Landlords living outside Hsin Hsing village as well as outside the area.

chia or 79.8 percent of the total was owned by 23 private outside landlords. Thirteen of them, owning over 19 *chia* of this land, lived in the two villages adjacent to Hsin Hsing, Ta Yu and Yung P'ing. The other ten, owning 9 *chia*, lived in more distant villages or in the cities and had little direct contact with their Hsin Hsing tenants. The remaining two *chia* of tenant land was public land, owned by public enterprises such as the Taiwan Sugar Corporation.

By 1954, the three-step program of land reform had been completed, and the almost 36 *chia* of leased land that had been cultivated by Hsin

Hsing villagers had been reduced to slightly over 16 *chia*. Almost 4 *chia* of the privately owned portion of tenant land had been sold by the owners to their Hsin Hsing tenants after the 1951 Rent Reduction Act (and before the 1953 act of expropriation). More than 2 *chia* of public land, eight plots rented to four Hsin Hsing villagers, were made available to these farmers for purchase over a ten-year period by virtue of the 1951 Land Act which governed the sale of public farm-lands. And in 1953, under the Land-to-the-Tiller Act, the government purchased an additional 13.5 *chia* (in forty-six plots) of privately

TABLE 16

AREAS AND TYPES OF LAND CULTIVATED BY 90 HSIN HSING HOUSEHOLDS
AFTER LAND REFORM, 1957

	Paddy field	Dry field	Total (*chia*)	Percent (*chia*)
Owner-cultivated	42.2345	2.6938	44.9283	73.4
Tenanted	14.9100	1.3825	16.2925	26.6
Total	57.1445	4.0763	61.2208	100.0
Percentage	93.3	6.7	—	—

TABLE 17

AREAS OF CULTIVATED LANDS IN HSIN HSING VILLAGE BEFORE AND AFTER
IMPLEMENTATION OF LAND-TO-THE-TILLER PROGRAM

	Before implementation		After implementation (1957 records)	
	Area (*chia*)	Percent	Area (*chia*)	Percent
Owner-cultivated	25.8	41.9	44.9	73.4
Tenanted	35.7	58.1	16.3	26.6
Total	61.5	100.0	61.2	100.0

owned Hsin Hsing tenant land from the landlords and made it avail-able to the 33 former tenants for eventual ownreship. One of these 33 families had also purchased public land under the 1951 act.

With the completion of the Land Reform Program of 1953, the land tenure picture for Hsin Hsing village had changed radically. Accord-ing to the September, 1957, records, as a direct or indirect [3] result of the land reform, the amount of land leased by villagers was reduced by almost 55 percent from 35.7 *chia* of land in 1949 to 16.29 *chia* in 1957. Whereas in 1949 land leased by villagers had represented 58.1 percent of the total cultivated land, by 1957 it was reduced to 26.6 percent of the total. (See Tables 13, 14, 16, and 17.) (See Map 4 for distribution of village landholdings.)

Prior to land reform, 14.6 percent of the leased land in Hsin Hsing was owned by Hsin Hsing villagers and 85.4 percent by outsiders, including public enterprises. (See table 14.) After land reform, in 1957, only about 9.1 percent of the leased land was village owned; 90.9 percent was owned by outsiders. (See Table 18.)

TABLE 18

Tenanted Land in Hsin Hsing Village, 1957

	Paddy (*chia*)	Dry (*chia*)	Total	Percent
Land surface tenanted	14.9100	1.3825	16.2925	100.0
Tenanted land owned by Hsin Hsing landlords	1.4753	—	1.4753	9.1
Tenanted land owned by land-lords outside Hsin Hsing	13.4347	1.3825	14.8172	90.9

In the pre-land reform period (1949–1951), of the 92 farming households in Hsin Hsing village, 58 households (63.0 percent) were tenants, and of these 30 (or 32.6 percent of the village's farming households) owned no land whatsoever. (See Table 19.) In the post-land reform

TABLE 19

Number of Farming Families in Hsin Hsing by Size of Cultivated Land, 1951

Amount cultivated in *chia*	Own all land	Mixed owner-tenant owns more than half	Mixed owner-tenant owns less than half	Pure tenant	Total number of farming families	Percent of farming families
Less than 0.1	4	—	—	—	4	4.3
0.1–0.3	6	1	1	7	15	16.3
0.3–0.5	8	—	6	8	22	23.9
0.5–1.0	9	2	11	12	34	37.0
1.0–1.5	4	1	3	2	10	10.9
1.5–2.0	2	—	—	1	3	3.3
2.0–2.5	1	—	—	—	1	1.1
2.5–3.0	—	1	1	—	2	2.2
Over 3.0	—	1	—	—	1	1.1
Number of families	34	6	22	30	92	—
Percent of families	37.0	6.5	23.9	32.6	—	100.1

period, the 1957 records show ninety farming households listed in the village of whom only 38 (42.2 percent) were tenant households; of these only 9 (10 percent of the total number of farming households) owned no land, while the remaining 29 tenant householders were partial landowners as a result of the Land Reform Acts. (See Table 20.)

TABLE 20

NUMBER OF FARMING FAMILIES IN HSIN HSING BY SIZE OF CULTIVATED LAND, 1957

Amount cultivated in *chia*	Own all land	Mixed owner-tenant owns more than half	Mixed owner-tenant owns less than half	Pure tenant	Total number of farming families	Percent of farming families
Less than 0.1	4	—	—	—	4	4.4
0.1–0.3	12	1	—	3	16	17.8
0.3–0.5	11	5	1	3	20	22.2
0.5–1.0	18	9	7	2	36	40.0
1.0–1.5	5	2	1	1	9	10.0
1.5–2.0	2	—	—	—	2	2.2
2.0–2.5	—	—	—	—	—	—
2.5–3.0	—	2	—	—	2	2.2
Over 3.0	—	1	—	—	1	1.1
Number of families	52	20	9	9	90	—
Percent of families	57.8	22.2	10.0	10.0	—	99.9

TABLE 21

AREA OF FARMS CULTIVATED BY 36 FARMERS WHO PURCHASED LAND THROUGH LAND REFORM, 1957

Kinds of farmland	Area in *chia*		Percent
Land purchased under Land-to-the-Tiller Program		15.3716	59.6
Paddy field	13.0115		—
Dry land	2.3601		—
Land originally owned and cultivated by farmers themselves		4.5224	17.5
Paddy field	4.4374		—
Dry land	0.0850		—
Leased land		5.8980	22.9
Paddy field	4.7665		—
Dry land	1.1315		—
Total area		25.7920	100.0
Paddy field	22.2154		86.1
Dry land	3.5766		13.9

The rest of the land worked in Hsin Hsing in the post-land reform period consisted of the already mentioned 15.3716 *chia* purchased either under the 1951 act for the sale of public land or the 1953 Land-to-the-Tiller Act, plus the 29.5567 *chia* owned by the villagers as individual, joint, or corporate owned land. However, if one considers the 15.3716 *chia* of land which changed ownership under land reform as

TABLE 22

NUMBER OF FAMILIES PURCHASING LAND UNDER LAND-TO-THE-TILLER PROGRAM,
AND AREA OF FARMS THEY CULTIVATE
Part A. Pre-Land Reform (1949–1951)

| Size of class (*chia*) | Number of farmers later to purchase land | | Area of farms cultivated (*chia*) | | | |
	Number of families	Percent	Paddy field	Dry field	Total area	Percent
Landless: farmers owning no land	19	52.8	—	—	—	—
Less than 0.1 (*chia*)	4	11.1	—	0.0610	0.0610	1.3
0.1–0.3	7	19.4	1.0425	0.0240	1.0665	23.6
0.3–0.5	3	8.3	1.0784	—	1.0784	23.8
0.5–1.0	3	8.3	2.3165	—	2.3165	51.2
1.0–1.5	—	—	—	—	—	—
1.5–2.0	—	—	—	—	—	—
2.0–2.5	—	—	—	—	—	—
2.5–3.0	—	—	—	—	—	—
Over 3.0	—	—	—	—	—	—
Total	36	99.9	4.4374	0.0850	4.5224	99.9

TABLE 22

NUMBER OF FAMILIES PURCHASING LAND UNDER LAND-TO-THE-TILLER PROGRAM,
AND AREA OF FARMS THEY CULTIVATE
Part B. Post-Land Reform (1957)

| Size of class (*chia*) | Number of farmers to purchase land | | Area of farms cultivated including previously owned land (*chia*) | | | |
	Number of families	Percent	Paddy field	Dry field	Total area	Percent
Landless: farmers owning no land	—	—	—	—	—	—
Less than 0.1 (*chia*)	2	5.5	0.3369	0.0130	0.3499	1.8
0.1–0.3	7	19.4	1.3773	0.2600	1.6373	8.2
0.3–0.5	10	27.8	3.6438	0.2482	3.8920	19.6
0.5–1.0	13	36.1	7.7481	0.5918	8.3399	41.9
1.0–1.5	3	8.3	3.5210	—	3.5210	17.7
1.5–2.0	—	—	—	—	—	—
2.0–2.5	1	2.8	0.8218	1.3321	2.1539	10.8
2.5–3.0	—	—	—	—	—	—
Over 3.0	—	—	—	—	—	—
Total	36	99.9	17.4489	2.4451	19.8940	100.0

the equivalent of owner operated land (and legally this is how it is considered), then it is notable that of the 61.2208 *chia* operated by the villagers in 1957 44.9283 *chia,* or 73.4 percent, was privately owned and the remaining 26.6 percent tenant operated.

Thirty-six families, about 40 percent of the Hsin Hsing village farming families, were benefited by the Land-to-the-Tiller Act of 1953. Before the reform program, 19 of these 36 families owned no land at all, and their livelihood depended strictly on the land they rented and whatever outside income they had. However, the other 17 families, besides their rented land, owned only about 4.5 *chia* of land, most of which was paddy field. After the Land Reform Program, which affected almost 15.5 *chia* under the 1951–1953 acts, land that these 36 families cultivated as owners increased to 19.9 *chia,* of which about 17.5 *chia* was paddy. In 1957, 19 of these same 36 households continued to work a little below 6 *chia* of land as tenant farmers. (See Table 21.) This tenant land is cultivated under the strict enforcement of the 37.5 percent Rent Reduction Act.

The change in the landholding status of the 36 families directly affected by the reform program is shown in Table 22, Parts A and B. Before land reform only 3 of the 36 owned more than 0.5 *chia* of land, but in the post-land reform period, 17 of the 36 owned more than 0.5 *chia*. The average area purchased by Hsin Hsing tillers under the reform was 0.44 *chia,* usually in one and sometimes two plots of land per family. This means that in Hsin Hsing village, of the 54 plots of land sold to the tillers by the government, the size of the average plot sold was less than 0.3 *chia* of land.

Chang Yen-t'ien (1954:86) writes that in Taiwan about 46.44 percent of the total pre-reform tenants, including part-tenants, purchased land through the reform program. But he notes that "more than half of the former tenant families . . . are still entirely or partly under the influence of tenancy."

For Hsin Hsing village, the records show that 62 percent of the 58 pre-reform tenants purchased some land reform land, and the figure is probably this high because of the higher rate of tenancy in Hsin Hsing than in Taiwan as a whole. Thirty-six households, or 65.5 percent, of the 58 are still to some extent tenants, however. This is mainly because the land they rented happened to be part of the 3 *chia* of land the landlord could retain under the 1953 law. While this was true for landlords in all of Taiwan, the average land purchase figure may be larger for the whole of Taiwan than for Hsin Hsing because elsewhere in Taiwan there were large tracts of public land available for purchase and, in addition, at the time of the restoration there was little Japanese-cultivated land in the immediate area of Hsin Hsing for Hsin Hsing villagers to take over. These factors have generally contributed to a lower average amount of land tilled by owners in Hsin Hsing than in other villages and areas.

The two major improvements in the land tenure situation as seen in Tables 19, 20, and 23 are: first, the significant increase in landownership and decrease in tenancy, especially the decrease in the number of pure tenants; and second, the large increase in the number of Hsin Hsing mixed owner-tenants, who in 1957 owned more than half the land they cultivated.

It can also be seen from Table 23 that, in 1957, 70 of the 81 land-

TABLE 23

Statistics on Landownership Classification for Hsin Hsing Village:
Pre-Land Reform (1951–1952) and Post-Land Reform (1957)

	1951–1952		1957	
Size of class (*chia*)	Number of farming households	Percent of households	Number of farming households	Percent of households
Own no land at all	30	32.6	9	10.0
Own less than 0.1	12	13.0	9	10.0
0.1–0.3	18	19.6	18	20.0
0.3–0.5	12	13.0	19	21.1
0.5–1.0	13	14.1	24	26.7
1.0–1.5	4	4.3	6	6.7
1.5–2.0	2	2.2	2	2.2
2.0–2.5	1	1.1	3	3.3
Total Landowners	62	67.3	81	90.0
Total farming households	92	99.9	90	100.0

holding families still owned less than one *chia* of land, and 46 of the 81 owned less than a half-*chia*. Thus, the land reform brought about virtually no increase in the total amount of land cultivated by Hsin Hsing villagers or increases in the number of families cultivating the land in each size category. While the reform produced important changes in the internal nature of the land tenure situation, it did not and could not solve the basic problem—an insufficiency of cultivable land coupled with rapid population growth.

Of the 115 households registered in the village in 1957, only 90 households can actually be considered farming families. The 25 registered households of Hsin Hsing village which do not cultivate land at all must be classed as village nonfarming, landless families. The breadwinner in such families may work locally as a hired farm laborer or may have gone off to work in Taipei because of the land scarcity. Once assured of an adequate living in the city, a few of such men sold off or gave up the very small portions of land they were cultivating. Once well settled in Taipei, a few brought at least part and sometimes all of their families to live in the city, although they still maintained registration in the village. Others still maintain a household in the village, leaving an old mother or perhaps even a wife and daughters in the village house.

Other landless households consist of old people who, in the course of family division, left themselves landless by dividing their land among their sons. Such old people usually continue to live in their own house or apartment in the village and eat with their sons' families on a rotation basis.

In Hsin Hsing village there are many farming families who, like the landless, must engage in some form of supplementary activity to earn additional income. Of the 90 farming households, 40 cultivate less than 0.5 *chia* (1.2 acres) of land. (See Table 20.) Many of these families, and even some families which cultivate more than 0.5 *chia*, are too large for the income from so little land. To augment their income, some work as farm laborers and others as itinerant merchants, but most go to Taipei to seek work. In the near future the continued population increase and fractionalization of the land may force more and more of these families into the ranks of the landless.

Many of the benefits which should have resulted from the land reform—the rent reduction, the increased incentive to work the land, the increased crop production and the higher income from a greater application of fertilizer—are negated by a general rise in operating costs for the tiller. This is especially true for former tenants who bought land through the 1953 Land-to-the-Tiller Act; their annual payments on land purchased from the government come to a higher amount than would have been charged in rent (37.5 percent) for similar land. In addition, they now also bear all the operating costs on the land, which formerly were largely borne by the landlord. At the time of the research (1958) at least, this act in itself had not brought about any noteworthy increase in the standard of living.

Although the annual payments on the mortgage to the government do not exceed the 37.5 percent rent paid as tenants on private land or the 25 percent rent paid as tenants on the formerly public owned land, the financial burden is actually heavier than it was when the farmers were still tenants paying reduced rents. As Chang (1954:89–91) has pointed out,

A new owner, so far as he has not fully paid the land price, is in fact a tenant. He has to assume a burden of duties and land price more than that of a bona fide tenant, and has to pay the operating expenses equal to those of a tenant, which are generally higher than those of owner-farmers. His income, too, like that of a tenant, is lower than that of owner-farmers. . . . The situation of new owners, within the coming ten years, will certainly be no better than that of tenants. But looking forward to [being a] full owner-farmer after ten years, when his burden will be only 14.32 percent of his annual main crop, the new owner is mentally in a better situation, and socially he has climbed to the rank of owner-farmer.

Often, villagers who have purchased land under the reform program do not really consider themselves its owners. Besides knowing that they are not yet reaping any increased income from the land, many have a "seeing is believing" attitude. They will believe that the government has made it possible for them to own the land when they no longer have to pay on the mortgage and when they earn an income from the land equivalent to what an owner-farmer earns. They recognize what the future may hold for them as "real owners," but, in the meantime, the burden is extremely heavy.

Villagers who work outside Hsin Hsing have done more to raise the standard of living than has the decrease in tenancy. The increased use of cash has also led to an apparent rise in living standards. In Japanese times, villagers tended to save their money toward future land purchase. Today, people no longer save money for fear of inflation; instead, they are using their cash to purchase tangible goods—bicycles, more and better clothing, and so on, are increasingly in evidence in the rural area.

THE NATURE OF PRIVATE-OWNERSHIP LAND

The 29.5567 *chia* of privately owned land in Hsin Hsing village falls into three categories: (1) individually owned, 35.3 percent of the total private land; (2) jointly owned, 61.5 percent of the total; and (3) corporate or community owned, only 3.2 percent of all the private land owned. (See Table 24.) This classification and the percentages for each type in Hsin Hsing approximate the situation in Taiwan as a whole (T'ang, 1954:98–107).

The system of individually owned land is rather simple, since it consists of portions of land legally owned by one individual who, in most cases, represents a family. On all land records this land is always listed in the name of that one owner. As can be seen in Table 24, very little of the land individually owned in Hsin Hsing is house or road land; it is almost all cultivated land.

Joint-ownership land in Taiwan is one of the most complex forms of private ownership to record and keep track of. It is a common phenomenon making up the largest percentage of the privately owned land in Hsin Hsing as well as in Taiwan. A plot of land is owned jointly by from two to hundreds of individuals. Each joint owner will own a portion of the plot—one-third, one-fifth, or one-twelfth, and so on. In many cases, in Hsin Hsing at least, the joint owners do not own equal shares. Each joint owner may work his share independently or in small groups according to family relationship.

Under the land reform record-keeping system, rather than registering each tiny share of land separately in its owner's name at the Land Office, "it was decided that all plots of land under joint ownership would be classified under the names of all the joint owners, and not under the names of each owner separately" (T'ang, 1954:100). By this system, then, the land was recorded as joint land under the name of one person who acted as legal representative for all the joint owners. Even in Japanese times the government did not interfere in this system, and the representative was supposed to see to the regular payment of the farmland tax for all the joint owners.

TABLE 24

AREA OF PRIVATE LAND UNDER INDIVIDUAL, JOINT, AND CORPORATE OWNERSHIP IN HSIN HSING VILLAGE, 1957

	Area in *chia* of cultivated land	Percent	Area in *chia* of house, land, and road	Percent	Total of each type of land area owned	Percent of total private land
Individual	11.1006	34.1	0.3946	1.2	11.4952	35.3
Joint	17.9196	55.1	2.0768	6.4	19.9964	61.5
Corporate	0.5365	1.6	0.5195	1.6	1.0560	3.2
Total	29.5567	90.9	2.9909	9.1	32.5476	100.0

Regarding the reasons for the existence for so much joint-ownership land in Taiwan, T'ang (1954:101–102) writes:

The causes that have given rise to joint ownership are three; reclamation of land through common efforts in the early history of Taiwan; joint purchase of land; and inheritance of ancestral landed property by brothers. . . . The landowners themselves preferred joint to individual ownership in order to avoid the incidental troubles of subdivision, surveying, and the red tape of transfers. Under such circumstances, it frequently happened that a piece of land originally under individual ownership might come to be jointly owned when it was transferred or inherited; and that a piece of land originally under joint ownership might have a larger number of joint owners as time went on. The number of joint owners of a plot of land varies from three or five to scores or hundreds of persons. This state of affairs not only is a positive hindrance to cadastral management, but also obstructs land improvement and gives rise to innumerable disputes.

The forms that joint ownership take in Hsin Hsing seem to correlate with T'ang's explanation of the causes that have given rise to it. For example, most of the house land in Hsin Hsing is land jointly held among relatives. There are also instances in Hsin Hsing where the land is listed under the representative name of a Hsin Hsing villager, but the joint owners are farmers from neighboring villages as well as from Hsin Hsing. The reason for such diversified joint-ownership groupings may very well go back to the initial period of settlement in the area.

However, the most common type of joint ownership in Hsin Hsing is holdings of groups of cousins or brothers. Inheritance of family land is generally the reason for such ownership groupings. Usually, cousins who are joint owners are members of separate households. The land originally belonged to their fathers as joint land, or to their paternal grandfather, or perhaps to some even more distant relative.

On the other hand, the situation varies when the joint owners are brothers. If family division has already taken place, then each brother will cultivate his share of the land independently. If division has not occurred, the brothers work the whole plot as a common unit, just as they manage all of the economic affairs of such a household. Sometimes brothers may have recently inherited the joint shares from their father. In other cases, the brothers may have recently purchased the land as joint-ownership land. Some have officially listed the exact share of each brother to eliminate any problems or disputes over the land when the family divides.

The joint ownership of land became a serious disadvantage for some farmers as a result of the Land-to-the-Tiller Act of 1953. Owners of joint-ownership portions of land are really no different from the owners of individually owned plots. However, according to the reform act of 1953 (T'ang, 1954:186, Chapter II, Article 8), any joint-ownership land which is not tilled by the owner but is rented out instead, and is not owned by certain specified helpless people, e.g., the old, the infirm, orphans, is liable for expropriation by the government or purchase by the tenant. This singling out of joint-ownership land was done by the government in an attempt to do away with this very common but administratively complex type of ownership which is "primitive and confused" (Chang, 1954:80). While individually owned land could be retained by the noncultivating landlord in amounts up to three *chia* (if medium-grade land), the law did not provide for retention of any portion by joint owners of land.

As a result of this purely technical difference, the law has worked a hardship on many owners who owned small shares of joint-ownership land which they rented out. One such example in Hsin Hsing village was a man who owned a few small portions of joint-ownership land. Since he held an outside job, his family worked one of the small plots and rented out the other; the income contributed to their livelihood. This rented-out land, on which a share of the family's income depended, was expropriated by the government.

Corporate or community-ownership land is the third type of private-ownership land. In Hsin Hsing village, as in most villages in Taiwan, this type of landholding belongs to a *tsu* group. The *tsu* may be a very large one which dominates a whole village, as in many Taiwanese villages, or it may be one of many small *tsu* groups in a village such as Hsin Hsing. In Hsin Hsing only a few of the *tsu* groups own such land, which represents only 3.2 percent of the total land owned by Hsin Hsing villagers. Almost half of this corporate land is the house land for *tsu* members. Almost all of the cultivated corporate land, about 0.5 *chia*, belongs to one of the larger *tsu* in Hsin Hsing, the K'angs. Most of their land is unofficially rented out to two of the *tsu's* own members, who then pay rent of 37.5 percent to the *tsu*. The money is used for some of the *tsu* expenses such as religious ceremonials or the repair of the *tsu's* main ancestral-worship room.

In the official land tenure records, the corporate land is listed in the name of some members of the *tsu* group; it is not recorded as rented-out land. In the several cases of corporate landholdings in Hsin Hsing, the *tsu* members listed as owners in the records are long since deceased, but their names are still carried in the books. The cultivated portions of the corporate lands are administered by respected *tsu* elders. Generally, in Hsin Hsing the *tsu* group pays little concern to its corporate lands, since the amount of them is actually insignificant.[4]

LAND REFORM AND THE LANDLORD

The government compensated landlords for lands expropriated in 1953, but because of the unstable economic situation the compensation was not in cash; 70 percent was paid in land bonds and 30 percent in Government Enterprise Stockshares. In order to insure the value of the bonds against the fluctuations in currency values, they were issued to the former landlords on a commodity basis and, at maturity, were to be paid in kind instead of in cash. Rice was to be paid in return for expropriated paddy land and sweet potatoes for dry land. The principal and interest at 4 percent per annum on the land bonds are being paid to the former landlords over a ten-year period in twenty equal semiannual installments (a payment schedule notably similar to that made by the purchasers of the land from the government). The land bonds are transferable and can be sold on the open market or used as security in financial matters (Chang, 1954:76–77; T'ang, 1954:147–151; 154–163).

After the restoration the national and provincial governments owned 70 percent of the industrial enterprises in Taiwan. These had been taken over from the Japanese at the end of the war. At that time, it was the desire of the Nationalist Chinese government to transfer all public enterprises to private owners except those relating to national defense, those of a monopolistic nature, and those affecting utilities.

For the most part this was achieved after 1953 by transferring the stockshares of such enterprises as paper, mining, and cement to former landlords in payment for their government-purchased land (Chang, 1954:77–79; T'ang, 1954:164–173). But it was clear from the outset that some of these enterprises were less profitable than others and, as far as the landlords were concerned, less acceptable (Chang, 1954:79). Although it was common knowledge that many of the stockshares they received were not worth face value, the landlords could do little but grumble and complain.

After the issuance of the stockshares, business speculators frequently toured the countryside, telling the unwary stockshare holders that the value of the shares they held was very low. They offered cash for these shares at a slightly higher price than they were actually worth, and some landlords in the Hsin Hsing area sold out. Later, they learned that the stock values had risen and that they had been "cheated." This happened mostly to small landlords who lacked business experience. It added to dissatisfaction over the land reform and the feeling that the government had ruined the landlords.

A middle-aged man from one of the formerly big landlord families in the Hsin Hsing area spoke critically of the Land Reform Program and of how it hurt the landlord. Despite his bitterness, however, he admitted that "now the landlord no longer can spend all his time playing around drinking, gambling, and seeing shows. Now, in order to live, he must go out to work and do business. In the old days if the landlord played a lot and needed more money to finance his entertainment, he could just raise his rents."

But, much more important, the Land Reform Program had a major effect on the landlord class in the Hsin Hsing area and possibly in Taiwan generally, and as a result a major effect on the general economy of Taiwan and thus on life in many villages. Before land reform it was traditional in China for the wealthy to buy land for investment or simply for purposes of security. To these landlords, and especially to many urban people, the Land Reform Program made it evident that it was no longer profitable nor even safe to invest their capital in the land. Instead, these people, in addition to their forced participation in industry through being paid in shares of stock for expropriated land, have now in many cases begun to shift their excess capital willingly into industrial, commercial, and small business activities in urban centers and in the smaller market towns. When money was invested in the small market towns, it usually went into financing light industry or small businesses and often meant that the investor needed new technical knowledge. In some cases, the landlords or their sons became greatly involved in business activities, gradually sold off portions of the three *chia* of land which they had been allowed to retain under the land reform act, and used the money for additional investments.

Many former landlords have done poorly at business, and some have even failed because of their lack of experience and training. Others have maintained their economic investments in the villages. Several formerly large landholders in the two villages adjacent to Hsin Hsing continue their activities in their villages and the surrounding area very much as before. Although their landholdings were cut significantly by the land reform, they nevertheless retain their maximum three *chia* of land. Also, in some instances, a number of landlords prior to the 1953 act managed to retain control of more than the three *chia* limit by legally dividing their family and then transferring portions of their land to the names of other members of their family. By virtue of their positions many landlords, especially those who worked as minor officials or civil servants in the local administration or who were well acquainted with officials, became aware of the ins and outs of the proposed land reform laws and so knew exactly how to manipulate their landholdings legally in order to retain as much land as possible.

Even today landlords may, and do, buy land in excess of three *chia* and then hire laborers to till it for them. As long as they do not rent the land out they seem to be safe from legal action. A few landlords who manage to buy additional land are still doing so in the names of other members of their family and in such cases then actually rent the land out to tenants. But it appears that the fear of another Land Reform Program in the future, as well as the increased movement of the landlords' economic interests outside the rural area, serves to deter many landlords from attempting to reaccumulate landholdings, even by the devious but legal means.

Another frequent activity of landlords who have chosen to maintain their economic interests in the Hsin Hsing area is that of moneylending. The small farmer, having little to offer as security, still continues to resort to the local moneylender for cash or other loans. The local moneylender lends fairly large amounts for longer periods of time than any agency of the government or association but, of course, at extremely high interest rates.

The landlords will continue to engage in moneylending as long as the farmer has credit difficulty. If a good profit can be made from moneylending, it is evident that the wealthy landlords will not willingly transfer their economic interests into more productive economic activities.

Traditionally, the village landlord has played a major role in the leadership of his village and its immediate vicinity. During the Japanese period, such leadership roles were greatly reinforced by the Japanese, who preferred to handle village problems through the wealthy landlord class rather than by dealing directly with the "peasants." The Hsin Hsing villagers readily recall that the local Japanese police and officials showed respect only for the well-to-do landlords. Consequently, if the villagers were to get along successfully with the Japanese, they had to work through their landlords. They usually elected a landlord to handle local village affairs and to represent village interests in dealing with the Japanese authorities.

The arrangement was also to the landlord's advantage. As the official leader, he wielded greater power by which he could more easily manipulate the villagers, and even the tax collector, to his own advantage. His recognition as a leader by his fellow villagers and by the authorities also increased his prestige.

Not only was such a landlord the elected village political leader but he might often be an informal leader as well, a person who took an active part in most of the social and religious affairs of the village. He usually contributed money and time to help make these affairs a success. The efforts of the landlord helped to build up his reputation as a public-spirited citizen. Frequently, he assumed the role of mediator in discussions of village and intervillage problems and in disputes between his own villagers or even between members of other villages. When the landlord's efforts as a mediator extended beyond his own village, he enhanced his own reputation in the whole area and that of his village as well.

These conditions continued after the restoration into the post-land reform period. Today, the landlord class continues in the rural area and wields power in local grass roots politics as well as in socioeconomic affairs. In most villages the recognized leaders are still those who are rich, maintain big landholdings, and have had a fairly good education. Such people may also have influence—perhaps by virtue of a relative—in some government agency. It is still a great advantage to a village to have a wealthy representative of the landlord class to deal successfully with authorities. Many, if not most of the government officials, are drawn from this class, since they are educated and usually wealthy.

However, this picture is beginning to change. Village affairs are being profoundly affected as many former large landlords and traditional local leaders transfer their economic interests and activities away from the land to new business interests elsewhere. When a landlord gives up his major economic interests in the area, it is usually not long before village social, religious, and political activities become much less important to him. Because the personal advantage is gone, he is no longer concerned with maintaining his status or leadership role. He may even move his residence out of the village in order to be closer to his new economic interests.

Villages suffering such a loss of local leadership have reacted in two different ways. The first reaction has been apathy—a reluctance to occupy positions of formal village leadership. The other reaction has been for villagers who have more time and money than their fellows and who may aspire to improve their status, to assume formal village leadership.

The first reaction is best evidenced by a new problem in recent village elections, and especially in the 1958 election. In six of the twenty-two villages in Pu Yen Hsiang, there was no candidate for mayor. According to the district officials, the problem in those six villages was that no one was willing to spend the time and money required of the position. Several villagers pointed out that "The office of village mayor must be filled by a person who is not bound to his fields or other work to support his family. He must have an interest in village affairs and enough money to meet the expenses of the traditional functions of the office. He must be able to entertain any public officials or police visiting the village; he must have enough education and social acumen to carry on successfully the necessary relationships with villagers as well as outsiders with whom he is in frequent contact as village head." However, here it may be noted that the office of mayor no longer requires that an individual have a relatively high degree of education and literacy; village records and paper work are now maintained by a minor official from the district Public Office who acts as village secretary.

In other villages, the reaction to the withdrawal of landlords from participation in village affairs has been that other people have attempted to fill the position of mayor, who is general village leader. In some villages, men who have the basic qualifications for the office, as well as a sincere interest in working for the village, have gained the respect of their fellow villagers and have been successful as mayor and village head.

There are also villages—and Hsin Hsing appears to be one of the few in the area—in which the individuals elected to the office of mayor have failed to win respect or acceptance as village leaders. Although they have the qualifications of money and time, and often were the only candidates in the village, their motives are suspect. The man who was mayor of Hsin Hsing during my stay there is perhaps a good example of this. He is a man whom most of the villagers fear but do not respect. They point to his inadequate education—"He knows very few characters!" They say that he has kept more than one wife at a time by taking other men's wives. They feel that he does not really want to work for the village, but only to increase his own power and status. Nevertheless, in spite of all this, he was elected. The main reason he was elected, apparently, is that he has enough time and money to carry out at least the superficial functions of the office, and village cleavages worked for his advantage, as did his membership in one of the larger village *tsu* groups with a following that worked hard in the election.

In Hsin Hsing, then, although this man bears the official title of mayor, he is not really accepted as village head. Today, Hsin Hsing village, like many other communities, seems to be virtually leaderless. In Hsin Hsing and in some other villages observed, this has led to a state of civic disorganization in meeting many village problems, especially those concerning relations with other villages. (An example of just such a problem will be discussed in Chapter 6.)

The post-land reform period in the rural area shows signs of being one of social as well as economic transition. Although the landlords still form a definite and important class, the changes taking place may mark the beginning of a decline in the almost exclusive leadership of the landlord or gentry class. There are incipient signs of instability in a traditional social system which had grown out of an unequal distribution of rural wealth and income as a result of the land tenure system. The Land Reform Program which has led many landlords to withdraw their interests from the rural villages appears to be leading to some equalization of social status in rural Taiwan, which may in turn enable new village leaders to become effective.

In the past and, to a lesser degree, in the present, there have been capable villagers who had no opportunity to compete with the landlord class for primary village leadership. Now, perhaps for the first time, these people will have some opportunity to manifest their leadership abilities. But many traditional attitudes must be cleared away before such new leaders can gain widespread acceptance. In addition to actual economic equalization, there must be a more complete equalization of social status in the village. There must be a change in the villagers' own attitudes toward leadership and authority, for they have not yet been emancipated from their respect for wealth and power and the use to which these two can be put in the manipulation of people and politics.

Although the accomplishment of change in this attitude toward leadership and authority is still a long way off, it should be noted that respect for a man is not based entirely on his wealth and power. These qualities in themselves are not enough, but must be accompanied by evidence of responsibility toward the village, active participation in village affairs, and at least an outward appearance of "not looking down on less fortunate fellows."

The consequences of village social disorganization are not fully apparent. However, definite signs of such disorganization were seen in the last chapter in the problems of community organization and cooperation over irrigation, and will be seen in later chapters in the problem of village solidarity. It is perhaps too soon to tell how success-ful these new leaders will be, but it seems likely that if disorganization continues as a result of the gradual withdrawal from leadership by the landlord class, the most capable among the aspirants for village leader-ship may find, by necessity, increasing acceptance from their fellows.

EFFECT OF LAND REFORM ON THE LAND MARKET

In the Hsin Hsing area, another effect of the Land Reform Pro-gram appears to be a decrease in the free circulation of land, especially in land for rent. Because the 1951 Rent Reduction Act is still in effect, tenants who have contracts are remaining on the land and not giving up their right to tenancy. The landlord can no longer freely change tenants, even when the contract period ends, unless the tenant wishes to give up his rights. At the same time, as the value of rents decline, "the value of leased farm land . . . [is] lower than that of owner cultivated-land" (T'ang, 1954:63). Thus, many landlords do not want to sell their land when its value is low. But even more, under such conditions prospective buyers would gain little from buying land oc-cupied by a tenant who has a contract and a fixed rent.

Landlords who have been tilling some land themselves will very rarely rent it to anyone now. To do so would mean that the landlord, although receiving his 37.5 percent rent, would have little control over his own land. As a former large landlord put it, "Before the Land Reform the landlord made the rules if he wanted more rent. Today the government makes the rules." If the landlord should find that for some reason he no longer can till the land himself, it is more likely that he will hire laborers to work the land. Formerly, he would prob-ably have rented it out. Thus, there is very little land available today for anyone wishing to rent it.

There also seems to be little turnover of publicly and privately owned land which was purchased from the government by former tenants under the 1951 and 1953 acts. Only under great financial stress will such villagers give up their rights to assume full ownership at the end of the ten-year amortization period. According to the 1953 act, a farmer who is unable to continue payments on such land may ask the government to repurchase the land for resale to other farmers. "The Government shall in such a case reimburse to the purchaser in one lump sum the purchase price already paid" (T'ang, 1954:191, transla-tion of the Land-to-the-Tiller Act, 1953, Chapter IV, Article 29). How-ever, despite the law, when such instances have arisen in the Hsin Hsing area, the land has not been resold through the government but by the farmer directly to another farmer who has approached him for additional land to support a growing family.

Such purchases have a surface appearance of legality, but, strictly speaking, they are not. According to the 1953 law, land purchased from the government under the act can be sold by the original purchaser only after he has become a full owner by completing the twenty payments to the government. In current practice, the purchaser, using a middleman or a land broker, secretly gives the owner enough rice or money to cover the outstanding payments to the government. In addition, he gives him more money or rice to cover the payments already made, plus a substantial bonus. When all the remaining payments have been made, usually in one lump sum, the land is officially turned over to the new owner. By law he must be able to till the land himself. This should eliminate the likelihood of landlords engaging in such transactions. In Hsin Hsing village this method has so far been limited to the small landholder who through expanding financial resources has been able to buy additional land to support an expanding family. Such people cannot easily acquire land through completely legal means because of the decreased turnover of land since land reform.

However, some landlords in the area not only manage to purchase such land reform land by this method but manage to buy back their own land which, expropriated by the government, has since passed through several hands. They may then even rent it out, even though the law says that such expropriated land can only be sold to someone who will till the land himself. According to a reliable informant, this can be managed when the land has passed through several hands since 1953, so that the government agencies have lost track of it and are no longer aware of the history of its transfers. The Land Office responsible for such land can easily lose track of it. The land tenure data are recorded in the Land Office in so many different books and cards that it is difficult to maintain any adequate check on the transfers of individual plots of land. Besides this, not all the data are accurate, or even kept together in one office. In the Hsin Hsing village area for example, some records are kept in the Lukang Land Office and some in the Pu Yen Hsiang Public Office, according to a system for recording land tenure data prescribed by the provincial Land Office in Taipei. In addition, there seems to be little investigation by land agents of the ownership of lands in the area.

Probably the greatest source of purchaseable land since the land reform is private-ownership land which formerly belonged to large landholders. At the time of the expropriation in 1953, many landlords got their start in outside business or commerce, and many have since proved successful. As a result, many of them have sold more and more of the three *chia* of land which the 1953 law allowed them to retain, using the money for further investment in business or light industries. In the Hsin Hsing village area the lands of such former landlords have

recently represented the largest portion of land available for purchase
on the open market. Even such land, however, does not necessarily add
a great deal to the land market, since much of it had already been
rented out.

The result of this static condition in the land market appears to be
an ossification of socioeconomic mobility *within* the rural area. The
traditional means for improving one's family's status by acquiring
more and more land and the advantages which accrue to the landed
are no longer so readily attainable. The main outlet now available for
those who have hopes of improving their economic condition is to
acquire some kind of business interest, usually outside the Hsin Hsing
area, and, in such a case, those people rarely remain part of their
native village.

LAND SCARCITY IN HSIN HSING AND ITS
CONSEQUENCES

We see that in spite of the Land Reform Program (and perhaps
in part because of it) and in spite of the apparent increase in the
productivity of the land, there has been a continuing land-population
imbalance and hence an increasingly serious land scarcity in the rural
area. Some of the attempts to solve this continuing problem have
already been discussed here. For the remainder of this chapter we will
examine in some detail the consequences of one solution to this
problem—out-migration—for the villagers, their families, and for the
village as a whole, particularly in role behavior and attitudes toward
the land.

Even now the problem of a growing population and a resulting land
scarcity in the area has greatly affected the lives of many villagers. The
most important effect has been an increased mobility to new centers of
employment such as Taipei, where villagers carry on small business
enterprises or more usually work as unskilled laborers. This trend
toward increased mobility has already spread to other villages of the
area, and is likely to become more extreme all over the island as the
population pressures increase.

The lack of any extensive light industry in the area which could
absorb excess local labor leaves little alternative for families which do
not have enough land to support them. Even a Hsin Hsing village
family which has enough land to support all its members and keep
most of them occupied for the greater part of the year must nevertheless contend with the problem of agricultural slack seasons. Some of
the young men and women of such families may possibly find employment in the local menthol oil factory or brickworks. Whether full- or
part-time, the job is close enough to home so that the villager can go

home whenever his labor is required by the family. Other young men peddle vegetables in the slack season. The only equipment necessary is a strong bicycle. The young men go to the market town of Yuan Lin early in the morning to buy vegetables and then sell them along a regular route of villages. Very often they peddle in villages where they have friends or *ch'in ch'i* relatives who can introduce them to potential customers. A young man peddling vegetables can earn NT $10 or more a day, which he will give to the head of the household.

A few village men earn money as rice or land brokers in the local area. There are also several village men who earn extra income as professional cooks at weddings or other local festivals. A few of the older men may on occasion still go up into the interior mountains or hills for several days to find herbs which they sell to Chinese druggists, but this part-time occupation is not as commonly engaged in now as it was in the past.

Several girls and young women of the village have recently gone away from home to work in a sugar factory in the mountains. The sugar companies send men to the villages to recruit them; later a company truck comes to pick up all the recruits from the area and take them to the factory, where they live in dormitories.

Village women and girls also weave fiber hats at home in their spare time. The white fiber, made from the bark of a tree, is supplied by factory agents from Lukang who travel from village to village leaving the fiber with the women, picking up the completed hats on subsequent stops. The women, who may work on one hat sporadically for several days, receive between NT $6 to NT $12 for each hat depending on the quality of the fiber worked. These hats are then finished in small factories for export.

The most important outlet for the excess labor of the Hsin Hsing village area since the late 1940's has been employment in Taipei. The income for the villagers earned by work or business in Taipei has been steadily increasing, as has the number of villagers going there. The village representative and his son, who is employed in the district Public Office, estimated that 35 percent of the total village income in 1957–1958 was derived from work or business outside the village area, mainly from work in Taipei. Most villagers send their earnings home in small sums, either by registered mail or by a fellow villager. The remaining 65 percent of the village income was estimated as follows: about 45 percent from rice production, 6.5 percent from the marketing of vegetables, 6.5 percent from the sale of menthol oil, 3 percent from farm labor, and 4 percent from other sources. The income which the villager earns as a laborer in Taipei is not included for tax purposes with the farm income.

In 1958 there were about one hundred Hsin Hsing village residents either working or doing business in Taipei. This group was composed mostly of men, although a large number of boys above the age of sixteen and also some women and girls were included. Other than a small minority who have their own business, most of these men worked as pedicab drivers, coolie laborers, or clerks in stores. Men who have some land in the village usually have jobs driving a pedicab or pulling a vegetable cart which permit them freedom to return home for the harvest or other busy agricultural seasons. Some villagers, who have been in Taipei long enough to save some money, manage to buy their own pedicab or vegetable cart. Those who do not usually rent them by the day.

It is common for girls or women to work as cooks or domestic servants. Villagers who work as house servants or clerks have frequently been referred to their jobs through a relative, friend, or fellow villager before leaving the village. The villager usually lives in the home or store of the employer. On the other hand, the villager engaged in the other forms of labor usually shifts for himself. In such cases, if the man does not have his family in Taipei, he often shares a small room with several other villagers who also work in the city. The men share the room rent and get their meals at restaurants or sidewalk food stands.

If the young male villagers live in their employer's quarters, their activities are usually rather closely supervised. However, young males, especially those who work as pedicab drivers and live on their own, often get into trouble—drinking, gambling, frequenting bars, and visiting prostitutes. Sometimes they fall in with groups of boys who engage in gang fights. The boy's family first notices something is wrong when he fails to send money home. The family either questions other adult villagers who have returned from Taipei or writes to a villager in Taipei to discover what is wrong. When they find out about the boy's activities, they send word to him to return home.

Another group of young villagers likely to get into difficulties in Taipei is the younger married men who leave their wives in the village. Sometimes, they become involved with other women in the city or even take a second wife. This results in family conflict and occasionally leads to divorce and bad feeling between the husband's family and that of his first wife.

While most parents are aware of the possibly corrupting influences on their sons who go to Taipei, they nevertheless rationalize their fears because the additional income is so useful to the family. It is only after something happens and the boy is actually in trouble that they call him home.

Not only has working in Taipei had direct gross effects on the men who go there but it has also greatly affected the role of women and children who remain in the village. Although the women often help out in the field when the men are in the village working the land, their main concern is still running the households and tending the livestock. However, once the husband is gone, the wife must take on added responsibilities for the farm operations. She must hire people to plow, transplant seedlings, weed, and perhaps harvest the crop if the man cannot leave his work in Taipei. She must pay wages and arrange for the payment of taxes and exchange of rice for fertilizer. She must make many decisions, frequently without the benefit of her husband's counsel and opinion. In addition, she herself must spend a good deal of time in the fields supervising laborers or checking the flow of irrigation water. Her role in the household is greatly changed, as is her relationship to her children, since it is she alone who is responsible for their care and discipline (the problem is not so serious in extended family households where there is more than a single adult couple in the family).

Even the role of the older children is affected since they must assume tasks at much younger ages than they normally would. There is more work for them in the fields, and perhaps there are younger children to take care of while the mother is in the fields. Sometimes, children are kept so busy that they cannot attend school regularly.

Frequently, the separation of the husband from the family may prove unsatisfactory for everyone. The woman, burdened with added responsibilities of both household and land, may prefer to move to Taipei with her husband and so keep the family together. At the outset she may make occasional short visits to Taipei, and finally, if her husband has established himself in either a good job or a small business in Taipei, he will send for her and perhaps the children to live with him in Taipei. However, women whose husbands are not so well established in the city must continue in their unstable situation in the village.

Most village families or parts of families which have moved to Taipei live together in the Wan Hua section in a very small community of their own. In addition to the more than twenty Hsin Hsing village families congregated together in Wan Hua, there are more than sixty families in this section from the general area of Hsin Hsing. Before 1955 these village families were scattered all over the city, but now the Hsin Hsing village families and many families from nearby villages join together as a group to perform some of the same religious ceremonials they did in the village itself.

Once the whole family moves to Taipei, there seems to be a general weakening of ties with the native village, and they usually go back only for special festivals. In addition, it appears to be more and more usual for families who have made a success of a small business in

Taipei to sell out their land and leave the village entirely. Such cases have even included joint families, where the whole family, including the old parents, have made the move.

Such increased out-migration of whole families has thus resulted from both the scarcity of available land and the apparently adverse effect of the Land Reform Program on the possibility of acquiring land for purchase or especially for rent. Just as many landlords now realize that the accumulation of land is no longer a safe capital investment, many villagers, who in the past sought social mobility through increased landholdings, now see this avenue as relatively limited. Increasingly, they now look to other nonagriculturally-based sources of livelihood and social mobility.

It appears then that much of the villager's traditional sentiment for his land and, to a lesser extent, his ancestral home not infrequently takes second place if there is a surer way of earning a livelihood and accumulating status and wealth. Again, as we have seen, even landlords who traditionally had the greatest sentiment and attachment for family and ancestral home have now in many instances been selling off their remaining landholdings as more secure and lucrative economic opportunities present themselves in the city.[5] This pattern is not perhaps so unusual; after all, many overseas Chinese in Southeast Asia as well as in Taiwan who left their homes on the mainland and made their fortunes abroad never returned to China but later had their families join them.

The families which prosper in Taipei undoubtedly prefer life there to what they had in the village, but there are still many villagers who work and live in Taipei only because they cannot manage to earn enough to support their families on the land. With very little land in the village, they have no capital to invest, and once in Taipei they must take whatever work is available. The people say that a villager who goes to Taipei as a coolie laborer, as most do, "usually goes as a water buffalo." Such men may very well prefer to stay on the land, but they have no alternative. Although they dislike working in Taipei as "beasts of burden," they frequently complain (along with the villagers who remain tied to the land) that a farmer's life is hard and bitter. "A farmer must go to the fields and work very hard even in rainy or windy weather. He must irrigate the fields if the crops need water, and sometimes pedal water all night to irrigate the fields. In addition, he must pay rice to the Farmers' Association [meaning the Provincial Food Bureau] for taxes and in exchange for fertilizer. In other words, the Farmers' Association takes the rice away from the farmers after they harvest their crops."

At the same time, the villager who remains on the land has dreams of "glory" for the next generation. He usually does not want his son to be a farmer like himself and "suffer on the land." He wants him to become a businessman or teacher for "although teachers and minor officials don't make much money, their work is easy." He wants his daughters to marry businessmen since "rather than having money only after the harvest, the businessman always has money coming in." Unfortunately, the farmer cannot always afford to educate his son beyond the primary grades. The family may not be able to afford middle school fees, or there may be a need for the boy's labor on the farm or for the income he can earn in some kind of menial work in Taipei. As for a daughter, in the traditional way of arranging marriages in rural society, often the best a father can do is marry her to the son of another poor farmer like himself. There is an old saying *"Men t'ang hu tuei,"* which means that a suitable marriage joins families of the same social standing. Thus, as the farmer sees it, his situation is a vicious circle: his socioeconomic condition itself bars any hope for improvement for himself or his children.

Yet, for most who remain in the village, there is a certain ambivalence in attitude. In spite of the statements just quoted, for many of them sentiment still runs high for life in the village and on the land. There is a certain amount of security on the land and in the village where life has meaning and regularity. There is a time for work and time for play, and the villager is somebody with a definite place in the scheme of things.

This sentiment is shared and actually more explicitly expressed by the group of families in the village earlier described as unable to reap an adequate living from their small landholdings. Of this group of perhaps no more than ten families, the adult male members had previously sought supplemental income in the city but were either unable or unwilling to adjust to city life. Some could not find secure jobs which would enable them to support their families there, and feared the effects, especially on their children, of the split household. Others had misgivings about exposing their families to the corrupting effects of urban life, even though it would have been financially feasible to move the whole family to the city.

It is the families of this group which have been influential in making the growing and marketing of vegetables as a cash crop an important part of village livelihood. They are willing to take the gamble still present in vegetable growing, since they see it as the only possible way of earning enough money on their insufficient landholding to enable them to remain in the village.

Thus, not only does out-migration of Hsin Hsing villagers to the city have direct consequences for village life but the attempt of several families to find ways for the whole family to remain in the village has its effects on the village as a whole. Some of these farmers are success-

ful, and their example influences other farmers in the area to change
their form of land utilization in order to raise their standard of living.
They have been an important internal influence toward acceptance of
change in the village, just as the out-migrants, linking village and
urban center, have been an important external influence toward
change in village life.

[5

Family and Kinship

The scope of the changed and extended relationships beyond the village is very evident in the examination of the family and kinship system, the life cycle, and religious and magical beliefs to which we now turn. As in the preceding chapters, it will be observed that many of the relationships that extend beyond the village, such as certain economically based connections and relations with matrilateral and affinal relatives, are not new phenomena either for the inhabitants of Hsin Hsing or for other Chinese villagers. The Chinese village has seldom been an isolated unit, and many traditional types of extended relationships common to the mainland will be evident in the structure of social relations in Hsin Hsing village. However, there are changes and modifications in these aspects of village life which can be directly related to the recent socioeconomic developments and increasing urbanization which were discussed earlier.

Chapter 5 will describe the nature and functions of the family and kinship system in the village area, while Chapter 6 will examine interfamily and interpersonal relations, especially as they extend beyond the village and affect intravillage cooperation. Chapters 7 and 8 will indicate the interaction of the above relations and the economic factors of life with the life cycle and the magical and religious beliefs and practices.

THE *TSU*

Fukien, the ancestral province of the residents of Hsin Hsing, is known for the predominance of the large common descent groups called *tsu* organizations. As a number of writers have pointed out (Hu, 1948:14; Chen Han-seng, 1936:37; Lang, 1946:173; de Groot, vol. I, 1892:191) many villages in the provinces of southeastern China are inhabited exclusively by families bearing one surname, so that *tsu* and village are coterminous. In other villages which contained several *tsu*, each kept to itself in a separate neighborhood. So predominant

127

was the institution that perhaps four out of every five persons were
members of an organized *tsu* (Lang, 1946:173).

Tsu organization performed many important activities and functions, as Hu Hsien-chin (1948:10) has pointed out:

The *tsu* keeps a record of its descent lines by the compilation of genealogies.
It is endowed with property by well-to-do members and uses the income to
defray the expenses of ancestral ritual, to assist young members to attain an
education, to help out destitute members in old age or when orphaned, and
to provide burial space for the dead. Where the *tsu* constitutes a community,
community affairs are managed by its leaders. Furthermore the *tsu* is interested in promoting the social standing of its members, as their prestige raises
the reputation and influence of the group, and it is much concerned with
straightening out differences between members and with keeping up the
sense of moral values with the family and the *tsu*.

These features have allowed the *tsu* to develop considerable solidarity and
have enabled it to compete successfully for prestige and power against similar
groups in the same neighborhood.

These activities and functions were performed by a highly structured and highly segmented organization with a population of two or
three thousand people, as Freedman (1958:132) has noted. The membership is characterized by broad social differentiation including

families of bureaucrats, . . . some well-to-do merchants, a proportion of
small traders and craftsmen, and a mass of cultivators, the greater part of
whom work land held in the name of the lineage or its various segments.
The majority of the members of the lineage are poor, but the lineage as a
whole is corporately rich in land, ancestral halls, and such other items of
property as rice mills. Men tend to stay within the community, and even if
they go out of it in order to take office or engage in business they leave
their families behind, return when they are older, and send money back.

In fact, Hu (1948:10) notes that although the membership of the *tsu*
may be "spread over a wider region, it has its focus in one community
which is always associated with the ancestral graves and the ancestral
hall where the memory of the ancestors is venerated."

The *tsu* as Hu (1948) and Freedman (1958) describe it is elaborate
in structure, function, and activity. Freedman, however, suggests that
loosely structured organizations are still to be considered *tsu* and accordingly constructs a scale on which localized lineages may be placed,
differentiating them in social status along a "continuum from A to Z"
(1958:131), representing "models of the polar opposites of the scale"
(1958:131). Thus, the *tsu* pictured above by Hu and Freedman would
be the "Z" model while "A" model is

small in numbers, with a population of two or three hundred souls. Apart
from one or two small shopkeepers and a few craftsmen, its members are
cultivators of small pieces of land which they own outright or rent from

external landlords. Their general level of income is low. They own no common property except for a plot of land which is the grave site of the founding ancestor. . . . Apart from domestic ancestor worship, which is conducted before the simplest instruments, and annual rites at the tomb of the founder of the lineage, there is no ancestor cult. There is no recorded genealogy, individual men being placed in the system merely by their generation (which is indicated by their personal names) and their ascription to one or the other of the sub-lineages which trace their origin from the sons of the founder. No genealogical unit stands between the sub-lineage and the household, nor is there any tendency for groups of closely related households to co-operate economically and ritually. Headship of the sub-lineages and the lineage passes to the oldest men in the senior generation of these units, no other formal leaders being recognized. Disputes are brought before sub-lineage heads, but when they cannot be resolved a gentleman from the protecting community is brought in to try to reach a settlement (Freedman, 1958: 131–132).

The continuum can be even further extended to include the very small localized kinship organizations found in many villages in Taiwan (such as in the Hsin Hsing area) and probably also on the mainland of China. Before going on to a discussion of family I will attempt to demonstrate this. In both structure and function, these small localized kinship organizations go beyond what Freedman refers to as "inflated families" [1] and which he warns us not to confuse with lineages (1958:2). Such kinship organizations as exist in Hsin Hsing do not quite approach either the size or structural complexity even of Freedman's "A model" *tsu*. Nevertheless, these kinship organizations —on the basis of their activities and functions—are *tsu*, since they are more than simply patrilineally related families. They do operate as local organizations which are aligned on the basis of patrilineal kinship and attempt to wield sociopolitical influence in the village and area.

The Single-Tsu Village

The general social organization of a village made up exclusively of one *tsu* group is likely to be rather different from a village like Hsin Hsing, which contains a number of smaller *tsu* and unrelated family units. The village with a single large *tsu*, as has been pointed out (Hu, 1948:9–11), tends to have a unified organization which dominates most of the village's activities. No matter how many village "social associations" a villager belongs to, he finds that the members of each are all part of the same kinship group. While this does not necessarily eliminate interfamily or interfactional rivalry and friction within the village, such *tsu* organization nevertheless does tend to create an unusually firm basis for group solidarity. The *tsu*, in effect, is the village and is thus very easily able to present itself as a unified body against pressures from outside. It has, in addition, a much stronger basis for internal unity and cooperation. Thus, families which belong to such single-*tsu* villages gain a substantial amount of security from the situation.

While there are now few single-*tsu* villages, and apparently few fully active *tsu* organizations in the Hsin Hsing area, during late Ch'ing times and even into the early Japanese period there seem to have been many *tsu* groups with unity and power which were active. Most of the large *tsu* organizations were confined to individual villages, although some extended into several. At the earlier date, it appears that these organizations were either overseas sections of large mainland *tsu* or had at least been formed on the basis of their earlier ancestral affiliations in China (Barclay, 1954b:47). In the Hsin Hsing area these affiliations were probably reinforced by the relative ease and frequency of communication between the mainland and the nearby port of Lukang.

Hsin Hsing villagers still tell how these *tsu* organizations and single-*tsu* villages frequently took part in inter-*tsu* rivalry and fighting. Barclay (1954b:47) has noted how these groups (which he does not define, but refers to as "clans") engaged in "indiscriminate civil disorder" along the line of the cleavages and antagonisms brought over from the mainland. Older villagers say that during the late Ch'ing period there were few government officers in the rural area to control these *tsu* groups, and if an officer did appear, he could easily be bribed. With the advent of the Japanese, however, the situation rapidly changed. The Japanese police were not "polite" when a *tsu* organization "insulted or beat other villagers." If *tsu* members "did wrong," they were beaten by the Japanese who, unlike the Ch'ing dynasty officers, "could not be bribed." The *tsu* members feared the Japanese officers just as any ordinary villager did, and for this reason the *tsu* organizations were often reluctant to support members who got into trouble. As a result the *tsu* began to lose their unity and power: ten to twenty years after the Japanese had taken over the government of Taiwan, the activities of the *tsu* villages and organizations had significantly decreased in the Hsin Hsing area. As we have already seen in Chapter 2, the port of Lukang lost its importance as a channel of communication with the mainland soon after the Japanese arrived. As the movement of people between Taiwan and the mainland ceased, relations between the Taiwanese *tsu* and the paternal *tsu* on the mainland broke down. This was very likely another factor contributing to the weakening of Taiwanese *tsu* organizations after the Japanese occupation.

There are now few *tsu* organizations which are strong enough to be of major influence in the Hsin Hsing area as a whole, and only three of the approximately twenty-two villages are inhabited exclusively by one *tsu*. The single-*tsu* village is known locally as *"yi hsing ts'un"* ("one surname village"), and in the literature is commonly called a "clan village."

The Multi-Tsu *Village*

Today, most of the villages in the Hsin Hsing area are populated by several *tsu* groups, plus a number of families not affiliated with any of the village *tsu;* these are called *"tsa hsing ts'un"* ("mixed surname villages") and are sometimes referred to in the literature as "multi-kin villages" or "segmented communities." In the Hsin Hsing area they are of the type with a marked tendency toward local exogamy. In these villages, unlike the single-*tsu* village, no individual *tsu's* activities coincide with those of the village organization.

Hsin Hsing, a multi-kin village, was first settled by immigrants from Fukien who came to Taiwan in small groups of three or four men. After examining the area, these men finally founded the village of Hsin Hsing. Soon after this, and throughout the years that followed, people of other surnames came to this easily accessible plains area and settled down in the village. As time passed, the families of some of the earliest arrivals grew into what now comprise the several village *tsu* groups. Of these, the larger *tsu* are the ones which go back to the early period of the village founding and have therefore had the time as well as advantageous circumstances which have enabled them, relatively speaking, to increase their number of member families and population. Others with perhaps equally long village histories are still small because circumstances somehow prevented their expansion. Some of these have few members in a small number of related families; several are still in individual unrelated family units. The latter have simply produced too few surviving children, so that they have never expanded their numbers sufficiently to have more than a single male heir in a generation to carry on the male line. Others are of relatively recent origin in the village, some only three generations, not yet long enough to have expanded their membership and number of associated family units.

However, in Hsin Hsing village even the relatively older and larger *tsu* are far simpler and less elaborated organizations than Freedman's (1958) somewhat less complex "type A" *tsu*. But as we shall see, they share many features of structure and function which differ primarily in degree rather than in kind. The *tsu* organization of Hsin Hsing, in this respect, is rather representative of the general area and more than likely of much of the mainland.

The lack of elaboration of the size and organization of the Hsin Hsing *tsu* can be attributed to two main causes. The relatively short history of both the village and of the *tsu* organizations has meant a lack of depth in generations and therefore a lack of breadth in collateral relatives. Then, economic pressures and the resulting rather high degree of out-migration, often of whole family units, has restricted the expansion of local *tsu;* in fact, the size of village *tsu* may have almost reached a point of relative stability.

Part of the lack of an elaborate *tsu* organization in Hsin Hsing can be seen in the absence of significant formal *tsu* segmentation, i.e., into *fang*—a sub-*tsu*—or *chih*—a *tsu* branch. The lack of formal segmentary organization is most likely a function of small size—even the largest *tsu* organization has a population of only over one hundred, and several others are considerably smaller. All village *tsu* embrace groups of families in several lines of descent (Freedman might call them "sub-lineages" since each traces its origins to a son of the *tsu* founder) within which are families of more closely related kinsmen, such as the families of brothers. However, these sub-lineages neither have nor attempt to exert sociopolitical influence in the village; they depend upon their *tsu* organization to do this in their behalf. Again, this is a result of their relatively small size; it has prevented the evolution within the *tsu* of broad social differentiation and thus of sub-lineages wealthy enough to form new or separate formal segments by setting aside or donating property as corporate lineage property or for an ancestral hall. The fact is, formal segmentation of *tsu* as small as those of Hsin Hsing would "reduce the groups below the minimal functional size" (Geddes, 1963:30).

Before examining something of the activities of the Hsin Hsing village *tsu* organizations, let us first turn to their composition. As noted earlier, there are twelve surnames among the ninety-nine family units in the village.[2] Four of these—Huang, Shih, K'ang, and Shen (in order of number of people)—make up 82 percent of the village population and 81 percent of the village households. Nearly every fourth villager is named Huang. Most of the Huangs belong to one *tsu,* tracing their common ancestry to one of the village founders. Aside from two small member households which live elsewhere in the village, the whole *tsu* membership lives in one large compound made up of two buildings, where each household has its own apartment. Three small Huang households do not belong to this *tsu* and live elsewhere in the village. (See Map 2.)

Each of the three other most common village surnames is found in at least two different kinship groups, some of large size and others of moderate size. But regardless of the number of member families, the members of such groups maintain themselves in some form of kinship organization and live in a compound together or in a small cluster of separate houses. Thus, the two kinship groupings with the surname Shih can be said to form two *tsu* organizations of an incipient form;

each lives in its own section of the village. Hsin Hsing also contains two very small Shih households which are not related to each other nor to either of the Shih *tsu* organizations.

The families with the surname K'ang form three separate kinship groups (one of them is the second largest *tsu* in the village) plus a few isolated households. The large K'ang *tsu* occupies a compound made up of one very large extended house and a smaller structure and two other smaller buildings in other sections of the village. The other K'ang kinship groupings occupy their own compounds in other parts of the village. The K'ang households which are not members of any of the other kinship groupings in Hsin Hsing also live separately. One of these families actually traces a common ancestor with one of the smaller K'ang kinship groupings but because of internal conflict participates in none of its functions. One of the isolated K'ang families is headed by a man who was formerly the wealthiest landlord in the village; his predecessor, the old family head now deceased, was village mayor in Japanese times. The family moved into Hsin Hsing about thirty years ago from the small neighboring village of Lo T'se, where there is still a large K'ang *tsu* organization with which the Hsin Hsing landlord maintains close relations and in which his family continues to participate.

The majority of the Shen families comprise one *tsu,* and most of its members live in one corner of the village, although a few member families live in a single building in a different part of the village. One unrelated Shen family lives in still another part of the village.

Thus, various independent households in Hsin Hsing bear the same surnames as some village *tsu* organizations. On this basis they are considered *ch'in t'ang* (relatives of the ancestral hall) and therefore might at times be given some slight preferential treatment by the *tsu* with which they share a common surname. In this sense they might be treated somewhat differently from the families which bear the eight other village surnames and form unrelated households. But a number of village families have few or no patrilineal kinship relations within the village.

Tsu *Activities and Functions*

To accomplish their ultimate goal of benefiting their members through the organization's sociopolitical influence, the Hsin Hsing *tsu* perform a number of activities which help to provide the necessary group solidarity. And while they have not succeeded as completely as they might with more resources—for example, in population and wealth—*tsu* solidarity and members' total identification and loyalty are notably more complete than the villagers' greatly diminished solidarity and identification with the village itself as a community.

(This latter point will be further discussed in Chapter 6.) The village *tsu* organizations do continue to maintain a certain solidarity in the ceremonial, social, and political areas.

In Hsin Hsing the *tsu*, in terms of its actual activities, is very clearly a ceremonial group. As we will later see in greater detail, the *tsu* comes together for ancestor worship: sometimes for worship of an early ancestor by the representatives of all the *tsu* families and other times only segments, such as the families of several brothers, who alone come together to worship their own more recent ancestor. On the other hand, representatives of the entire *tsu* membership participate in funeral rituals in one capacity or another, depending upon their relationship with the deceased. However, the actual mourning during and after the funeral is actively participated in only by the much smaller immediate family of the deceased, including all lineal relatives, and perhaps extending out to no more than the first or perhaps second degree or grade of collaterality. Thus, the *wu fu* (or five mourning grades) at best operates in Hsin Hsing in a much watered-down version. The other ceremonial and festive or social occasions in which the entire *tsu* membership, or representatives of each member family, participate or cooperate is at the time of a marriage and certain other life cycle events, such as the rite when a boy reaches the age of sixteen.

But what we have seen among the Hsin Hsing *tsu* is quite beyond what Fei relates about patrilineal kinship groups in Kaihsienkung (in the Yangtze valley) which he calls "*Tsu*." The *Tsu* in Kaihsienkung, Fei tells us, "can be taken as no more than a ceremonial group which assembles periodically at wedding and funeral occasions, taking a common feast, offering sacrifices to the common ancestors together, and contributing a small sum barely enough to cover the food. Real social obligations of mutual aid exist between smaller groups, such as brothers with newly divided households" (1939:85). Therefore the *Tsu* as a larger kinship group appears to take little part in nonceremonial activities such as the economic or especially the sociopolitical activities and functions in which the Hsin Hsing village *tsu* actually do participate as single organizations.

To a degree, however, there is similarity between the Kaihsienkung *Tsu* and the *tsu* of Hsin Hsing in their nonparticipation in economic activities. As we have noted, most of the Hsin Hsing *tsu* are small, not particularly well-off financially, and have a minimum of social differentiation. Only the large K'ang *tsu* has maintained any corporate landholdings, and even there the income is so small that no ancestral hall has ever been built, nor has the income been used for educational or welfare purposes beyond allowing its own poorest member families alternately to rent the lineage land when land was at a premium. Primarily, the income has gone to help in maintaining the *tsu* ancestral-worship room in the main *tsu* house. (When other *tsu* need special funds for work in the room or for the worship itself, member families are usually taxed.) Whether village family groupings form a large or small *tsu,* or even smaller groups of related families, they do not function as central economic units for their member families. Each family or household is an independent economic unit.

While in many ways these seperate economic units do act in unison, such as for exchange labor on the basis of their kin or *tsu* relationships, for the most part their actions as economic units are fairly independent. This means that in many areas of activity the family operates with relatively little regard for their patrilineal kin in other households. Consequently, family economic and social relationships are not limited to patrilineal relatives. As in the single *tsu* village, many Hsin Hsing villagers belong to a number of both formal and informal social associations. However, in Hsin Hsing these activities bring them into regular contact with fellow villagers with whom they have no kinship relationship. Such a diversity of activities with both relatives and nonrelatives in the village does have a tendency to undercut the solidarity of the *tsu* or kinship organizations. In addition, family activities and relationships, both kin and non-kin, also extend beyond the village. (The latter will be discussed in greater detail in later chapters.)

Still, the member families of each Hsin Hsing village *tsu* organization, including some which have no more than sixty to seventy people, do band together in many other village sociopolitical activities. Therefore, when we examine elected offices we see that the village mayor is one of the financially better off and influential members from the large K'ang *tsu*. The village representative to the *hsiang* council is an older "gentleman" from the big Huang *tsu;* he is considered well educated and (on the basis of the three *chia* [7.2 acres] maximum landholding allowed since the land reform) is a fairly large landowner who hires laborers to work his land. The elected agent and head of the village small unit of the district Farmers' Association is an influential member from the large Shen *tsu*. The villagers' choice of one relatively important man from each large *tsu* organization is clearly not a concidence.[3] Villagers definitely align themselves on the basis of *tsu* in such situations. Each *tsu* attempts to work for its own socioeconomic and political influence in village affairs, or at times in cooperation with other village *tsu* when that proves more advantageous. This is true in village elections or even in what appears to be occasional *tsu* block voting in district or county elections. According to the villagers, this would occur if one of the *tsu*'s own members is a candidate, but actually occurs more usually when a *tsu* member's *ch'in ch'i* or even friend is a candidate.

That Hsin Hsing *tsu* are more than merely ceremonial is seen in the way various individual unrelated families, because they share a common surname with a *tsu*, try to identify with it and, to a small degree, do absorb some of the hoped for and actual sociopolitical benefits and security which seem to accrue to members of the larger village *tsu* organizations. (This is discussed in greater detail in Chapter 6.)

Each village *tsu* can therefore be seen as attempting to exert sociopolitical influence in the village and sometimes also in the immediate area in competition with other *tsu*. So as not to weaken its position in face of the rest of the village, each *tsu* works hard to confine its internal conflicts within the *tsu* itself. Therefore, their own respected (and usually well-off) elders serve as mediators for the solution of intra-*tsu* conflict. In case of inter-*tsu*, general village, or intervillage conflict, these same *tsu* leaders have usually been recognized by the villagers as the most likely people to be able to bring a conflict to a successful solution.

As we have seen above and will see more of here and in Chapter 6, the Hsin Hsing village area kinship organizations, despite their relatively small size and minimum formalization, nevertheless do display a relative functional equivalence to Hu's (1948) and Freedman's (1958) images of a *tsu* and thus are clearly to be considered as *tsu* organizations, as they are by their members. One might further note that for the *tsu* organizations in Hsin Hsing village, there appears to be no inherent relationship between structure and function. The most important feature of such groupings is that their activities (such as their sociopolitical ones) be carried out within the local community and perhaps the larger area, and these seem to be carried through here with a minimum of formal structure. Since *tsu* is not to be thought of as a static organizational phenomenon but rather as having a kind of evolution with stages going from incipience through decay, a *tsu* in its early or incipient stages of development could then exist on a very small scale, be rather weak in its formal organization and activities and even in its functional effectiveness, and yet still maintain itself as a *tsu*.

What is also worth noting (and what we will see more of in Chapter 6), is that conditions in the Taiwanese rural area have been working against the likelihood of these unelaborated *tsu* ever developing into truly mature *tsu*. This seems to be true in the case of the adverse effect on the rural *tsu* organizations by the Japanese during their period of occupation of Taiwan and the recently changing socioeconomic conditions, such as the Land Reform Program, which prohibit the *tsu* from acquiring corporate landholdings and inhibit *tsu* members from achieving great landed wealth within the rural area. In addition, it also appears that as a result of these past and recent developments the villagers feel a need to turn outward away from the village. Therefore, although the villagers themselves continue to see their local kinship-based organizations as *tsu*, not simply groups aimed at preserving a patrilineal tie, and also continue to try to make them function as *tsu*, their strong identity with, dependence on, and submission to the authority of their *tsu* organizations is now being undermined.

THE ECONOMIC FAMILY

In Hsin Hsing village the economic family, the *chia*, is the basic socioeconomic unit. It is "a unit consisting of members related to each other by blood, marriage or adoption, and having a common budget and common property" (Lang, 1946:13). The household or *hu* may in theory include temporary residents such as relatives or servants in addition to the members of the economic family. Since there are seldom additional people in Hsin Hsing families (or in families in the area generally), the *chia* and the *hu* almost always coincide in the village, and the average number of persons in it for Hsin Hsing is 6.1. It is the *hu* which is officially registered at the local Hsiang Public Office and as such is considered the official tax unit.[4]

The economic family in Hsin Hsing may take one of three forms—conjugal, stem, or joint; sometimes a family may change through all three forms over a relatively short period of time. The most prevalent type of family in Hsin Hsing is the conjugal, the *hsiao chia-t'ing* or "small family." This family "consists of man, wife or wives, and [unmarried] children. Families of this type may be either complete or 'broken;' the category includes childless couples, families consisting of . . . unmarried brothers and sisters, single persons . . ." (Lang, 1946:14). Others prefer to consider the latter two forms of unmarried siblings or single persons as subconjugal families. Thus, in Hsin Hsing village, sixty-five households (about 66 percent of the total) are conjugal. These comprise only about 55 percent of the total population, since the average conjugal family consists of only 5.18 persons.

For the villagers, the ideal form of economic family is the joint family (*ta chia-t'ing*), usually comprised of at least three generations, and preferably more. According to Lang (1946:14) the joint family includes "parents, their unmarried children, their married sons (more than one) and sons' wives and children" and sometimes other relatives. Or there may be only one of the older parents and the married sons and their families; in another variant the oldest brother "presides over his [unmarried sisters], married and unmarried brothers, with their wives and his children and their children . . ." (Lang, 1946:14).[5] One can more specifically refer to this type as a fraternal joint family.

However, in Hsin Hsing village the *ta chia-t'ing*, although usually thought of by the villagers as an ideal type, is low in frequency of occurrence, as has been true for most of rural China. On the basis of the 1959 official population records for the village, only about 5 percent of the 99 households in the village could be considered joint families according to the definition. These five households consisted of 59 persons, about 10 percent of the total village population. The average joint family in Hsin Hsing contained 11.8 persons, considerably more than is found in the other family types.

The third type of economic family in Hsin Hsing is the stem family. In form, this lies somewhere between the joint and conjugal family types. The stem family in Hsin Hsing, following Lang's definition (1946:14–15), "consists of the parents, their unmarried children, and one married son with wife and children. The family of this type, too, can be broken, e.g., when only one of the parents is alive or the son has no children." Lang goes on to note that

In China the stem family is not infrequently a reduced joint family. Some of the married sons break away from their parents after having stayed with them in a joint family; one of the sons and his wife and children continue to live with them until their death. But often the Chinese stem family is also an enlarged conjugal family. . . . A Chinese conjugal family which has only one son is enlarged when the son marries and brings his bride home, without being even temporarily separated from his parents.

According to this definition there are 29 stem families in Hsin Hsing, which make up about 29 percent of the total number of households. With an average of 7.3 persons per family, these comprise almost 35 percent of the village population. However, only a few stem families in Hsin Hsing represent a reduced joint family. Most are enlarged conjugal families in which one son has married and then had children. However, the process should be seen as cyclic. In many cases the head (*chia chang*) of a stem family was originally a member of a joint family which divided into conjugal families and then expanded into the present form of stem family.

Whatever form the economic family in the village may take, many of the basic features of the *chia* remain the same for all three. All the members of the *chia* live under one roof, except for a few who may work outside to supplement the family income and therefore live away from the village. The latter, however, are still part of the *chia*, although perhaps not part of the official household *hu*, depending upon where the individual is registered for residence. The *chia* is in theory supposed to function as a single cooperating unit in all of its activities —economic, social, religious, or any of the other areas of daily living. Therefore, all property—land, house, farm equipment, and general household furnishings—belong to the *chia* as a whole. Only personal clothing and items a woman brought into the house as part of her

dowry are considered to belong to the individual. Consequently if
there is a divorce, the woman may take these things with her. Under
such a system in the Hsin Hsing area, when a *chia* is dissolved as a
cooperating economic unit, all sons are entitled to an equal share of
all family property.

The structure of all types of economic family is hierarchal according
to generation and age, and the oldest male, at least until his retirement, serves as family head (*chia chang*). However, the wife of the
chia chang usually plays an important part in the making of family
decisions, especially those related to household affairs or to important
financial matters. Thus, in the joint family, while the authority within
each of the several conjugal units lies with the husband and father of
that unit, the ultimate authority for all members of the larger family
theoretically lies with the *chia chang* and his wife.

In the joint or stem families of Hsin Hsing, however, it is common
for all married sons (or the married son in the stem family) to share in
most of the family's decision-making. This seems most true in the
larger families where each adult male's financial contribution is indispensable to the continuation of the stem or joint form which the
parents, above all, wish to maintain. In such situations, when making
an important decision the *chia chang* willingly confers with the other
adults in the family and may actually yield to their wishes. On the
other hand, in larger families which are economically secure, since the
chia chang has complete control of the family's economic assets, he
appears to be much more dominant and authoritarian in imposing his
will on the members of the *chia*.

Normally, as a *chia chang* in Hsin Hsing grows older, he gradually
relinquishes his responsibilities to his oldest son, slowly training him
to assume full family authority. Sometimes, however, the old *chia
chang* is unwilling to retire and give up his authority. In such instances, the oldest son must gradually usurp the old man's powers, but
this must be done delicately, or the village will criticize him as an
unfilial son. Here, the old *chia chang's* loss of authority does not imply
any loss of respect for him.

Even after his full retirement and the transfer of actual family authority to a son, it is quite common for the old man to retain the title
of *chia chang* while the son performs all the duties. In such cases, the
villagers are aware of the situation and respect it. Therefore, if they
must choose or elect someone to fill a village office, they may name the
old *chia chang* who is officially family head, understanding that it will
be his son who assumes the duties of the position.

While each stem and joint family consists of at least two conjugal
families, these conjugal families have, for the most part, a merely
biological identity. All the functions it might have in other circum-

stances are almost completely subsumed within the structure of the
larger economic family of which it is a part.

When a son or brother marries and forms another nuclear or conjugal family within the joint or stem family, the newlyweds are given
their own small apartment or room within the larger house. If there is
no additional space and the family can afford it, a small room or set of
rooms may be added on to the house, possibly in the form of an
additional wing. In any case, the new couple always has its own sleeping quarters.

However, even though the son, his wife, and children, if any, live
together in their separate quarters in the large house, all of them are
expected to function primarily as members of the larger family. Ordinarily, if the members of any of the conjugal families which make up
the larger *chia* begin to or attempt to function as an independent unit
rather than as members of the joint or stem family, it is not long
before family division takes place. Therefore, whatever their private
relations within the confines of their own quarters, a husband and
wife, at least until they become older, relate to one another almost
strictly as two members of a larger family rather than as husband and
wife. In public the two never display any affection or, in fact, have
much to do with each other beyond the contacts necessary to carry on
the family's affairs.

A husband and wife, until they are middle-aged, rarely go anywhere
together. If circumstances require them to go to the same place, they
usually go and return separately. When an outsider is present, husband and wife do not eat together, and, in fact, only the men sit at the
table; the women remain in the kitchen. At family mealtimes the men
usually eat informally, often not at a table, while the women busy
themselves with the cooking and cleaning up, taking their own food
when they have a chance after the men are through.

While the adult males of the *chia* take care of most of the work on
the land, the women are responsible for household duties and many
other chores—tending livestock, drying and preserving certain crops,
and performing lighter agricultural tasks in the fields. In the joint
family, the wife of the *chia chang* usually spends much of her time
supervising her daughters-in-law, helping to tend to the grandchildren
and doing other light tasks. In a joint family the daughters-in-law
usually rotate the tasks among themselves. For several days in a row
each in turn will rise before dawn, tend the fire, and prepare the food
for the entire family. The other daughters-in-law meanwhile do other
tasks either around the house or in the fields. When a mother must be
away from the house, her unweaned child is at times nursed by one of
the other daughters-in-law or even by a neighbor who has milk.

The unmarried younger daughters of the *chia chang* usually keep to the house and are not given very much free time. They work in the kitchen and around the house, assisting their mother and sisters-in-law and helping to take care of younger siblings or nieces or nephews. In their spare time they usually make fiber hats. Unlike their young brothers (who spend much time playing and little helping in the house or fields), the girls, partially as training for their eventual marriage, are burdened with a good deal of responsibility from morning until night.

In the joint or stem family, the discipline of children is theoretically performed by any adult who happens to be present. However, in Hsin Hsing village it is considered better for a child's own parents to discipline him when at all possible; a paternal uncle may correct his nephew only if the boy's parents are absent. It is well realized that antagonisms between members of the larger family can too easily arise over this problem.

Although the discipline of daughters-in-law is traditionally a prerogative of the mother-in-law (the *chia chang's* wife), she imposes her authority through her son, the girl's husband. Thus, if a daughter-in-law steps out of line—especially if she is new in the family—her mother-in-law will call her husband in and demand that he beat his wife or otherwise discipline her. The *chia chang* himself has almost nothing to do with his sons' wives. He not only does not concern himself with their discipline but he seldom talks with them, and would not remain alone in the room with one of them.

However, the *chia chang* shows little overt feelings towards any member of his family. While he is likely to fondle his infant son or daughter, and especially a grandchild, in public, such open display of affection ceases completely when the child is several years old. After that a man's relationship with his children becomes quite formal.

Many villagers still feel that when each person in the joint family fulfills his role properly, this form of family structure has great advantages. They say that only the large family can "become wealthy" and have "power." The large family makes it possible for people to work at a combination of occupations. While most of the family lives in the village and works the large landholdings which villagers believe only a large family can accumulate, some of the members may work in the town or perhaps locally as minor civil servants. Only a large family can have numerous contacts outside the village with relatives by marriage and with friends. To the Hsin Hsing villager, these extensive relationships with outside people, and frequent visits from these people, symbolize the family's status and enhance its reputation and prestige.

The villagers' views about the advantages which accrue to the large family which make it their ideal are not without foundation. There are families in the Hsin Hsing area, usually landlord families, which the above description fits perfectly. While the large joint families in the village constitute only a small minority, the form is nevertheless within the realm of achievement for a family which can manage to have enough children who work hard and cooperate toward this end.

As was pointed out earlier, although the majority of the economic families in the village are conjugal, there is a natural cyclic process through which any family may evolve three different forms in a few years. Many conjugal families do develop into the stem form and some into the joint, but usually it is not long before division takes place and the family is once more reduced to a simpler form.

FAMILY DIVISION

There are certain inherent difficulties in the large family form which almost inevitably lead to eventual division of a large family. An insufficient economic base and land scarcity are probably the most common reasons for division. A *chia* may have enough sons to form a large family, but there may not be enough land to maintain a group of several small families, and it may be difficult to obtain the additional land needed for their maintenance.

The family's economic inadequacy frequently gives rise to many devisive forces. A son, and especially his wife, may come to feel that the other family members are not contributing equitably to the family maintenance and are thus the cause of the inadequate family income. These feelings may be based on fact. One son may not be working as hard as the others, and have more children than the others, or a son or brother may be absent from the village, leaving his family behind. For example, in 1958 several twenty-nine-year-old men with families were conscripted for military service for two years. The district Public Office decided in some cases that the conscriptees' brothers who had separate *chia* could help support their families. But in all of those cases where conscriptees belonged to joint families, the *chia* is not only deprived of the man's usual contributions but always has to support his wife and children and, in addition, send him a monthly supplement to his inadequate army pay. It is considered selfish under such circumstances for the rest of the family to wish to divide the economic household and land because one member is not earning his keep, but, as evidenced in Hsin Hsing, it does happen.

Usually, there is no problem if a son goes to Taipei to work, leaving his wife and children behind with the joint family, as long as he regularly sends money home. However, there have been incidents where a man was caught up in the ways of the big city—perhaps with another woman or merely with its entertainment—and sent little or no money back. Under such circumstances the idea of family division is likely to come up, probably initiated and encouraged by the daughter-in-law who feels that her own husband works the hardest and contributes most to the family's income. The daughter-in-law's reason for wanting the division may, of course, be much more basic, such as being treated badly in the house or wanting independence, but situations like these give her a good excuse. The villagers feel that it is usual for the daughters-in-law to want to divide the family even though their husbands do not. "This is because the woman's mind is smaller than the husband's."

When division-provoking situations do arise, they are frequently aggravated by the desire of the *chia chang* and his wife to minimize strain by distributing the family's wealth and chores equally. They usually see to it that each small family in the *chia* is given food and money for clothing equally and that all the family members, including daughters-in-law, share equally in the work. While this policy is especially designed to prevent jealousy among the daughters-in-law, it can lead to greater ill-feeling when a daughter-in-law, and possibly her husband, contribute much more than the others and yet receive no more for their work.

Under such circumstances as these, then, a family division may occur. It takes place after a general agreement by the whole family that each son will after all work harder and do better for his own small family when he is independent and on his own. However, division is not inevitable. Sometimes one son of a large family may work in Taipei to supplement the family income. If he does well there, an ideal situation for the family may develop, with part of its income coming from the city while the rest of the family stays and works in the village. It has also happened that the son in the city gradually brought his other brothers into the city business and finally, after selling the land in the village, brought the whole family to live in the city. They often remain a single economic household there—at least for a short time. However, on other occasions a son doing well in Taipei has decided that it is best for his own wife and children to benefit by his good fortune, and, by bringing them to live in the city, he has forced the division of the large family.

Sometimes other factors contribute to the early division of large families. Since some of the taxes paid to the government are progressive, a large family with a higher income may divide in the hope of lowering its total taxes. Occasionally, a landlord may wish to accumulate more land and so divides the family and registers the land in different names, which can be done under the land reform laws. Other families may divide in the belief that there is more danger of conscription for men in a large family. Such a recent division, however, is not recognized by the authorities as negating the possibility of kin in other households supporting the soldier's family.

A very strong and authoritarian *chia chang*, or even his wife, can frequently postpone the division of a family for a number of years. Contrary to Freedman's findings (1958:21) that "as long as at least one of the parents is alive, married brothers were more likely to remain together," family division in Hsin Hsing village usually takes place before the death of the old father. Frequently, it occurs soon after the sons of the family are married and sometimes after the first son has married. In such an early division the parents, who are sometimes not very elderly, may join the conjugal family of one of the sons, thus forming a stem family. More frequently, however, the parents themselves form another conjugal family as do each of their sons. If the parents do form a stem family with the oldest son, he may be granted a somewhat larger portion of land in the division than his brothers, in order to care for the parents.

In either case the parents remain in their own living quarters. If the parents form their own conjugal family and the father is still able to work in the fields, he is likely to retain a small portion of land for himself at the time of division. If the parents officially become a conjugal family, they will be fed and cared for on a rotation basis, usually for ten or fifteen days, by each of the new *chia* formed by the sons. They receive a certain amount of pocket money from each son, sometimes in cash but frequently in rice, after each harvest. (They can then sell the rice when they need cash.) Should they need medical care, it is the sons' responsibility to contribute equally towards its cost. If division takes place before all the children are married, the parents form a conjugal family with the unmarried children, retaining a large enough share of land to give the unmarried daughters a dowry and the unmarried sons a land parcel equal to what each of the married brothers received.

From fear of public criticism as well as from filial piety a son rarely fails in his obligations to his parents. A son who has moved his conjugal family to Taipei may sometimes be delinquent in sharing the costs of his parents' care, but more often the problem is his inability to do his share of parent-feeding in the monthly rotation. Under such circumstances the other brothers often refuse to take over the absent one's duties, dividing the month up among all the brothers as if the Taipei brother were still in the village. The parents, then, much to their annoyance, have to cook their own food in the absent brother's part of the rotation, even though he sends them money from Taipei to pay for it.

After the family division, if one of the sons (and his family) who received a portion of land is working in Taipei, the father may spend a good deal of his time farming the land for his son. An old father who has a family large enough to care for him in his old age may spend his time occasionally helping his sons on their land, doing odd jobs around the house, or just relaxing. A man with few sons and very little land will have to continue to work the land well into his old age.

Although the reasons for family division are varied, there are standard procedures for implementing the process. The actual division is carried out through the customary process of mediation by a person called in to help work out an amicable settlement. This man may be a *tsu* relative, a respected fellow villager, or a maternal relative. Family division entails the equal division among all sons of all property belonging to the large family. All the land must be evaluated according to its productive capacity and location. Where the amount of land cultivated is very small, the members of the family may in rare instances agree to draw lots. The winner of the drawing gets all the land and pays his brothers for their share; they may then go to the city to support their families.

In the division of the house, each new *chia* retains its own apartment or rooms. The family's large brick stove usually goes to the oldest son, while the others use small charcoal stoves until they can build their own brick stoves. Sometimes, until they are well settled under the new family arrangements, the *chia* of the younger brothers may continue to use the original family kitchen and stove.

Although the division often results from or causes bad feelings between the newly formed *chia*, there is a great deal of interaction among the members of the family even after the family property has been divided. Such related families frequently share in the use of certain tools and farm implements, either through mutual lending or joint ownership. Since they are both relatives and neighbors, such families may also continue mutual aid and cooperation with one another in everyday tasks.

THE "ANCESTRAL GROUP" [6]

Perhaps one of the most important unifying factors which joins divided families, as well as *tsu* organizations, is their joint religious activities. Although economic reasons may have divided the larger family, certain religious ceremonies continue to be a joint function. Ancestor worship and participation in funeral rituals for patrilineal relatives are two of the most important religious activities for the family. The one part of the house excepted from the division is the central room known as the *kung t'ing*, which contains the family's ancestral tablets, altar, and sometimes statues of gods which are owned jointly by the families. The room and its contents continue to be the common property of all the members of the separated families.

The conjugal families which now form independent *chia* (economic families) in their turn begin the process of expansion into joint or stem families as sons marry and have children; they may ultimately go through a similar process of division. In this manner, over a few generations a larger patrilineal kinship group develops which takes on the activities and functions of a *tsu* organization and is considered to be such by its members. The original *kung t'ing* is retained and continues to be used for the common religious activities of the enlarged kinship group. In Hsin Hsing, as the patrilineal kinship group expands, brothers often keep their own immediate ancestors' tablets, such as that of their parents' and sometimes grandparents', in a semiformal *kung t'ing* in their own quarters. However, ceremonies honoring the earliest ancestors are still held in the main *tsu kung t'ing* and are attended usually by representatives of all the *tsu* families. If a family moves permanently from the village to the city, it might make an entirely new copy of the ancestral tablet so that all of its own recent ancestors can be worshipped in the family's new locale.

Thus, the kinship group or, when it grows large enough, the *tsu* remains unified or at least is regularly unified on certain occasions as a "religious family." Kulp (1925:145–146) has called it "the practical unit of ancestral worship." The religious family "becomes a conscious unit only during the ceremonies of ancestral worship and varies according to the ancestor worshipped at any one time. It thus includes all those persons who ordinarily come together for ancestor worship." Only direct ancestors (or forebears considered to be such) are worshipped. A religious family is thus composed only of relatives who share common descent from a direct ancestor. The size of the family varies accordingly. While a *tsu* of over a hundred people, like the Huangs in Hsin Hsing, form a religious family to worship their founding ancestor, only the several *chia* of several brothers make up the religious family which combines to worship their deceased father, since he is not the direct ancestor of his brother's children or the other members of the *tsu*. The size and composition of a religious family is thus a function of the ancestor worshipped on any occasion. Thus, one notes that in Hsin Hsing village, when the members of a *tsu* worship their founding or earliest ancestors (whom they share in common), the *tsu* and religious family are identical. At other times a functioning religious family may be only a small portion of the *tsu*.

The newly separated households of the religious family function as a conscious unit for more than the actual ceremonies of ancestral worship. Although attendance at the ceremonies is frequently limited to representatives of each *chia*, other family members are drawn together by the organization, planning, and economic cooperation frequently necessary for such worship. An *esprit de corps* unifies the families in ancestor worship as well as in their mutual participation in rituals upon the death of a *tsu* relative.

This appears to be especially true in Hsin Hsing village where the *tsu* groups are small and so have little, if any, income from corporate land holdings. A large *tsu* with income from corporate land has a formal organization for the carrying out of ancestor worship or funeral arrangements. The more causually organized *tsu* of Hsin Hsing, however, must organize themselves for each occasion, and most *chia* must actively contribute both time and money.

Therefore, whenever worship of an early ancestor is to take place in one of the larger Hsin Hsing *tsu* compounds like those of the Huang or K'ang groups, each smaller *chia* sends incense, yellow paper money, and food to be used as sacrifices. There is no system of rotation under which each household in turn furnishes the sacrifices for all, although the care of the ancestral-worship room rotates from one *chia* to another at yearly intervals. In the Huang compound, for example, each of the four branches of the *tsu* which descend from the four sons of the *tsu's* founding father takes over the responsibility for the *kung t'ing* for a year and then passes it on to the next branch. The Huang *tsu*, though the largest in the village, has no income from corporate land. The *chia* which has the annual responsibility for the *kung t'ing* must therefore buy incense and paper money for the regular worship in addition to keeping the room clean. The large K'ang *tsu*, on the other hand, has corporate land; the income from this property, through the agency of one of the elders of the *tsu*, covers any additional expenses in the operation of the *kung t'ing*, such as the repair of any religious objects belonging to the *tsu*. The men in a religious family or *tsu* who are respected and act as advisors on *tsu* matters are those who give their time and who are the first to do any necessary work or to give money for *tsu* purposes. However, whatever the type or size of *tsu* group, the worship of the ancestors follows a standard pattern, the only difference being the number of *chia* which participate.

Thus, it is only on limited occasions that the entire *tsu* worships the early ancestors held in common by all *tsu* members. These infrequent rituals are held in the main *kung t'ing* of the *tsu* compound, and male representatives of the *tsu's* member families then seem to be the main participants. On such occasions, the main *tsu kung t'ing* serves as a kind of informal ancestral hall. However, on many other occasions, a small group worships their own more recent ancestors in this same main *kung t'ing* where their ancestors' tablets are housed and which then serves as a kind of private family or sub-*tsu kung t'ing*. Frequently, however, smaller sub-*tsu* groupings or families house the ancestral tablets of their recently deceased personal ancestors in their private, small, informal *kung t'ing* within their own apartment.

Most of the actual ancestral-worship rituals in the village are for the benefit of more recent ancestors of the sub-*tsu* groupings, and these are performed in either the private or main *kung t'ing* by the smaller group. Usually, it is the women who have married into and become part of the *tsu* who perform most of the actual ancestral-worship rituals in Hsin Hsing and other villages of the area. M. Freedman (1958:85) also notes that "The rites performed in the [ancestral] halls [of the *tsu*] were conducted by and in the presence of men; their daughters and wives played no direct part in the proceedings. In the home, in contrast, it is clear that, whatever the theoretical inferiority of women in the sphere of ancestor worship, they occupied a central position in its performance."

Since there are no ancestral halls in Hsin Hsing village or in the local area, this was the case. Worship of ancestors takes place exclusively in the *kung t'ing* of the *tsu* or family. Ancestor worship performed in a hall or in the *tsu kung t'ing* on certain few occasions would be public, a formal observance for all to witness and theoretically conducted by men. But more often in the Hsin Hsing area women conduct it. Ancestor worship, as it generally takes place, is on a small scale, is private, and tends to be rather informal. As a result, the women, in the presence of their children, usually take the main part in carrying out ancestor worship. As some of the villagers noted, "The men are busy, and the women are more religious anyway."

It is partially the unity of the religious family organization, which continues even after the legal economic division of a larger family, that gives the several newly independent *chia* a definite basis for cooperation and a sense of common identity. Of this Freedman (1958:23) has noted that the

newly separated households were at least potentially members of one ancestor-worshipping unit in relation to recent forebears, and some forms of *ad hoc* economic co-operation might be instituted between them. In other words, while the formal division of house and land, which was a ritually established rupture at one point in time, created legally independent households, the relations between these households might diminish gradually in time rather than undergo a sharp transformation from involvement to indifference.

Although a joint family may not continue for many generations as a single unit, it derives continuity from the maintenance of the religious family, with its function of ancestor worship. To ensure such continuity, marriage and adoption are a primary and conscious concern. In addition to providing the family with the necessary descendants to worship the ancestors, the institutions of marriage and adoption ensure the security of the family through growth and expansion. For the parents these institutions mean security and care in old age as well as in the afterlife. "One's future is in one's children" is a common saying which has had much meaning in traditional China and which is still no less important in the changing Taiwanese village. Besides these

ABOVE: Housebuilding in Hsin Hsing. BELOW: Bedroom of a village landlord's married son.

ABOVE: Itinerant beautician. BELOW: Itinerant artisan making steamers.

ABOVE: Stacking rice straw after harvest. RIGHT: Grinding glutinous rice for holiday cakes.

ABOVE: "Good-luck lady" leads typical Hsin Hsing bride to sedan chair. LEFT: Son of successful Hsin Hsing village migrant and his bride. BELOW: *Pai-pai* to T'ien Kung for sixteen-year-old boy.

ABOVE: Ancestor worship.
RIGHT: Altar in kung t'ing
with statues of invited
gods. BELOW: *Tao shih*
begins *pai-pai* at midnight
before arrival of bride.

ABOVE: Transporting pig to market.
BELOW: Worship after sale of pig.

ABOVE: Neighboring village comes to Hsin Hsing to pick up bride. BELOW: Sending boys off to army.

Possessed *t'iao t'ung* and his assistant recording "god's words."

Matsu procession: a successful call for rain.

future and long-term considerations, in Hsin Hsing the needs of the present are by no means overlooked. When a family enters into marriage or adoption proceedings, the parents make the arrangements with great care, because taking another person into the family may mean extra hands for the work of the household or merely an extra mouth to feed. The new person can facilitate the building and continuation of a stronger and larger family or hasten the family's division or destruction. One other important factor to be considered is that through the extension of relationships with *ch'in ch'i* (matrilateral and affinal relatives) beyond the village by either marriage or adoption, the family can enhance its socioeconomic security and political position. For these reasons, marriage and adoption are contractual matters in Taiwan, determined by whole families rather than individuals.

MARRIAGE

While surname and *tsu* exogamy is universal in the Hsin Hsing area as well as in traditional southeast China, marriage within one's own village is not uncommon, but is clearly preferred outside the village. It is considered incestuous for any person to marry another who bears the same surname. Whether the other is actually a member of one's own *tsu* (a *ch'in tsu*) or a perfect stranger, possibly even from another part of Taiwan, the rule still holds. One may still read stories in the newspapers of the suicide in the city of two lovers whose families forbade their marriage because they bore the same surname. In the village even a mention of such a marriage is frowned on.

Except for this prohibition, however, there are no rules against marriage within one's own village. Of course, in a single *tsu* village the individual has no choice but marriage outside the village. However, in villages like Hsin Hsing with a number of surnames, marriage between villagers is not unsusual. In 1958 there were about twelve cases in which the families of both husband and wife were Hsin Hsing villagers.

There are a number of reasons why, even in a multi-*tsu* type of village such as Hsin Hsing, the villagers prefer marriage with someone from elsewhere. One is that the small population of the village and the presence there of only twelve surname groups limits the individual's choice of a mate. Another less practical reason lies in the general village attitude that "It is better to marry outside of the village since marriages between two families of the same village are just not as interesting." When the bride lives in another village some distance away, the marriage procession with its musical accompaniment from the groom's village to the girl's village and back again carrying the gifts and dowry, goes through or past several other villages, drawing crowds of people as it passes. To the villagers this is all exciting and something which should be part of a marriage. At the occasional marriage between two Hsin Hsing villagers, the wedding procession with sedan chairs, dowry, and music goes along a regular route through two neighboring villages and back to Hsin Hsing. Villagers do not consider this quite as stimulating.

The preference for marriage beyond the village limits also rests on the feeling that it is not a good thing to have one's in-laws too close or to have the bride in too close proximity to her parents' home. When the two families live nearby, there is too much opportunity for bad feeling to develop between them. When the two families are in the same village, every detail of how the daughter-in-law is treated by her husband's family immediately reaches her own family, and it is far too easy for the girl to run home with complaints about every hardship, real or imaginary, in her new family. This sort of thing can easily cause interfamily conflict. In intravillage marriages in Hsin Hsing there have also been instances where a daughter-in-law has spent too much time in her old home, helping her mother instead of always being available in her husband's house to do whatever work is asked of her. Of the twelve marriages between Hsin Hsing families, relations between the two families in five cases were not considered good for a variety of such reasons.

Another factor favoring marriage outside the village is the village parents' fear of gossip about the cirrcumstances of the marriage. If both families live in Hsin Hsing village there is a good chance that the boy and girl knew each other before marriage; this in itself is considered improper, and people are very likely to say that this was a "love marriage" forced upon the two families because the young couple had been secretly seeing each other and having sexual intercourse. When one hears village discussions of marriages which have taken place between Hsin Hsing villagers, one gets the idea that almost all of them have been the result of a secret love affair. Such secret affairs do usually force the two families to agree eventually to a union between the two young people. Thus, in most instances, neither the couple nor their parents will willingly discuss the reasons for an intravillage marriage. When they do, they usually say that the marriage was arranged because both families felt the boy and the girl were well suited. They feel it is necessary to defend such a marriage from the inevitable talk. Family members usually remark that they had firsthand knowledge, without needing the word of a matchmaker, that the girl would be a good worker and an asset to the family. However, no matter what reasons are given, other villagers openly discuss the matter, often good-naturedly teasing those involved and making jokes about the "real" basis for the marriage.

Thus, while marriage outside the village is preferred, it is far from being a strict pattern in the Hsin Hsing area. Villagers do not frown upon nor criticize intravillage marriages, though they good-naturedly joke about the manner in which they were supposedly brought about. This, however, in no way appears to injure the status of the families or of the couple.

The most basic factor favoring marriage outside the village is the family's desire to extend and solidify its connections with new families in different places, most preferably with families with which there is no already existing *ch'in ch'i* relationship. Families in a village like Hsin Hsing, where they have a limited number of *tsu* relatives, feel it a definite advantage to extend their connections to families with which they can have relationships not marred by the enforced intimacy which so often spoils the relations between *ch'in tsu* or fellow villagers. Marriage between two Hsin Hsing families technically produces a *ch'in ch'i* relationship, but proximity tends to produce an enforced intimacy which has the disadvantages without the advantages of the *ch'in tsu* bond. The courtesy and warmth normally typical between *ch'in ch'i* is eroded by the frequent contact and increased opportunities for conflict.

Cousin Marriage

Although, as already indicated, there is a definite surname exogamy and a preference for marriage outside the village, there is no preference for any form of cousin marriage over noncousin marriage in the Hsin Hsing village area of Taiwan. It would be convenient if, on the basis of investigations made on the mainland, such a nonpreference as found in this area of Taiwan could be shown to be universal for Chinese society; however, the relatively few published studies that deal with aspects of cousin marriage in mainland China differ greatly in their findings. For example, the literature indicates that of the two possible forms of cross-cousin marriage—with mother's brother's daughter (matrilateral) or father's sister's daughter (patrilateral)—in some mainland areas considerable feeling is expressed against one or the other or both, but particularly against the patrilateral form. In many parts of China the latter is technically allowed, but not socially acceptable in practice. Thus the over-all picture is both confused and confusing, and the only present certainty is that the patterns of practice and acceptance vary widely throughout mainland China.[7]

In the Hsin Hsing village area, while there is acceptance of some forms of cousin marriage, no single type is actually preferred to noncousin marriage, and although most forms of cousin marriage are technically allowed, they are not equally acceptable. It is thus apparent that in this area, like many on the mainland, the allowance of cross-cousin marriage is certainly not symmetrical.[8] In any case, in Hsin

Hsing village the number of cousin marriages of any kind is small. Rather than cousin marriage, Hsin Hsing villagers prefer marriage with an outsider of no blood or previous affinal connection, i.e., with a family with which they do not already have a *ch'in ch'i* relationship, as was explained above. This results from their strong desire to extend their circle of family or *ch'in ch'i* relationships to new families in other villages with whom there is *no* prior *ch'in ch'i* relationship.

As several people of the area pointed out, "the villagers prefer to arrange marriages between families whose relationships are good." Although they think it may be all right to let their children marry a relative (*ch'in ch'i*) if the relationship between the families is good, at the same time they are not particularly interested in arranging such a marriage and usually do *not* do so. There are many villagers who have stronger feelings on the subject and think it unwise to arrange a marriage with the family of a *ch'in ch'i*, since "they are afraid bad *kan-ch'ing* may develop between the two families if the daughter-in-law and her husband's family do not get along well." They do not want to risk endangering an already good *ch'in ch'i* relationship. As long as the two families are on good terms, they think it is wise to leave well enough alone, and this added to their preference for building new *ch'in ch'i* relationships through marriage outside the village provide strong support for outside marriages.

As already mentioned there are some marriages between cousins, however, in the Hsin Hsing area. When it comes to cousin marriage, though, there are very definite opinions as to which forms are acceptable and which are not. There are three possible kinds, though they are not equally regarded: (1) patrilateral cross-cousin marriage (*ku piao hsiang ch'in*); (2) matrilateral cross-cousin marriage (*ku piao hsiang ch'in*)—in Hsin Hsing, at least, these first two elements (*ku piao*) are again used rather than those of *chiu piao,* as sometimes reported by anthropologists for mainland China areas and other parts of Taiwan; [9] and (3) matrilateral parallel-cousin marriage (*i piao hsiang ch'in*). Patrilateral parallel-cousin marriage is, of course, out of the question because both young people bear the same surname.

In a patrilateral cross-cousin marriage a young man marries the daughter of his father's sister, bringing her back to live in the home of her mother's brother. She now bears the same surname her mother had before marriage and belongs to the same kinship group; worse, in village opinion, her husband and her mother in this sense share the same name. The relationship is felt to be so close that the marriage is almost incestuous. Such marriages are thus frowned upon, and people talk about and criticize the two families for making such arrangements. Some people even believe that when the blood ties between families are so close, the children born of the union are likely to be mentally defective ("stupid"); one villager said that the "former Japanese emperor Ta Cheng was a stupid person because his family always arranged marriages with their own kinsmen."

In a matrilateral cross-cousin marriage a young man marries the daughter of his mother's brother, bringing her back to live in the home of her father's sister. The villagers call this "following the aunt." In village opinion this kind of marriage is all right as long as there is good *kan-ch'ing* between the families. Since mother-in-law and daughter-in-law were both born in the same village and the same patrilineal kinship group, they are likely to have much in common and, thus, perhaps have a warmer relationship than usual, which tends to reduce the possibility of domestic conflict. To the villagers this kind of marriage is similar to a match arranged between the children of two families which are friends; no one criticizes or gossips about such marriages.

In a matrilateral parallel-cousin marriage a young man marries the daughter of his mother's sister, bringing her home to live in the house of her maternal aunt. This kind of marriage is generally approved, since to the villagers the kinship ties between the two families barely exist. Kinship terms for matrilateral parallel-cousins do exist, but not many villagers use them. A partner in such a marriage is thus not necessarily marrying someone designated by label as a kinsman. The bride has been born into an entirely different kinship group than her mother's sister, and before marriage she did not refer to her aunt's husband or son by formal kinship terms; they were only recognized as unlabeled *ch'in ch'i*. In village opinion, therefore, marriage of a girl to her matrilateral parallel-cousin is almost like marriage to a stranger. This is much different from marriage with either cross-cousin, "who are always clearly thought of as some kind of relative by birth." (See Appendix 2 for a further discussion of cousin terminology and for a listing of kinship terminology in Hsin Hsing village.)

Hsin Hsing village's representative to the *hsiang* council provided the following estimates which bear out the villagers' attitudes towards cousin marriage noted above.[10] By his estimate, in Hsin Hsing village, and probably in the area generally, less than 0.5 percent of the village males marry their father's sister's daughter (patrilateral cross-cousin). About 1.5 percent marry their mother's brother's daughter (matrilateral cross-cousin), and about 2.0 percent marry their mother's sister's daughter (matrilateral parallel-cousin). In other words, it is this informant's opinion that "Only about 4 percent of the marriages are with *ch'in ch'i;* the remainder [or 96 percent] are marriages with strangers or friends."

Just as the people of the Hsin Hsing village area think it preferable, for the most part, not to have cousin marriage, there also seems to be no attempt either by Hsin Hsing villagers or other villagers in the area to develop any definite system of connubium between particular *tsu* groups. This is similar to what Freedman (1958:98–100) finds for Kwangtung and Fukien. It is especially true for the Hsin Hsing area, where most *tsu* groups are so small relatively that their size would tend to limit marriage choices too narrowly. *Tsu* groups therefore have little interest in cementing mutual relationships through marriage patterns. Instead, marriage arrangements in the Hsin Hsing village area are "cast in many directions" (Freedman, 1958:100).

The unstructured habit of marriage arrangement is evidenced by the great range of villages, cities, and areas from which wives in the village came. The 154 married women in the village in 1958 whose origin was traced came from a total of 52 different places. Sixty-six came from 19 different villages (including Hsin Hsing) in Pu Yen Hsiang. Fifty-four came from 18 different villages in the neighboring *hsiang* of Fu Hsing. Eight women came from Lukang and 6 from the market town of Chi Hu, about five miles away from Hsin Hsing. The remaining 20 came from 13 other places which ranged from villages in other nearby *hsiang* all the way to the distant cities of Taipei, Kao-hsiung, and Hsin Chu.

There does not even appear to be any real patterning in the birth-places of the women who came to Hsin Hsing from villages in Pu Yen Hsiang and the neighboring Fu Hsing Hsiang. Although 24 women, or more than one-third of all who came to Hsin Hsing from Pu Yen Hsiang, are from the one village of Hsi Shih Hu, this seems to be mainly because it is the largest village in the *hsiang*. In addition, the women from Hsi Shih Hu frequently act as matchmakers between other girls from their own village and Hsin Hsing village families. The same seems to be true for the large village of Fan She, from which 25 percent of all the girls marrying into Hsin Hsing village from Fu Hsing Hsiang come. Their common origin affects in some ways the relations between the Hsin Hsing families into which these women have married. In the early years of marriage the women of about the same age tend to be more friendly. In addition, when either Hsin Hsing or the native village of these women observes a religious festival occasion, the men from Hsin Hsing who are married to women from the same village may go there together, just as the male relatives from the wives' village may come as a group to visit Hsin Hsing.

It was possible to trace in the records and through interviews the place of marriage for only 41 Hsin Hsing village women; again there was no particular marriage pattern. Of the 41, 9 were married into 5 villages in Pu Yen Hsiang, 14 into 8 villages in Fu Hsing Hsiang, 9 into Lukang, and the remaining 9 into 5 other places which included more distant *hsiang* and cities such as Taipei and Taichung. It is interesting that of these 41 cases traced about 14 women, almost 35 percent of the total, were married into relatively urban places, including the 9 who went to Lukang. This is consistent with the attitude expressed by many villagers, that they prefer to marry their daughters to men doing work other than farming, since they feel that farming is a hard and insecure life.

Siaosiv and "Adopted Husband" Marriage

There are two other forms of marriage in the Hsin Hsing area. Both of them have decreased in frequency but are nevertheless still relatively important. These forms are especially important to relatively poor villagers, since they offer an institutional means of facilitating the marriage of people who might otherwise have financial difficulty.

One form which has been popular and frequently occurs in the Hsin Hsing area is what Fei (1939:53), writing about Kaihsienkung on the mainland, refers to as the

siaosiv system, siaosiv meaning small daughter-in-law or more precisely the foster daughter-in-law.

The parents of the boy will take a girl as foster-child at a very early age, the future mother-in-law even feeding her at her breast, and will take care of her up to marriage. All the elaborate proceedings such as match-making, marriage gifts, the sending of the meeting-boat and sedan chair, will not be needed, if the daughter-in-law has been brought up in her husband's house. Some of the siaosiv do not know their own parents. Those who have still maintained contact with their own parents, owing to early separation, will not be of special interest to them.

The system in the Hsin Hsing village area, although not referred to as the siaosiv system, has basically the same form and function. However, because there are certain important differences in attitudes and details of operation between it and its Kaihsienkung counterpart, the system as practiced in the Hsin Hsing area will be taken up later in the discussion of adoption.

The other form of marriage, and the least common, is a matrilocal (or more precisely uxorilocal) type in which a man marries and goes to live with his wife's family. He is usually referred to by the villagers as an "adopted husband." At the time of the marriage, the two families assume a ch'in ch'i relationship just as in any ordinary marriage. The boy's family sends a small dowry, and the girl's family provides the couple with the necessary bedroom furniture, which is the reverse of the practice in an ordinary marriage. In the Hsin Hsing area, unlike similar practices on the Chinese mainland and in Japan, the husband always seems to retain his own surname, but in going to live with his wife's family he accepts the authority of his father-in-law.

Therefore, there is a certain social stigma attached to the adopted husband. The villagers often refer to such a husband as a *chui hsu* or a *chao fu,* terms which in themselves may indicate some feeling of derision. While the terms, as compounds, generally mean a son-in-law who lives with his wife's family, taken separately there is a derogatory quality in the individual components of the compounds. For example, *hsu* means son-in-law, but the literal meaning of the other word of the compound, *chui,* is irrelevant, useless, or a parasite. In the second compound, although *fu* has the general meaning of husband or man, *chao* means to beckon, to call, or to give notice.

Although the institution of husband adoption is recognized as a necessity in some cases, most villagers look down on such a husband and, in a sense, consider him an incomplete man. There are jokes made about adopted husbands, sometimes even in their presence, and if a man is henpecked or does chores for his wife which a woman would normally do for herself, the villagers are likely to say he is "being like an adopted husband." The attitudes of the other village men toward the adopted husband vary according to the kind of person he is, but generally such a man finds it difficult to win the respect of his peers. Unless he is an aggressive person, he is unlikely to speak out in a male group, since he knows the other men will pay little attention to him. For this reason, few men or their families will agree to a marriage by adoption unless the family is very poor, has little or no land for the son to inherit, and cannot afford a regular marriage for him. The men in Hsin Hsing village who have become adopted husbands were usually at the average marriageable age for men at the time of adoption; they were not adopted into the girl's family in their youth or at any time before the actual marriage.

The family wishing to adopt a husband for their daughter must offer some firm reward such as land or money. Then, sometimes a poor and perhaps ambitious but "thick-skinned" man will agree to become an adopted husband. The boy may know and like the girl and so be willing to give himself for adoption as a husband.

The family which brings in a husband for their daughter may do so out of a need for the man's labor or from a desire to have descendants. Perhaps the more common situation solved by such an adoption is when a family has a marriageable daughter and a much younger son who, because of his youth, will be unable to work the family land for a number of years. Frequently, there is a written or verbal contract which stipulates the terms of the marriage by adoption. The agreement in a situation like the one just described is usually effected for a specific number of years, or at least until the wife's younger brother is old enough to take over the management of the family's land. The husband agrees to live in his wife's family home, accept the authority of his father-in-law, work for the family as he would for his own, give at least the second-born child the wife's surname, and sometimes even promise that he and any offspring from the marriage will worship the wife's ancestors. In return, the adopted husband's family is spared the usual heavy expenses of marriage, and the man himself gets a wife whom he could not normally afford. He can raise a family, even if it will not be fully under his own authority for a number of years. Most important of all, he is promised either a definite sum of money or rice or a certain amount of land at the expiration of the contract period.

At the end of the contract period the adopted husband with his wife and children may remain in the wife's family home if they get along well with them, especially with her younger brother's family. More often, the family will divide into two separate units, although the wife with her adopted husband and children may remain in the same house or village with her family. However, when the two families do not get along well and the husband is too bothered by his inferior status in his wife's village, he may move his wife and children to his own village if there is room in his family's house or village and if he can manage to earn a living there. It seems to be more common for the adopted husband to take his wife and children to another place after fulfilling his contract than to remain with his wife's family. Although an adopted husband who has a forceful personality may assume actual authority over his family, after the separation from the wife's family, it is the wife and not the husband who is officially recognized as the *chia chang* of the family.

Sometimes a husband is adopted into a family which has no sons in order to furnish descendants. The adoption of a husband for this purpose differs in one important way from the adoption of a husband when the wife has a younger brother. The living arrangement of the adopted husband in the girl's family is likely to become permanent. Since there is no younger brother and his family to complicate family relations, the adopted husband and his wife and children may simply continue to live with the wife's family and therefore transmit the names of both families through their children.

Whether the family of the wife and her adopted husband remains in her family's house or goes to live in his natal village or family home, the general manner of naming children and assigning descent lines is the same. Usually, the first child is given the father's surname, and the second child—whether it is a boy or a girl—receives the mother's family name. All subsequent children bear the father's surname. The one child bearing the surname of the mother's family will inherit property through that family, and is responsible for carrying on the mother's line and the worship of her ancestors. If, however, no child is given the mother's family name, as is sometimes the case if there is no property to be inherited from her family, then no matter where the family lives, all the children are supposed to worship both sets of ancestors. If there is property, once the second child has received his inheritance he or she and the mother worship the mother's ancestors, while the father (adopted husband) and the children in his descent line worship his ancestors. When the second child (who has been given the mother's surname) is a girl, it is not unlikely that a husband will be brought in for her in order to carry on the maternal line. There are cases in Taiwan, and one in Hsin Hsing village, where a village family for several generations has become in a sense matrilineal as well as matrilocal, at least until a male heir is born.

Barclay (1954b:228–229) finds that this matrilocal form of marriage, where the husband is adopted and lives with his wife's family, has been very common in Taiwan for many years; between 1906 and 1930, 15 to 20 percent of all Taiwanese marriages were of this matrilocal type. However, the frequency of the practice has been decreasing, until in 1943 only 6.2 percent of all marriages in Taiwan were of this form (Barclay, 1954b:229, Table 69). Barclay notes that this decrease has been constant, for "when men were no longer obliged to marry on these degrading terms, they began to shun this type of marriage. Because it was inconsistent with the rest of the family system, matrilocal marriage presented a special occasion for discord—men were led to expect one kind of familial role as husbands, but required to accept another one that was inferior."

There are only six adopted husbands recorded for Hsin Hsing village. It is thus difficult to see any tendency toward or against the practice in Hsin Hsing village itself. These six adoptions have taken place since approximately 1900, and according to the present ages of the surviving men, four were adopted into the village well before World War II and only two were adopted afterward. These same records show that only one Hsin Hsing villager was adopted out of the village between 1949 and 1957.

Remarriage

According to the ideal norms of Chinese society a woman should marry only once, and a young widow who does not remarry is often greatly honored. A woman's natal family is responsible only for arranging her first marriage; any subsequent marriage is theoretically her own responsibility. The family of her first husband, whether he died or there was a divorce, also bears little responsibility for helping her to remarry.

In actuality, however, many divorced or widowed women do remarry. And a second marriage, although never given the same honor as the first marriage, may nevertheless be sanctioned by society according to the circumstances of the particular case. The woman's economic circumstances and her age are the basic determinants of whether or not she will remarry and whether or not her marriage will be accepted or criticized. A young divorcee or widow who has very young children or none can do little but remarry unless she is wealthy. A second marriage for her is generally acceptable. The woman with young children must have someone to support her and her children until they are old enough to contribute financially to the family. It is also felt that a young childless woman, and even a childless rich widow, should remarry, if for no other reason than to bear children who can later care for her and worship her after her death.

A woman wealthy enough to support herself and her children, or over thirty-five with older children who can or soon will be able to work is not considered honorable if she remarries. Since there is no pressing economic reason for her to marry again, if she manages to find a husband—and this is certainly difficult—she will be generally criticized. People usually assume that her only reason for remarrying was to fulfill her sexual passions, and they joke and laughingly speculate about her sex life. Therefore, such a woman does not usually remarry.

In the infrequent cases in the rural area today when a man and woman are divorced—often because the man has found himself another wife in Taipei—the woman will probably return to her native home if they will have her. An alternative solution is for her to go to the city or town to work and earn her own living, which is an innovation for women. If she returns to her native home, as happened in the one recent divorce case in Hsin Hsing, her family will probably attempt to arrange for her to remarry as soon as possible in order to rectify such an unnatural family situation. If a divorcee has children by her first marriage, any male children would almost automatically remain with their father or at least with his family. The divorcee from Hsin Hsing had one young daughter and was considered by everyone to be blameless in the divorce. She had been advised by the police— who had helped work out the terms of the divorce and make the final settlement [11]—that she would be better off if she made her husband keep the little girl, since otherwise the child's presence would make it that much more difficult for her to start a new life either working or finding a new husband. In a sense, then, it was considered that she had won the divorce, since her husband had to take their little girl. The woman, of course, took back all the furniture and other items of her dowry which she had brought into the marriage.

Since the Hsin Hsing villagers realized that she was not at fault, although she was much talked about, she was not criticized. Nevertheless, even though she was still only in her middle twenties, she was now very limited in her choice of a marriage partner. The only men who will marry a divorced woman are usually a widower with his own children, an older man, or sometimes a physically handicapped man. The Hsin Hsing divorcee married a widower with one child.

Such a second marriage is sanctioned by society, but its ceremonial observance is very unlike a first marriage and does not follow the traditional pattern. Rather than being brought in a sedan chair from her village to her husband's home, the woman makes the trip quietly with the matchmaker very early in the morning so as not to be seen by other people. While the necessity for the second marriage is realized and therefore accepted, it is not considered good taste to make a public display of an act which defies the ideal norms and traditions. It would show a definite lack of respect for custom and propriety and would be subject to criticism.

From middle age on a woman who is widowed usually prefers to remain in her husband's village, especially if she has been there a long time. If the family is undivided, she and her children will continue to live with her deceased husband's family, or if the family has previously divided, she and her children may continue to live as a separate household. A younger widow with young children is more likely to be a drain on the family's economy. Her deceased husband's family, frequently with the help of her own people, may soon very seriously consider her remarriage. A widow, like a divorcee, is limited in the types of husband she can find. If she is considered a good daughter-in-law and gets on well with the deceased husband's family, a marriage may be arranged with a younger unmarried brother. Although there is presently only one such case in Hsin Hsing village, this form of second marriage is not uncommon in the area and is perfectly acceptable.

In other cases, if a younger widow does not get on well with her deceased husband's family, has no financial resources, and cannot be supported by his family, she may go elsewhere to work in order to earn a living for herself and her children. (This is possible today because of job opportunities for women.) Or she may even return, with or without her children, to stay with her natal family at least until she can remarry. The question of the disposition of her children must be settled with her deceased husband's family, though it is more common for her children to accompany her as she enters her new life. Thus, although divorce causes the break-up of the family, the death of a husband does not necessarily cause any major change in the functioning of the family, especially if the woman is older and has grown children.

ADOPTION

Two major types of adoption are recognized by the villagers in the Hsin Hsing area according to the particular reasons for the adop-

tion. Adoptions, like marriage, require a go-between or broker to make
the necessary contacts and arrangements. The most frequent adoption
is that of a girl. There are two forms of this, although the forms are
not always differentiated at the time of adoption. One is the adoption
of a girl as the future wife of one of the sons of the family. (This
arrangement was briefly mentioned earlier as the *siaosiv* system of
marriage.) Upon adoption the girl, in the Hsin Hsing area, is called
either a *hsi fu* (a daughter-in-law) or *tung yang hsi* (a girl brought up
in the home of her fiance). The other called a *yang nu* (adopted
daughter), is the adoption of a girl who, much like a regular daughter,
will live with the family until she reaches the age to be married out.

The other major adoption type is that of a son to worship the
ancestors and to perpetuate the family by producing descendants. Although such a son is called a *yang tzu* (adopted son), he has all the
rights of inheritance of a natural son of the family, at least by local
practice.

Both types of adoption are socially accepted and legally recognized
and are entered in the official village and family records in the Pu Yen
Hsiang Public Office. In each case the child is listed according to the
special term designating that specific type of adopted person.

Adoption of a Daughter

Of the many reasons for the adoption of a daughter, one of the
most basic is that the adopting family has no children while the girl's
family either has too many girl children or is simply unable to afford
the expense of raising her. Sometimes, when an infant has died and its
mother is despondent, the family may adopt a baby girl to comfort the
mother for the loss of her own child. In other cases a couple which has
not been able to produce a first child may decide to adopt one (usually a girl), believing that having a child in the house will make it
possible for the woman to conceive, or more accurately, that the
adopted girl is supposed to invite in a baby boy (*chao ti*).

Another common reason for adopting a girl child, especially among
poorer people, is as a future wife for one of the sons of the family. Such
a marriage is much cheaper for both families, since it makes it unnecessary to have the usual expensive wedding. Other families who
have no girls to do the family housework may adopt a girl with the
idea that she will work for the family until the time she is married.
However, if such a family has subsequent financial reverses, or if everyone becomes attached to the girl and finds that she is such a good
worker that she could contribute much as a permanent part of the
family, they may marry her to one of their own sons to keep her in the
family. The feeling here is that so long as the family knows and values
the girl, there is no sense in marrying her off to some other family only
to bring an unknown girl into the house as a wife for their son. The

girl is already accustomed to the ways of the house, and has probably developed a mother-daughter relationship with the wife of the *chia chang*.

At the time of adoption, the family may have no intention of bringing up a wife for their son, although they may change their minds later. Whereas an apparently definite distinction between simple adoption and adopting a girl as a future wife for a son in the *siaosiv* system of marriage (discussed below) was made by Fei's mainland China Kaihsienkung villagers (1939:53–55), in the Hsin Hsing village area no distinction based on reason for adoption need be made when the girl is adopted. A girl adopted to be a daughter may later be married to the family's son, and a girl adopted as a future wife for a son may ultimately be married out just as if she were the adoptive family's own daughter. And whatever the original intent of the adoption, or what kind of marriage is eventually arranged for her, the girl is usually treated very much as if she were a natural daughter of the family that adopted her. It is for this reason that I have treated both kinds of adoption under the same general heading.

A family which offers its daughter for adoption must usually give the adopting family a payment of "milk money" at the time of adoption, whether the girl is to be a regular daughter or the future wife of a son of the new family. Both the natal and adopting families consider themselves to be *ch'in ch'i* as a result of the adoption. In fact, when the girl reaches marriageable age the adopting family will frequently consult with her natal family about the potential husband and the marriage negotiations. In many such instances the affinal relationships then become a three-way affair between the girl's natal family, the adopting family, and her husband's family.

When the girl is definitely being adopted into a family as a servant, her family will often be given some money as recompense for the loss of her services. In these cases, the girl is usually at least eight or nine when adopted, old enough to be immediately trained and do useful work in her new home. The Chinese law in Taiwan recognizes such adoptions; however, it recognizes the girls as adopted daughters (*yang nu*), not servants, and stipulates that they must be well treated and be married out at marriageable age. When a girl is adopted to be a servant, there is obviously little likelihood that the two families will maintain a *ch'in ch'i* relationship, since the adoption is recognized as a purely business transaction. Such adoptions are no longer as common as they used to be, although they still take place among some rich, rural people. The sister of the former large landlord in Hsin Hsing had been "given such a girl as a wedding present." The practice is especially common in market towns and cities where girls are "sold" to wealthy families as servants or where they are adopted by a family to

be hired out to houses of prostitution or bars. These girls are still
recognized as *yang nu.*

The majority of girls adopted in Hsin Hsing or adopted from the
village either come from or go to villages in the Hsin Hsing area. Of
the 39 recorded cases of girl adoptions (over a period of some 50
years), 29 of the girls came from villages in Pu Yen Hsiang or nearby
Fu Hsing Hsiang; an additional 3 came from Lukang and 1 from the
nearby market town of Chi Hu. The other 6 girls came from more
distant places such as Taipei or other cities.

Of the 39, only 5 were between two families within Hsin Hsing
village. In most cases of girl adoption, as in almost all adoptions in or
away from Hsin Hsing, the two families involved in the adoptions
are not related. That most girl adoptions take place between families
from other villages is a clear indication that these families are not
ch'in tsu of the Hsin Hsing village families. In most cases they also do
not have a *ch'in ch'i* relationship until after the adoption. Even adoptions between Hsin Hsing families were not between related families.
At most the families are simply friends.

Siaosiv *Marriage*

In a discussion of problems Chinese families have in securing
brides for their sons, Olga Lang reports that it is not uncommon for
them to "arrange to have their sons' future brides brought up in their
homes—a practice especially widespread in the South" (1946:127). She
also observes (in a footnote) that "the custom was well known in old
China (it was mentioned even in the legal code of the Yuan dynasty).
Though it did not become universal, the number of arrangements of
this kind always increased in hard times" (1946:127). She attributes
the necessity for such arrangements partially to the common shortage
of marriageable women and partially to the high cost of marriage, that
is, the expense of obtaining a wife for a son as well as the cost of the
marriage festival itself (1946:125–127).

Although Fei finds the practice of adopting a girl as a future wife
for a son (the *siaosiv* system) to be a new institution for Kaihsienkung,
his theory of its economic *raison d'être* coincides with Lang's explanation. Fei, however, goes a step further:

> The *siaosiv* system is despised, since it develops at times of economic de-
> pression and is usually practiced by poorer families. Moreover, its effect in
> loosening ties of affinal relationship, affects the normal working of kinship
> organization. It is also unfavorable to the status of women and to the pos-
> sibility of the young couple forming an independent family, since they lack
> the contribution of their parents in marriage gifts and dowry (1939:54–55).

When one examines the conditions under which families in the Hsin
Hsing area adopt a girl as a future wife for a son and the frequency

with which these adoptions occur, it is obvious that the *siaosiv* system of marriage is not "despised," even though economic circumstances are an important motivational factor. Nor does it seem to loosen the ties of affinal relationship; on the contrary, it seems in some ways to strengthen them. Since the *ch'in ch'i* relationship is accepted as a consequence of either a marriage or an adoption, the *siaosiv* system simply has the effect of establishing it earlier than a regular marriage would.

In the Hsin Hsing area I have found no evidence, either, of any real dislike for the system by either set of parents. The girl's parents benefit by saving the expense of rearing an extra girl child whom they are unable or unwilling to support as well as by saving the cost of a wedding or of providing a dowry. The boy's parents gain a household worker, are spared the normal marriage expenses, and, in addition, have the advantage of raising their future daughter-in-law under their own roof. Since the villagers feel that the most common cause of family division is a dissatisfied daughter-in-law, a son's wife who has grown up since childhood as a member of the family is much less likely to want or to try to force a division of the family. In effect, the *siaosiv* system is felt to conduce to the attainment of the ideal joint family, while not in the least impairing (in Hsin Hsing) the usual establishment of *ch'in ch'i* relationships.

Despite all this, there are indications that the *siaosiv* system is becoming less frequent in Hsin Hsing and other areas of Taiwan. Further, even where such adoptions have taken place in recent years, it is noticeable that more and more often the girl is married out when she reaches normal marriageable age, rather than being married to the son of her adoptive parents. The trend seems to be quite recent, and there are a number of possible reasons for it.

Keeping in mind Lang's (1946:127) and Fei's (1939:54–55) explanations for the *siaosiv* system of adoption and marriage, we can observe resemblances in several important recent developments in rural Taiwan. First, there have been notable changes in demographic patterns there, in recent decades especially, which have affected sex ratios (see Chapter 2) for both Hsin Hsing village and area and for Taiwan generally (Barclay, 1954b:212, Table 60). The ratio of women to men has gradually increased until there is by now almost an equal proportion of each, which makes the problem of finding a suitable wife for a son much less serious than it used to be. This great increase in the proportion of females is closely related to the decline of infant mortality rates as a result of better public health facilities and of the generally better economic climate and consequent higher standard of living which has been notable mainly during the past decade. The economic circumstances to which Lang and Fei attribute the persistence of the *siaosiv* system are thus moderated. Both of these factors, the increased

number of females and the improved financial conditions, mean that
brides are both easier to find and easier to afford. As a result, *siaosiv*
adoptions are less and less frequent, and girls originally adopted under
the system tend more and more to be married out. Contributing to this
latter tendency is the increasingly open opposition of young people to
having their marriage partners imposed upon them arbitrarily by their
parents. The opposition is likewise made possible by the improvement
in economic opportunity for young people, in this instance by the
growing ease of urban migration.

Probably some dislike for the system has always been present among
the young people for whom *siaosiv* marriages were arranged. From the
time of adoption the girl is treated as a member of the family—in
other words, like a daughter, not a daughter-in-law. In the Hsin Hsing
area, when the marriage is definitely decided upon the young couple
are apprised of it. The girl is usually in her early teens at this point.
Suddenly, then, the young people are confronted by a change in their
relationship; no longer are they brother and sister, but potentially
man and wife, with a whole new set of behavior and attitude patterns
to absorb. At the very best, the situation is awkward for them. Much
like a normal engaged couple, they develop an avoidance relationship;
they may no longer remain alone in the same room and show increasing embarrassment in each other's presence, especially when others are
around. If they are seen together anywhere, they are usually subjected
to a good deal of teasing by friends and neighbors as well as their
relatives. And, living in the same household, the pressure of maintaining the avoidance pattern is much greater than anything ever experi-
enced by the usual engaged couple, who may scarcely know each other
by sight before the wedding day. The couple entrapped by the *siaosiv*
system undergo constant embarrassment, and as a result they often
develop a resentment against each other that culminates in a strong
preference for marriage to someone else entirely.

Formerly, the young people could not easily or openly express their
opposition to the match, since they had almost no option but to do
exactly what their families and elders had planned for them. Furthermore, they knew that if a *siaosiv* marriage had been arranged for
them, this was usually because there was no other form of marriage
possible, given their circumstances.

The recent demographic and economic changes in Taiwan have
radically changed things for such young people. Now, thanks to the
decreased necessity for such adoption marriages and the concomitant
increase in economic opportunity for the young, they are increasingly
able to express their opposition to a system which is not consistent
with the modern tendency for allowing young people a much greater
say in the choice of their marriage partners.

In Hsin Hsing, for example, one current reason why *siaosiv* adoptions less often lead to marriage is that the girl objects to marrying the family's son and insists on being allowed to marry outside her adoptive family. The more equal balance of the sexes and the increased economic opportunities for outside work, even in the rural towns beyond the obvious opportunities of urban migration, have given the young people a mobility never possible before, in addition to loosening the family's economic hold on them. An unwilling young woman or man can now threaten to go to the city to work if a projected marriage is for any reason distasteful. And even if the family, by extreme coercion, should attempt to force through a *siaosiv* system marriage, the young people now have a further protection, since such forced marriage arrangements are not upheld by law.

The changed economic situation with its concomitant effects on mobility and increased independence from the traditional authority of the family makes it possible for young people to resist prearranged marriages as they were never able to do before. It seems likely that these factors underlie the apparent decrease in the number of marriages between son and adopted daughter.

Adoption of a Son

The kind of family most likely to adopt a son is generally one which has no sons of its own. The fears of such people that there will be no one to take care of them in their old age or to worship them after death, or to furnish descendants to carry on the family line, are the basic reasons for such adoptions. This kind of adoption is still common on Taiwan, in urban as well as rural areas. For example, during our stay in Taipei, my own family had a servant from the mainland. She was childless, divorced, and saw little chance that she would be able to remarry. Thus, when she was about thirty years old she adopted a three-year-old boy, boarding him with friends while she worked. Her explanation was that she would need someone to take care of her in later years and to worship her after she died.

A family willing to give up a son for adoption is usually under the pressure of financial necessity and has more than one son. The necessity must be serious, since a family "selling" its son for adoption gives up all claim to him. The adopting family gives the boy's family money for him, and the villagers say, "When a son is adopted out, it is like cutting off one's finger" and, further, "when one sells [adopts out] a son, one no longer has any relations with him" ("*Mai tzu wu yu tzu chiao*"). The family adopting the boy naturally wants his entire loyalty, the kind of familial closeness their own son would have had. For this reason, not only are his ties to his natal home supposed to be completely broken but the age of adoption of boys is as young as possible, at least below the age of four. In Hsin Hsing there were only a few instances in which boys were older when adopted, and of the eighteen adoptions recorded in the village, three boys were under a year old and most of the remaining were under four when adopted.

Although the records show such a boy as a *yang tsu* (adopted son) his surname is legally changed to that of his adopting family. He may never be told about his natal home or his real family, since his extreme youth at the time of adoption makes it possible to keep the identity of his own family a secret from him. If the boy does find out, as sometimes happens, who his own family is, his adoptive family may attempt to prevent him from visiting them for fear he might refuse to come back or transfer his allegiance to his own natal family and thus refuse to be obedient.

In Hsin Hsing a poor, childless couple, having adopted a young boy, later adopted a young girl with the intention of marrying the two. This boy, who was a bit older than usual when adopted, managed to learn who his natal family was and insisted on visiting them. He found that his brothers had recently become fairly well-off financially, and he entertained ideas of returning there permanently. His adoptive parents, fearful that their plans and future security would be upset, beat him and forbade him to visit his natal home. The boy's natal family could or would not do anything to interfere with the authority of the adoptive family, and he had to remain with his new parents.

For similar reasons, and because adoption of a boy is considered a business arrangement, the two families do not maintain *ch'in ch'i* or other relations between themselves. However, in a few cases in Hsin Hsing where the two families were previously friends or *ch'in tsu,* or were fellow villagers, the relationship was maintained, and there was little attempt to keep the truth from the boy. Of the eighteen cases of boy adoption in Hsin Hsing, in five of them both families were from Hsin Hsing, though almost all were adoptions between unrelated villagers. However, when I was about to leave the village, plans were being made for the adoption of an infant son between the families of two brothers who had formerly been the large landlords in the village. The older brother had four sons and three daughters, while the younger brother was childless. No money was to be paid, and, of course, the adoption would not be kept secret from the boy when he grew up.

The villagers consider the adoption of a patrilateral nephew as a son an ideal form of adoption, but it is nevertheless rare. Usually, only large, wealthy families which have a strong regard for the traditional ideal of the joint family plus the means to maintain the ideal patterns are in a position to arrange such adoptions. The average village family, as we have seen, is usually weak in landholdings, financial resources, and numbers. It is generally of the conjugal type. In such

families, neither of two brothers is likely to have enough sons or sufficient financial stability to risk giving up the potential income and
future security a son represents by allowing even a brother to adopt a
male child. These small village families generally find it impossible to
manifest many of the patterns of the traditional family ideal, with the
result that son adoption in the Hsin Hsing village area usually takes
place between families which are not related by blood.

[6

Personal Relationships and Cooperation Within and Beyond the Village

We have seen that one of the most important relationships for villagers is that which exists between families who claim a common ancestor in the village and who consider themselves to be members of the same patrilineal group, i.e., *ch'in tsu.* On the other hand, a villager who happens to bear the same surname without claiming descent from the common ancestor in the village is called a *ch'in t'ang,* the same term one would use for a complete stranger who happened to bear the same surname. However, in the belief that there was an original common ancestor on the mainland, *ch'in t'ang* in the same village or perhaps also in the immediate village area are felt to be much more closely related than *ch'in t'ang* from other places. And although the relationship is not considered to be one of actual patrilineal kinship, there is nevertheless some special feeling between village families bearing the same surname who believe that they share a common mainland ancestor. But generally, the majority of Hsin Hsing villagers can easily trace their common ancestry in the village itself as a result of its relatively short history.

INTERFAMILY AND INTERPERSONAL RELATIONSHIPS

Since most patrilineal relatives either live in the same house or at least in the same part of the village, this relationship is in turn reinforced by physical proximity. At the same time, although the larger *tsu* of Hsin Hsing do not have ancestral halls (nor do even the three *tsu* villages of the area), the *tsu* do form religious families for the purpose of ancestor worship, as we have already observed. This is another factor which strengthens the bond between members of the same patrilineal group.

169

Thus, by reason of their *tsu* or other patrilineal relationships and their physical proximity, such groups within the village tend more easily to become cooperating units in many phases of their daily lives. In addition to the small amount of corporate land which one of the village *tsu* groups owns, some *tsu* (and, more frequently, patrilineal relatives who have recently divided into separate households) may continue to share certain expensive farm implements or may even buy them cooperatively. Such implements will usually be rented out to a nonrelated villager, but they will be lent out without charge to a *tsu* or other patrilineal relative as long as there is no bad feeling between the two related families. Therefore, a member of one of the two Shih families which is not affiliated with the other two Shih *tsu* and which lives in a separate part of the village—but which recognizes a shared mainland ancestor with one of the Shih *tsu*—receives the loan of the latter's threshing machine without charge. Although they do not recognize an actual *tsu* relationship with him, they do feel he is more than simply an ordinary *ch'in t'ang,* and thus they lend him things which others would normally pay to use.

Patrilineally related families are also more frequently willing to lend each other small amounts of money without any interest charge, and it is very common to find such families, again especially those which have recently divided, cooperating in odd chores which demand more labor than any individual economic family may have available. As mentioned in Chapter 3, they frequently exchange labor at harvest-time—possibly without counting a day for a day. In one case, a joint family which had a married son in the army divided itself economically, thus leaving the soldier son's wife and child on their own. This division was initiated by the wife, who did not get along with the family and thought she could manage better alone. After the division, however, she very soon found herself unable to manage, and it was necessary for her husband's father and brothers and *ch'in tsu* in the village to help her. The villagers were critical of her; they felt that before division, as one family, the others had to help her as a matter of course. But once the bond was broken, she had to seek their help and in so doing incurred an obligation to them and lost some face.

Weddings bring forth the most obvious form of cooperation between patrilineal relatives. There are great festivities on such occasions, and the family of the bride or groom entertains many people, especially *ch'in ch'i* and friends from outside the village, at a banquet. At such times the family needs a great deal of extra help in serving the food to the many guests and in acting as hosts. Patrilineal relatives play an important part on these occasions, since they do not need to be formally entertained as do *ch'in ch'i* and friends from outside the village with whom there is a more formal relationship.

Perhaps the most important form of cooperation between patrilineal relatives occurs when one of them has any problem with a nonrelated villager or outsider. Even though the patrilineal relatives may not be on the best of terms, when trouble comes they can usually be depended upon to rally to the support of their fellow kin.

However, while patrilineal kinship is extremely important, it is far from being the only relating factor operative in the village. Often the families within any particular patrilineal groups in Hsin Hsing are not on the best of terms. Hsu (1949:129) points out for West Town, Yunnan, that "Even among families whose heads are brothers and first cousins (patrilineal) there is little solidarity. Most of them do not like each other. Only when there is trouble with outsiders do they tend to unite to some degree. But such unity is very temporary." Hsu's statement has some validity for Hsin Hsing; the overintimacy and also the frequent feeling of competition between related families often tends to cause conflict between them.

In discussions with Hsin Hsing villagers, the relationships between all village families tend to be described in terms of *kan-ch'ing*, good or bad. As already noted in Chapter 3, Fried (1953:226–227) defines *kan-ch'ing* as a concept or code of relationships between non-kin of different status, which differs from friendship in that it "includes a recognized degree of exploitation." However, in the Hsin Hsing area, I have found that the term is extended to cover the quality of kin relationships as well. In other words, the Hsin Hsing village area people use *kan-ch'ing* to describe the quality of any relationship between people whose relative positions are in some way differentiated in a hierarchy, whether in class, economic, family, or kinship structure.

Thus, in the Hsing Hsing area, I found that villagers not only refer to their *kan-ch'ing* with a landlord, a tenant, and so on, but also use this same term to describe their relations with *ch'in tsu* and *ch'in ch'i* relatives. We have already seen that when a tenant reports that he has bad *kan-ch'ing* with his landlord it means that he and the landlord are not behaving toward one another in accordance with the relations prescribed or expected on the basis of their relative positions as landlord and tenant in the socioeconomic system. Similarly, when a villager cites his bad *kan-ch'ing* with a relative, for example, he means that for whatever reasons they have not been displaying the kinds of behavior toward one another prescribed by their relative positions in the hierarchal kinship system. As a result, the feeling or sentiment (the *kan-ch'ing*) is not good between them. Close patrilineal kinship, therefore, does not necessarily determine the nature of one's personal feelings and overt behavior within the relationship.

In Hsin Hsing village, as we have already noted, the *tsu* groups do not hold in common any significant amount of corporate land which could function as a source of unity by necessitating organization to administer such lands. Such *tsu* organization might easily tend to extend to other phases of *tsu* relationships and so possibly act as an additional unifying factor. On the other hand, Freedman (1958:63–76) points out that on the mainland large *tsu* holdings have often been controlled by the wealthier members of the group, which sometimes results in conflict rather than unity. But again, as Hsu (1949:129–130, note) points out for West Town and other places, such a lack of significant *tsu* corporate land is very common.

Because Hsin Hsing village *tsu* groups are relatively small and generally not prosperous, they are limited in their ability to meet all the economic needs of their members or to fulfill the social needs of all the different personality types of the group. The small size of these *tsu* and other patrilineal kinship groups as well as the personality differences between some *ch'in tsu* relatives make it desirable for the cooperative ownership of machines and also cooperative work efforts to extend to non-kin friends and neighbors in the village if work is to be done effectively.

Even a member of a *tsu* group frequently forms close friendships from childhood on with non-*tsu* fellow villagers. For example, friendships through age groups of children and young people are quite common in Hsin Hsing. Children's play groups to a great extent are composed of children of the same sex and age. Because they necessarily live near each other, they are therefore most often relatives. In addition, however, they frequently include children who are neighbors but not kin-related and, as the age of the group increases, also non-kin children who come from other parts of the village. The latter may be schoolmates whose friendships become very deep and last into adulthood.

Some of the groups of boys who have been close friends since childhood become sworn brothers (*chieh pai hsiung ti*) in their late teens or early twenties. In doing so, such boys—usually in groups of about five to ten—make an informal pact which is often celebrated by a dinner. In their organization as sworn brothers they agree to help each other, cooperate in many of the ordinary chores of life, and aid each other in any emergency. There are also certain occasions, such as the birth of a child or the death of a parent, when the sworn brothers band together to render assistance above and beyond that expected of ordinary villagers. The membership of such a group for the most part crosses kinship lines, since as some sworn brothers once observed, "There is no point in *tsu* relatives becoming sworn brothers."

All of these friendships and special relationships, if continued into adulthood, often lead to important relationships between two unrelated village families in the economic and social aspects of life. The frequently formed non-kin relationships may also be based upon a common interest in the production and marketing of certain crops, common irrigation problems on land in the same area, or membership in the same water pumping station cooperative. On such bases, then, villagers have the opportunity to make contact with non-kin fellow villagers, and sometimes with people from neighboring villages, and to establish strong friendships and mutual visiting relationships over long periods of time. On the other hand, some villagers who have these relationships in common never develop a real friendship on these bases alone.

VILLAGE SOLIDARITY

What exist, then, in Hsin Hsing village, and apparently in most of the surrounding villages, are many diversified groupings which cross kin lines. A single family is usually a member of more than one such group. Although the feeling of membership in a *tsu* group is often strongest, the feeling of solidarity with any grouping will vary according to the particular situation. Hsin Hsing is therefore unlike the *tsu* village with its large single *tsu* organization in which relationships are primarily based on kinship, and which may perhaps lend some over-all unity to the many smaller groupings. Hsin Hsing does not have this all-encompassing and overriding kinship organization or feeling of solidarity to provide real unity to the internal diversification.

The village is not entirely lacking in solidarity. There are many occasions, mostly religious or festive, when a basis for village unity does exist. Such events are the birthday of the village god, certain religious processions and *pai-pai* occasions, and often a village marriage or death (all of which will be discussed in detail in Chapters 7 and 8). But feelings of village unity do not necessarily extend to the rendering of substantial assistance to any particular village family or household in need of aid, and in Hsin Hsing the result is a general insecurity and fear by most villagers that in times of personal distress aid may not be forthcoming from within the village.

Because the village has no single uniting thread to minimize natural cleavages, it is often difficult for the many different kinship groupings to cooperate in meeting an unusual problem which may arise for any village family. Many of the villagers would be unwilling to exert themselves, even if the mayor were to ask for help for any one family. If the family in need is opposed to the mayor politically, not in his *tsu* group, or is a smaller individual family with little influence in the village organization, even the mayor may give only limited help or at best only go through the motions of organizing the entire village to act together.

An individual family, then, when faced with a crisis situation, can usually expect aid from its own *tsu* or smaller kinship group but not from the entire village. On the other hand, the comparatively smaller kin groups of the village frequently do not have the power of the larger village *tsu* to give effective aid to an individual faced with problems. Individuals in such small groups therefore tend to limit their involvement in the problems of others, and most such families suffer frequent anxiety and insecurity. In their attempt to ensure some support from the village when in trouble, they put an extremely high priority on the maintenance of good *kan-ch'ing* with everyone in the village. They are always extremely careful of what they say and do for fear of injuring their village relations. Although no kin relationship may exist, if one of these families should by chance have the same surname as one of the village *tsu* groups, it often attempts to identify itself with that *tsu* group and so derive some of the benefits of membership in it.

Small individual village families can frequently be observed ingratiating themselves with village *tsu* groups with the hope of maintaining good relations. They are also often known for their extreme courtesy with regard to relations with other villagers. The head of one such household confided to me in an interview that only by maintaining especially good *kan-ch'ing* with his fellow villagers could he expect their aid if he needed it. For this reason, he pointed out, he agrees to perform many annoying village tasks and generally goes out of his way to participate actively in village affairs in order to prove his family an asset to the village.

Within the structure of village relationships, the members of the larger *tsu* groups often show a fair degree of self-confidence—at least in their relations with the isolated families or even with families of small *tsu*. In any village discussions of problems, members of the larger *tsu* often suggest that the bothersome tasks be done by someone from one of the smaller or isolated family groups. The latter, usually after some mild objection, almost always acquiesce. But this feeling of confidence that the members of the larger *tsu* groups have is unquestionably limited to their relations with the organizationally weaker and poorer village families. In facing the outside world and the general problems of life, all the villagers suffer from insecurity and anxiety as a result of the village's limited sources of solidarity.

This is why new relationships made outside the village through marriage with nonrelated families take on added importance. The villagers naturally value their *ch'in ch'i* relations and, to a much lesser degree, friends made through business dealings and other means outside the village.

INTERVILLAGE RELATIONSHIPS

In the ethnographic and other literature on Chinese social organization, only passing reference has been made to the significance of matrilateral and affinal relationships in Chinese life. The possible reasons for this are summed up by Fried (1953:95) when he writes that "kin relations which are beyond the clan . . . are quite difficult to describe, since they lack institutionalization and present few sweeping regularities on which generalizations may be based." He also notes that they should not be overlooked, "since in individual cases they may be of great value."

Most anthropological studies of the Chinese village have emphasized interfamily relationships within the *tsu* or smaller patrilineal kinship group. These are somewhat institutionalized and usually within the confines of the village. This is especially so in a *tsu* village where intra-*tsu* ties tend to overshadow any outside relationships. Writers such as Lin (1947) have discussed matrilateral and affinal relationships in the case of an individual family. In his book *The Golden Wing* we find much of the story revolving around the main character's economic relationships with matrilateral relatives outside the *tsu* village. In this study, however, the relationships are dealt with on the individual rather than on the general village level.

On a more general level, Freedman (1958:104) has noted the extension of the relationships of members of a lineage group through marriage outside the village. On the basis of the available literature, he writes, "Marriage opened up for any family possibilities of social contact with people in other communities . . . men were brought into touch with matrilateral kinsmen and affines, and the relations set up on these bases could clearly serve an important foundation for political and economic activity." But Freedman's main emphasis is lineage organization, and he offers neither much descriptive detail nor analysis of the relations with non-*tsu* kinsmen. This may be due in part to the meagerness of examples available in the literature which point up the actual extent of matrilateral and affinal relationships.

Matrilateral and Affinal Extensions of Hsin Hsing

The general pattern of close relationships of Hsin Hsing villagers with their outside matrilateral and affinal relatives is reciprocal, and would hold true for all the villages in the area with which Hsin Hsing has marital and adoption contacts. For this area at least, Hsin Hsing is far from unique. The relationships have practical value in three main fields: the economic, the social and religious, and the mediatorial and political. The relationship between *ch'in ch'i* depends upon propinquity; ideally, *ch'in ch'i* live close enough so that contact with each other is not a hardship, and yet preferably not so close as in the same village. Most marriages and adoptions usually involve persons within an area which can be readily spanned by bicycle. Another factor is *kan-ch'ing* with one's *ch'in ch'i*. Here it should be noted that the *ch'in ch'i* relationship in itself is ordinarily the best basis for good relations. The continuance of good relations is probably aided by the maintenance of social distance or, in other words, a lack of the overintimacy which so often causes ill-feeling between *tsu* relatives. As already indicated, it is perhaps for this reason that ties established by marriage within the village often become more similar to those of *ch'in tsu* than of *ch'in ch'i*. This in itself reinforces a preference for marriage outside the village. Good *kan-ch'ing* is also maintained as a result of a determined effort on the part of *ch'in ch'i*. *Ch'in ch'i* are almost always ready to help each other in times of any kind of need.

The very fact that one's *ch'in ch'i* usually do not live in the same village, although in the same general area, is of major significance economically. In a wet-rice growing area, where paddy fields must be flooded several times during the course of the growing of each rice crop, irrigation is very important. Because of the nature of the irrigation systems, two adjacent villages, although geographically very close, may be weeks apart in their agricultural cycles if they obtain their water from two different irrigation systems. For example, one village may be at the end of one irrigation system, while the next village down the road may be at the beginning of another irrigation system. At the time the village on the beginning of the irrigation system has already transplanted its rice seedlings into the flooded rice paddy fields, and is perhaps already preparing for the first weeding, the neighboring village on the other end may still be waiting for the water to come through so that the fields may be flooded and prepared for transplanting the rice seedlings. Although not all of one's fellow villagers have land in the same immediate area or within the same irrigation system, it is nevertheless unlikely that many cycle differences will be greater than a few days for most of one's fellow villagers. Therefore, the greater difference in agricultural cycle between *ch'in ch'i* living in different areas makes possible an amount of economic interchange usually not possible between fellow villagers.

The outright gift or sale at a comparatively low price of rice seedlings by one *ch'in ch'i* to another living in some other area has direct bearing on the cyclical differences resulting from differences in irrigation systems. A Hsin Hsing villager on the end of the irrigation system who loses his rice seedlings in the seedbed as a result of insufficient water may turn to one of his *ch'in ch'i* whose area has an earlier cycle. Since it is not unusual for a farmer to have an excess of seedlings after transplanting, he will usually give his *ch'in ch'i* the seedlings for the asking. If extra seedlings are not available through a *ch'in ch'i*, it then becomes necessary to purchase the seedlings, often at a high price.

If a villager should for some reason be unable to arrange for the necessary labor to harvest his crop, he knows that he may call upon some of his *ch'in ch'i* who are not at the time engaged in their own harvesting to come to his aid. Since a whole area must usually be harvested over a period of a single week, labor shortage is a frequent problem. The latter is especially serious if a typhoon threatens; then a crop may have to be harvested immediately. Under such conditions, one's *ch'in ch'i*, if available, come to help without expecting wages. The *ch'in ch'i* who gives his labor knows that at some future date he can expect to receive similar help. This is not only true in times of emergency; there is frequently an informal exchange of labor in house building or other economic functions. If at all possible, a *ch'in ch'i* always holds himself ready to extend such aid.

The availability of a *ch'in ch'i*'s aid also extends to money loans. When a villager is in financial need and wishes to organize a money-lending club he may ask several of his *ch'in ch'i* who live nearby to take part in the group of ten or more *tsu* relatives and fellow villagers who usually make up such a club. There are also cases in the area where villagers have gone into joint business ventures with *ch'in ch'i* much like those which Lin (1947) described in *The Golden Wing*, although on a far smaller scale.

As mentioned in Chapter 3, Hsin Hsing villagers' *ch'in ch'i* living in other villages are frequently helpful during harvest seasons as contacts in finding work for Hsin Hsing villagers on harvest labor teams in other places. Perhaps more important, they contact labor teams from other villages to come to harvest in Hsin Hsing. Still another type of help given by *ch'in ch'i* is to introduce Hsin Hsing village vegetable peddlers to customers in other villages.

Ch'in ch'i relationships are not only important economically but have social value as well. As will be seen later, social activity in Taiwan is intertwined with religious activity. The activity in the villages of Taiwan is marked by many *pai-pai*, which frequently involve large numbers of people and great quantities of food. When a large *pai-pai* is held in the village, every family participates. An occasion for a *pai-pai* in one village does not usually coincide with a *pai-pai* occasion in another, which makes a certain amount of visiting possible.

Usually, the most festive *pai-pai* is that for the village god. Since all the village families celebrate it at the same time, it is impossible to invite one's fellow villagers to the family feast. This means that if one is to have guests, and this is most desirable, it is usual to invite one's *ch'in ch'i* and friends from other villages. In a sense, the *pai-pai* furnishes the villager with an opportunity to entertain his *ch'in ch'i*. In any village, no matter how poor, such occasions are frequent and, most important, reciprocal, so that on this basis alone there is much visiting back and forth. On such visits among the *ch'in ch'i,* there is usually a good deal of warm feeling, often helped along by alcohol. Sometimes a *ch'in ch'i* may even remain overnight, not necessarily by intention.

This same type of visiting takes place at the marriage festival of a son or daughter, when the principal guests are usually *ch'in ch'i*. At a wedding festival of a son the most important guest is felt to be the groom's oldest maternal uncle, who sits in the seat of honor. The importance of the maternal uncle at the wedding reception as well as other similar relationships with this uncle have been pointed out by Fei (1939:87) and other ethnographers working in mainland China villages.

Women, whenever possible, like to return to their natal home for a visit, but such occasions are limited by household duties. In a smaller and poorer household such visits may be relatively infrequent, but in a large joint family, especially if it is well-to-do, daughters-in-law take turns so that the visits may be both frequent and prolonged. Consequently, much of the visiting between *ch'in ch'i,* especially in poorer villages, is limited to the male members of the family. If the family is small, i.e., not of the joint-family type, it is usually difficult for a woman to leave her house and young children in order to return to her natal home at the frequent *pai-pai* and other visiting occasions. And so frequently we find the curious situation of the husbands and sons and often the husband's father going alone to the wife's or mother's natal home.

If on certain occasions the woman does accompany the men back to her natal home, she then dresses up and spends most of her time talking and helping in the kitchen and back rooms with her female relatives. The men, on the other hand, are warmly entertained in the mainroom of the house and are introduced to other guests, usually the host's *ch'in ch'i* through other relatives. Such meetings often lead to new contacts and friendships.

But the mutual visiting by *ch'in ch'i* is not limited to formal occasions like the *pai-pai* or marriages. Villagers, especially when they happen to be in the vicinity of a *ch'in ch'i's* residence, miss no opportunity to visit; there may sometimes be a planned visit when one is not busy with chores. In addition, when traveling to other areas, the home of a *ch'in ch'i* is usually a good stopping-off place where one will probably receive a warm reception. On these visits, which are talked about later with great pleasure, the villager is made welcome as a guest. He is usually served with whatever delicacies are available and treated in an extremely warm and cordial manner. (When one visits a *ch'in tsu,* even when he is not busy, one cannot expect to be served any refreshments or be treated in any special way.) In speaking of visits to *ch'in ch'i* or of their general relations with them as compared with their *ch'in tsu,* most villagers describe them as being much warmer.

However, as is true of the *ch'in tsu* relationship, there are situations in which conflict does exist between *ch'in ch'i.* There can be conflicts over the exchange of wedding gifts and dowry or tension over the poor adaptation of the daughter-in-law to the new family. Certainly *ch'in ch'i* relationships are not totally without bad feelings, but great care is taken to minimize conflict.

It is because these relationships are so good that *ch'in ch'i* often play an important mediatorial rule. When ill-feeling develops between *ch'in tsu* in Hsin Hsing, the elders of the *tsu* group may be called upon to mediate and settle the dispute. A respected man of the village or the mayor may be called upon, especially by the very small kinship groups. If these means fail it is common to invite a respected *ch'in ch'i* male, who is related to both disputants, to mediate. Such a mediator is considered the person most likely to be able to settle the dispute successfully. Although related to both, this *ch'in ch'i* is somewhat less familiar and greatly respected. If for no other reason than his "face" or his reputation in the eyes of others, his *ch'in ch'i* usually settle their dispute peacefully. The villagers generally feel, then, that disputes between members of the same *tsu* are best mediated by highly respected *ch'in ch'i.*

Politically, the *ch'in ch'i* activities have unquestionable importance during elections beyond the village level. Since the restoration of the present Chinese government in Taiwan, elections of one sort or another have become important annual events in the area. Whether the election is only on the *hsiang* level or as high as the *hsien* level, great interest is built up in the village. Often, several people from the local area or village run in county and district elections. An individual candidate in either, living in a village or nearby market town, must depend upon votes from the entire area in order to win the election. This, then, necessitates a large circle of campaign managers—people spread through the area who will campaign for the candidate among their fellow villagers and their own relatives. For this purpose, one's *ch'in ch'i* are often the most important single source of political support.

Ch'in ch'i are generally spread over the local countryside as a result of the marriage and adoption patterns. Large family groups, which are often the ones most likely to produce a candidate for a political office, are usually noted for the large number of their *ch'in ch'i* extensions. This tends to give added advantage to their candidates. The candidate

with a large circle of loyal *ch'in ch'i* campaigners tends to win added
personal respect in the area as a result, and when a man does not
support his *ch'in ch'i* in an election, it is likely to prove embarrassing
to both the candidate and his relatives. The recent importance of
elections in Taiwan has unquestionably added to the cementing of
good *ch'in ch'i* relationships.

It is not only the official governmental elections which depend heavily on *ch'in ch'i* relationships. There are other elections in the local
area which are important to the villagers and in which the candidates
again often depend heavily on their relatives. Local nongovernmental
offices like those in the Water Conservation Association are extremely
important to the area. This association has a great deal of control in
the building and repairing of irrigation works and in generally controlling the flow of water to the rice paddies. There are also important
elected officials in the district Farmers' Association, and *ch'in ch'i* play
an important supporting role in the campaigns for these positions.

The support by people for their *ch'in ch'i* candidates for various
offices is, of course, not based solely on loyalty to one's relatives. Like
all *ch'in ch'i* relationships, these too are expected to be reciprocal.
When a village or small group of neighboring villages has problems
such as a court case or repair of a faulty irrigation system or a regularly flooded road, the suggestion is frequently made to send a certain
villager to ask the aid of his *ch'in ch'i* who happens to hold some office,
however minor, in which he could conceivably exert some influence on
the government or private agency. Well-placed *ch'in ch'i* can be of
great help if there is good *kan-ch'ing* and a feeling of obligation exists.
Of course, a *tsu* relative in an official position is even more desirable,
but in an area of small kinship groups one's *ch'in ch'i* may tend to
outnumber one's patrilineal relatives, extend into a wider geographi-
cal area, and so offer greater possibility for aid. Even when a *tsu*
member runs for public office in the local area he can ask and expect
each of his many *tsu* relatives to solicit aid from *ch'in ch'i*. Although
few villagers are actually involved in elections, the *ch'in ch'i* relationships which may be activated in behalf of a candidate are many and
far-reaching.

The matrilateral and affinal relationships which have been described for Hsin Hsing village are not unique to particular families
but are general throughout the village. And since such relationships
are reciprocal, the same *ch'in ch'i* relationships described for Hsin
Hsing village would tend to exist in at least as many villages in which
Hsin Hsing people have contacts through marriage and adoption. The
extravillage *ch'in ch'i* relationships thus tend to give the villager an
additional source of security which can supplement what he derives
from his intravillage relationships. Although they are not institution-

alized in the Chinese social organization like *tsu* relationships, still it is noteworthy that in a village like Hsin Hsing and the surrounding area matrilateral and affinal-based relationships, that is, with *ch'in ch'i,* are much more functionally important than previously indicated in the literature.

This is not to underrate the importance of patrilineal or *tsu* relationships. Where these exist, they are unquestionably the most important, the most relied upon, and the most meaningful relationships. My intention has been to point out the possible extent and importance of the heretofore unrecorded *ch'in ch'i* relationships. By their very nature *ch'in ch'i* relationships, unlike *ch'in tsu,* are seldom carried beyond two or possibly three generations. However, during the period when recognition is still attached to such relationships, they may be of great importance and value to their reciprocal members.

The widespread and important *ch'in ch'i* relationships of Hsin Hsing villagers throughout the area greatly affect village life. The value attached to *ch'in ch'i* relationships extends the villagers' interests beyond their own village, gives them contacts with people beyond their own boundaries, and furthers their opportunities for new experiences.

Dual loyalties may arise with regard to one's own village and one's *ch'in ch'i.* While a villager can almost always be relied upon to give his primary support to his *ch'in tsu* relatives in any conflict with a fellow villager or even with a *ch'in ch'i,* such support is not necessarily extended to a non-kin person with whom he only has an ordinary village tie. Therefore, especially in any situation of conflict between one's own villager and a *ch'in ch'i* in another village, the villager is beset with a conflict of loyalties. Caught in such a dilemma, the villager frequently does nothing openly rather than take a position and antagonize either side. Even if a situation of this kind occurs only occasionally, it tends to reinforce the villagers' belief that in case of trouble they cannot fully rely upon aid from their village alone.

While carrying on field work in Hsin Hsing, I observed a case which serves as a good example to point up several things which have been discussed—the importance and some of the effects of *ch'in ch'i* relationships, the problem of irrigation as a source of social conflict, the lack of strong village leadership and organization in a multi-*tsu* village such as Hsin Hsing, and how these reinforce the villagers' estimation of the limited sources of available support to the individual family.

THE LI FAN INCIDENT: A CASE STUDY

Early in the spring of 1958 a Hsin Hsing villager and his elderly father were severely beaten in their fields by two men from the neighboring village of Ta Yu. The reason for this was that Li Fan, the Hsin Hsing man, had taken water from a public irrigation ditch which was at the time considered to be carrying privately owned rather than public water. The men from Ta Yu claimed that the water which Li Fan had taken was from the cooperative pumping station of which he was not a member. As they were beating him senseless with a metal hoe, his father tried to come to his aid and was also beaten.

The cooperative station, which pumps water from a nearby river, is located in the larger and wealthier neighboring village of Ta Yu. Most of its members are from Ta Yu village, although there are several members from other nearby villages, including a few from Hsin Hsing. Because the great majority of the pumping station members are Ta Yu villagers, these members have the controlling hand. Members from other villages have little if any voice in the making of cooperative policy. The cooperative's large size caused the Ta Yu members to feel that they had little to fear from outsiders. Apparently, the cooperative had unofficially agreed that any outsider caught taking the cooperative's water should be beaten as an example to others and that the association would fully back whoever did the beating in case any trouble should ensue. Before the beating of Li Fan and his father several other such incidents had gone unchallenged.

When Li Fan and his father were carried back from the fields, word quickly spread through Hsin Hsing village. The villagers were at once incensed and felt that those responsible for the brutality should be punished. The police were notified at once, and a doctor was called to treat the men's severe wounds. But until the doctor or police arrived, I was called in to administer first aid—mainly to stop the bleeding—and also to photograph Li Fan in his beaten condition.

The two police officers who soon came on their bicycles from the local police station were also angry at this new violence and recorded the stories of the two victims and the witnesses. Later, however, when an attempt was made to arrest the two Ta Yu villagers, they insisted that they had not started the fight, had only fought back in self-defense, and in fact had themselves been beaten by Li Fan and his father. This, under the law, meant that the accused would not necessarily be held by the police, especially since a wealthy and influential man in the area who was a friend of the Ta Yu pumping station cooperative had acted as guarantor for the two men. The men were therefore released and immediately pressed counter charges against Li and his father with the greatest haste and efficiency. The wealthy Ta Yu landlord and other leaders who were important persons in the cooperative as well as influential in the area and the local office of the government district knew how to handle such matters. And although the policemen themselves saw that the two Ta Ya men were not hurt in the fight, the two men were nevertheless able to purchase false affidavits of injury from a notorious doctor in a nearby market town.

Meanwhile, the Hsin Hsing villagers faced problems. They did not have anyone who could help write up the accurately detailed letter of accusation required under Chinese law. When they finally found someone to write the letter, it was submitted through the local police and had to go through a long series of channels before it finally reached the courts.

Several days went by and nothing seemed to happen in the case. When the Hsin Hsing villagers—mainly the few relatives and close friends of Li Fan and his father—went to ask the police what was happening, they were told that such things take time and that it would perhaps be better if they tried to settle the case with the Ta Yu villagers through mediation.

About this time, the Ta Yu villagers who were in the pumping station cooperative and who represented the two assailants made overtures to mediate. The reason they offered was that since both sides were hurt in the fight, they should forget the whole matter instead of pressing further and going to court. To this suggestion there was, of course, no agreement.

The Hsin Hsing villagers were in an awkward position. Although most of them would have liked to help Li Fan and his father win satisfaction and compensation for their injuries and to teach their assailants a lesson, they could do little. One of the main problems was that they had no one who would or could act as their leader. They were an unorganized group, and did not know what to do or how to go about handling the case. This was unlike the men from Ta Yu, who not only had a large powerful pumping station organization to support them, but also had the wealthy and influential village landlord who was a key figure in the cooperative and an influential and powerful man in the area to act in their behalf. Hsin Hsing village no longer has capable and interested village landlords who can lead them in times of trouble. As mentioned in Chapter 4, this may well be a general problem in villages where land reform has at least indirectly caused the downfall in wealth and prestige and especially the community interest of many of the former landlords.

Had Hsin Hsing been a single *tsu* village, Li Fan and his father as part of such a *tsu* might have received more active support from the village as a whole. A *tsu* village's organization and leadership, which grow out of family relationships, would undoubtedly have been much more centrally structured than this small multi-*tsu* village with its highly devisive units. To make the matter even worse, Li Fan and his father are from one of the smallest family groups, which made it all the more difficult for the village to marshal and organize its leadership, since there is no formal organization to handle such matters.

Another problem was that many of the villagers who were at first much aroused by the beating of their fellows, later became wary when they began to realize that many of the Ta Yu villagers taking an active part on that side were their own *ch'in ch'i* relatives. To participate actively thus meant fighting against relatives with whom it has always been considered important to maintain good relations. Although these people still wanted to help Li Fan and their own village, they could not do so openly, but rather had to do it in secret.

Other villagers, because of their *ch'in ch'i* relatives in Ta Yu, could not or would not help even in secret, although some continued to pay lip service to the cause of their fellow villager. There were, however, a few villagers who could not even do this. They felt such strong loyalties to their *ch'in ch'i* that they acted as "spies," telling their Ta Yu *ch'in ch'i* of the plans being made in Hsin Hsing to fight the case. Obviously, they considered their relationships with their *ch'in ch'i* more important than those with their fellow villagers. This was realized by the Hsin Hsing villagers who, although somewhat angry, could do nothing more than attempt to keep these people from learning their plans for the case.

The village mayor and several others who might otherwise have been organizers in Li Fan's behalf were among those who could give only limited open help. Therefore, on the Hsin Hsing side there was a complete absence of organized leadership. For want of someone who could or would lead, the village did little except talk about the case.[1]

Not very long after the day of the beating the story of the incident had spread through the whole area. People were talking about the case so much that the winning of it by Hsin Hsing now became as much a matter of face as anything else. Hsin Hsing villagers began to express fears that "if these two Ta Yu villagers were to go unpunished, it would mean that anyone could beat Hsin Hsing villagers or their children at will." No one would respect their rights or face any more if they did nothing about the case.

As some days passed without anything being accomplished in the matter, some villagers who could openly show concern in the case (for example, a few *ch'in tsu* and *ch'in ch'i* of Li Fan and his father and also some of their close friends in the village) became active in Li Fan's behalf. They managed to gather together the village men to discuss the matter at a meeting. During the course of the meeting, it became evident that the villagers generally did not know what course of action to take. Their main hope was to settle the matter through the traditional process of mediation rather than take the case through the courts. They feared that going to court would be expensive and take a great deal of time before settlement. But, perhaps even more important, they felt that because they were a small and poor village which was up against a large village and a wealthy, influential pumping station association, the whole case would be of no avail. They had always held the idea that the poor man without influence could do nothing against the rich and influential. The latter two elements, money and influence, seemed to them to constitute ultimate power. To attempt to do anything against this power was useless. For them even the law was subject to influence by the individuals who hold the power. (This belief was undoubtedly reinforced during the period of Japanese rule, and the present government has done little to remove it.)

At the same time, the villagers felt that since Ta Yu was a neighboring village in which many Hsin Hsing villagers had relatives, if they were to continue to live in peace with Ta Yu and their relatives it was necessary to avoid doing anything which would contribute further to the tensions. After much discussion it became evident that the villagers preferred first to try again to mediate the problem. However, if this did not work out satisfactorily then the case would have to go to court, although they very much doubted that anything could be gained from a court trial.

A few days after the village meeting was held, the Ta Yu side again approached the village—this time through the mayor—asking that they again try to mediate the case. One of the influential men of the area had offered to be mediator at his home in another village about two miles down the road. Mayor K'ang of Hsin Hsing, an educated member of the large Huang *tsu* in Hsin Hsing village, and others of its villagers directly involved in the case attended the mediation meeting.[2] The mediator was a man who was considered to be biased in favor of Ta Yu, and he displayed his bias in the manner in which he tried to mediate the case. Still, since the role of the mediator is a very respected one, the Hsin Hsing villagers agreed to attend the meeting and stayed throughout the proceedings. They felt that it would have been disrespectful to the mediator to leave too soon and that, in addition, it would cause him to lose face, which was to be avoided. Nothing came of this meeting, since the mediator suggested that the Ta Yu side pay Li Fan and his father only a small amount of money as compensation for their injuries.

After several such futile attempts at mediation, the case was finally called up for investigation in the courts. The court procedure called for the accused and the accusers and their witnesses to appear in a special investigative court somewhat similar to a grand jury. The purpose was to investigate the charges, hear the witnesses, and then decide if the court should indict the accused.

The investigation is highly formalized. Since neither the accused nor the accuser may have their lawyer present, the only document on which the investigators base their inquiry is the original letter of accusation. On the basis of the information furnished in this statement, it is up to the investigator to get at all the facts in the case.

Unfortunately, on the basis of the Hsin Hsing side's letter of accusation, the court investigator's questions to the witnesses were such that the investigator felt that there was not enough evidence for an indictment to send the case to court, since each pair of men insisted that they had been beaten. Instead, he, like the police earlier, suggested that the two parties involved mediate their differences. Unfortunately, he did not know many facts in the case, including the fact that mediation had already failed and that the local police could be called upon to testify that the Ta Yu men had not been beaten.

Later, however, additional facts were made available to the examiner, and upon learning of these, another investigation was immediately held and an indictment was brought against the assailants. Several weeks later the case came to court, and Li Fan and his father were awarded an amount of money large enough to cover doctor and hospital bills.

When village loyalty threatens ch'in ch'i loyalty, there is bound to be conflict in the minds of the villagers. Unlike the set institutionalized patterns for behavior regarding patrilineal relatives, there is no real institutionalization of behavior on the basis of village membership or ch'in ch'i relationship. This leaves ultimate behavior up to the individual, totally unstructured and influenced only according to situation. Although villagers do feel that one should not side with ch'in ch'i from elsewhere over one's own villagers, nevertheless, since one's village does not coincide with one's kinship group, villagers do not feel bound to support a fellow villager as they would if he were a patrilineal relative.

As a result, villagers realize that one's dependence on others must not be limited to certain people or groups simply because of the chance relationship of village membership or even, for that matter, by membership in kinship groups which may be either too small or economically too weak to be of real help. Instead, it is considered necessary to extend one's possible sources of support beyond village and patrilineal relations, by building one's network of reciprocal relationships to include people such as friends, neighbors, and ch'in ch'i. Then, the relationship can be based on good kan-ch'ing, and on such a basis people often show a greater willingness to become involved in each other's problems and to render full support.

This attitude about the importance of extensive relationships outside the village, plus the expansion beyond the village that general economic change is forcing on so many villagers, tends to produce a more independent and less village-bound economic family group. It is this increased independence which in turn both allows and at the same time forces the economic family to move further away from the village and even, although to a lesser extent, from the *tsu*. The process further weakens the actual unity and solidarity of the village and the *tsu* as organized bodies. But each *tsu* organization remains a competitive sociopolitical force in terms of most internal village affairs.

As we will see in the next two chapters, although the life cycle of the villagers and their supernatural and ritualistic activities (like the family and kinship system) show the effects of change and extensions of relationships beyond the village, village solidarity, unity, and cooperation are still being reinforced by these same activities. Their manner of implementation, ritual especially, continue to crosscut the various kin lines (on all levels) and to offer one of the important remaining sources for the reinforcement of village ties.

[7

Life History of the Villager

ATTITUDE TOWARD CHILDREN

The notion of limiting the number of their offspring is quite alien to Hsin Hsing villagers. They greatly desire children and feel that to have none is the saddest thing in life. This attitude is entirely in keeping with the general cultural emphasis on family continuity and care for aged parents which is summed up in the saying, "A husband and wife without children are people without a future." A son is of greater importance and value than a daughter, simply because it is the male who remains with the family and ensures its continuity; his sister's marriage inevitably takes her away from her natal family and ties her future to that of her husband and his kinship group.

Nevertheless, girl children are considered necessary in any household, and the ideal family consists of four or five children, of which two are girls. There are countless chores around the house for which daughters are needed, and today unmarried girls often contribute financially to the family income. Even the daughter's marraige plays an important part in helping to extend the family's relationships with others. When a parent dies, daughters return to mourn and wail at the funeral. As some villagers said, "If you have girls, then they will cry for you on the road one day." In addition, there is little doubt that most parents are sincerely saddened when their daughters marry and leave home. Parents are genuinely devoted to their children, regardless of sex. The children are welcomed and loved and treated equally, especially in early childhood. Even a physically handicapped child receives loving care, and no matter how inadequate the food supply may be, all will share it equally.

However, under a patrilineal system the boy child is always more desirable, and the parents' love for all their children does not mean that a daughter's ultimate value is considered equal to that of a son. As several villagers said in more or less the same words, "When a married couple has no children, they just want a child, be it a boy or a girl, and when they have a boy they want a girl. But if the parents have too many girls, they say they don't want any more girls because too many girls are no use. The difference is that people don't ever say too many boys are no use." These villagers hastily added, "People just say that girls are no use; they don't really mean it or do anything about it. They only adopt out girls [give their daughters for adoption] if their economic condition demands it." It is rare for a boy to be sold or adopted out, and if he is, it is because of direst economic necessity. Although most families do not like to give up a daughter, either, and tend to resist making such a commitment, one of several girl children is often given for adoption under much less urgent financial pressure. The figures for Hsin Hsing show that more girls than boys there are adopted or given for adoption.

Giving up a child for adoption is one way of alleviating economic difficulties perhaps aggravated by too large a family, but the villagers make no attempt to limit the number of children they have in order to forestall such a contingency. Some villagers realize that the tremendous increase in population discussed in Chapter 2 is the reason for the economic conditions which make it difficult to get land or a job, but they give little thought to birth control as a solution. As one informant put it, "Some people do think about birth control, but rural people still want many children. Even if a couple has ten children, if they have another they are still so happy. The villagers just like children. Mr. Shih, who is fifty years old, had another baby son and was so happy. He couldn't expect that boy to support him since he is already so old, but perhaps he feels this son will have many descendants to worship him and carry on the family."

While many village men are aware that there are ways of preventing conception, only a few are familiar with specific methods. Some of the men remember that the Japanese soldiers used condoms during sexual intercourse, but for the most part they thought this was basically a method of disease prevention rather than a contraceptive device. However, some of the younger men who have lived in Taipei and have had premarital or extramarital relations with prostitutes, have thus been informed that the condom can be used as a means of contraception.

Even the villager who is aware of this use of the condom does not find them readily available, and when they are available, they are too expensive for regular use. In general, if a village man feels he has more children than the family can support, he abstains from sexual relations—at least with his wife. On rare occasions he may go for sexual satisfaction to girls in Lukang. Such men usually share a bed with some of their older sons, while the wife sleeps with the younger children.

PREGNANCY AND BIRTH

The villagers believe that pregnancy lasts ten lunar months and is signalled by the initial interruption of the menstrual cycle. It is rare for a village woman to see a doctor at all during her pregnancy. The villagers consider it unnecessary and say that only the rich people go to a doctor. Even though there is a government-run health center in the *hsiang* which offers some pre-natal care, modesty prevents village women from visiting the clinic although the excuse they give is that they do not have the time.

The expectant mother receives no special care during pregnancy; she eats no special foods and goes about her household and field tasks as usual. The women fear that if they eat special foods the baby may get too big and that the delivery will be difficult and dangerous. They wear no special maternity clothes, but wear either larger and fuller skirts or leave the top buttons of their regular skirts open. During the last month of pregnancy and the first month and a half after the birth, the parents abstain from sexual intercourse. This, the villagers explain, is for the protection of the mother's health.

Today, most village women employ a midwife at the birth of their first child. Midwives first began to be used about twenty years ago, but "then it was only rich people." The regular use of a midwife by ordinary villagers has been common only since the postwar period or the late 1940's. It is interesting that one of the important advantages of having a midwife, according to a group of village women, is that "If we call a midwife, it is easier to register the baby in the Hsiang Public Office since the midwife will then write out the certificate of birth. Othewise a birth certificate must be obtained through the village mayor."

Previously, the older women of the family delivered all babies. Today, these same women may be present to assist the midwife at the time a first child is born, and they usually assist in the delivery of subsequent children when a midwife has not been called. The husband is not present when his wife gives birth.

The midwife who works at the Pu Yen Hsiang Health Center is usually called to Hsin Hsing village. She has been trained by attending several classes for midwives. "She charges NT $30–40 [about US $1] for a normal delivery, or more if she has to give an injection to stop excessive bleeding." The midwife makes two house visits, one at the time of the birth and the second when she washes the baby on the third day after the birth. When the child is born, the midwife applies a silver nitrate solution to the eyes only if it appears that there might be something wrong.

The birth takes place in the bedroom of the house, usually with little illumination available. Sometimes only one small electric bulb or a kerosene lamp is lit. In labor and during the birth, the woman seems to be relatively quiet, refraining from cries of pain. This may result from the usual stoicism of Chinese women, who are trained to show as little emotion as possible no matter how great the pain. To have other people hear any cries would be embarrassing, and thus cries are avoided.

A woman must not give birth to a child in her natal home. It is believed that such a birth would bring bad luck to her brothers' wives when they give birth and might even result in their being unable to have children. In one case, the married daughter of a Hsin Hsing landlord family did not get on well with her husband's parents. After a number of years of marriage she returned to live in her parents' home while her husband worked in the city and occasionally visited her. When it came time for her to give birth to her third child, she had to leave her brother's home and go to a hospital to have the baby, a most unusual occurrence in the village. She could not give birth in a neighbor's house, of course, since this might damage the birth prospects of the women of that house.

After the birth, according to a custom whose reason and origin are now unknown, the umbilical cord and afterbirth are wrapped in a rag and buried in the river bottom. Anything related to the birth, especially if it has been in contact with the woman's blood, is considered unclean.[1] The very room in which the birth takes place is likewise considered unclean, and anyone who enters the room for a month after the birth cannot then attend a wedding, since this would mean bad luck for the bride.

The baby is fed "sugar water" (sugar boiled in water) immediately after birth and until nursing begins. The baby begins to nurse about the end of the second or third day, when lactation begins.

After the birth, the new mother eats with the family at the next regular meal, and there is no change in her meal schedule. The food she eats, however, is special, and often consists of fresh fish, chicken, wine, and other such "good and rich foods." These are felt to encourage the production of milk and, more important, to help the mother regain her strength. These foods are usually gifts sent during the first month by the new mother's brothers and sisters. Neighbors and friends may also send such gifts, and the household of the new mother gives them "oil rice" (fried glutinous rice) in return.

It is felt that the new mother should do as little work as possible and rest frequently during the first month after the birth. If she belongs to a joint or stem family, this period of rest is virtually assured. If, however, the family is small, she must depend upon help from *ch'in tsu,* neighbors, or friends in the agricultural slack season or, if she can afford it, a hired woman from Hsin Hsing or another village to come daily to do the heavy household work. However, it is not at all unusual for the new mother to begin to do heavy housework within a week after giving birth. It is interesting to note that *ch'in ch'i* relatives rarely, if ever, come to help the woman with her household tasks.

During the first month after the birth, the new mother may not go outside of the house between sunset and sunrise "because she will make heaven and earth dirty, and because she is also afraid of devils at night." This belief is said to be quite widespread throughout the local area and even in nearby towns. The prohibition also applies to the woman's laundered clothing, which must be taken inside the house by sunset even if still wet. If the new mother were to show herself or her clothing outside the house at night, the next child born to her might be abnormal—a "devil baby" or a "dirty baby."

According to the villagers, such devil babies may also be born under other circumstances. For example, "stubborn people or those who do not believe or follow traditions can have a devil baby." In one case of such a birth, a woman's husband had insisted on building their house on a spot which the geomancer had deemed unsuitable. The birth of an abnormal child may be brought about by other actions as well: the villagers believe that if a woman is pregnant neither she nor anyone near her should cut things, bang nails with a hammer, or bore holes. If either of the latter acts is performed, the baby may be born with a hole in its head. If one cuts such things as cloth, the baby may be born with a cleft palate. Once when a pregnant woman in Hsin Hsing passed under a bamboo tree which someone was cutting down, she "gave birth to a baby with a deep opening in its head so that one could see the brains. The baby died." The explanations are obviously rationalizations for birth abnormalities and, at the same time, tend to reinforce social conformity and the maintenance of the traditional beliefs and customs.

On the third and the twelfth days after birth of the child, the husband's family offers their ancestors and the gods fried glutinous rice. This ceremony is held more frequently for boys than girls. When the baby is a month old the family again worships, this time offering dough cakes as sacrifices.

On the ninth day after birth the infant is given a name. In Hsin Hsing this is usually done by the older members of the patrilineal family such as the grandparents. According to several villagers, the given name must not be the same as that of any living relative or friend of the family, as it would be disrespectful to the older person.

In typical Chinese fashion, it is common in Hsin Hsing and the surrounding area for the first character of the given name to be the same for all children of the same generation in a single *tsu,* or at least in the same *chia*. But there are also a number of families in the village which customarily give their children a single character for the given name, omitting the first character which normally designates generation. For the most part, they seem to do this simply as a matter of convenience.

Customarily, the natal home of the new mother sends gifts for her first born son and daughter. Such items as gold jewelry and clothing are sent at the time the baby is one month old. It is also at this time that the baby is first taken outside, often dressed in all his new finery.

The infant is usually nursed for two years or more, or until the mother becomes pregnant again. Mother's milk is the main item in the child's diet during this period; it is supplemented after the eighth or ninth month by rice gruel. At about the age of one the child is given additional solid foods. During this period, the baby may be nursed occasionally by an aunt, a *ch'in tsu,* or even a close neighbor if the mother happens to be away or in the fields and unavailable. Generally speaking, it is very common for female members of the same joint family or kinship group, and sometimes even neighbors who are close friends, to take turns caring for each other's children so that one mother at a time can be released for work away from the house. However, in some small families where there are no other women or young girls such as a daughter or younger sister-in-law, the mother has to carry the child slung on her back while she goes about her work.

Weaning does not seem to be a problem, since in most cases children are weaned fairly late. Village mothers report that in the few instances where a child resists being weaned, the mother may finally put red pepper on her nipples to discourage him. However, such action does not seem to be necessary very often.

CHILD REARING

Toilet training, like weaning, is not considered a problem by the villagers. It is not emphasized until the child is considered ready for this new stage—that is, until he is physically capable of controlling the sphincter and bladder and able to understand what is expected of him. By the time the child is six-or-seven-months-old, his diaper is replaced by training pants—pants slit open at the crotch. However, toilet training does not begin until the child is almost two-years-old, walking, and beginning to talk and understand what he is told. At this time he is taught to ask to be taken to an inconspicuous spot to perform. Eventually, he will go there by himself. If the child has a lapse, he is slapped on the hand. Village mothers note that toilet training is usually accomplished in about a week after it is begun and that the child usually offers little resistance.

A young child is in the care of older siblings during much of the

day, thus relieving the mother for her tasks. It is common to see girls of
six or older, or boys if there are no sisters, carrying younger children
on their backs. While this prevents older children from participating
in many activities with their age mates, there are usually enough children carrying little brothers or sisters around to allow the formation of
separate play groups. A boy saddled with a younger sibling is, of
course, much more restricted in his activities than a girl in the same
situation.

The young child is thus rarely left by himself; he gets a great deal of
attention and much affection. One seldom hears a child crying. Since a
young child is seldom permitted to crawl about on the ground freely
except when he is within sight of someone older, there is also little
chance of his being injured. Some village families do have bamboo
playpen-carriage combinations in which a child can be kept while the
mother is busy with other things.

Generally speaking, very young children have a great deal of freedom and are given few responsibilities. Boys and girls, until the age of
five or six, play together and can be seen running about the village in
small groups. At about six, they begin to be assigned minor chores
about the house such as sweeping, care of still younger children, even
care of the fowl. Little girls are given responsibilities earlier than boys,
and their activities are thus restricted much sooner.

Children may be disciplined by either parent. Frequently, this task
falls to the mother when the father is away working. On occasion,
when the father has been the primary disciplinarian in the family, his
absence may affect the behavior of his children, and they may refuse to
obey their mother. In such cases village *ch'in tsu* may speak with the
child, but only if the child's father has expressly asked them to do so.
Even brothers do not like to interfere in the training of each other's
children since quarrels may develop out of such interference. It is even
less likely that a *ch'in ch'i* would discipline a relative's child. This is
natural, since most *ch'in ch'i* live outside the village and thus are
distant both geographically and in blood relationship. At the same
time the *ch'in ch'i* relationship is a notably warm one, and it is unlikely that relatives would care to disturb it by attempts to discipline
others' children.

Young children are not frequently disciplined physically and are
never disciplined in this way when they reach their early teens. If
parents had to beat a child over fifteen, people would say that they
could not have "brought him up properly if they still had to beat
him." Only on a couple of occasions did I see a child being beaten. In
one case a girl of about ten had been caught stealing fruit from a
villager's tree. A big disturbance followed, and the girl's father beat
her in front of the many villagers who were present. It appeared that

the father was perhaps more angry with the child for causing him to lose face than for taking the fruit—something which children frequently do.

Ordinarily, when discipline is called for, the parents threaten their children. Such threats are based on things the children have had experience with, as for example, "If you are not good I will sell you out [to another family]." This is done since "children know it is a terrible thing to be sold out." The villagers point out that they never threaten children by saying, "the demons will take you away," for such warnings lack the reality necessary to intimidate the child.

Respect for elders is mainly taught by the example set by parents and older siblings. Children are frequently told stories which focus on acts of filial piety and are also warned of the tortures that await the unfilial in the underworld. This makes a great impression on most children. Such training is reinforced by the funerals which the children attend, both in their own village and in the villages of their *ch'in ch'i*. On these occasions the tortures of the underworld and the favorable and unfavorable kinds of rebirth after death are emphasized.

In general, however, children have a great deal of freedom of action, and to a large degree they get their own way with their parents or are at least made to believe they do. Village adults often find it difficult to refuse the requests of their children, and rather than say no, will commonly *p'ien* (fool) their young child. For example, a parent will convince the child that the unpleasant task to be done or medicine to be taken is really something quite special, a treat or a privilege.

EDUCATION

Primary education in Taiwan is now "compulsory." Schools operated by the provincial government are open to all children. There is a small percentage of village children who for various reasons do not go at all and a larger group who attend sporadically. There are several schools scattered throughout each *hsiang,* and each is attended by the children of a few villages. The children from Hsin Hsing along with the children from seven other villages in Pu Yen Hsiang attend a school in Hao Hsiu village, about two miles down the road from Hsin Hsing. While most of the students walk to and from the school each day, some bicycle and a few occasionally go by bus. The school enrollment for 1958 was 1,293, including 666 boys and 627 girls. Of this total enrollment, 88 students were from Hsin Hsing—39 boys and 49 girls.

Officially, children must attend school from the ages of six to twelve, but there are many students at the Hao Hsiu primary school who are as old as fourteen and fifteen. The latter are usually students who had to drop out for a while, and have now returned to complete their schooling.

During 1958, there were fourteen other Hsin Hsing village children of school age—two boys and twelve girls—who did not attend the primary school. The girls had either not attended at all that year or had dropped out during the course of the school year. The number of students from Hsin Hsing not attending school is proportionally higher than the number from other villages in the Hao Hsiu primary school area. This is probably attributable to one or both of two factors: the impoverished condition of some families and the negative attitude of some parents toward the necessity of schooling, particularly for girls.

The economic factor is undoubtedly more important, especially in Hsin Hsing village, which suffers most from a land scarcity. More of the male adults, both young and old, must go to Taipei to work on at least a part-time basis. Consequently, the women must take a much greater part in cultivating and harvesting, which means that school age children must care for their preschool siblings. This applies mainly to girls in Hsin Hsing and helps account for the much larger number of girls not attending school. However, the negative attitude toward education also plays an important part in keeping children from school. The mother frequently feels this way about schooling because, unlike her husband, she has had few outside contacts or experiences to show her the value of education. However, to answer the social pressure to send their children to school, villagers who refuse to do so tend to use the economic factor to justify their actions. They point out that the child is needed at home to care for younger siblings while the mother works in the fields. And they add that "it is not important for girls to go to school and learn to read." Since village children are not required to wear uniforms in primary school, and since the cost of books and supplies is small, parents do not usually cite these expenses as a reason for keeping a child home from school.

Although primary school education is compulsory, parents who refuse to send their children are not forced to do so. At the very most, the local school teacher may pay the family a visit and make a tactful attempt to persuade the parents to send the child. If they still refuse, the school drops the matter until the next year, when the personal request by a teacher is repeated.

Most villagers however, do realize the importance of education. While they feel that schooling is more necessary for boys, many also recognize its value for girls. Adult Hsin Hsing villagers, most of whom are illiterate, often say that "one suffers if one cannot read and write." It is generally the educated members of the village who are most

LIFE HISTORY OF THE VILLAGER

highly respected. When a letter from a relative in the city arrives, most villagers must go to one of their literate neighbors to have it read.

Today, most village children do complete primary school. Kuo-Yu (Mandarin) is used almost immediately from the first year, even in the rural primary schools. Primary school graduates and those in the lower grades can therefore speak Mandarin. In addition, because of the increased contacts with urban centers and also with Mandarin speakers in the rural areas, most of the young people retain a speaking knowledge of Mandarin. This holds true even for the majority, who remain in the villages and do not go on to middle school.

However, the ability to read Chinese characters is frequently not retained for very long. Primary school graduates can usually read simple texts, although much of this material is often memorized. Even those who do fairly well in reading forget characters very quickly unless they go on to middle school or continue to take an interest in reading after graduation. The reading of simple material soon becomes difficult with lack of practice.

Unfortunately, the primary schools, whose books and courses of study are furnished by the provincial government, make no attempt to teach the children material which would equip them to read simple agricultural magazines. Consequently, the upper classmen or primary school graduates who try to read *Harvest Magazine,* a useful agricultural magazine for the farm population, have found even this simplified though specialized material frustrating. Most of the young people who do make an attempt soon give up and all too often read almost nothing at all. The end result is that several years after they graduated from primary school, many of these young people are again functionally illiterate.

In Hsin Hsing village only a few primary school graduates go on to junior and finally senior middle school each year. They usually go to a community school in Lukang, since it is located close to the village. Students attending this school can live at home and make the three-mile trip each way by bus or bicycle. During the period of this research, the two Hsin Hsing village girls attending middle school went to the Lukang school, along with three boys from the village. A few other boys attended middle schools near Chang-hua, less than ten miles from the village, and one village boy was studying at a middle school in Taichung about twenty-five miles away. The boys at the Chang-hua and Taichung schools had to live away from home.

The Lukang middle school gives a general education; the one near Chang-hua gives specialized training in agriculture; the Taichung school is considered academically superior to the others. All middle schools, however, charge tuition and can be entered only after passing an examination. Each year many graduates of area primary schools are denied entrance to the middle schools for lack of room. Students are eliminated on the basis of the examination system. Therefore, the choice of which middle school a student will attend frequently depends entirely upon which school admits him.

Regardless of the course of study, most parents hope that a middle school education will enable their son or daughter to secure some kind of minor white-collar job such as clerk in the local government agency. One Hsin Hsing villager struggled financially to send his son to middle school because he felt the boy was a weakling (he was extremely thin and small for his age and wore glasses) and therefore would never be able to farm. The father felt that the only hope for his son was to go on with his schooling so that later he might possibly obtain some kind of minor position with the government. In a few cases, the parents may aspire to a college education for their child.

It is compulsory for all middle school students in Taiwan to join certain school organizations. Boys and girls in junior middle school are members of a youth organization somewhat similar to the American Scouts. Senior middle school students join the Youth Corps, an anti-Communist organization dedicated to retaking the mainland. Boys and girls in all the colleges in Taiwan must also belong to this organization.

By means of the centrally organized Youth Corps, the government is able to give young Taiwanese military, political, and physical preparation against Communist attack. The many after school meetings and outings which members must attend give the government the opportunity to propagandize the young members in anti-communist thought and inculcate in them patriotism towards President Chiang Kai-shek and the Nationalist government in Taiwan. The government has had some success in this effort in the Hsin Hsing area, but elsewhere a great resentment has been built up. The resentment appears to be manifested more by the Taiwanese in the colleges and universities than by the middle school students.

A village middle school student rarely keeps up his earlier close associations with other village children unless they too attend middle school. By the time the students enter senior middle school their childhood contacts are almost forgotten as they join cliques of their classmates; the disruption of old patterns is so sharp that they almost snub their former friends in the village. Their new associates are almost always students from other villages and from the town or city in which the school is located. The association pattern in primary school is quite different. The children from one village tend to stay together, even though the school includes students from other villages.

Not only do these middle school students usually fail to maintain associations with their fellow villagers but they seem also to divorce themselves from the village itself. As they progress in their schooling, they become more and more antagonistic toward many of the village traditions, particularly those with a magical or religious basis. They have learned to regard them as superstition, and feel they are unworthy of their participation. Often, at religious and magical rituals in the village the middle school students, sometimes accompanied by their classmates from other places, can be seen on the sidelines laughing at the "superstition and backwardness" of the participating villagers. This attitude is in part fostered by what they are taught first in the elementary schools, then in the middle schools, and reinforced by their many new contacts with people and ideas from urban centers.

The village seldom has the opportunity to learn new ideas and ways of doing things from these students. Even if some of the students happen to be willing to share their knowledge, the other students' obvious snobbishness and lack of interest hinders the receptivity of the nonscholars to anything the students may propose. Consequently, the advanced education of some of their number produces few direct benefits for the village.

There are also educational offerings in the area which are nonofficial and informal. Among these are sewing classes, either private or offered by the local Farmers' Association for members' daughters. The private schools charge tuition, but the Farmers' Association classes are free. The Farmers' Association also holds classes in farming techniques for village boys. Boys may also be apprenticed to a craftsman for training. Since the practice is not too common in Hsin Hsing village, the few apprentices in the village have been boys of poor and almost landless families. One village boy was apprenticed by his father to a carpenter in Lukang and another to a carpenter in Taipei. Sometimes, village boys or girls are apprenticed to craft shops in Taipei.

ADOLESCENCE

When a boy reaches sixteen[2] an elaborate religious festival marking his transition from child to adult may be held in his honor. This may be done if the boy had been ill as a child and his family in asking the god for help had promised to perform such a ritual or if his family can afford it or wishes to display their economic ability to do so. If the boy had been sickly, thanks are given to the gods at the festival, especially to T'ien Kung (the highest of all gods) for bringing the boy to this stage of development, and requests are made for further help. When such a festival is held, a *tao shih*—a Taoist priest—is called to the village to officiate. (The ritual is similar to the one held at the time of a marriage, which is described in that section of this chapter.)

Many *ch'in ch'i*, friends from outside the village and some fellow villagers are invited to share the food and drink which were offered to the gods. For the most part the *ch'in tsu* and other villagers who are present are there primarily to help serve and entertain the guests from outside. Women, who never serve food at village festivals, work in the kitchen, helping to prepare the food for the male chefs.

At sixteen a boy is, in theory, considered an adult, ready to take on adult responsibilities. Although he does have some new responsibilities and privileges, he is nevertheless not really considered an adult until he becomes a father and may frequently not be treated as an adult until he is himself the head of a household. However, at sixteen there are certain changes in social status for the boy. He may, for example, now represent his father and his family at village meetings, voting for his father if the occasion should arise and even speaking for his family. In addition, it is considered proper for the head of a household to leave his sixteen-year-old son to act as host and entertain the family's houseguests.

A boy of sixteen is considered old enough to leave home by himself to work in the city. Although there are boys under sixteen working in Taipei, their parents are quick to point out that their fathers are there to watch over them. It would be considered highly irregular for a village family to allow a younger boy to be in the city unsupervised. Villagers are always concerned about possible criticisms of the way they bring up their children. If something should happen to an unsupervised boy in the city or if he should get into trouble, people immediately say that the parents are at fault because they neglected their duty and did not take proper care of their son. Therefore, the social recognition of a boy as an adult at age sixteen in a sense protects his parents from criticism and alleviates their pangs of conscience should something happen to the older boy who is away from home alone.

As boys move into their mid-teens they begin to take on added responsibilities in the economic life of the family. More and more of their labor and their earnings, if any, are contributed to the family treasury. At about eighteen the boy begins to do many of the field chores. At this time he also may hire out as a field laborer, receiving a man's wages. Sometimes a fellow villager may teach him how to transplant rice seedlings, for which training the boy receives meals but very little financial remuneration. Once he has learned this skill, however, the boy can hire out as a laborer at NT $20 to $25 per day.

Although the boy now begins to take on many responsibilities, he still spends a great deal of time playing with his friends. Village boys in their late teens and early twenties form small groups and spend much time together telling stories, going into town, and generally enjoying themselves. At times they may also help each other with their field chores.

At about the age of twenty, boys who are extremely close may become sworn brothers. This group of six to fifteen village boys may, at times, include some who are *ch'in tsu* and perhaps a few from other villages. But most often, the boys come from the various kinship groups in the village. A small dinner party may be held in the village to commemorate the formation of such a group. There are a number of different groups of sworn brothers in the village, each usually representing a different age group of village men, although sometimes there may be two different sworn brother groups within a single age group.

A sworn brother group has an important function in adult life for its members and their families. When a sworn brother marries or has children, the group is expected to give a gift to mark the occasion. When there is a death in the immediate family of one sworn brother, the others send sacrifice foods and come to the funeral to mourn for the deceased. Sworn brothers may also come to each other's aid in times of need. These groups are rather popular in the area, and the members of such groups may maintain a close relationship for many years. It is not unusual to attend a small *pai-pai* dinner in the home of a middle-aged villager and meet a sworn brother from another village or nearby town.

In general, girls have many more responsibilities in the home than their brothers do, and therefore once in their teens have much less free time for play. The limited freedom they get and the work load which they must assume is intentional training for marriage. If a girl is given too much freedom at home, the villagers say that "she will be unhappy when she later marries and finds she has a strict mother-in-law." At the same time she must learn how to work "so her parents-in-law won't get angry with her. It is also easier to marry her out if she learns to work well, since a boy's family wants a good worker." Thus, in addition to helping with household chores and caring for younger children, girls also do some work in the fields. In their spare time they usually sit in a small group with other girls and women of their own compound or sometimes neighboring houses and make fiber hats which are sold to augment the family income.

However, the daughters of financially secure village families are not given so much responsibility, and their activities are much less restricted. The teenage daughter in such a household may do very little household or fieldwork, especially if there is an older sister-in-law in the house. These girls may, of course, continue their education in middle school or attend a private sewing school. Such was the case with the young daughters of two village families. One of these girls, a good student, was sent to the Lukang Community Middle School. The

other girl was not interested in continuing her education after graduation from primary school and so first attended a sewing school in the
area, then went to work in Taipei under the guidance of a relative,
and was finally called home where she began to make clothes for pay.
Since this girl's family did not need the income from her work, she did
not take the work seriously and spent much time amusing herself in
the village and in Lukang where her older married sister lived. Although the girl's father was extremely strict with his sons, even with
one who was married and himself a father, this daughter was allowed a
great amount of freedom.

The sexes begin to be more and more segregated once village children reach the age of eight or so, and this continues on throughout
adulthood. It is, of course, much less true for those who attend middle
school, where there is much more opportunity for boys and girls to do
things together. However, except for a few occasions when they work
side by side, as in weeding operations, the ordinary village adolescents
have little contact with others of the opposite sex, particularly in
public places.

The sight of a boy and girl together in public can be the basis for all
kinds of rumors about the nature of their relationship. The fear of
criticism and ridicule by fellow villagers is more than enough to prevent open associations. However, there is frequently talk in the village
about secret love affairs between young villagers. Sometimes such
young people are actually seen together near the river in the dark of
night, and their secret meeting is immediately publicized in the village. According to many villagers, the talk precipitated by such relationships has been the cause of those marriages arranged between Hsin
Hsing villagers.

CONSCRIPTION

Since about 1953, young Taiwanese as well as mainlanders have
been conscripted into the Nationalist Chinese armed forces. The
length of service is normally two years, and the usual and preferred
draft age is twenty-two. However, as late as 1958, twenty-nine-year-old
married men with families who had somehow not been called up
earlier were still being inducted into the service. Supposedly, a married man with a family is drafted only if his nuclear family is part of a
joint family. Sometimes, however, even if the joint family is divided a
man may be drafted if the local public officials feel that the man's
brothers can help support his family. Each district has its own quota of
conscripts.

For purposes of communication and training it is important that the
soldier have some fluency in Kuo-Yu. However, there are many boys
in the rural area who either never went to school or who did not

complete their education and so speak little if any Kuo-yu. Therefore, sometime during the preconscription age of twenty to twenty-two the government requires all males who have not completed primary school to attend special Kuo-Yu classes at the local primary school. The local police see to it that these boys attend the classes by imposing fines on the families of the negligent.

In general, the villagers disapprove of forced military service and deeply resent the conscription of men with families. The service imposes many hardships on the families, since it means a loss of farm labor and actual income. While the government assumes some financial responsibility for the families of such men, the aid is slow in coming, and when it does arrive, it is usually insufficient. Moreover, the soldier's pay is so small that rural families have to send their sons or husbands in the army additional spending money almost every month.

In addition to their concern about the hardships conscription imposes on the families, the villagers also fear for the safety of their sons and husbands. Many of the boys from the area are stationed on the offshore islands of Quemoy and Matsu, rightly considered dangerous places. However, in spite of the many problems, one attitude the villagers express, at least in public, is that "like taxes, military service is every man's duty."

In most instances, before a group of villagers leaves to begin service in the army, several functions are held to "send the men off." The night before the departure a village *pai-pai* is held in which the gods are asked to speed the safe return of the conscripts. Every village family participates, each bringing a basket of sacrifice foods to the court of one of the larger village *tsu* houses. Here a shaman (*fa shih*) performs a ritual, inviting the gods to come and partake of the food offerings. At the conclusion of the ritual, each family takes its own food home and eats it for their evening meal.

That same night before the men leave, a large subscription dinner may be held in honor of the draftees. While every village family participates in the *pai-pai*, many families do not take part in this large dinner. Usually, only families which are friendly with the draftees' families will pay the subscription price and send a representative to attend. The representative may be the family head himself or a young son of sixteen years or more. One or two of the village men who earn extra income as cooks on various occasions prepare this dinner at no charge, and several village men and/or boys volunteer to serve the food. Some of the women usually help in the kitchen. At the dinner there is a good deal of drinking and drinking games, joking, and storytelling. In addition, some of the more respected *tsu* leaders or elected officials make speeches.

The next morning the men are sent off by most of the village. The

village orchestra plays amid banners wishing each man luck and a
speedy return or general congratulations on going into the army.
These banners are sent by *ch'in ch'i* and friends, and the number of
banners each man receives is often considered an indication of his
family's popularity. The villagers form a procession and accompany
the draftees for more than two miles to the *hsiang* Public Office where
young men from several villages meet to be taken away to the army
camp in government trucks. The departure of men to the army is thus
made into a rather grand and colorful occasion. The villagers report
that this tradition began during Japanese times, and it bears many
similarities to Embree's (1939:195–203) description of such celebra-
tions in Suye Mura.

The two years or so of military service are full of new experiences
for many of the village boys, since it is their first opportunity to travel
to other parts of Taiwan and come in constant contact with men from
other areas of the island as well as mainlanders. But once his term of
military service is over, a man usually returns to his earlier occupation
and, if he is single, he can expect to have a marriage arranged for him
soon after his discharge. The activities of these ex-service men in
civilian life are not noticeably different from what they were before
military service.

MARRIAGE

Today, in Taiwan the average age for marriage is twenty-four
for men and twenty-two for women by Chinese reckoning. Before the
1950's the ages at marriage were two years younger: twenty-two and
twenty. The obvious reason for this change is military conscription.
Usually, men enter the army when they are twenty-two, and although
this is still considered the proper age for a man to marry, families with
sons about to be called into service tend to postpone marriage arrangements. In most cases they prefer not to have the son marry, enter the
army, and leave the new daughter-in-law behind, since the villagers
feel that the son should be present, especially early in a marriage, to
establish the wife in habits of good behavior and obedience. In general, while the mother-in-law holds authority over her daughters-in-
law, in actuality it is the girl's husband who best enforces this authority. In Hsin Hsing village, for example, there have been cases in which
a daughter-in-law disobeyed or was disrespectful to her mother-in-law.
In such instances it would be quite unusual for the mother-in-law to
attempt to impose her authority by physical means. Instead, she is
likely to speak with her son and demand that he force his wife into
line. The son uses whatever means he feels necessary—speaking firmly
to his wife or, sometimes, even beating her—to make her obey his
mother. Parents fear that their inability to control a daughter-in-law

when their son is absent may cause irreparable harm to family relationships.

There are a few cases in Hsin Hsing and other villages in the area where an early marriage was arranged because a boy was to be called into the army. These are usually small families which must replace the loss of a son's labor with that of his wife. While the girl may not be able to perform as well as the man, the family tries to choose a strong, capable, and obedient girl who knows farming and whom they feel they can control during her husband's absence.

In recent years another factor which has played an important though not so direct a part in the postponement of marriage has been the increased economic value of girls. A daughter now can contribute substantially to the family income. She may earn money as a seamstress at home, as a field laborer during weeding operations or harvests, or even as a factory laborer in the city. Her marriage now means an economic loss to the family, and it is therefore not unusual for parents to postpone the event for some time. A pretty and capable daughter of one of the K'ang families was not married until she was almost twenty-three-years-old. When she was finally about to be married, her father said that he had held off arranging her marriage as long as possible because she had contributed much to the family income by sewing.

As noted earlier, the emphasis on the importance of family continuity requires that marriages be carefully arranged. However, the interpretation of what is a careful and good method of marriage arrangement has been changing through the years, and today, it is quite different from what it was early in the century. Forty to fifty years ago the arrangements were made solely on the word of a marriage broker, and not even the parents saw the prospective spouse of their son or daughter. Today, it is common for the couple to get a glimpse of each other and, in addition, to have some part in the decision as to the desirability of the marriage.

One of the first changes in the system was that the parents, instead of depending completely on the word of the matchmaker, began to insist on seeing the prospective bride or groom and the family in order to have a sounder basis for making a decision. The matchmaker was asked to effect a meeting of the two sets of parents, at which there were delicate and indirect discussions about their respective families and the possible marriage. Of course final decisions were not made until the matchmaker had discussed privately with each family the other's attributes and transmitted proposals and counter-proposals about the engagement gifts and dowry. At the same time both families took the opportunity to learn as much as possible about the other family from neighbors and friends. The young people had little to do with either discussion or decision.

In the past seven or eight years it has become possible for the young people to get a glimpse of one another, and perhaps even to meet in a very formal situation. This most recent development has been precipitated by the general changes in the economic and social life of the village as a result of the great increase in mobility and contacts with urban centers.

Two different factors are responsible for the increase in mobility; men are conscripted and leave the village or go alone to urban centers to seek employment. These men, whether single or married, tend to become more independent of family discipline. They have opportunities to meet women, and perhaps to have an affair. The unmarried man may well become less willing to be ordered back to the village one day in order to marry a girl, sight unseen and chosen for him by others. But the situation is even worse when a village man, married to a girl he had never seen and had not chosen, whom he does not yet care for, finds himself suddenly in love with a girl in the city. In such a case it is not unusual for him to stay in the city and live with the woman, refusing to go home to his legal wife. Today, this situation could end in divorce, which creates additional problems because of the need to return the engagement gifts and dowry. In addition, it is likely to inflict serious guilt feelings on the parents. On the few occasions when a village marriage has been dissolved, the parents who arranged the marriage seem to be the most seriously affected, questioning whether or not they had made a poor marriage choice for their son or daughter. It is consequently considered very important to avoid such situations, and many parents have expressed the feeling that since things are now different it is better to share some of the responsibility for arranging a marriage with the young people themselves.

The young people who are allowed to share in the responsibility do so in several ways. Frequently, once the arrangements for a marriage are under way and the parents of the two families entertain favorable feelings towards one another, a meeting is arrranged at which the young people can at least see each other. A favorite rendezvous is some large shop or theatre in Lukang. The two sets of parents arrive, each accompanied by the son or daughter. One family is escorted by the matchmaker who, from a distance, points out the girl to the boy and his family. Sometimes the boy and his family may visit the home of the girl. When they arrive, the girl may appear briefly and offer them tea and cigarettes.[3]

In each case, both the boy and, in turn, the girl are asked for an opinion about the tentatively chosen mate. The young people cannot really judge each other, except perhaps by looks, and if he or she is at all filial and respectful of the parents, can say little more than, "the girl looks all right," or "she is not too pretty, but if you [parents] think she is acceptable, then it is all right." In this way, the parents relieve themselves of some of the responsibility in the ultimate choice, and if something goes wrong with the marriage, the parents can always remind the young people that they agreed to the match.

In actuality, even though many young people want some voice in choosing a mate, most attempt no further contact after the "initial meeting." The boy usually makes no effort to see the girl even if he knows she works in a field near the road, fearing that if anyone sees him they will laugh at him.

The parents of the boy make their choice on the basis of qualities which they feel will best benefit the family. Thus, they usually seek a healthy, strong, and capable girl who can do the necessary work in the house and the fields and seems able to bear children. They also want a girl who can get along with people well and who can thus adapt easily to the new household into which she comes as a stranger. The girl's family wants a son-in-law who is economically and emotionally stable and can therefore provide adequately for their daughter. Both families place equal importance on the economic condition of the bride's or groom's family and the kind of ch'in ch'i they are likely to make.

The choices available to a family trying to arrange a marriage are limited by their own socioeconomic standing, and the families of a newly married couple are usually as evenly matched in this regard as the bride and groom are matched both physically and intellectually. On occasion, hoping to arrange a better marriage, one family and the matchmaker may conspire to deceive the other family as to economic standing or the intelligence or ability of the son or daughter. One such marriage was arranged by a matchmaker from Hsin Hsing village between a local girl and a boy from another village. No mention was ever made to the groom's family that the girl was rather dull, not capable at housework, or even at work in the fields. The justification the matchmaker offered for her behavior was that "after all, if the couple is actually married, then it must mean that they were fated for each other, and therefore there is nothing wrong." This same attitude is occasionally adopted by people who feel they have been similarly cheated; it enables them to accept the *fait accompli* and make the best of it.

However, such attempts at deception are not at all common, and "usually a stupid person marries a stupid person; otherwise they can't get along." The villagers feel that a marriage between people who are too different is likely to lead to the girl's unhappiness. More important, they know it may wreck the relations between the two families. For example, it may end with the girl being sent back home. Another important deterrent to attempts at deception is the danger to the family's reputation and general status if they do something so generally considered improper. However, most village families hope that

their daughters' economic and social position will be improved by
marriage or that their son will marry a girl with a large dowry. One
reason the villagers give for not attempting to arrange marriages
within their own village is that "after all, everyone in one's own village knows exactly how poor you really are."

It is only after the amount and kind of engagement gifts and dowry
have been settled through the matchmaker's negotiations that the
marriage agreement is considered definite. These gifts are, then, "like
a marriage contract." The engagement gifts the boy's family sends to
the girl and her family may consist of cash, a common figure being
about NT $2,000, plus cloth and jewelry for the girl. When these gifts
arrive, her family sends back gifts of gold, clothing (a belt, purse, and
so on) and sometimes some cash. At the wedding the girl's family may
return most of the gifts to the husband's family in her dowry of
furniture, clothing, and even cash. However, as the villagers point out,
"Usually in a marriage, all gifts considered, it costs the boy's side more
than the girl's. If the boy sends gifts of cash, much of it will come back
from the girl's side since her family will use the engagement money to
furnish the dowry. If the girl's dowry includes a radio or bicycle,
however, then her family might spend more." A family's reputation
may be enhanced or lowered by the worth of the engagement gifts or
dowry it provides. In the unusual case that the girl's dowry is smaller
than the boy's side expected, his family may treat their new daughter-
in-law badly, thus adversely affecting relations between the two families. When the arrangements for a marriage are completed, both
families send money to the matchmaker. Usually, the groom's family
sends twice as much as the bride's. The matchmaker is also remem-
bered on the occasion of the birth of the couple's first son, when the
couple sends her fried glutinous rice to thank her for arranging their
marriage.

Several months at least separate the official engagement from the
wedding, for which preparations are quite elaborate. Formal invitations are sent out by the boy's family to those *ch'in ch'i* and friends in
the area who have already sent gifts to commemorate the occasion.
"To send invitations to anyone else would be like asking for money,
and that would be embarrassing," say the villagers. The invitations
are delivered personally by members of the boy's family, *tsu,* or close
family friends in the village. The groom's house is decorated with red
streamers, wall and door hangings, and scrolls bearing lucky sayings
and good wishes for the occasion. Lengths of cloth with money and
messages of good wishes pasted on them are sent by friends and relatives and are put up on the walls of the ancestral-worship room. If the
groom's family is a member of a *tsu,* the *tsu's* main ancestral-worship
room is used for this purpose as well as for the ritual, even if the
family has its own private room.

The night before the wedding day, starting at midnight, a *pai-pai* is held at the boy's home. A Taoist priest (*tao shih*) officiates at the ceremony, held in honor of T'ien Kung to thank him for guarding the boy so that he could reach marriageable age, and prayers are said for the future of the boy and his family. At the same time, many lesser gods are invited to the *pai-pai* to be worshipped, and statues of these gods (which may belong to other villagers) are brought to the ancestral-worship room of the boy's home. The village orchestra performs during most of this ceremonial to entertain T'ien Kung. Many expensive foods, including at least one whole dressed pig and goat, bottles of wine, and a good deal of paper money are offered in honor of the gods and their soldiers and horses. (A description of the Taoist pantheon is found in Chapter 8.)

The *tao shih* invites the gods to partake of the sacrifices and transmits to them the prayers of the family. In the course of the ritual the *tao shih* and the participating members of the family, including the groom and his father and brothers, simulate trips to heaven and to the underworld to communicate with the gods. A shaman, known as *t'iao t'ung* (his broader functions are also described in detail in Chapter 8), accompanies them on these "trips." He is possessed by a local, less powerful, and important god known as an ambassador god and thus acts as the intermediary between the family and the higher gods. "After all," queried a villager on this point, "can a common man go directly on his own to see and talk with an emperor?"

Much of the food offered at the *pai-pai* is sent the next day as gifts to the girl's family; during the next several days it is fed to the guests who attend the wedding festival as well as the many people, usually *ch'in tsu* or fellow villagers, who help in the preparations and entertainment of the guests at the girl's village. The cost to both sets of parents is very great, and the poorest families save for a long time or borrow money in order to have a proper wedding festival.

While the boy's family is holding the *pai-pai* on the night before the marriage, the girl's family is busy with preparations for the next day. When the marriage broker, accompanied by the carriers bearing more gifts, and the village orchestra arrive, they are fed in the girl's village. Then, they help the girl's family load the many carts with her dowry and the sweet cakes which accompany the bride when she goes to the groom's village in her sedan chair.

The vehicles which carry the gifts to the bride's family and take the dowry back to the groom's village are either rented wheeled carts drawn by men hired in Lukang or trays carried on poles by the groom's *ch'in tsu* and/or fellow villagers. Only a wealthy family can afford to use the many hand-carried trays, since all the carriers must be fed banquet food and those who carry heavy items are given *hung pao* (money wrapped in a red paper packet). Far fewer wheeled carts are required to transport the gifts, and fewer men are needed to pull them. Hired men must be paid wages and fed simple food, but since there are so few of them the over-all cost is much less. When a prosperous villager asks his *ch'in tsu* and fellow villagers to participate and help carry the gifts and dowry, the occasion becomes much gayer since so many members of the village are taking part.

In most marriages in the village area today, two sedan chairs are used, each carried by two hired men. One transports the marriage broker to and from the bride's village, and the other carries the bride to the groom's village. During the prewar Japanese period when gasoline was plentiful and inexpensive, a taxi was more commonly used. Today, labor is cheaper than gasoline, and therefore it is only the wealthier or more modern villagers who use a taxi.

When the dowry is loaded on the carts in the girl's village, the villagers all turn out to watch the proceedings and scrutinize the articles. The dowry generally includes furniture, new clothing, and jewelry, as well as certain ordinary household cleaning items to symbolize the tasks the girl will perform in her new home. A portion of a dressed pig sent by the groom's family is cut up, and much of it goes back to the groom's family along with the dowry.

While the carts are being loaded, the girl bids farewell to her family and the ancestors of her natal home. For the last time she goes with her parents and worships the ancestors. Then she is led into the waiting sedan chair by a "good-luck lady," who must be an old woman with a living husband and many descendants. It is she, therefore, who finally sends the bride off alone, in the hope that the girl will have a similar good fortune. The good-luck lady also gives the bride a red string and instructs her to hang it over her bed to insure the fidelity of her husband.

The departure is accompanied by a good deal of crying by the girl, her mother, and other women of the immediate family. These tears, of course, reflect sincere regret at parting as well as the girl's fear at leaving the familiarity of her home and family. There is no doubt, however, that much of the girl's weeping is a conventional display of filial piety to show that she regrets leaving the home where she has been brought up and treated so well all her life. To smile on this occasion or not to weep for all to see would be extremely disrespectful toward her parents.

The bridal procession, consisting of the two sedan chairs, the vehicles carrying the dowry, and the accompanying village orchestra, then takes leave of the girl's village and begins its journey to her new home. The whole procession is preceded by a man carrying a bamboo pole some twenty-five feet long with a piece of meat tied at its tip as an offering to the mythical tiger which would otherwise devour the bride.

The bridal train follows a predetermined route, passing through several villages to display the dowry for all to see, even if the bridal couple live in neighboring villages and even if they happen to come from the same village. All along the route the special wedding music of gongs and horns attracts villagers who wish to see the procession.

The time of arrival in the groom's village, usually in the afternoon, has previously been fixed by a geomancer. Most of the villagers are outdoors waiting to examine the dowry. The bride's sedan chair is placed before the door of the boy's house, but the girl may not leave the chair and enter the house until the dowry has been ritually examined and accepted by the groom. Once this is done, a child of the household formally welcomes the bride to her new home, and she is led from the sedan chair and escorted into the house by the matchmaker. On entering the house the bride steps over a burning brazier and steps on and breaks a piece of red tile. The first act symbolically cleanses her of any ill fortune she may have picked up accidentally along the way (an example of such an accidental contamination is for the wedding caravan to pass a funeral along its route). The second act symbolizes the bride's willingness and her intention to obey her new family. These acts completed, she is led to a private room where "according to custom" she spends the next several hours alone except for occasional visits from the matchmaker.

That evening a festive banquet is held to celebrate the marriage. An even number of courses is always served, sometimes as many as sixteen to eighteen, and a great deal of wine is consumed. The banquet is attended by many guests, male and female, old and young, for the most part relatives (*ch'in ch'i*) and friends of the boy's family only. The adult males eat apart from the women and children. Either a *ch'in tsu* of the groom or else a fellow villager plays host at almost every table of male guests to see that the guests eat and drink and are generally entertained. Finger games to promote the drinking of wine are usually played. Other male *ch'in tsu* and village friends and neighbors serve the food to the guests, while the women help in the kitchen. The male cooks are hired from the village or from the local area. Dishes, tables, and chairs are hired for the occasion in Lukang and brought into the village by oxcart.

About halfway through the banquet the bride is brought out and, together with the groom and his parents, is formally presented to the assemblage of guests and villagers by a highly regarded elder *ch'in tsu* or a respected villager. After this introduction, many respected guests are called upon to give brief speeches; in these they remind the young couple of their duty to their parents and express hopes that children will soon result from the marriage, especially boys. The speeches completed, the groom goes from table to table, drinking with and accepting toasts from all the guests. The bride returns to her room, where she often receives guests who wish to meet her. She serves them "bride's tea," for which the guests give her a small red packet of "bride's money." (This is considered to be her own to do with as she pleases.) The bride's tea is sweetened, and the sugar in it represents everyone's wish for her: "Sweet, sweet, have a baby boy."

Since there is no religious or civil ceremony to mark the occasion, it is difficult to say exactly when the couple is considered to be definitively married. Villagers themselves disagree on the point. Some feel that the couple is married once the engagement and marriage arrangements have been made. Others say that the marriage occurs when the couple is presented at the marriage festival. Still others feel that there is no marriage until it has been consummated, and some even say that the couple is not formally married until the union is registered at the Public Office. While no single answer was agreed upon, several villagers pointed out that the marriage begins once the engagement is agreed upon, "since at this time the two families are tied together as *ch'in ch'i,* and this, after all, is one of the most important factors in any marriage."

Taiwanese marriage has a broader social function than marriage in contemporary Western culture. It establishes *ch'in ch'i* relationships between families, it brings a new member into a boy's family, and it joins two people who then produce children. A Chinese marriage, then, does not take place as a result of a single religious or civil ceremony. Instead, a series of events, beginning with the engagement agreement and culminating in the sexual union and production of children, mark the establishment of the married state.

On the day after the bride arrives at her husband's village, a good-luck lady introduces her to relatives and neighbors and tells her how each person should be addressed. Some people call on the family to be introduced to the bride. The girl is also taken to the other side of the village to meet any *ch'in tsu* who may live there. Later on this second day, the couple returns to the girl's natal home to attend a banquet very similar to the one held at the husband's home the day before. When she returns to her family on this occasion she is frequently all smiles, in sharp contrast to her tearful departure. The cheerful aspect, like the previous day's public woe, is probably conventional, a demonstration that she is happy in her good fortune at having made such an excellent match. But it is perhaps also due to the fact that she has been to her new home, gone through her first night of marriage, and now feels that the worst is over.

The couple either travel together, in a taxi, to the girl's village or separately, the bride in a sedan chair, the groom by bicycle. Usually, several of the groom's male friends and relatives accompany him.

While the girl spends most of the evening in the kitchen or back rooms of the house with her female relatives, the boy and his companions are formally entertained by the bride's father and other male relatives at the banquet. Most of the banquet guests are *ch'in ch'i* and friends of the girl's family, and the men who serve the food and entertain the guests are *ch'in tsu,* close friends, and neighbors.

Before many hours have passed the bride, the groom, and his companions take leave of their hosts. Since this is their first formal visit, it is important "to eat little and leave early" to show their politeness, although the party continues after they have left.

The guests who are formally invited to this banquet and to the wedding festival in the groom's home are those who have sent a gift. The form of the gift usually depends upon the relationship the guest has with the family. Close *ch'in tsu* or *ch'in ch'i* commonly send lengths of cloth with several hundred NT dollars and messages of good wishes pasted on them which are displayed on the walls. Other guests may simply send money wrapped in a red paper packet. Regardless of the kind of gift or who it comes from, the receiving family informally records the name of the donor and the amount of the gift. This is done so that later, on a similar occasion, an approximately equivalent gift can be returned.

On the third day after the wedding the new daughter-in-law begins to work in her husband's house. From the outset she is carefully supervised by her mother-in-law and usually does much of the cooking, washing, and general housecleaning. "If the daughter-in-law is good, she will listen to and obey all the family, including her sisters-in-law and even her husband's younger sisters." This is the best way for her to demonstrate that she is anxious to learn the ways of her new home and please her new family.

A girl's parents cannot visit their daughter in her new home for the first four months after she is married. While the girl can pay them brief visits during this period, such visits are dependent upon the economic condition of her husband's family and the number of people who can perform the necessary household tasks in her place. If she were to leave her household duties undone she could easily anger her mother-in-law. To avoid such a contingency, many newly married girls rarely see their parents during the early months of marriage. However, if a girl marries within her home village, she may easily be tempted to visit her parents frequently, and perhaps even to continue to do some of her old tasks for her mother—all at the expense of the work she now owes her husband's family. Such a situation can provoke the mother-in-law to treat the girl harshly and may eventually lead to bad feeling between the two families, since they live in close proximity and therefore know everything that goes on in the other's house.

ADULTHOOD

Marriage does not affect substantially the customary daily routine of a young man, for as a new husband he continues to spend as much of his free time with his friends as he did before his marriage and almost never allows himself to be seen publicly with his wife. (This would be embarrassing both to himself and his wife, since people would say they must be in love and laugh at them.) The boy does not usually achieve higher status nor assume many more responsibilities upon his marriage. In general, he continues to function under the authority of his father, unless a family division takes place. Many older villagers point out that the boy does not become an adult by virtue of his marriage.

Usually, it is not until the birth of the first child, and perhaps even a division of the joint or stem family, that the boy begins to settle down. He then achieves more status in both his family and the village; he feels a resonsibility for his family and ceases to spend all his spare time with his friends. He also begins to voice strong opinions about the running of the household. There are exceptional boys who, even before marriage, assume a great deal of responsibility and spend little time with their friends. Once married, such boys become even more responsible.

Unlike her husband, the bride is immediately saddled with work and various responsibilities and has even less time for recreation than she had before. Like her husband she gains little increase in status from her marriage. For her, adult status is not achieved until she has established her position in the family by bearing a child, preferably a male child. Until then she is not really part of the family.[4] The villagers tell a story of a girl whose family did not send an adequate dowry with her when she married. Her husband's family was dissatisfied, and eventually she was sent home. However, when the boy's family realized that she was pregnant, she was immediately brought back and made welcome in their house. Real status and authority are achieved by a daughter-in-law when she finally assumes the role of the wife of the head of the family upon family division or the death or retirement of her mother-in-law. It is thus easy to understand why daughters-in-law often agitate for family division.

An adult male's leisure is usually determined by the agricultural season. However, even during the harvest, when people are busiest, there is seldom rushed or harried activity. Since men can do their work only during the day, the evening is a time for relaxation during both the busy and the slack seasons. Many men spend their free time visiting each other at home or at the village store where one can buy a stick of sugarcane or some flavored ice in the hot weather. Wherever they may be, the men usually sit about smoking, talking about their crops or work, or telling stories and jokes. Some men play Chinese chess or listen to the radio at the village store.

The women have less free time during the day regardless of the agricultural season. During the slack seasons women are occupied steadily with ordinary household tasks. During the busy season they are simply busier, taking on additional work in the fields, cooking food at home for any hired laborers, or drying rice or vegetables after the harvest. When women do not have pressing work, they often spend their time in small groups working on fiber hats or mending clothing. At times as they work they may listen to Taiwanese opera on a radio, but more often they simply talk or gossip. Women also spend some of their free time visiting with neighbors or *ch'in tsu* in the village. If their own parents or brothers live in villages nearby, they may visit them on occasion for several hours.

OLD AGE

As old age approaches—and a person is considered old after fifty—both men and women gradually retire from farm work and household tasks if they have children who are able to take over the work and care for them. While this is usually the case, in these days there are also times when married sons go off to work in Taipei, and it then becomes necessary for the old man and the daughters-in-law to work the land. In such cases even the old mother has to do a great deal of work in the household.

In general, however, old age is a time of great freedom and leisure for men and women. Since they have few pressing responsibilities, they are free to wander about the village and visit each other. At most, old people of either sex may help watch their young grandchildren during the day. Some of the older people, especially one or two grandmothers in Hsin Hsing, are known for their ability to tell wonderful stories based on Taiwan opera or puppet shows which they have seen in the surrounding villages or in Lukang.

Unlike younger people, the old are not under pressure to adhere to the proprieties of life. Old women smoke in public, appear at public dinners normally attended by men only, and are generally outspoken. Old men frequent banquets and festivals held in Hsin Hsing and even surrounding villages. On such occasions they care little how much they eat and frequently gorge themselves with the good food. Their juniors watch and say nothing, and in fact seem to enjoy watching the old men behaving in ways that they cannot. At most they may laugh and make good-natured jokes at how much the old man is still capable of eating, while continuing to push more food on him. When old people talk, even though the younger people may consider their words pure nonsense, they merely smile and agree. When the evening is over there is usually some young grandchild waiting to lead the old man back over the dark paths to his house.

Frequently, even though the older man has virtually retired as head of the household, he may still bear the title of *chia chang*. In such instances, it is usual for him, rather than for the son who is actually head of the house, to be elected to village positions. These positions may be political, religious, or social: the man may be charged with the arrangements for the *pai-pai* for the village god or elected *lin chang*, and so on. Although everyone knows that old men are not able to handle the extensive duties of these jobs, they are nevertheless elected by their fellow villagers out of respect. The selection is made with the knowledge that the duties and responsibilities of the position will be carried out by the man's sons, but his election tends to give the old man a great deal of face in the village. This arrangement is made possible by the manner in which elections are usually conducted in the village. Although there is an election, the outcome is usually pretty well predetermined by the families concerned, who agree before the vote is cast who will be elected and who will actually serve in the position.

ILLNESS, DISEASE, AND MEDICINE

As has already been shown in Chapter 2, the tremendous increase in population on Taiwan is a reflection of the great reduction in the death rate, which results, primarily, from the lower incidence of fatal diseases. The control of disease has been effected by such factors as public health programs which have helped eliminate diseases like cholera and malaria, an increase in the number of Western-style doctors, an increased reliance on Western medicine and medical techniques, and somewhat better sanitation as a result of education of the public and governmental enforcement of health standards.

It was during the Japanese period that Taiwan saw the advent of Western-style doctors and medicines, especially in the 1930's. However, they were few, and their practice was limited mainly to the wealthy. The benefits of their knowledge, therefore, and the everyday use of Western-style medicines did not reach many of the rural people. During this period the rural people continued to rely primarily on Chinese doctors and herbal medicines, as well as magical cures effected by shamans and healing priests. (The magical techniques are discussed more fully in Chapter 8.) However, public health measures introduced by the Japanese government to combat epidemic diseases did benefit the rural people. Some forms of improved sanitation reached the rural areas through the schools and, perhaps more effectively, through the publishing of government edicts enforcing practices of sanitation. Semiannual government inspections forced villagers to clean up their houses and the villages twice a year. The inspections were carried out by the Japanese police and civil officials, and any family which did not pass the inspection was subject to fine and to reinspection, which meant that "the party was punished by having to clean up all over again." The policy of inspections instituted by the Japanese has been continued under the Nationalist Chinese regime.

During the latter part of the war, and especially after the restoration of Chinese rule to Taiwan, there was a marked increase in the incidence of disease, particularly communicable diseases. There was even a recurrence of cholera. This was a direct result of the poor living conditions brought about by the war and, with the coming of the Chinese government, a chaotic administration which was unable or unwilling to deal with health problems. However, the situation gradually began to improve after 1948 and 1949 when Taiwan became the new stronghold of the Nationalist Chinese regime. This improvement is evidenced by the general situation in the Hsin Hsing area. Beginning in the early 1950's the number of Western-style doctors practicing in the area increased. At this date, there are a number of such doctors, and the villagers consider their fees reasonable and within their means. The reason for this great increase lies in the different licensing practices of the Japanese and the Nationalist governments. Under the Japanese a man had to be a graduate of a medical school before he could practice medicine; under the Chinese government, the applicant is required only to pass a practical examination. This means that people who have worked in hospitals as aides or technicians and have had some opportunity to observe others practicing medicine may have accumulated enough knowledge to pass the examination and obtain a license. Therefore, while there are now a large number of licensed doctors practicing in the Hsin Hsing area, only a few who went to school in Japan have had formal medical training.

In addition to the great increase in the number of doctors practicing in the local area, in recent years there has also been a marked expansion in the number of private and public hospitals in the cities. These hospitals, which are sometimes very large, can accommodate many patients, house relatively modern facilities such as operating rooms, X-ray and other equipment, and provide modern drugs for patients. Although most of the patients treated in these hospitals are city people, village people sometimes go to them for treatment. They are usually referred there by a local doctor who is capable of diagnosing an illness as one requiring hospital care or who is honest enough to realize the limitations of his own medical knowledge and so recommend that his patient seek medical care in the hospital.

Besides these hospitals, the government has established a clinic or public health center in each district. The center in Pu Yen Hsiang has usually been understaffed or lacking a doctor entirely for long periods of time thus making it impossible for villagers to be sure they can obtain treatment at the center. The result has been that since some villagers wasted time going to the center without receiving treatment, most have come to ignore it completely.

The advent of modern drugs has also helped improve health conditions in the local area. Western-style doctors practicing in the area utilize a great many drugs in treating illness. Penicillin is now so plentiful and inexpensive that most of them are almost automatically expected to administer the drug to their patients. Indeed, the drug has become so well known in recent years and is so readily obtainable in Lukang drug stores that it is not unusual for ordinary villagers to buy it and administer it with a hypodermic needle to their own family members or, more often, to a sick pig. The drug stores in Lukang and other towns and cities which sell penicillin and other Western drugs also usually have a counter in the shop which features Chinese herbal and root medicines. These are still used by many Taiwanese as well as mainlanders.

In addition to the drugs or antibiotics, village families keep various kinds of Western-style patent medicines in the house for treating stomach upsets, headaches, colds, backaches, and so on. These are left with them on consignment by traveling medicine merchants. The medicines are separately wrapped and placed in a kit or bag, and every few months the peddler comes through the village, examines the contents of each bag, collects for what medicine has been used, and replenishes the supply. Many village families have several medicine bags on hand, each supplied by a different company.

A few times a year medicine shows featuring music, comedians, and even snake charmers, also visit the villages in the area. The companies which sponsor these shows sell two or three medicines for special illnesses. Such groups usually draw great village crowds, and their sales are large.

However, in spite of all the improved medical facilities available and the somewhat better sanitation practiced in the local area, there is a high prevalence of disease. Skin diseases are common, especially among children, and intestinal parasites plague both young and old. Trachoma is not uncommon, but the villagers do little to counter it. The disease usually strikes older villagers who are unwilling to spend the time and money necessary to obtain proper treatment. One trachoma victim, a woman of about forty, stated that although she knew she would eventually go blind, "by that time my children will be grown and able to take care of me." In the interim she would not take the time nor spend the money to obtain treatment.

There are several reasons for the high rate of intestinal and parasitic diseases. Although the villagers are aware that water should be boiled before drinking, they actually merely heat it. At the same time they court danger by buying drinks from sidewalk vendors in town. Facilities for washing dishes and other utensils are limited; much of it is done in the nearby pond which serves as the laundry and a bathing place for buffalo as well. Intestinal diseases are also caused by eating raw vegetables which were fertilized with human excrement.

These disorders common in the village do not usually cause alarm. When a familiar illness strikes, the patient may be given some patent or herbal medicine and the illness allowed to run its course. Childhood diseases are common and produce little anxiety. However, there is a fear of diseases whose origin is poorly understood, which produce curious symptoms, and for which no cures are known. When one of these illnesses strikes, a Western-style doctor is called in to administer penicillin or some other drug. The general feeling is that Western medicines, if they are appropriate for the illness, effect fast cures. While many villagers insist that Chinese medicines are just as effective if not more so in the long run, in that they produce a more permanent cure, they readily admit that Chinese medicines are slower to work than Western ones. If the Western medicines fail to help and the patient does not seem to recover quickly enough, or if the illness is very unusual, the villagers conclude that the disorder is caused by some supernatural agent and must be dealt with by magical means. (A detailed discussion of supernatural explanations for illness and the remedies used to cure them is found in Chapter 8.) Most of the diseases prevalent locally are not fatal, and old age seems to be the main cause of death in the Hsin Hsing area.

DEATH, BURIAL, AND MOURNING

The villagers' attitude toward the rituals and ceremonials associated with death vary for the most part with the age and status of the deceased and the economic condition of the family. An old person is almost always given an elaborate, very expensive funeral which entails lengthy mourning rituals. This is also true for a younger adult who leaves children and therefore has status in the community. Young people and children are given a rather simple funeral unless the family is financially well-off. A funeral ceremony is very rarely held for an infant or child under a year old.

The villagers believe that the individual has three spirits. At death one spirit remains in the grave, another remains in the incense pot in the ancestral-worship room of the family home, and the third journeys to the underworld to be judged by the gods of the underworld for its past deeds in life. These gods determine the fate of the spirit, which may be eternal punishment and torture in the underworld, a punishment appropriate to the seriousness of past deeds, or rebirth in another world as anything from an insect to a member of the gentry or an even higher status. However, the spirits of people who have lived extraordinarily pure and good lives are permitted immediate entrance to the "Western Paradise," never again to undergo the uncertainty and misery of earthly life.

Death

Death is not always sudden and unexpected. Sometimes it becomes apparent that an old person is about to die "when his eyes no longer see or he can no longer eat rice." When this happens, the family is able to prepare for the occasion and, at the same time, eliminate the need to perform a ritual to rid the bedroom of the demon of death— necessary if someone dies in his bed. The dying person is washed and dressed in special clothes and moved from the bedroom to the family's or *tsu's kung t'ing*. Here he is placed on several wooden benches which have been covered with straw mats, and he and the family wait for death to come. Female members of the family take turns keeping watch in the room, passing the hours making fiber hats or doing other hand work.

On one occasion a very old woman was apparently dying and was thus washed and dressed in her burial clothes and moved into the ancestral-worship room. The family recalled that when she could still speak she had said she wanted to die on the anniversary of her husband's death so that the ritual of ancestor worship for herself and her husband could be carried out easily by the family on the same day. For four days the old woman lingered in a coma; finally, on the fourth day, there was "no more breath in her" and she died. I expressed amazement that the old woman had died on the very day she had predicted. The response was, "Well, of course, the old people are always right."

In cases of sudden death, the body is moved immediately into the ancestral-worship room, washed and dressed in burial clothes, and laid out on the mat-covered benches to await burial. Whether the deceased had been brought there to die or was placed there after his death, all chairs in the room are removed, mirrors are covered, statues of the gods taken down, and scrolls picturing the gods hung face to the wall. Straw is placed on the floor on which the mourners and visitors sit. At this time the family of the deceased must register the death at the *hsiang* Public Office and obtain permission to bury the body in the public cemetery. (Burial in private fields has not been permitted since early in the Japanese period.)

Relatives, including *ch'in tsu,* married daughters, and *ch'in ch'i,* are notified of the death and asked to come to the home of the deceased. Relatives in distant places are notified by means of telegram, special-delivery express letter, or telephone. If their relationship to the deceased was a close one, they too are asked to come to the village. Relatives who live nearby are usually notified of the death by messengers, such as a younger member of the deceased's family or some *ch'in tsu,* friend, or neighbor.

While they are still on the road approaching the village relatives begin to wail, and as they enter the village they fall to their knees and crawl to the house and into the room where the body lies. Someone who was present at the time of the death may crawl out to meet and welcome these relatives and then crawl into the room with them. *Ch'in tsu* relatives and married daughters are expected to wail and crawl both to show their respect for the deceased and to express their sorrow for not being present at the death. The villagers consider it unfilial to be absent when a parent or *ch'in tsu* relative who is older or of a higher generation dies. Many villagers look on and may criticize the arrivals for not wailing loud enough or for not getting down on their hands and knees to crawl soon enough. One may also hear old village women note how filial someone is because of the distance she crawls or the way she wails.

Preparation for the Funeral and Burial

Immediately after the death, arrangements are made for five *tao shih* to come to the village from Lukang to officiate at the funeral. A village funeral may be delayed because the *tao shih* are participating in a funeral elsewhere and are not available immediately. Usually, five *tao shih* form a group and work together with a small orchestra of three or four men who normally accompany them to the ceremony. The group of about eight men usually charges approximately NT $380 (US $10.50).

It is very rare that a Buddhist funeral is held in Hin Hsing or other villages of the area. While most of the villagers worship Buddha and Kuan Yin along with the Taoist hierarchy of gods, they are not Buddhists, and the one such funeral held in recent years was for the old mother of the largest landlord family in the village. This woman was a Buddhist, and while she was still alive had Buddhist nuns come to the village to pray for her.

Virtually all village families willingly assist in the funeral preparations. Most village families are members of one of several "Father-

Mother Societies" organized to provide help for member families at
the time of a death. Membership in a society is a kind of insurance
which helps the bereaved family through the ordeal. The members of
a father-mother society stand ready to handle the many tasks which
must be carried out for the funeral ritual and burial, and each contributes a sum of money to the family of the deceased. This amount is
calculated on the basis of the current cash value of a given quantity of
pork.

Usually one or two male members of the society take informal
charge of the many arrangements and tell each person just which tasks
he should perform. This "organizer" usually is self-appointed and
assumes this responsibility "because he likes to run things, regardless
of the amount of time and work it involves." The village storekeeper,
a member of the Shen *tsu,* is such a man. He is also a part-time farmer,
the elected head of the village Farmers' Association unit, and a
shaman. He "pushes himself" into many such positions and, although
the villagers feel that he is rather aggressive along these lines and not
necessarily the most capable person available, they nevertheless accept
his leadership since he handles so many unpleasant and time-
consuming tasks.

In addition to those in the father-mother society, almost all the
other villagers hold themselves ready to aid a bereaved family. While
the members of the society are called upon to do the most time-
consuming and hardest work, any villager must be prepared to
help. If a death occurs at harvest time, the village farmers may have to
postpone the harvesting of the crops, because if a man is requested to
participate in and help with the funeral, he can do nothing but accept
and do the tasks assigned to him. The time of death is therefore a time
of village unity. No matter what feeling may have existed between a
villager and the deceased or the members of his family, the villager, if
called upon, cannot refuse to help. "One cannot have bad feeling
toward the dead."

Among the tasks assigned to the helpers are: notifying relatives and
friends of the death; constructing an outdoor altar for the funeral
ceremony; buying, preparing, and cooking the food which is served to
all who participate in the funeral; sewing mourning clothes; and
bringing the coffin from Lukang to the village. Villagers also help in
digging the grave and carrying the coffin to the cemetery later.

For the most part the members of the family have little work to do,
and at most the immediate family may be found helping to make
mourning clothes or preparing vegetables for the cooks. Usually, they
are kept busy mourning and wailing and greeting relatives and friends
who arrive from elsewhere.

During the period of the funeral and attendant rituals, the family of the deceased and their friends who participate in the funeral wear mourning clothes or armbands. The type of clothing worn by the relatives is determined by the nature of their relationship to the deceased. When a parent dies, sons and their wives clothe themselves completely in coarse white sackcloth, belting the garment with a hempen rope. They also wear a white cloth hat banded with hemp. The daughters and grandchildren of the deceased also wear garments of white cloth. The daughters and the female grandchildren wear hoods, and the male grandchilren wear white headbands. More distant relatives and friends who participate in the funeral usually wear an armband made of the same coarse white cloth.

Narrow strings of colored yarn several inches long worn on the mourner's arm band, headband, or hood are an additional way of indicating the mourner's relationship to the deceased. The color of the yarn or combination of colors worn indicates whether the mourner is related through the same patrilineal line, through the matrilateral or affinal side, or whether he is simply a friend. In these days most of the villagers are no longer clear which color indicates which relationship and have to ask the older people who should wear what color. However, frequently at different funerals in the village and area there appears to be no uniformity in the wearing of the colored yarn as a means for identifying the wearers' relationship to the deceased. These strings of yarn are worn by all relatives of the deceased throughout the mourning period.

Funeral Ritual

The funeral usually takes place within one or two days of the death. Most people prefer to complete the funeral as soon as possible to avoid undue expense and to enable things to return to normal, but some wealthy families prolong the funeral ceremony and delay the burial as a means of conspicuous display.

Prior to the arrival of the *tao shih,* a roofed three-walled shelter of bamboo and canvas is constructed to house their paraphernalia and an altar. When they arrive, they hang on its walls paper streamers lettered with moral sayings and a number of scrolls. These scrolls, often numbering thirteen or fifteen, depict the main Taoist and heavenly gods, the twenty-four filial acts (*erh shih sze hsiao*), and scenes of the underworld showing the courts of justice for the dead. The latter depict the punishments and tortures inflicted on the immoral and the various forms of reincarnation possible depending on the kind of life the deceased has lived.

Throughout the funeral ceremony, small children are led from scroll to scroll by their elders, usually their grandparents, while each scroll is explained to them. Great care is taken to explain the nature of the rewards for filial and moral behavior and the retribution for unfilial and immoral acts. It seems likely that these gruesome pictures of the punishments and tortures, as well as those which show the forms of reincarnation, make lasting impressions on the young children. In fact, throughout the funeral ceremony there are a variety of opportunities for instructing the young people and children in the moral and filial forms of behavior.

There are usually two parts to the actual funeral ceremonial. One is the ritual conducted by the five *tao shih,* in which they pray for and safely guide the spirit of the dead person through the underworld to the Western Paradise *(hsi fang lo yuan).* The second part is the actual burial ritual. Adjuncts to the first part of the funeral ritual are entertainment performed for the spirit of the deceased and a ceremony to send the spirit on its way. These can be and are performed in either order, and it is not infrequent for the ceremony sending off the spirit to be held after the burial—sometimes as much as a week later. The length of time devoted to these rituals depends on the availability of the *tao shih* and the financial circumstances of the family of the deceased. A prosperous family (like that of a landlord) which is willing to spend a great deal of money on an elaborate ceremony usually takes several days or even a week or more to complete the ceremony. During the entire period many guests are housed and fed, as is expected of such a family. A poor family, on the other hand, may complete the entire ceremony in one day and one night, ending the next morning with the burial. This short form of funeral is the most common in the village.

In the Hsin Hsin area, the funeral sequence usually begins with the *tao shih* beating on drums and shooting off firecrackers in order to "frighten away bad spirits." This is done in the courtyard, and both adults and children hide inside the house so they will not be "hit by [come into contact with] a bad spirit." During the first phase of the ritual, the *tao shih,* often accompanied by musicians, chant and pray for the deceased. They wear colorful hats and robes decorated with designs such as the eight trigrams *(pa kua).* They change their robes as they move to successive parts of the ritual. A member of the family is present throughout the rituals, taking part by kneeling behind the *tao shih* and burning incense. This role is assumed by the chief mourner, usually the eldest son, although another member of the family may substitute for him as a representative for the entire family.

The chanting and prayers of the *tao shih* are interrupted in the late afternoon when entertainment is provided for the spirit of the deceased. The performance of the juggler or acrobat is traditionally paid for by the married daughters of the deceased. Generally, the charge for such entertainment is NT $180 (US $5). This entertainment is held outside in the family's or *tsu* compound's courtyard. A table is set up and a paper ancestral tablet for the deceased is placed on it. Usually, this paper tablet is used by the family for the first year after the death, after which the deceased person's name is transferred to the family line's main wooden ancestral tablet. Today, in addition to the paper tablet a photograph of the deceased is also placed on the table. Then, in order not to expose the spirit of the deceased to the heavens, an open, large black umbrella is tied to the table. The mourners gather at the sides of the table, joined by most of the villagers, who sit or stand in the courtyard to watch the entertainment. Even passersby from other villages join the large audience, and the cheerful reception given the entertainer by the outsiders and even sometimes by the mourners makes it apparent that the spirit of the deceased is not the only one being entertained.

With the completion of this part of the ritual, the members of the *tao shih* group and the several mourners resume chants and prayers in behalf of the deceased which continue long into the night and through to dawn of the next day. This is done in shifts so that the various participants can take time off to eat food furnished by the family and to nap.

During the course of the night a series of ceremonials takes place outside the house and in the *kung t'ing* of the house in preparation for sending off the spirit of the deceased. One ceremony, held outside, simulates the transmission of a letter from the family of the deceased to the underworld. The letter, prepared by the *tao shih*, describes the dead man's life, speaks of his good as well as bad points, and ends with a plea for clemency and forgiveness toward him. All five *tao shih*, carrying flaming torches, conduct the ceremony. One *tao shih* acts as the "forgiveness governor" and carries a paper symbol of the forgiveness governor and the "forgiveness letter." He is followed by three "aides"; together these four men actually run and try to catch the fifth man who is supposed to represent a horse and who carries a *papier-mâché* horse on a pole. The forgiveness governor wants to catch the horse in order to ride it to the underworld to present the forgiveness letter to the gods.

The colorful and exciting ceremony usually attracts a large number of villagers, both adults and children. During the whole spectacle the *tao shih* joke and laugh, which suggests that the ceremony is designed to entertain the audience and the mourners. Some villagers observed that "This ceremony in this very form was passed down from our ancestors, and it is natural and interesting to be so playful since the sad mourners then won't worry so much." When the *tao shih* chase each other and weave in and out they often get tangled up, and each time this happens the horns in the small orchestra are purposely blown

off-key to add to the comedy. Usually, during the last part of the
ceremony, when the forgiveness governor chases the horse at full speed,
all the children present applaud and scream with glee. The adults
laugh and say "it is all right for the children to do this, since it is so
exciting."

After the forgiveness letter has been delivered, final preparations are
made to simulate the trip of the spirit to the underworld and finally to
the Western Paradise. A check is written and signed with the names of
relatives and friends, and this, along with millions of dollars of imitation paper money, is burned by the nearest *tsu* relatives, usually members of the immediate family, in the ancestral-worship room. Throughout the ceremony, the room is guarded by two male lineal descendants
or close patrilineal relatives of the deceased. They stand covering the
door with a straw mat and each holds a large knife in his upraised
hand. The purpose of their vigil is to prevent the spirits of any other
dead persons, especially if not of the same descent line, or any of
various demons, from stealing the money. The ashes of the burned
paper money are wrapped up and weighed by a *tao shih* on a standard
wooden balance scale as proof to the gods of the large quantity of
money offered them. The *tao shih* also pretends to add up the amount
of money by using an abacus. Many villagers watch these proceedings
with great delight since the *tao shih* clowns about while doing them.
The ashes, with a number of other items, are later placed in the coffin
and buried with the deceased.

With the offering of the money to the gods, the spirit of the dead
begins its journey to the underworld and, it is hoped, its eventual
journey to the Western Paradise. The ceremony is only a simulation of
the trip, and the villagers explain that it is hoped the rite "will have
the effect of later easing the spirit's actual trip by showing it the way."
A *tao shih* and all descendants of the deceased who are present make
the journey, carrying a white banner which represents the spirit of the
deceased, an incense pot, the paper ancestral tablet, paper servants,
and a paper puppet of the dead person. The group walks in a circle,
crossing an imitation bridge over and over again, and as they walk the
tao shih tells the people of the "ten acts"—how children should act;
how daughters-in-law should act; how servants should act; how neighbors should act toward one another; how brothers should act; how
wives should act; and so on.

When the underworld has been reached, two *tao shih* and all the
mourners and many village adults and children gather in the ancestral-
worship room. The *tao shih* act out long dialogues and stories which
tell about the trip and the many people, obstacles, and underworld
gods which the spirit has encountered along the way. Many of the
incidents related are steeped in moral precepts, but they are also
humorous and often exciting.

That these stories, as well as the entire funeral ritual, serve several purposes is recognized by the *tao shih* and many of the villagers. First, the stories tend to stress the importance of filial piety and morality. They teach the villagers that "Parents should love but not spoil their children, because a spoiled child becomes stupid"; "Since the parents take care of the child—the parents feed, school, and find a husband or wife for the child—the child should therefore be filial"; "People must marry, since the parents have given us our bodies and we must give the parents another body—a descendant"; "If you are unfilial to your parents, then your son will be unfilial to you, and besides that you will be punished in the underworld." Some stories emphasize the necessity for cooperation between brothers to hold the family together. These stories draw attention to the importance of filial piety, but their moral precepts are presented in such a way as to poke fun at those present whose behavior has in any way been known to be unfilial. The barbed humor is frequently directed at daughters-in-law who do not sufficiently respect their husbands' families, for example, and who therefore talk too much and so neglect their household duties and family responsibilities.

The second recognized purpose of these rituals is to provide a release for the mourners' grief. The emotional intensity of bereavement is moderated by the humorous stories told by the *tao shih*, as well as by the excitement sometimes created by the ceremonies. One *tao shih*, who also operates a small tailoring shop in Lukang, explained, "I don't really believe that the things we do in these funeral rituals actually do anything for the spirit of the dead person. But since the villagers believe in it and want it done, and will pay for the performance of such rituals, I come and do it. It makes them feel better and besides, when we perform all these exciting ceremonies and tell the funny stories, it makes them laugh and helps them forget their sadness." The extent to which the *tao shih's* opinion is valid is seen again and again during the course of the evening's events, as well as during the performance of the juggler. Often, even the most sincerely grief-stricken are unable to refrain from smiling at some of the stories and comical situations. Some stories are so filled with slapstick comedy that they bring almost hysterical laughter from the mourners.

On the trip to the underworld, the spirit of the deceased is judged. A favorable decision is inevitably reached, and the spirit is given permission to go to the Western Paradise. Once again the participating group goes outside, this time to complete the ritual with the journey to the Western Paradise. A paper sedan chair is set on the ground and an incense pot placed next to it. Then a paper puppet of the deceased, paper servants, and paper money are burned while the mourners wail.

It is nearly dawn when all of this is completed, and afterwards everyone present eats a large breakfast prepared by the village men, who act as cooks for the occasion. The meal is elaborate and consists of many of the same meats, soups, and other dishes normally served at a festival dinner.

Burial

During the course of the next day the actual burial takes place in the public cemetery at a time and place determined by a geomancer or *k'an feng shui te jen*. A number of tables are set up in the courtyard of the house beforehand, with many baskets of food prepared as sacrifices to the spirit of the dead displayed on them. These baskets of food, as well as lengths of dark colored cloth covered with written messages of condolence and money, have been sent by relatives and friends. The money and cloth are sent to the family almost immediately after the death. The baskets of food and wine are sent the day the burial takes place.

Once the sacrifices and incense have been set up on the tables, the coffin is carried out of the house and placed at the head of the tables. Many male mourners, including sworn brothers of members of the bereaved family, *ch'in ch'i*, friends, and neighbors—or representatives from the families of these people—then "worship" the spirit of the deceased, each performing an elaborate sacrificial rite on his hands and knees. One of the "heaviest mourners" (those with the closest patrilineal ties to the dead man) accompanies each one in the ritual in order to thank him. Throughout the worshipping the women relatives, especially the daughters of the deceased, lean against the closed coffin and wail aloud.[5]

While this ritual takes place outside the house, a small group of village men goes to the cemetery to dig the grave. When it is time for the burial, the coffin is carried on the shoulders of several men to the cemetery, followed by the mourners. Usually, only the heaviest mourners and close friends accompany the coffin the whole distance (about two miles) to the cemetery. However, many others who attended the funeral come out to the road to send off the coffin and mourners. While still on the road near the village, the closest lineal relatives of the deceased suddenly turn to these others and crawl on their hands and knees toward them. This is done as a form of obeisance, to thank them for their participation and to beg them not to bother to go to the cemetery. Then the mourners are helped to their feet by friends and more distant relatives such as *ch'in ch'i* and run to catch up with the coffin and the other mourners.

At the cemetery an elaborate ceremonial is conducted by a man who is often a combination geomancer and shaman (*fa shih*). In his capacity as geomancer, he is present to see that the coffin is placed in the proper position, and as shaman he is expected to invite the gods to the ceremony and, especially, to obtain the god of the earth's permission to break the earth and to ask him to accept the body. Once the burial is completed, all return to the village where an elaborate dinner is held for all those who participated in any stage of the funeral.

Several weeks after the burial, on a date set by a geomancer, the members of the mourning family reconvene at the cemetery to dedicate the tombstone. They again wear white mourning clothes, and a ritual is conducted by the same geomancer-shaman.

Mourning

After a death, the descendants usually observe heavy mourning for forty-nine days (seven weeks). During this period they worship the spirit of the deceased twice each day, at sunrise and sunset, coming together to wail and chant as they did on the day of the funeral.

On the hundredth day after the death, or sometimes after one year, another mourning ritual is held. On this day it is common to burn the temporary paper ancestral tablet and transfer the dead person's name and death day to the family's permanent wooden ancestral tablet. Until very recently, the name was placed on a small permanent wooden tablet instead of on the temporary paper one, which made it unnecessary to transfer the name to the main family tablet. It is also on the hundredth day that the mourning family sends sweet cakes to everyone who sent money or gifts at the time of the death. The sweet cakes are a symbolic message "that things are now better."

For three years after the death, patrilineal descendants of the deceased are supposed to wear the lengths of colored yarn to show they are mourning. At the end of this period, they usually wear red yarn for a few days just to show that things are now good again. Actually, in the village the colored mourning yarn is most frequently worn for only a year. It is also customary during this three-year mourning period for the women to wail at the grave when the family goes to the cemetery each Ch'ing Ming Chieh (a holiday early in April) to clean the graves and offer sacrifices.

If in the years following a death the family has not been able to produce a boy child or has been in financial difficulties or poor health, they may have the grave dug up and the coffin moved to a new and more propitious spot determined by a geomancer. This takes place at least three years, but usually more than ten years, after the death. Specialists from Lukang or from some other village are hired for such an occasion. These men, in the presence of the closest relatives of the deceased, pick out each bone, clean it, and attach it in a special order to a short charcoal pole which is placed in a tall ceramic pot. The pot is then reburied in the new grave and a new tombstone, engraved with the date of reburial, is set up.

Actually, few people go to the trouble and expense of reburial. Those who take this unusual step do so only because they believe that their misfortune is attributable to one or both of two causes: the initial burial was made in an unlucky spot, so that the spirit of the earth was disturbed and is therefore troubling the family, or the spirit of the dead person is unhappy in that spot.

The rituals connected with death are numerous and complicated, and most of the survivors, not understanding why they are supposed to do many of the things required during the funeral ceremony, simply follow directions given by the old people and the *tao shih*. In most instances the old people themselves disagree about the meaning of the various parts of the rituals. However, whether or not they understand the reasons or purposes of the rituals, the village families follow directions "because it is filial to do these things, and it is also good for the ancestors and for ourselves."

[8

Religion and Magic in Hsin Hsing Village

The importance of religion in Chinese life has long been under-
estimated by many Chinese and Western scholars. This underestima-
tion is due in large part to the apparent lack of a formally organized
religious system characterized by sacred and pious activities. In truth,
though, a very structured system of religious (and magical) belief does
exist and is functionally important in the life of the people.

In the Hsin Hsing area (and apparently in most of rural Taiwan)
this system is characterized by a strong belief in a supernatural or
spiritual community which is composed of the spirits of natural objects, the spirits of ancestors and deified heroes, and evil spirits or
demons, all of them able to influence or affect the lives of the villagers.
The system functions to merge these entities "into a harmonious
whole. The individual person not only has to fit himself into customs
and institutions of the living but must adjust himself to the needs of
the members of the spiritual community in order to remain *en rapport*
with them so as to win the happiness he longs for" (Kulp, 1925:284).

We have already seen something of how the material and spiritual
communities are functionally integrated in various aspects of life in
the Hsin Hsing area. We saw, for example, how the religious family
and its associated religious rites function to buttress the precarious
solidarity of the families and *tsu* groups through their periodic divi-
sions, and how the various rites of passage, marking off the transitional
phases of the villager's life cycle, help to reaffirm his identity within
the family, its extensions, and the community. In this chapter, we will
observe the religious and magical practices common to the area: the
frequency of the supernatural rituals and the extent to which they
pervade and influence village life, and the degree to which some have
been modified in participation or performance or in the significance
the villagers attach to them as a result of changes in other aspects of
the society, especially in socoeconomic developments.

231

We will also see that although some religious or magical act is performed in the village almost every day of the week, either by a family or by the village as a whole, this is not necessarily an indication of piety and veneration as the West understands religion. For the Taiwanese villager, the observances are not necessarily sacred only; many villagers have pointed out that they "make life interesting and exciting, and the people look forward to them with great enthusiasm." Not only do such activities have a significant function in Taiwanese society but, as we shall see, many villagers are extremely aware of the importance of many rituals to the continuity of their society and patterns of living.

CONCEPTUALIZATION OF SUPERNATURAL BELIEFS AND ACTIVITIES

The villagers' practices are not based on a strong belief in any single concept of the supernatural. There is, in fact, so complete a mixture of religious and magical beliefs in the village that it is often difficult to determine where one form ends and another begins. While elements of popular Taoism and ancestor worship are the strongest and most apparent, there is a clearly Buddhist influence, and the moral and ethical teachings of Confucianism are extremely evident. There are also important elements of animism out of which has "grown a complex of attitudes and values" (Kulp, 1925:284) and a system of divination by which the "spirits of wind and water" (Kulp, 1925:284) may be controlled; this is referred to as geomancy (*feng-shui*).

The funeral ceremony (described in Chapter 7) clearly shows the presence of this admixture in the villagers' beliefs. There are elements of Taoism and Buddhism in the ritual of the journey of the spirit of the dead to the underworld for final judgment, punishment, and rebirth in the next world, but there are also evident Confucian teachings and even remnants of animistic beliefs. It is perhaps most accurate to say that all these beliefs have been combined into a single loose system, and the average believer makes no attempt to define or distinguish the different elements of the whole.

Confucianism

While Confucianism is closely integrated within the religious system, there is no formal cult or official Confucian ritual in Hsin Hsing village. Although there is a Confucian temple in Lukang, usually only residents of that city worship there.[1] However, the moral and ethical teachings of Confucianism are present in the rules of correct behavior which have been passed down from generation to generation of villagers. Filial piety, respect for age and authority, and worship of the ancestors are all considered both important and fundamental to correct behavior. Aptly expressing a rather general feeling, one villager said, "Everyone knows it's natural to act this way. What other way is there to act?"

The development of this attitude is promoted chiefly by examples in everyday life which are a part of a child's general upbringing. Children are frequently told stories which emphasize the rewards of filial and virtuous behavior. The scrolls displayed and the stories told by the *tao shih* during funerals (see Chapter 7) contribute greatly to the indoctrination. In addition, the use of formal kinship terminology constantly reminds children of the importance of proper behavior towards their superiors or elders. Terms of respect (utilizing kinship terminology) which take into account the relative age and generation of all relatives and even friends and neighbors are learned early and indicate the way one person is expected to act toward another.

Children and adults are also constantly reminded of the "moral way" by door hangings whose elaborate calligraphy exhorts them to proper behavior as well as wishing them good fortune. While most villagers cannot actually read the characters, they know what they mean. These scrolls are usually purchased in Lukang; nowadays many of them bear anti-Communist, nationalistic slogans which mean little to most of the villagers who buy them.

The schools consistently emphasize many of the basic traditional moral values. Textbooks present stories about acts of filial piety or respect for elders and those in authority and emphasize the value of reasonableness, compromise, and cooperation, and, of course, patriotism and even extreme nationalism. In addition, special topics or themes are stressed during certain weeks. For example, the schools observe "filial piety week," during which they stress obedience and respect for age, teachers, and parents. Other weeks are devoted to the importance of love and charity, respect for country, and the national flag. Thus, we find the moral and ethical teachings of Confucianism constantly reaffirmed in everyday life.

Ancestor Worship

Ancestor worship, which is closely related to Confucianism and the mystique of filial piety, and whose rituals actually reinforce it, is a form of religious belief to which virtually all Hsin Hsing area villagers adhere. The believers are not, however, in agreement about the effect ancestors have on the lives of their descendants. Many in Hsin Hsing do not agree that ancestors provide positive aid to their descendants, but few would deny the misfortunes that are sure to fall if neglected ancestors vengefully fail to protect their unfilial descendants from the many negative spirits.

Since ancestral spirits live in the other world much as they did in this one, they must be fed, cared for, and propitiated. "If these things are not done, the ancestors will be hungry and dissatisfied and in a sense themselves turn into negative spirits, known as Good Brothers (*hao hsiung-ti*). They then wander about causing trouble for any humans with whom they happen to come into contact."

The firm belief in the dangers of neglecting the ancestral spirits seems, in itself, to be an important contributing factor to the failure of Christianity to establish itself in the area. While there are no Christians in Hsin Hsing or in surrounding villages of the immediate area (which has prompted missionaries to label the area "the infidel strip"), certain residents express anxiety over the proximity of several Christians in villages not more than three miles away. They particularly fear danger from the Christians' ancestors. When people are converted to Christianity, they destroy their ancestral tablets and cease to worship and care for their ancestors. Naturally, these neglected ancestors are expected to wander around the area, causing trouble for anyone they come upon and stealing the food and other things people offer to their own ancestors. Since there are few pressures the community can exert to make these Christians continue their ancestor worship, they are a source of constant danger and apprehension to their neighbors.

They are also a source of bewilderment. Villagers find it difficult to understand why anyone would want to assume such an "uninteresting" and unfilial religion and consequently miss the great interest and excitement of the *pai-pai* and the thrills of shamanistic rituals. One village woman remarked that "It must be very dull to be a Christian; all they do is go to church and sing songs." In fact, this same woman advised me "to practice the religion of the people of America when you are in America, and to practice the religion of the people of Taiwan when you are in Taiwan. That is the only way to get fun out of life."

Since the belief in the potential influence of ancestral spirits for good and evil is so strong, the relatives of a dead person who has left no descendants will often adopt a child to worship the deceased. An example of such a case was cited by a villager: "There were three brothers and one died before he could have any children. The second brother gave one of his own children to worship that dead brother, as a descendant worships an ancestor. This child then also inherited the brother's property. There are very few cases in this village or anywhere where a strange child is adopted for this purpose. Thus, after a person has died it is common to give the dead person a relative as an adopted child for the purpose of worship and inheritance." However, if a family lacks the forethought to adopt a child, they may find it necessary to do so at a later date. If they are unfortunate in their affairs, the cause of their troubles is often laid to a relative who left no descendants to care for his spirit. It then becomes necessary for the family to placate the spirit by adopting a child as his official descendant and worshipper. All such adoptions are eventually recorded on the ancestral tablet. The name of the adopted child is engraved next to the name of the deceased, along with a note stating that he was adopted for the purpose of continuing the line (*ch'eng szu*).

Buddhism

In the Hsin Hsing village area, Buddhism, at least as an independent religious system, is of negligible importance. While there are visible elements of Buddhism such as the scroll bearing the image of the goddess Kuan Yin, it is difficult to distinguish features of Buddhist ritual from Taoist features. Women take the most active part in all forms of Buddhist worship, and once each year they worship at scattered temples located in the *hsien*. In spite of the mixture of religious images in Buddhist temples, the Buddhist rites are distinctly identified as such.

Popular Taoism

Of the various religious practices discussed thus far, popular Taoism may be said to occupy the most time and attention of the Hsin Hsing villagers. Popular Taoism is a debased derivative of Lao-tze's "Way" and centers around a hierarchy of gods infiltrated by many diverse supernatural beings or forces. Belief in these supernatural entities is derived from the Yin-Yang principle, the concept of the universe as the sum of the infinity of all the positive and negative forces that comprise it. In popular Taoism, the positive and negative forces have become personified; thus, it is not only necessary to have priests (*tao shih*) but shamans (*fa shih* and *t'iao t'ung*) too are needed to conduct religious ceremonies to worship the gods and to perform magical rites to propitiate the evil supernatural beings who might otherwise harm the believers.

The hierarchy of gods in popular Taoism is ranked in order from the highest T'ien Kung, the heavenly God (also referred to by the villagers as Yu Ti, the Jade Emperor), down through others of lesser importance, to an assortment of village gods and private, individual gods at the bottom of the hierarchy. Many are historic personages of the early dynasties, particularly the Sung and T'ang, who have been deified for their remarkable deeds. Their feats are well known, although the stories of some apparently have mythical backgrounds.

The villagers consider the hierarchy of gods to be fashioned on the order of the imperial court of traditional China. They are thus, as described by one of the better educated older villagers, "what would be the equivalent of an emperor, ministers, marshalls, and generals. In this hierarchy T'ien Kung is the emperor. Right under T'ien Kung are the three brother gods, San Chieh Kung: (1) T'ien Kuan, the god of heaven; (2) Ti Kuan, the god of earth; and (3) Shui Kuan, the god of water." In addition, the gods which reign in the underworld are regarded as high and powerful gods.

After these there is a whole lesser series which inhabit local areas such as villages. Some of these lesser gods have specific functions in which can be seen the mixture of magic in religion, for example, providing aid to the villagers when they are faced with illness in the family or fire in a house. Others help when general misfortune befalls the village or an individual family. (These will be discussed in detail below.) The lesser gods also function as intermediaries or "ambassadors" between ordinary people and the higher gods, since mere mortals cannot take their prayers or wishes directly to the highest gods but must transmit their prayers through these lesser gods, just as they must employ certain priests or shamans in order to communicate with the lesser gods; this was seen in the premarriage ritual described in Chapter 7, when a *t'iao t'ung* performed in this way.

The parallel between the system of gods and that of imperial China is heightened by the attribution to the gods of their own armies of soldiers and horses. Each god's importance and power, of course, determines the size of the army he possesses. Since the soldiers and horses protect the gods and carry out their work, sacrifices offered to a god must include food for his soldiers and hay and water for the horses.

The villagers [noted one informant] believe that the gods within the hierarchy, much like ancestors, do not punish people when they do not worship. Instead the gods' action is positive, since if the people do worship the gods, they will protect the people and help make their lives run smoothly. If they do not worship, the gods will neither bother them nor help them. This is equivalent to giving them trouble since the people believe that without the gods they will have trouble in life and nothing will run smoothly. The gods are not considered possible sources of doing bad since they are holy men (*sheng jen*) and therefore won't hurt the people. People do not think of the forces of nature as good or bad. They only know from experience that life is hard and that they need the gods to help make things run a little more smoothly. Therefore, worshipping the gods is traditional, and so long as life is difficult, people will grow up generation after generation worshipping the gods in the same way.

For these reasons, the villagers worship the gods not only when they desire aid but also on the gods' birthdays and other special occasions.

Statues of the gods are usually carved by master craftsmen in Lukang, a well-known center for such work in Taiwan. They may be owned by individual families, by a *tsu*, or jointly by the entire village population. Hsin Hsing village owns the statues of two gods: one of the main village god, Ta Shih Kung, who is said to have accompanied the original founders of the village from the mainland, and one of the Earth God T'u Ti Kung. These statues were purchased with "public money" collected for religious purposes.

Some individual families have statues of personal or private gods whom they worship. There are two families in Hsin Hsing which have private gods: one of these gods, Er Shih Kung, has become very important in the village. He is considered powerful, his aid is frequently sought, and many of the villagers worship him on his birthday. The other private god is worshipped by only the one family. Their origins are unknown; according to the owners, the gods came from the mainland with their ancestors.

Origins of such private or personal gods are varied. Sometimes the origin is a vision. This is the case with one man in the area. For years he had been plagued by bad luck. He had no children and could not make an adequate living. One stormy night, walking through a wooded area, he was frightened by a flash of lightning, which showed him the form of a man in ancient costume high up in a tree. Fearing for his life, he claims that he immediately vowed to build a statue in the image of the vision and worship it as a god. In the twenty years since that day his fortunes have changed, and today he is a wealthy man with many children.

The great importance one of the private gods in Hsin Hsing has taken on has enhanced the prestige and prominence of the K'ang family which owns his statue. The majority of the villagers worship Er Shih Kung each year and frequently go to him for aid in time of illness or other emergency. Each time this is done, the contribution of the K'ang family to the village welfare is recognized. The family receives certain material benefits from the villagers, and families which feel they have benefited from Er Shih Kung's help feel a sense of obligation to the K'ang family. As a result, they feel obliged to help whenever the K'ang family needs some kind of favor. Each of the many village families which join in the *pai-pai* held by the K'ang family for Er Shih Kung on his birthday contributes several large, sweet, steamed cakes as sacrifices. These are kept by the K'ang family as custodians of this useful deity.

However, some village families feel a degree of antagonism towards the K'ang family; they feel that the K'angs are abusing their position. The most bitter antagonism is that of the Huangs, the family which owns the other personal god, which the village does not recognize. The Huang family is bitter about the situation and is joined in its antipathy by some others who appear to have been stirred up by its many criticisms of the K'angs. However, despite the bitterness, the two families do not express their antagonism openly, for this would be a serious breach of etiquette. Interestingly enough, neither of the two families which personally possess these private gods is a member of any *tsu* organization in the village. It appears that the possession of these gods by the two families is a means that each family has used to establish a place for itself in the village. The family in possession of Er Shih Kung, the god which has become popular in the village seems to have actually achieved this goal.

Other Supernatural Beings, Forces, and Beliefs

In addition to gods and ancestors the villagers believe in evil supernatural beings. They are known as demons or *kuei*, but, out of fear of their malevolence and respect for their power, the villagers more often speak of them as gods or *shen*. The already mentioned Good Brothers belong to this group of *kuei*. "When one hits such a bad thing," one's spirit becomes possessed or is taken away by the supernatural being, and sickness, ill-fortune, or even death may result. It then becomes necessary to secure the services of a shaman or diviner to determine the cause of the trouble and appease the spirit.

Fate and Divination

Beyond and stronger than the influence of gods and spirits is an all-pervasive force, fate. It affects and predetermines the over-all direction of life and events. The fate of an individual is determined by his eight birth characters and "the set of forces of Yin-Yang and the Five Elements, which were connected with the movement of the stars in directing the mystical operation of time, which, in turn, determined the nature of personal events" (Yang, 1961:135). The Hsin Hsing villagers' belief in the concept of fate was well described by Kulp (1925:171) for Phenix Village when he wrote,

Fate decides all things. Fate determined the time of birth and it will determine the hour of death, the manner of death and the experiences between birth and death. It is useless to strive against fate. All one can do is to learn the will of fate and conform in the best possible way. One may try to outwit fate but sooner or later one is doomed to defeat. Such are the attitudes that people hold regarding the great events and experiences of life.

This belief leads to various forms of divination that are designed to determine what the individual has in store for him and what, if anything, can be done about it. Thus, if resort to ancestors, gods, magic, or medicines fails to produce results, the difficulty is accepted as predetermined by fate. The concept is especially valuable in preventing a weakening of the general belief structure, for if all attempts at manipulation through supernatural influence should fail, the concept of fate offers an acceptable explanation of the failure within the framework of the system.

THE ANCESTRAL-WORSHIP ROOM OR *KUNG T'ING*

The village family or *tsu* perform most religious and magical activities in the *kung t'ing* where the statues of the gods and the ancestral tablets are housed. This is a central room in every village house (see house diagram in Chapter 2), whether it is a large *tsu* house with many apartments belonging to component families or the small house of a nuclear family. Some households which reside in the apartments of a large *tsu* house reserve a small part of one of their own rooms as a kind of *kung t'ing* where they maintain ancestral tablets bearing the names of their own deceased parents or their own most recent ancestors. However, these households continue to share in the maintenance of the main *kung t'ing* of the *tsu* where a tablet recording all the names of the *tsu* ancestors is housed.

The *kung t'ing* of a Hsin Hsing village house is fairly representative of those found in the homes of the area and the homes of urban Taiwanese. (Today, usually it is only the mainlanders in Taiwan who do not have such a *kung t'ing* set up in their homes.) The appointments of the room include an altar which stands against the wall opposite the main entrance. Above the altar may hang two calligraphy scrolls which flank a scroll depicting the Buddhist goddess Kuan Yin. Statues of the main Taoist gods, a few in glass boxes, and the ancestral tablets stand on top of the altar. Incense receptacles and wine cups are placed before the statues of the gods. In front of the altar stands a large table on which food offerings are placed during worship. On ritual occasions this table is moved away from the altar and used as a dining table. The last appointment is an incense pot which hangs from the ceiling a few feet from the entrance to the *kung t'ing*, wherein the spirit of T'ien Kung, the highest god, is said to reside. He is not represented in statue form.

In many respects the care and function of the *kung t'ing* indicate the nature of village religion and its relation to other aspects of village life. Although this room is the most important single site for the performance of ritual activities, it is by no means limited to "sacred" events. The family entertains guests here on both religious and non-religious occasions, and it also serves as a meeting place for the family to sit and talk. Because it contains an electric light bulb, children play or do their homework here, and women gather here to work on fiber hats. Perhaps the most "profane" of the uses to which this room is put, particularly if the *kung t'ing* belongs to only one or a few households, is its use as a storage place for sacks of rice or fertilizer and mounds of sweet potatoes. In the case of a jointly owned *kung t'ing,* several members of the large *tsu* who share in the ownership of a harvesting machine or winnower may store the machinery in the room.

The multiple uses to which the *kung t'ing* is put account for its usually untidy and cluttered condition. It is seldom cleaned or dusted. Dust and ashes from burned paper money and incense accumulate during the period between the New Year's clean-up and the sanitation inspection of the village by the police and public office people.

In the Hsin Hsing area, statues of the gods are housed in the *kung t'ing* of village families or in temples. Actually, only the very powerful gods, such as the goddess Matsu and some of the underworld gods, are housed in individual temples, usually in Lukang or some other town. The Earth God is the only god who has his own small temple in each village. His temple is known as the T'u Ti Kung Miao. In a few larger villages a temple sometimes is built to house all the statues owned by the community. But Hsin Hsing and other small villages of the area have no such temple, and village-owned statues are therefore maintained in the *kung t'ing* of private homes. When it is necessary to worship many gods at one time, the gods are invited to come from their resident *kung t'ing* to the single *kung t'ing* which is to be the center of worship for the occasion.

Each year two different Hsin Hsing village families are charged with the responsibility of housing and caring for the statues of Ta Shih Kung, the village god, and T'u Ti Kung, the Earth God, and for arranging any events which concern these particular gods. Each family head is in charge of a single statue and is called a "pot master" (*lu chu*). (The term "pot" apparently refers to an incense or fire pot often used in the worship of a god.) The pot master is usually assisted by several men.

The pot masters and their assistants are said to be chosen by the gods themselves at the annual formal celebration of the village god's birthday. On this occasion, the names of all the village family heads are read out singly "to the gods," who are asked to make their choice. To determine the god's answer, kidney-shaped blocks are thrown in turn by each family head. The ways in which the blocks fall are interpreted as either an affirmative or negative reply. A third possibility is that the god is laughing at you. The men who are rewarded with the most positive responses are named pot masters and assistants. Not infrequently, the old head of the household who is selected as pot master is already virtually retired. In such a case, it is realized that a son will handle the great responsibilities of the job.

Occasionally in Hsin Hsing, pot masters have taken their responsibilities seriously enough to spend a great deal of their own money to refurbish an old and worn statue of the god. In one such instance, a very poor but devout pot master for the Earth God realized that the villagers did not intend to contribute to the care of the god's statue. As a pious act he used his own money for this purpose. He was apparently motivated in part by his need for security within the village community. His family is poor and unrelated to any of the other large or small patrilineal kin groups in the village. He appears to have counted on this act to assure his family of assistance at any time of need in the future. And, in fact, his gesture was much appreciated by the village as a whole. It greatly improved his reputation and strengthened his family's relations within the village.

In addition to the village-owned statues which are cared for by the pot masters, there are also several statues of public gods which are owned by individual families and kept in their own family *kung t'ing*. Some families are more devout than others and may spend a great deal of money, sometimes as much as NT $300 to 400 (US $8–11), to purchase a statue of a god. These families generally own a statue of the Earth God and may sometimes purchase the statues of minor local gods to which they have taken a special fancy.

PRIESTS AND SHAMANS

The villagers depend upon specialists to communicate and deal with the gods and other supernatural spirits in their behalf. These specialists are either the Taoist priests known as *tao shih* or the shamans known as *fa shih* and *t'iao t'ung*. Since the powers of these men are not the same, the manner and degree to which they are able to function as intermediaries between the ordinary people and the supernatural varies widely.

The *tao shih*, as a member of a religious priesthood, functions purely as a religious practitioner. He is able to conduct rituals and ceremonies, but has no supernatural powers. The *fa shih* and the *t'iao t'ung*, on the other hand, have definite personal supernatural powers which enable them to cope with evil forces. Of the two, the villagers consider the *fa shih* the more powerful, because he himself has powers which enable him to confront the demons and exorcise them. The *t'iao t'ung* has no power himself but "only borrows his power from the gods"; it is only while he is possessed by a god that he has any supernatural powers.

There are no *tao shih* living in Hsin Hsing. Those who conduct services in Hsin Hsing are usually residents of Lukang. Almost all of them are ordinary family men who do not earn their livelihood by farming but have shops of some kind in the city. They are, so to speak, "their own boss"; their businesses can either be closed temporarily or some employee or member of the family can be left in charge for one, two, or even three full days at a time when a funeral or some other ceremony must be performed. It would, of course, be impossible for a farmer to engage in activities which might call him away from the harvest or other such imperative activity. Furthermore, most farmers lack the modicum of literacy necessary for the performance of certain ceremonies.

The *tao shih* in Lukang received their training from older members of the priesthood. These men do not belong to an organized church, for there is none in Lukang. In fact, the priesthood itself is loosely organized and informal, although all its members in the area do wear a special signet ring. A man who wishes to become a *tao shih* declares his intention to an established priest and, with the latter's permission, joins his group as a novice. He is given instruction in the various ceremonies and learns how to use the special ritual instruments. As his training progresses, he accompanies other members of the group on their trips into the countryside and assists as they perform ceremonies. Eventually, he either becomes a member of the group in which he received his training or conducts ceremonies as a independent priest.

There are three *fa shih* and three *t'iao t'ung* in Hsin Hsing village serving it and neighboring villages. Actually, these men seldom perform outside the village, and shamans from other villages are occasionally called into Hsin Hsing by people who were not helped by their village shaman or who, for personal reasons, prefer a shaman from another place. This is especially true in the case of a nonresident *fa shih,* an older man, who is considered more powerful than the ones in Hsin Hsing. However, such cases are infrequent, and most people find their own village shaman sufficiently able to meet their needs.

Too, most villagers find it economically advantageous to engage the services of a local shaman rather than an outsider. When the *fa shih* or *t'iao t'ung* is a fellow villager, one is not expected to pay him any fee for his services, but need only feed him after he performs. The food is usually a simple noodle dish or rice and meat soup. Although it is prepared in large quantities in order to feed all the villagers who were present during the shaman's ritual, the cost to the host is small. But when a shaman is called from outside, he must be paid a fee in addition to being fed with the other participants. The money is normally wrapped in a packet of red paper and handed to the shaman. The villagers usually know how much they are expected to pay, and both parties assume that the amount will be adequate. If the family does not give the shaman enough money, the villagers note that "the shaman probably will say nothing, but will not return should he be called."

Most families make every effort to compensate the shaman amply and are just as anxious to satisfy their village shaman. The family feels some debt of gratitude when he performs a ritual for them without payment. In some cases they even feel obliged to repay him in some way and may be unusually cooperative when he needs assistance. They may help him with some minor work in his fields, or may patronize the store which is owned by one *t'iao t'ung,* or buy meat from the intinerant butcher, also a local *t'iao t'ung.*

Thus, a shaman does receive certain indirect compensation for his work in his own village, but since there is so little opportunity for actual or direct financial recompense, one wonders what moves a man to take up such an occupation. In the cases of the *fa shih* and *t'iao t'ung* in Hsin Hsing and neighboring villages, the motivation clearly is not any mental or physical abnormality. These men are male members of the community without observable afflictions who only in their performance as shamans become anything out of the ordinary. At all other times they function in what appears to be a perfectly normal manner.

However, the shamans of Hsin Hsing do seem to share one trait which is less evident in their fellow villagers. They all are somewhat aggressive men seeking to raise their status and prestige in the village. Apparently, the greatest inducement for them to become shamans was the opportunity the occupation presented for gaining position and recognition. Since the status of a villager depends at least in part upon his rendering public service to his village and area, every time a shaman performs he receives recognition for his contribution.

The most frequently employed *fa shih* in Hsin Hsing is a rather intelligent man presently attempting to accumulate some land, who recently built a small building in which he grows mushrooms. He seems to be trying very hard to raise his status in the village, and in his active role of *fa shih* he manages to keep in the public eye. The villagers feel that he gives a great deal of his time for the village and for his fellows. The two other *fa shih* in the village are older men who for various reasons are called upon only to perform certain functions. One of them is frequently away from the village, since he works in Taipei.

The three *t'iao t'ung* in Hsin Hsing are men who are not exclusively engaged in farming. The *t'iao t'ung* for the village god Ta Shih Kung, a butcher who peddles meat on a bicycle and does some farming on a small piece of land, is a minor partner in a butchering company located in a village about two miles from Hsin Hsing. Unfortunately, this man has been ill a great deal, and since he has frequently not been available when the villagers wished to communicate with the god, his services are not often employed. In his stead the villagers call the *t'iao t'ung* for the important private god, Er Shih Kung, who makes himself readily available and is willing to perform. This is surely one reason for Er Shih Kung's growing popularity. This man, about thirty-four years of age, owns the village general store, does a little farming, and is the head of the Farmers' Association's village unit. In addition to these undertakings, he also takes an active part in all village events such as the coordination of village funeral arrangements.

The third *t'iao t'ung* for the less important village private god, Chu Wang Yeh, now has a vegetable stand in Taipei. His family still resides in the village, and he travels back and forth between the village and the city. However, he usually is not available in the village when his services are needed. On occasion, other Hsin Hsing villagers living in Taipei call upon him to help them communicate with the god.

It appears, then, that the two most active shamans in the village are the young *fa shih* and the *t'iao t'ung* for Er Shih Kung. These men apparently enjoy the popularity and increased contact with the villagers which their work affords them. At the same time, they undoubtedly recognize that their position in the community is enhanced each time they perform "a public service."

Any village man may become a *fa shih* if he is willing to devote time and energy to the intensive training involved in this undertaking. Master *fa shih* in Lukang or elsewhere are available as instructors. Under the tutelage of such a master, the novice learns how to conduct magical rituals and use potent charms and instruments of coercion with which he is able to exorcise malevolent demons or other spirits. In addition, the novice is taught the "special language of the gods," which enables him to communicate with them through the medium of a *t'iao t'ung*.

The latter has the ability to go into a trance and become possessed by a particular local god who, when he enters the body of the *t'iao t'ung*, speaks to the people in his own tongue. Only the *fa shih* can interpret this special language. Supposedly the *t'iao t'ung* does not understand it, and, like Western mediums, he claims he is unaware of what has taken place while he was in the trance.

The *t'iao t'ung* in the service of a local god is "chosen by that god" to serve him much as the god chooses his pot master. However, in this case, the candidates include only men who are interested in serving the god and the village, rather than representatives from all the village families. The prospective *t'iao t'ung* receives his training from, and is taught the god's language by, a master *fa shih* from Lukang. The training is conducted in complete secrecy and lasts for seven days.

Once the training is completed and the shaman is considered able to cope with the supernatural, he can be called upon to perform magical rituals when an illness strikes, particularly one which cannot be explained easily or cured quickly by present-day medicine, or for any other problem in which the cause is believed to be supernatural.

The *t'iao t'ung* also sometimes deals in divination while in a trance. At such times the god speaking through him may, for example, give advance notice of future events such as the visit of a "guest god" from a distant area like the mainland of China or even some coming change in the life of a villager or in the village itself.

Perhaps the most important specialist in divination, however, is the geomancer. As we have noted earlier, he determines the auspicious time and place for important events like marriage, burial, or building a new house. He does this through the use of his special almanac, which is based on astrology, the conceptions of Yin-Yang, the Five Elements, and so on. The geomancer himself is usually an ordinary man, very often a farmer, whose divining activities are performed in his spare time for a small fee. He has generally been trained by an older geomancer, very often a relative. The training consists mainly in gaining a mastery of the uses of the almanac and in acquiring a familiarity with the formalities and proper sequences of the events which he must give advice about. One geomancer in Hsin Hsing village is scarcely literate, yet he has apparently mastered enough knowledge about his almanac's contents and the proper sequences of events to be employed frequently, especially in surrounding villages outside of Hsin Hsing. Hsin Hsing villagers, however, seem to prefer to call in an outside geomancer rather than to consult their own fellow villager. The villagers' awareness of the relative illiteracy of geomancers in general (who are nevertheless still called in for consultation) makes one suppose that the formal qualifications of the practitioner are less important than his acceptance as a recognized geomancer. His powers may not be considered to depend entirely on the amount of formal training he has had, or his function in relieving the members of the family from the responsibility of making a difficult decision may be sufficiently valued to make his actual qualifications unimportant in their eyes.

Other kinds of diviners, fortune-tellers, or people who are said to be able to communicate with the dead can be found in Lukang and other such towns and cities. Fortune-tellers are frequently itinerant, and occasionally pass through the villages offering their services.

When a fortune-teller happens to come through the village, it is not unlikely that he has heard that some family there has a problem in which a fortune-teller may be of assistance. In Hsin Hsing, for example, the very wealthy K'ang landlord family had nine daughters and two sons. Apparently, it was generally known that the family would like to give one daughter out for adoption, but was hesitating to do so for fear they would be criticized. It was at this point that a fortune-teller "happened" to come to the village and offer his service to the

K'ang family, which immediately consulted him. In the course of reading the family's fortune he conveniently found that portents for the
future were unfavorable but could be positively influenced if one
daugher were given up for adoption. This course was adopted and
quickly acted upon. There was now little fear of village criticism, since
the action was clearly necessary to preserve the family's good fortune.

SUPERNATURAL RITUALISM

All religion exists to provide at least an illusion of protective
control against the uncertainties of nature. Although efforts to draw a
clear line between religion and magic are usually not successful, certain differences can be pointed out. Generally, religion has some
ethical or moral content, while magic contents itself with a more limited scope. Religion functions to preserve a concept of the universe in
which man can survive (almost always including after death) so long
as he obeys the rules; and the rules are those which his religion teaches
him. Depending on the complexity of his particular religion, his
priests may or may not be able to intercede directly for him with the
mighty supernatural beings who are his gods.

Magic, on the other hand, does not usually have a strong ethical
content; generally, it is completely pragmatic. In its concepts, supernatural forces or beings exist; they may be relatively indifferent to
man or may be beneficent or malevolent. The essential thing about all
of them is that they are subject to certain controls which can be
wielded by man (often by specially gifted individuals only). As
Malinowski (1948) has often pointed out, the art of magic is the
manipulation and coercion of impersonal supernatural powers in
order automatically to bring about a definite and desired end. In the
Hsin Hsing village area, although it may be at times difficult to draw a
clear line of distinction between religious and magical rituals, both
types are nevertheless identifiable.

As to clearly religious rituals, I found that Hsin Hsing area villagers
usually draw a distinction according to the cyclic or noncyclic nature
of the religious rite. The normally expectable events like birth, marriage, death, and some other such "rites of passage" or "crisis rites"
which are noncyclic have already been discussed in Chapter 7. I will
now discuss the fixed, recurrent group rites, usually referred to in the
literature as "rites of intensification."

Cyclic Rites

The villagers' calendrical schedule of *pai-pai* contains only rites
associated with formal religious holidays. However, there are other
cyclic rites whose time schedules are determined strictly by the individual family or *tsu* group; though cyclical, they fall into another

category which will be labeled for convenience noncalendrical. Both categories, whether the rites are performed by the village or community, or by the family or *tsu,* are rites of intensification which foster solidarity and reinforce social and cultural values.

Of the recurrent rites whose timing is determined by the family rather than the village, one type of non-calendrical *pai-pai* consists of those connected with the agricultural cycle which are held regularly by most village families at the same general times of the year—the rites to the Earth God, T'u Ti Kung (usually following the transferral of rice seedlings into the paddy field), those following the sale of one's pigs, and the like. In the former instance, the hired field hands who helped transfer the rice seedlings join the male members of the family in eating the sacrificial food offerings, including "meat, fish, wine and other good things." In the latter instance, after propitiating the Earth God, the family eats its simple sacrifices which may include wine if friends or nearby *ch'in ch'i* are invited.

The other kind of recurrent rite is the ancestral-worship ceremonies; these are not included in the category of such rites commonly carried out according to the calendrical schedule of religious rituals. However, a number of rites associated with ancestral worship, such as those held on the lunar New Year, the fifteenth day of the first month, Ch'ing Ming Chieh, and the fifteenth day of the seventh month, are regular cyclic rites performed by everyone at the same time. It is the anniversaries of the death dates of a family's ancestors (determined separately for or by the individual family or *tsu*) which are not considered part of the annual calendar of the community. On such an occasion, either the individual family, several patrilineally related families, or a whole *tsu* group or religious family will worship the deceased ancestor. The worship is always held in the *kung t'ing,* since not even the larger village *tsu* have ancestral halls. The number of family units which participate in the worship depends upon whether the ancestor is held in common by many families or considered the progenitor of only one particular family. As already explained in Chapter 5, in Hsin Hsing village the women usually take the leading part in the ceremonies, even though they are in a sense outsiders worshipping their husbands' ancestors.

The ceremony usually begins with the burning of incense at the time of day at which the ancestor died. The food offerings "sacrificed" are later eaten by the participants. The amount depends upon the economic situation of the family or families. Well-to-do families will offer larger quantities of food than poorer families, which usually means that a greater number of relatives and friends will be invited to share the feast. However, the food considered proper for sacrifice on any occasion is relatively standardized regardless of the financial condition of the family, varying only with extreme wealth or poverty.

Thus, most villagers sacrifice to the ancestors higher quality foods like pork, fowl (chicken, duck, or goose), fish, vegetable and soup dishes, steamed cakes, rice, and noodles. In addition, wine is offered, incense and paper money are burned, and firecrackers are set off. (On the occasion of other *pai-pai* held bimonthly, only minimum sacrifices of meat and fish, not fowl, are offered.)

The ancestral tablets indicate which ancestors should be worshipped. In addition, each religious family usually maintains a "remembrance board" as a reminder of the exact date on which to worship which ancestor. The death dates of all who must be worshipped are engraved on this board, which hangs on the wall of the ancestral-worship room. By relying on it, each family or group of related families is sure to fulfill its responsibilities to its ancestors. The board supplements the memories of the old people, who usually inform the family when it is time to worship some ancestor.

Generally, a single ancestor is worshipped for about two or three generations, or as long as someone remains who remembers him in his lifetime. When no one remains who remembers him alive, he, together with other more or less forgotten ancestors from times long past, is worshipped only on one designated day of each year, and then perhaps by the *tsu*.

The lunar calendar forms the base for the schedule of calendrical rituals—the *pai-pai* which are celebrated by the whole village on set days. One such important rite is the *pai-pai* for unworshipped, anonymous ancestors. Such forgotten and neglected ancestors wander about the countryside looking for sustenance, becoming negative powers or harmful spirits (*kuei*) which often make trouble for people. Although they are regarded as demons, the Taiwanese follow universal custom and refer to them euphemistically, calling them good brothers (*hao hsiung-ti*) to avoid antagonizing them.

Pai-pai for the good brothers are held regularly on the second and sixteenth of each lunar month by all the villagers of the area. On these dates each household worships individually, but outside of its house since "one does not invite negative powers or spirits into the *kung t'ing*." The sacrifices for this occasion are usually quite simple and consist of vegetable soups and perhaps some cut-up pork and/or fish. No fowl is sacrificed.

The villagers also tend the spirits of other unknown people. Skeletal remains dug up in a field may be placed in a small wayside temple; this is considered a "devil temple" but is euphemistically called a Yu Ying Kung Miao (temple of responding gods) and exists for the sole purpose of housing the bones and spirits of unknown people. The villagers annually go to the temple with sacrifices to feed the spirits of these unknown dead. At night many villagers consciously avoid the devil temple for fear that they may be harmed by its spirits.

In addition, the villagers also worship spirits of the unknown dead which have been confined for long periods of time or even permanently to the underworld for having led immoral lives. During the seventh lunar month these spirits are released and permitted to journey to the surface, where they roam about for the entire month. At this time they must be offered sustenance. The villagers refer to them as good brothers also, but, unlike the good brothers worshipped on the second and sixteenth of each lunar month, these good brothers are "criminal" good brothers.

Until a few years ago each community in the Hsin Hsing area and the city of Lukang worshipped them with large *pai-pai* on different days of the seventh lunar month. The many *pai-pai* held throughout the month made it possible for the people in one place to invite people from elsewhere to share in their feast. While this was very exciting, it involved a great deal of "waste," and so in the early 1950's, in the interests of austerity, the government decreed that the seventh month *pai-pai* must all be held on the same day, the fifteenth day of the seventh month. Today, therefore, since there cannot be outside visitors, each *pai-pai* is quite modest, with only pork, vegetable dishes, fruit, incense, and paper money being sacrificed. These are offered not only to the good brothers but also to an underworld god known as P'u Tu Kung who watches over the good brothers. The villagers call this occasion, the fifteenth of the seventh month, Chung Yuan.

The most frequent *pai-pai* which villagers define as calendrical are the four which are held independently by all village families on the same days of each lunar month. On the first and fifteenth all the gods and their soldiers and horses are worshipped. On the second and sixteenth days of each month, as mentioned above, offerings are made to the good brothers. These *pai-pai* are simple, and the villagers call the food sacrifices "rice and vegetables," meaning soups and cut-up pieces of pork or fish. No fowl, whole fish, or large slabs of pork are sacrificed on these occasions. Since all the families worship individually at the same time, there are no outsiders present to share in the food sacrifices.

One of the most important family holidays of the year is celebrated in winter in the first lunar month—the Chinese New Year. Although each family tries to have all its members together for this occasion, in the last several years a number of villagers who work outside have not returned home to celebrate this holiday on the excuse that the transportation facilities are too crowded and that it is difficult to travel. As a matter of fact, by remaining in Taipei during the holiday and continuing their work as pedicab drivers, these men are usually able to double their earnings because of the increased business. Nevertheless, many of the older people are quite unhappy about this situation. It is interesting that these same village men do come home in April to celebrate the birthday of the village god Ta Shih Kung, which they consider a much more exciting and gay (*je nao*) time to come home than the New Year.

The New Year's celebration actually begins on the twenty-fourth day of the twelfth month, when the villagers send the gods off to heaven. They burn incense and a special paper money called *chia ma* and shoot off firecrackers. The paper money bears a picture of a horse which symbolizes the horse on which the gods ride to heaven. The families sacrifice fruit and cake at a very simple ceremony.

On New Year's Eve the villagers worship their ancestors in the *kung t'ing.* "Since this is the last time of the year that the ancestors are worshipped, many sacrifices are offered." The next day the worship of the ancestors begins anew and is repeated daily until the third day of the first month. On these three days the villagers also worship the three brother gods (San Chieh Kung), and many of them, including men, young women, and children, spend their time gambling during the period of rest from work.

The fourth day of the first month is called Chieh Shen or "welcome the gods." On this day the gods who went to heaven come back to earth. The villagers offer sacrifices and burn incense and paper money to welcome them back.

The ninth day of the first month is the birthday of T'ien Kung, the highest of the gods. Although the villagers consider him a vegetarian, they nevertheless sacrifice pork, duck, and chicken in addition to vegetable dishes and cakes, explaining that T'ien Kung eats only the vegetables, but his friends and the other gods eat the meats.

The fifteenth day of the first month, called Shang Yuan or "the first full moon of the New Year," is the occasion for worship of all the gods and ancestors with sacrifices of meat, vegetables, incense, and paper money by each individual family.

Late in the second month or early in the third is Ch'ing Ming Chieh, "one hundred days after Tung Chieh" (the winter solstice). On this day, village families go to the cemetery to clean and sweep the graves and worship their ancestors. If a family has built a new house, married a son, or produced a baby boy during the year, they will hold a special ceremonial and offer many sacrifices at the grave site. In addition, for three years following the death of a member of the family, a special ceremonial takes place at which the female members of the family wail as they did at the funeral. Only the families which hold the special ceremonial invite guests to eat with them; this feast is held afterwards, at home.

The twenty-third day of the third month is the birthday of the goddess Matsu, who is said to have been a very good Fukienese woman deified because of her commendable deeds. Originally, she was the protectress of seafarers, and her statue was brought from the mainland by the earliest Chinese immigrants to Taiwan. However, over the years the residents of the Hsin Hsing area have endowed Matsu with considerably greater talents, and today she is considered capable of doing many things—curing the sick, aiding in the production of a boy child, bringing rain when it is needed, and even helping someone win the National Lottery. The villagers tell a story about a man from a village in the area who went to the Lukang Matsu temple and prayed for success in the lottery. When he did not win, he returned to the temple and with a sword lopped off one of Matsu's ears.

Middle-aged village woman often discuss seriously Matsu's magnificent feats. One day several women told "how, several years earlier, Matsu had saved some boys from drowning in the Strait of Formosa just off Lukang. When a sudden storm came up, the boys' boat sank and they were about to drown when Matsu came and saved them." The women debated the question of just how Matsu had accomplished this, one saying that the goddess had provided a bridge for them to get back to shore and another that the goddess had furnished another boat and pulled them ashore.

Numerous other Taiwanese also credit Matsu with enormous powers,[2] and each year many people from far-off villages and even cities travel to Lukang in long processions by hired trucks, bicycles, pedicabs, sedan chairs, and on foot to worship Matsu on her birthday. Some Hsin Hsing villagers also go to Lukang to worship Matsu on this day, but most worship her at home because they are too busy to travel to Lukang. However, Lukang is considered a very exciting place when it is filled with the tens of thousands of people who have come to worship Matsu, and many villagers, especially young people and women, go there in the evening to watch the festivities.

In addition to the recognition which is accorded Matsu on her birthday, for at least the last forty years Hsin Hsing and eleven other villages in the area have held a joint procession each year to worship Matsu some weeks after her birthday. About this time of the year, when the irrigation water is running low in the fields of Hsin Hsing and two neighboring villages of the other eleven, the occasion is taken to ask Matsu to bring much-needed rains for the rice crop. As far back as the late 1800's, these same twelve villages were allied together to provide mutual defense against the many bandits who then ravaged the area. While the necessity for such defense was eliminated soon after the arrival of the Japanese, the cooperative relationship between these villages has been continued through the annual Matsu procession. The Matsu procession, then, still provides an occasion which brings the people together, not only the residents of a single village, but those of many villages. In the Hsin Hsing area it is the only time in the year when the twelve former allies come together and reaffirm their traditional unity, even though some of them may have been at odds with one another.

Each year a different village of the twelve declares its willingness to be host and takes the lead in organizing and arranging the procession. Leaders of the twelve meet there and decide which villages will furnish the entertainment which is provided along the route to and from the large Matsu temple in Lukang. The individual villages then organize, assigning by lot the various duties among their families. Some villagers are called upon to carry the large sedan chairs which bear the statues of the village gods, and others prepare and transport refreshments to the prearranged places where the procession stops for rest and food. When the lots are drawn to determine which family will assume which task, the names of the village's large landholders are always included in the drawing. While they often willingly donate refreshments, they are loath to carry a sedan chair; now, as in the past, if selected to carry one, they usually pay another villager to replace them.

On the day of the procession, the villagers assigned to carry the sedan chairs assemble at a prearranged spot to begin the circuit through the twelve villages. A large statue of Matsu, borrowed for the occasion from her temple in Lukang, is carried in a big sedan chair by several villagers. As the procession passes through the village, the residents worship the goddess, and a local shaman invites her to eat. Village teams of performers accompany the procession. They dance, give exhibitions of traditional boxing and sword play, act out little incidents or excerpts from traditional Taiwanese operas or stories, or do a dragon dance in which a large, green paper dragon is carried over the heads of many men who weave in and out to simulate his sinuous movements. The whole occasion is extremely gay and entertaining and, it is felt, most rewarding. Many food offerings to the goddess are displayed in each village along the route. They are provided by each village family and are eaten at dinner in the evening, after the Matsu procession has passed. However, only the host village, where the Matsu statue remains overnight, or members of the wealthier or large villages invite guests from outside to share in the feast.

In the spring of 1958 the area was in dire need of water, since it had not rained for several months. Several hours after that year's Matsu procession began, the sky became overcast and by mid-afternoon a drenching rain was falling on the procession as it moved through the area. By the time the circuit was completed the rain had stopped, having flooded the rice paddies and saved the crop. It did not rain again for over a month. The villagers who do not believe in the power of Matsu were surprised. A few of the young men, some of whom are well educated, have told me that despite their skepticism they did feel that "Perhaps the rain on that day was more than just a coincidence."

The twenty-fourth day of the fourth month is the birthday of the Hsin Hsing village god, Ta Shih Kung. Those villagers who have been working elsewhere normally come home for this *pai-pai,* and even some of the members of village families whose business or work has required them to move to the city return for this day and stay overnight or several days with relatives in the village. The main reason for this influx is that the celebration is one of the gayest and most festive of all those held during the year.

All families worship Ta Shih Kung in a joint *pai-pai* held in the courtyard of one of the largest *tsu* houses in the village. A shaman is present to exorcise any devils that may be near and to invite the god to eat the sacrificed food, the best the villagers have all year. Guests are invited from all over the area to join in the festivities, and for weeks or even months in advance the villagers issue invitations to relatives and friends. At the time of the *pai-pai,* the villagers even invite their neighbors' guests, if they happen to know them, to eat their food. People walk through the village, pounce upon acquaintances who are ambling along or who may have just come out of the house of another villager, and tug at their arms and clothing to get them into their homes to eat. (My wife and I were virtually dragged through seven different dinners that evening.) The villagers generally prepare so much food for the occasion that there is always enough for a few more, and they talk for months about the number of people they entertained that day. One old woman, a member of a relatively poor village family, boasted that she had had seventy guests at her house and that she had fed three tables of guests five times. Some of these guests stayed overnight and had to be fed again the next day. She spent NT $700 (US $19.50) on food and wine and had been saving her money for months for this occasion.

For the most part, all these guests reciprocate and invite the Hsin Hsing villagers to join them at the *pai-pai* celebrating the birthday of their own village god at a later date. The *pai-pai,* therefore, functions to maintain relationships with *ch'in ch'i* and friends and to enable families to meet new people. In addition, since the villages hold these *pai-pai* at different times, the people of the whole area are assured of a continuing source of entertainment.

The entertainment includes not only the good food and the contact with different people but also a puppet show performed by a professional group hired from a city. The puppet show is based on stories from dynastic history and is a source of delight to the villagers and their guests. Adults and children from neighboring villages usually wander over during the course of the day to watch the show. The carnival atmosphere of the occasion is augmented by the presence of vendors of food, sweets, sugarcane, and betel nut who come from Lukang and surrounding villages to sell their wares.

The puppet show and other communal expenses of the *pai-pai* are paid for with money collected from each village family by the pot master for Ta Shih Kung and his assistants, who also arrange for the show. Each village household is assessed an amount calculated on the basis of the amount of land operated (whether owned or rented) and the number of people in the household. The families of village shamans are not required to contribute any money on such occasions. In 1957 and 1958 all other households contributed NT $7 for each *chia* of land they worked, NT $1 for each male member of the household, and NT $0.50 for each female member. The approximate amount of village money spent for each of these annual celebrations of Ta Shih Kung's birthday was NT $1,150 (approximately US $32).

As the day's festivities draw to an end, the pot master gives an accounting of the expenditures which is accompanied by much arguing and accusations when a controversy arises over the way he handled the money or how the arrangements for the *pai-pai* were made. It seems to be usual for the sides of the controversy to be drawn along *tsu* lines. The final event of the day is the selection by lot of next year's pot master and his assistants. Some villagers watch the throwing of the blocks hopefully, wanting to be allowed to assume this position of honor and responsibility; others await the outcome nervously, hoping they will not be selected. If a man is chosen to be pot master or assistant, he has no option but to perform the job.

During the fifth and sixth months, the busy agricultural season, there are no important village *pai-pai* other than the usual four to worship the gods, their soldiers and horses, and the Good Brothers. Most festive holidays and calendrical rites fall in months when the farmers are not busy with agricultural chores. (See Figure 3.)

The fifteenth day of the seventh month, called Chung Yuan, the day when all the villagers worship the good brothers and Pu Tu Kung, the god in the underworld who watches over them, has already been discussed. The usual worship of the gods and their soldiers and horses on the fifteenth (and the first) of the month is omitted in the seventh month, however, since the gods are thought to be absent from the village while the Good Brothers are there.

The fifteenth day of the eighth month is the birthday of T'u Ti Kung, the Earth God. On this day the villagers hold a *pai-pai* at his temple which is located on the road in front of the village. Each village family worships individually with sacrifices of pork, vegetable dishes, and moon cakes (*yueh ping*). No guests are invited to dinner on this occasion. However, if a family has a hired man working for them, it is customary to invite him to share the meal.

In the ninth month there are no special *pai-pai*, but around the middle of the tenth month, the village has one of its largest joint *pai-*

pai of the year on the occasion called *tso p'ing-an.* By the time of this *pai-pai,* the farmers have harvested their rice, and at the ceremonial worship of T'ien Kung, his soldiers, and many lesser gods, they thank T'ien Kung for giving them a good crop and "peaceful days." The ceremony is held in the courtyard of one of the largest village *tsu* houses, and a shaman invites the gods to partake of the sacrifices. Huge

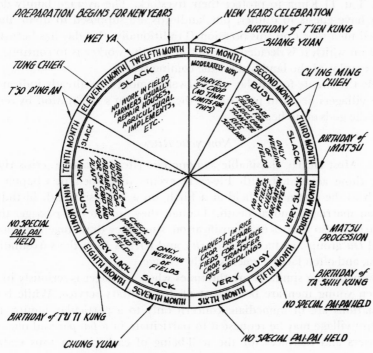

FIG. 3. A comparison of agricultural and religious calendars (lunar months).

amounts of paper money are offered to the god, but several informants noted that the village can no longer afford to hire a group of puppeteers to perform on this day.

Each village in the area arranges to hold its *tso p'ing-an pai-pai* on a different day. Thus, for a period of almost two weeks, the villagers busy themselves with visits to *ch'in-ch'i* relatives and friends to help them celebrate their *tso p'ing-an* festival. Hsin Hsing village alone entertains hundreds of guests on this occasion. But the amount of participation by village families in such socioreligious activities depends upon the number of friends and especially *ch'in ch'i* with whom they have maintained good relations.

Some time during the first half of the eleventh month, the villagers celebrate Tung Chieh. Each family worships its ancestors in the *kung t'ing* with steamed round dough cakes and other simple sacrifices. Some families also worship at the village Earth God temple, and others go to the Matsu temple in Lukang.

The sixteenth day of the twelfth month is called Wei Ya and is the last day of the year on which the Good Brothers are worshipped by each family. On this day the villagers also go to the Earth God temple to ask T'u Ti Kung to protect their livestock. The average family does not have guests to dinner, but landlords are supposed to invite their hired men to eat on this occasion. Traditionally, this day has been the one on which it is decided whether or not the worker is to continue in the employ of the landlord for the coming year.

By the twenty-fourth day of the twelfth month, as already indicated, the villagers begin to prepare for the New Year's celebration by sending the gods off to heaven.

Noncyclic Rites

Most clearly classifiable as noncyclic rites of passage (crisis rites) are those associated with life-cycle events (described in Chapter 7) such as the ceremonies held at a birth, on a boy's sixteenth birthday, upon marriage, and at death. Though they are rites of passage, they function also as rites of intensification, since they draw together family and *tsu* groups, including *ch'in ch'i* and friends from the surrounding area, and often large segments of the village.

Functioning similarly are the times when a villager is seriously ill or when young men are being sent off for military service. While both situations are of immediate concern only to a particular family, the entire village may be requested to participate in a *pai-pai* and offer its prayers and sacrifices for the well-being of each person thus endangered. In case of a serious illness, the patient's family requests the villagers' participation by sounding a gong at dawn of the day on which the *pai-pai* is to be held. It would be rare for any village family (no matter what its relationship with the sponsoring family) to be unwilling to participate.

Still another noncyclic *pai-pai* which clearly functions as a rite of intensification rather than a rite of passage occurs when a god from some distant place comes to the village for an unscheduled visit. The villagers may be notified of the impending visit by a local god speaking through a shaman (*t'iao t'ung*) while he is in a trance. On the day of the announced visit, the entire village holds a joint *pai-pai* to welcome and worship the god. The occasion may become a regular *pai-pai* event as a result of the shaman's earlier announcement and may eventually become a part of the village's regular cyclic calendar of rituals.

MAGICAL RITUALISM

As indicated earlier in this chapter, magic requires a distinctive type of ritual in Hsin Hsing village supernaturalism. Perhaps the most important single use for magical ritual in the Hsin Hsing area is the curing of illness. As we noted above, the increased availability of Western medicine, especially since the early 1950's, the accessibility of practitioners trained in these ways, and the evidences of their success have turned the villagers more and more away from traditional practices, at least as the major and usually the initial source of help. Thus, the villager now tends to turn to the magical ritual only when he feels that modern science has failed him. However, it remains true that the traditional ritualistic patterns fulfill social, psychological, and even therapeutic functions beyond what is possible for the scientific.

The Diagnosis of Illness

Nowadays, when illness strikes, the villagers observe its symptoms and try to determine its nature. From experience with certain basic sets of symptoms, illnesses are distinguished as being either in the realm of the physiological or supernatural, and therefore requiring a cure within that particular realm. Thanks to the villagers' new awareness of the germ theory of disease, most illnesses are immediately classified as physiological and, therefore, within the domain of science and medicine—primarily modern, Western-style medicine rather than Chinese herbal medicine. Such illnesses as measles, rashes and skin diseases, trachoma, colds, stomach disorders supposedly resulting from bad food or water, and the like, all fall clearly into this category. To treat these illnesses, it is now customary for the villagers either to call in a Western-style practitioner or to choose their own drugs or patent medicines.

There are still a few illnesses or symptoms, however, which are likely to be considered of supernatural origin—caused by a demon or one of the many spirits which are believed to inhabit numerous natural places and objects. These supernaturally caused ailments are best treated by supernatural means. Some forms of insanity, and the frequently unexplained crankiness in children—especially in cases where the child's spirit is believed to have been affected by a "frightening" incident—fall within this area.

It is a commonplace among villagers that "No medicine can help if a person runs into something evil," for example, one of the demons known as *kuei* or *mo shen*. Consequently, when the practitioner of Western medicine is unsuccessful in curing an ailment, the illness is clearly of supernatural origin and must be attacked by someone versed in supernatural methods—the shaman.

There is no particular problem with illnesses which can be clearly diagnosed as natural or supernatural. But there are many cases in which the diagnosis is not so easy or clear-cut. Mainly, the villagers rely on past experience to tell them which set of symptoms indicates which category of illness, and thus which kind of practitioner to call in. Naturally, there are considerable variations among the villagers themselves which may predispose a decision in one direction or the other—level of education, amount of experience, financial ability, and even types of social pressure. As one would expect, the actual availability of drugs and doctors affects choice. In recent years the dependence upon Western medicines and Western-oriented doctors has increased as a result of the increased supply of both at relatively low cost. The ease of access to antibiotics and patent medicines, their effectiveness, and the doctors' record of successes have given confidence in Western science, with the result that it is common today for the villagers to turn to Western methods first for most illnesses.

Many villagers now also feel that it is simpler to call in a Western-style doctor. A shaman often requires the assistance of two or three other people who must be asked in to help in the ritual, at their convenience. Further, when the Western doctor is called in, he charges a fee, and with its payment the transaction is completed. There is no residual feeling of obligation which must be discharged. The shaman, if he is a local one, usually charges nothing at all for his services, and often it is more comfortable not to incur such a feeling of obligation. Then, there are a number of incidental expenses connected with his visit—the cost of sacrifices and the food for all the participants and observers at the ritual.

Having two types of medical practice at one's disposal is not always an unmixed blessing, however, since the decision that an illness is natural or supernatural may be, or may be held to be, influenced by external circumstances. A case in point is the following which happened to a very poor family in Hsin Hsing. The parents were no longer young and already had three daughters and a small son when another daughter was born. Before the infant was named (naming takes place on the ninth day and is, in effect, when an infant becomes human) she became quite ill. Instead of calling in a practitioner of Western medicine, which many villagers insisted they would have done first, the family chose to consider the illness supernatural because the baby was not yet nine-days-old. They called in one shaman, and then another. Despite their efforts, the infant died. Under the traditional ideas the death was attributable to the will of the gods, and the family had done all it could do. The villagers gossiped busily about the event, however, noting that the family was poor and had too many girls already; implicit in their gossip was a recognition that the family may have preferred to have the female infant die.

The attitude of the villagers toward the old and new medicine is a useful example of the way in which practical, external factors can affect "folk" beliefs and values. Here availability, finances, and family circumstances have combined to promote the acceptance of a new body of knowledge. The rural community of the Hsin Hsing area has accepted Western medicine without damage to its value structure or to its beliefs, incorporating the new quite comfortably into the old framework. Thus, when the villager calls upon a Western-style medical practitioner first of all, and the illness is not cured, he can still reinterpret the symptoms and assume that the cause was supernatural after all—perhaps possession by a demon. Then, to cope with the supernatural, he calls in a shaman.

Shamanistic Curing

Probably the most common form of illness treated in this manner is that which the villagers call a "fright" (*ching*). In this "illness" a child or infant does not eat or sleep properly and cries a great deal. The mother may decide that the child "has hit into a bad thing" (*ch'ung*) and that some kind of malevolent demon is causing the trouble. Although she may call in a Western-style doctor, most villagers assume that such symptoms result from supernatural causes and therefore require supernatural treatment.

The many different kinds of charms and instruments at the disposal of the *fa shih* are designed to enable him to bring about the release of the child's soul or spirit. If the patient does not respond at once to treatment, it may be repeated in a day or two or a more powerful *fa shih* may be called in. For the most part, whatever was causing the symptoms, they usually disappear after a few days, and the villagers consider that the *fa shih's* powers have cured the child.

Sometimes in the case of a fright a parent will attempt to effect a cure without the aid of a formally recognized shaman, especially when it appears that the child has been frightened by a definite agent which has caused his spirit to leave his body. If, for example, a dog is believed responsible, the parent will secure some of the dog's hair, wave it over the child's chest, and repeat over and over, "child's spirit return to the child." Or, the parent may feel that the child was frightened by some person. This was the case when a bearded American friend of ours visited the village and frightened a child. The American was then asked to spit into a cup brought by the child's mother. The saliva was brewed with some soup, fed to the child, and incantations were repeated to help the child's spirit return.

Often the cause of the illness is not so easily discernible nor is its cure effected so simply. Even when a Western-style doctor is summoned, the anxiety of the patient's family may be so great that while the doctor is attempting to cure the illness, they may resort to supernatural techniques to discover its exact cause and necessary treatment. On occasion, a village family may either go to a fortune-teller in Lukang or consult one who happens to pass through at the time to learn the cause of the trouble. More frequently, however, they call in a *t'iao t'ung* to communicate directly with a god to learn what kind of supernatural being is involved and exactly how it may be successfully appeased or exorcised.

The *t'iao t'ung* goes to the family's ancestral-worship room and there sits among the people who, out of interest in the session or concern for the sick person, have gathered to observe the ritual. As those around him sit and talk, the *t'iao t'ung* stares into space; gradually, his hands, feet, and body start to shake. Usually, in fifteen minutes he is in a trance and possessed by the god. At this point he becomes extremely agitated and starts to scream and chant. He springs high into the air and blindly staggers around the room. One or two men hold a special cloth apron he wears in order to prevent him from injuring himself or those around him while he is convulsed. Within minutes his paroxysm subsides, and he is brought to the altar where he begins to chant in the language of the gods. An assistant (a *fa shih*), sits at a table in front of the altar and asks the pertinent questions in the special language. Through the medium of the *t'iao t'ung*, the god gives his answers. These are recorded by the assistant, who in some cases is known to be illiterate. The assistant writes certain characters with a brush and ink on a special paper. Once the god's words have been recorded he is presumed to depart, and the *t'iao t'ung* comes out of his trance. He usually is wet with perspiration and sometimes bears injuries incurred while he was convulsed.

In some cases of illness, the instructions the god gives to effect a cure can be carried out immmediately by the family itself. The god tells the cause of the ailment and gives directions for the appeasement of the spirits, e.g., the family must burn a specific amount of paper money as an offering for them. In addition, the family may be directed to feed the patient some herbal medicine prescribed by the god to eliminate the fever caused by the presence of the demon.

In some cases of illness, however, the god will inform the people that a cure can be effected only if the demon is not only appeased but also exorcised. In such an instance, it is necessary to call in a *fa shih* who has powerful means at his disposal to accomplish this feat, such as charms, a sword, and a whip with a handle shaped like a snake (symbolizing a mythical white snake which helps the gods fight the demons). In addition, the *fa shih* may make an agreement with the demon, who can be bought off with bribes of food and money, to make him release the victim's spirit and then leave.

If neither the supernatural efforts of the *t'iao t'ung* and the *fa shih* nor the medical efforts of a doctor produce a cure, the family may conclude that the supernatural causes of the illness require more than medical or magical means. Recognizing the inadequacy of man and shaman in the situation, they are forced to decide that it is necessary to appeal to the gods for help. The family then asks the entire village to sacrifice to the gods in the hope that they may intervene in behalf of the sick person. If even this effort fails and the patient dies, the villagers then conclude that the person was "fated to die at this time." While one informant noted that "Fate is a person's explanation of what has already happened," most villagers feel that "a person is fated to die at a certain time and the gods can do little to control or change that fate. If the person becomes ill when he is due to die, it is no use to call a *t'iao t'ung*. That person's life is already full and so there is nothing that can be done to make his life longer. If the gods could save those who are fated to die, then later there would be so many people that people would eat people."

A Case in Point

During my stay in Hsin Hsing village, I witnessed a case in which a family used Western- and Chinese-style doctors, several *t'iao t'ung* and *fa shih,* and eventually a joint village *pai-pai* to the gods in order to cure a sick member of the family. The family's twenty-year-old daughter had displayed signs of insanity over a period of several years. When she was disturbed she was subject to attacks of extreme depression accompanied by brief, but sudden, outbursts of intense crying, screaming, and cursing. When anyone, including her parents, attempted to quiet her, she would strike out at them wildly. For weeks at a time, the girl could scarcely perform her ordinary duties. Then her aberration would pass and for several months or nearly a year the girl would behave normally until she was taken with another attack.

The first of these attacks took place while the girl was living in Taipei, where she kept house for her father who worked there. The girl's mother and other siblings were living in the village, working the family's small piece of land. When the girl first became disturbed, a Western-style and then a Chinese-style doctor were called in to treat her.[3] When they were unable to help, a master *fa shih* was called in and, according to the villagers, cured the girl completely. However, the *fa shih* became angry when he was not given enough money as a reward for his aid. The family and villagers feel that as a result he put a curse on the girl and that since that time she has suffered these intermittent attacks.[4]

The girl was eventually brought back to the village to live, and it was during the period of one attack that I was able to observe the techniques used to deal with the disturbance. Over a period of weeks a series of *t'iao t'ung* were called in an attempt to determine the cause of the problem. After each visit by a *t'iao t'ung*, a *fa shih* was employed and every time some more powerful master *fa shih* was called upon. Finally, the family of the girl asked the entire village to take part in a *pai-pai* in order to ask the gods to help. Four or five weeks after the onset of the attack the girl's symptoms seemed to disappear, and she resumed her normal village life. The only explanation the villagers could offer for the recovery was that perhaps the powers of the shaman, combined with the help elicited from the gods, rid the girl of the demons which possessed her.

Other Forms of Magical Activities

In addition to the healing rituals, there are other magical activities frequently carried on in the Hsin Hsing village area. When a village house catches fire, prodigious energy is expended on rituals to rid the village of the menacing "fire spirit" or "demon" usually believed to have caused the conflagration. On one such occasion, a *t'iao t'ung* was called in to help the villagers find out how to safeguard the rest of the village from fire, and a *fa shih* was called upon to exorcise the malevolent demon. The fire spirit ritual was held late at night, and practically the whole village turned out to watch the proceedings. The *t'iao t'ung*, assisted by about seven other men, held a large wooden chair which was normally used to seat the statues of the gods during processions, such as that held for Matsu. At the *t'iao t'ung's* initiative, the men began to shake the chair as an invitation for the god to come and sit in it. Gradually, the *t'iao t'ung* went into a trance, and while the god was trying to take his seat in the chair, the men shook it more and more violently, so that it appeared to take the strength of all of them to hold on to it. Once the god was seated in the chair the shaking diminished. At this point the *t'iao t'ung*, possessed by the god, began to chant. A *fa shih* was present to record the god's words, which told the people how they could get rid of the fire spirit and protect the other village houses. The god directed the people to appease the demon by burning paper money in different parts of the village and also advised them to place protective charms on each house. These charms were made by the *fa shih* who had been called upon to exorcise the demon.

By the light of several lanterns and torches, the villagers, the *t'iao t'ung*, and the *fa shih* began to proceed through the village as directed. At intervals during this march, a man carrying the chair suddenly would become possessed by the god. Eventually, all these men became possessed and uncontrollably violent. They writhed and reeled and pulled the chair in different directions. At times the sheer weight of the moving chair caused them to fall to the ground in a heap. Villagers who had come to witness the ritual ran for cover for fear of being trampled by the frenzied men or struck by the chair they wielded. Finally, when the entire route had been covered, the god took his leave, and the men came out of their trances. Many of them bore bruises caused by their many falls under the heavy chair.

The villagers look forward to such exciting occasions and talk about them long after they are past. The exploits of the *t'iao t'ung* are a common topic of discussion among the villagers, and some consider them capable of performing superhuman acts while possessed. The magnificent feats of the *t'iao t'ung* in the old days are commonly recounted, and people admit that there are only a few *t'iao t'ung* in the area who now possess really unusual powers.

Of the magical rituals and shamanistic feats discussed by villagers, one of the most unusual is a feat performed by a *t'iao t'ung* while in a trance walking barefoot on hot coals without being harmed. The villagers note that few *t'iao t'ung* attempt this anymore. Some villagers claim that the *t'iao t'ung* used to walk on water. A young man related a story to me and several villagers about a *t'iao t'ung* who, while in a trance, had tried this several years earlier. Everyone present dissolved into fits of hysterical laughter at the last line of the tale—"When the *t'iao t'ung* tried to walk on the water he went under and was drowned."

However, there are certain classic feats which are performed successfully by the *t'iao t'ung* today. One of the most common is for a possessed *t'iao t'ung* to "cut his head open with a sword" without seriously harming himself. Commonly, this is done at a ceremonial called "taking water," which is performed only once in several years by any particular village, though within the immediate area each year there is usually one village which holds it. A *t'iao t'ung*, while possessed by a god, informs the villagers that they must schedule this ceremony for a specific date at a certain river. On the appointed day, most of the male villagers accompany the *t'iao t'ung* to the river, which may be several miles away. At the river, the *t'iao t'ung* goes into a trance and blindly staggers into the water. All the villagers run into the water after him. He is handed a sword with which he cuts his forehead, and the other men push his head to the surface of the water, allowing his blood to mix with the river water. Since the *t'iao t'ung* is possessed by the god his blood is sacred, and when it mixes with the water, the water is considered holy. At the moment of consecration, the villagers frantically fill the kettles, bottles, and barrels which they have brought with them. The water is carried home and used for its "curative and health-giving powers." Although the villagers of the Hsin Hsing area realize the importance of boiling drinking water, they will drink this holy water immediately after taking it out of the river and claim that they suffer no ill effects.

When the villagers have filled their receptacles, they depart for their own village. The *t'iao t'ung,* who is still in a trance, is carried on the top of a large sedan chair ordinarily used to transport the statues of gods. On his head is a large bandage. Although he has suffered only a superficial wound, the *t'iao t'ung's* actually cutting his head with a sword is impressive to the observers, since the blood flow increases when he dips his head into the water. All along the route homeward other villagers, already informed of the ceremonial, display sacrifices to the god who possesses the *t'iao t'ung* and bring out bottles and kettles in which to receive some of the holy water that is being transported in large barrels.

THE FUNCTIONS OF RITUAL IN HSIN HSING VILLAGE

Having examined the occasion and occurrence of many rites and rituals, we turn now to ways in which they function within the structure of village society and support it. Generally, their most obvious contribution is that participation in the ritual itself helps to relieve the anxiety of people who are desperately seeking to survive in a world of uncertainty or looking for solutions to otherwise insoluble problems. This is true whether the ritual is designed for protection or to moderate natural or supernatural disaster—illness, fire, or demonic possession—since at the very least the villager feels he is coming to grips with the problem. Other results of ritual are less obvious.

Curing rites, for example, resemble all medical practices in having useful side effects or fringe benefits beyond the actually therapeutic. Not only the patient but the whole family must be considered. The Chinese cultural focus on the family emphasizes the reciprocal responsibility of family and individual. Thus, a Taiwanese family must take advantage of every possible means to cure an ailing member or be looked down upon and criticized by the entire community for neglect, which increases the anxiety of the situation.

Therefore, when Western medicine does not work, the traditional-minded villagers turn at once to the shaman, feeling that the very failure proves that the illness is of supernatural origin. But even the skeptical families which have no firm belief in the potency of the magical rituals usually have them performed. This may be partly to avoid social censure, but, in fact, not even the most skeptical are entirely convinced that the rituals are ineffectual. Such villagers have been heard to say, "perhaps the ritual does help. And could one allow a member of one's family to suffer and possibly even die without trying every available means to save him?"

As is true of the curing rituals, the ritual that usually follows a fire in the village also has the important function of alleviating anxiety over this constant threat about which the villagers can do little directly. And, similarly, for another ever-present concern, the taking water ritual serves as a form of health insurance. Thus, these rituals also do much to relieve the constant anxieties of the villagers.

The psychological value of the curing rituals to the patient is very obvious. In Western society, when doctors and medicines cannot cure an illness, there is usually little room for further hope except for the minority who believe in practitioners like Oral Roberts or some other faith healer or miracle worker. In rural Taiwan, however, no one need abandon hope at this point, nor feel totally helpless in the face of the unknown. It is always possible and culturally acceptable to attribute the trouble to some supernatural cause and call in a shaman.

There is a possiblity of real psychological benefit for the patient who can be made to believe that the supernatural is truly the cause of his illness and that it is being dealt with by time-tested, traditional means. If he is, in fact, suffering from some psychosomatic illness, the reassurance that everything possible is being done can have very definite value. The shamanistic curing ritual, of course, also focuses attention on the patient. Family, friends, and villagers join together in the hope that their participation will bring about a successful cure. The attention, and the knowledge that the family has willingly assumed a heavy financial burden to have these services performed, can well give the patient a real feeling of worth and contribute to his recovery.

This kind of reaction can be seen in the case of the village girl, discussed above, who "went mad" (fa feng le). From the villagers' point of view the powers of the shamans, combined with the help elicited from the gods, together rid the girl of the demons that possessed her. Yet, from the Western point of view, it seems reasonable to assume that the rituals may have brought about their purpose in quite a different way—by making her a center of the attention not only of her family but the entire village, they made her conscious that the entire community valued her and hoped for her recovery. Their solicitude could therefore have relieved some of her anxieties and given her the confidence she needed to get well.

Another contributing factor is related to the very nature of the ritual which is used to exorcise demons. The vehemence of the shaman as he attempts to exorcise a demon is impressive enough to hear, but to be the object of his vehemence must be traumatic indeed. The shaman performs alone in the dimly lit house with the patient, while the family and villagers listen nervously from outside, not daring to come near for fear they will be "hit head-on by the demon" as he flees the shaman's magic. The awe and shock which he inspires in the patient could have actual therapeutic value, at least to the extent of bringing about temporary relief if not recovery, and may not be too dissimilar to the effect of electric shock. And fear of the "shock treatment," in either case, may provide as beneficial a result as actual recourse to the treatment.

A social function of ritual, and especially of shamanistic types of ritual, might be briefly considered here. This is its "entertainment" value in rural areas. Frequently, large numbers of people turn out to witness curing or fire rituals, which may last long into the night. They almost always regard the shaman's performance as an exciting event. Many attempt to become participants, and some in their enthusiasm and excitement may even become possessed. Most participate by merely presenting sacrifices. Frequently, large crowds come from surrounding villages to watch the often "amazing feats" carried out in the course of some shamanistic rites. In this process of drawing together for an exciting ritual event, the people gain a strong—if temporary—feeling of social cohesion. Even later, the rituals give the villagers an interesting topic to discuss and gossip about for many days. Thus, although there is little formal entertainment in rural Taiwan, the ritual act often serves to fill its place.

Even though these rituals are performed by so many villagers, it does not particularly indicate absolute faith in the supernatural. While a great number of old people still hold these beliefs without reservations, today most of the villagers express some degree of uncertainty. Generally, villagers say that "many t'iao t'ung are not as powerful as they used to be, and also there are some who are probably fakes, but who can really tell?" (This is a point frequently made in the past by the Japanese when they ruled Taiwan and again today by the present government through the school system.) In addition, the villagers ask, "Who can really know if the t'iao t'ung is possessed by a god and speaking the god's words?" But all the villagers "know from experience that life is hard," and they constantly seek ways to temper this harshness. Although their faith may not be absolute, they "would not dare merely to sit and do nothing" when a sick member of the family showed no improvement, or a child neither ate nor slept for days, or a fire destroyed someone's house. They are anxious, and their continued recourse to magical or religious rituals represents their attempt to do everything possible to allay their apprehension of the unknown.

Thus, even the most skeptical of the villagers will call on a shaman in an emergency. Though the importance of Western medicine has reduced the old primary reliance on ritual curing, social pressure as well as the desire to do everything possible if one method fails forces them to resort to ritual means. Neither their own nor their neighbor's consciences would allow them to let a member of the family die without the attempt to benefit from supernatural intervention.

It was probably these two factors, social pressure and fear of leaving any method untried, which opened the way for the very notable acceptance of Western medicine in Taiwan. While the skeptic is thus forced by them to call upon the shaman, the traditionalists are likewise forced to call upon Western medicine when traditional methods have failed. As we saw in the case of the baby girl who died, the village did not feel that calling even upon two shamans was a clear indication that the family wanted the child to live; it was strongly felt that a Western doctor should have been called in as well. The general disapproval is not simply an example of the increased faith in Western medicine, but a reflection of a total attitude toward the control of unknown and powerful forces. After all, the microbe theory of illness is often, even in the enlightened West, only another species of demonology.

Many of the functions of the magical rituals we have just discussed are also similar for the religious (*pai-pai*) rites. People look forward to the many *pai-pai* held in the village area. At the very least they offer a change in the daily routine of life. Many of them are occasions filled with thrills and excitement (*je nao*). This is particularly true of shamanistic rituals, and scores of villagers may flock to the scene of the performance. Young boys and men who have worked in Taipei and who, for various reasons, have been forced to return to the village almost always attend such events. These men seem to yearn for something to replace the excitement of the city.

Since community pressures for thrift also have tended to standardize the villagers' diet, even the most insignificant *pai-pai* represents an opportunity to eat better than ordinary food. A village family, unless wealthy, is criticized for eating any but the simplest food on ordinary days. People gossip behind their backs about their extravagance and general lack of thrift. Then, if the family should have to borrow money or need village aid at a future date, people may cite their extravagance and irresponsibility as a reason for refusing them. Thus, even the simplest *pai-pai*, like those held on the first, second, fifteenth, and sixteenth of each month, offer people a welcome justification for eating good food, and the bigger the *pai-pai*, the better the food.

The most obvious functions of the *pai-pai* are often recognized by the villagers themselves. There are several other important functions that the villagers may not talk about unless they are questioned about them.

Although in the process of organizing and administering *pai-pai* there may be certain devisive influences (usually along family or *tsu* lines), many Hsin Hsing villagers realize that the *pai-pai,* and to a lesser extent the magical ritual, are the main occasions for show of cooperation and unity within and between families and *tsu* groups in the village. Many independent, kin-related economic family units, which are more than ever before assuming greater economic independence, still come together for ancestor worship. Also, the whole village acts as a single unit when preparations are made for worship at large village *pai-pai* or a few shamanistic rites. Such widespread cooperation among the villagers of Hsin Hsing, and apparently among those in the other villages of the area, is not at all common on day-to-day occasions.

These *pai-pai,* as we have seen, also provide an opportunity for the extension of relationships beyond the boundaries of the village itself. Except for the occasional marriage, funeral, or boy's sixteenth-birthday celebration, the large *pai-pai* ceremonials are the only chances the villagers have to invite outside guests formally and to be invited in turn. Since all of these occasions stimulate reciprocal invitations and visiting, they therefore tend to facilitate contact and thus closer ties with *ch'in ch'i* in other places, which seems to be more and more emphasized in recent years. As we have already seen, the Matsu procession and *pai-pai* tends to foster cooperation and closer relations across village lines.

Even Christian families living in other villages in the area serve a large dinner and invite guests when their village holds an elaborate *pai-pai.* Although they themselves do not worship, these Christians realize that they have few opportunities to have guests and receive return invitations from relatives and friends. On such occasions they also feel obliged to do as the others do in order to avoid the laughter and criticism of their neighbors. People would say that they are either "too tight to spend the money" or perhaps just too poor. Such criticism tends to lower the reputation and general status of the family, and thus even Christians, on occasion, succumb to community pressures.

Religious and magical rituals in the Hsin Hsing area seem in general to be holding their own in face of the socioeconomic changes we have noted—changes brought about by increased economic security, higher standards of living and health, improved communications, and increased mobility. It is clear, though, that some practices of religion and magic have been weakened both in intensity and frequency. For example, many curative magical practices have been supplanted by Western medical practices as a primary means of curing. The significance attached to religious holidays such as the New Year and even some ancestral-worship ceremonies has actually decreased as urbanization and mobility to and from the city have affected village life; the urban-based villagers less frequently find it necessary or particularly desirable to return home for these occasions.

This is far from indicating, however, that all religious and magical practice is on the wane. While the traditional significance attached to some rituals has lessened, that of others has remained the same, and some have even, perhaps, increased in popularity. For example, the large shamanistic (sometimes almost orgiastic) rituals, and certain religious calendrical rituals such as the village god's birthday *pai-pai*, that draw the active participation of virtually the entire village population show no signs of weakening. Their continued and possibly even increased popularity, in fact, seems to go hand in hand with other changes in the society, including the growing influence of city life on the villagers. The same urban-dwelling villagers who can hardly be bothered to return for the more sedate New Year and ancestral-worship rituals continue to pay attention to these more dynamic rituals, as do villagers who have developed important urban ties by past residence or prolonged visits to the city. Perhaps these rites better satisfy the intensified need for excitement and entertainment stimulated by urban experiences.

But there are also other reasons for the continued importance of ritual activities in the life of the village. While the villagers are naturally unaware of the more subtle functions of ritual discussed earlier, they do recognize the part rituals can play in strengthening moral attitudes like filial piety and concepts like community cooperation. The *tao shih* priests, as we saw for example in Chapter 7, are quite open and willing at the least enquiry to tell people of the funeral ritual's multiple purposes, including those of reinforcing the moral system and relieving the anxiety which accompanies both life and death.

Other forms of religious and magical rituals serve to furnish a framework for unity and cooperation in village life whose economic and social bases have been deteriorating. The gradual breakdown of some traditional patterns, formerly based on village community life and socioeconomic necessity, has left an urgent need for some firm means to instill a sense of cohesion in the people who remain in a geographic unit. For this purpose even ancestor worship continues to play its integrative role at the family or *tsu* level.

Thus, with all the socioeconomic developments, despite some changes in form and emphasis, ritual generally is still a vital means of maintaining some semblance of communal life, even if these integrative ritual occasions are manifest only intermittently. It therefore seems reasonable to expect the performance of ritual to continue to have real importance in the lives of Hsin Hsing area villagers, although changes in emphasis are also likely to continue to occur.

[9

Hsin Hsing, Village in Change

In the preceding chapters we have seen how the Hsin Hsing villager, a peasant who was tied to the land and the village community and primarily involved in a basically subsistence type of agriculture, is being transformed to one who is becoming more and more involved in the market economy of the country and who has widespread contacts with an urban way of life. We have seen how such developments are affecting village social organization, community and kinship solidarity, and some of the general patterns of village life. We have also seen that although many features of traditional Chinese culture are still evident in the Hsin Hsing village area (especially in the realm of religion, which continues to be a source of community unity), the impact of increased urbanization in Taiwan in recent decades has brought about important and rather rapid socioeconomic and cultural changes. This has been especially marked in the roles of the village and kinship organizations that were previously the peasants' chief sources of identification and security. We now turn to a description of modifications and changes in traditional values and behavior that further indicate the inexorable direction of change in Hsin Hsing.

Social change is not new to Chinese society. It has been going on for a long time in Taiwan, as well as on the mainland of China, as a consequence of the continuing process of urbanization. However, the process in Taiwan has been accelerated as a direct result of Japanese rule followed by the present rule of the Nationalist Chinese government.

Until the early part of this century, rural society in Taiwan had been relatively stable for many years. Population growth was slow, and there was enough land for the people. Members of the economic families had close relationships with the village as a community as well as with their localized kinship groups. As long as communications were poor, banditry a constant danger, and mobility limited, village unity was essential to security and even survival. Cohesive, tightly knit single *tsu* villages were quite powerful and frequently the de facto govern-

270

ment of the local area. In such villages, composed of a single large *tsu* organization, the *tsu* could virtually control the lives of its member families, unite the entire village population on the basis of common kinship, and thus furnish security to all its members. But even villages like Hsin Hsing, fragmented into many small kinship groups, found their security in complete identity with the village, which made it possible for them to band together and cooperate for mutual security against the everday dangers and problems.

The coming of the Japanese at the end of the nineteenth century saw the introduction of a strong central government which led to an increased orderliness of life. The Japanese also introduced an expanded and efficient system of communications and public health and sanitation measures. These measures, coupled with a stable and secure life, made possible a radical increase in population which became even more pronounced in the late 1940's and 1950's under the Nationalist Chinese government. As all of these developments took place, particularly the maintenance of local order, the ties of the village began to loosen with the loss of its protective function and ability to initiate control beyond its own village boundaries.

In Hsin Hsing (and probably other villages like it), some of the numerous kinship groups began to increase in size and develop into *tsu* organizations as described in Chapter 5. With growth, each group became increasingly concerned with its own sociopolitical influence within the village and even in the nearby area, especially as the former imperative necessity for village unity declined. Thus, Hsin Hsing began to develop into a village with several significant competing *tsu* organizations which started, to some degree, to undercut the formerly necessary coalition of the different village kinship groups. So began the weakening of Hsin Hsing village as a unified community.

As the population increase continued in recent decades, and an already developing problem of land scarcity became even more extreme, it gradually became both necessary and possible for increasing numbers of rural villagers to migrate to the growing cities to find work to supplement their insufficient income from the land. This migration has broadened the villagers' urban contacts and relationships beyond the village. At about the same time, as we have seen in earlier chapters, the villagers have become increasingly more dependent upon and involved with the greater market economy. This has become especially true as patterns of land use have changed in response to all of the changing conditions, so that many villagers are increasingly shifting from what was primarily a subsistence form of agriculture to what is now participation in the market economy of the country. Therefore, there has been an acceleration of the impingement on the village by the outside world.

As the villagers have begun to extend their activities and interests beyond Hsin Hsing, the village's influence on the lives of its members has deteriorated even further. The increase in activities beyond the village means that the proportion of their total activites and hence their involvement within Hsin Hsing is decreased. While the *tsu* continues to perform many of its functions within the context of the village, when its members—by necessity—become more involved beyond the village, even the *tsu*'s role must be affected. The still relatively small and rather localized Hsin Hsing village *tsu* have very limited influence or means to support their members in their needs and relationships beyond the village. And as the villagers seek to establish outside sources of solidarity and security, the *tsu* is even further affected.

The most significant consequence of these socioeconomic developments in the Hsin Hsing area recently has therefore been an even more rapid functional deterioration in the internal village social organization. This is reflected in the decline of the village as a community and source of solidarity for its members. Along with this there has also developed a growing independence of the economic (usually conjugal) family unit from the village and even from the larger kinship group or *tsu* as well as a relatively increased independence of the individual from the family. The Hsin Hsing villagers have thus found it necessary to replace the supportive socioeconomic relations formerly based almost exclusively on village community life and kinship relationships (*tsu*) with relationships beyond the village.

The progress of such cultural changes has been suggested throughout the book. Now I will particularize, and indicate their existence in the context of modern-day attitudes, values, and behavioral patterns towards the family unit, the *tsu* organization, the village, the land, education, and conflict resolution.

Traditionally, the joint family was idealized. Although it often could not be realized in practice, as an ideal it was very highly valued. Division of joint families into individual small conjugal families was frowned upon, and when it did occur—as a result of internal family conflicts born of economically based problems and general poverty—it was quite common to attempt to disguise the split. Often, only the smallest degrees of division were permitted as a means of alleviating the sources of strain between the conjugal units, and when eventually a complete division had to be made, it was usually only after attempts had been made to mitigate the causes prompting it.

Thus, although the small family was most common and the rate of family division was high, great theoretical importance was attached to the large joint family and was reflected in the villagers' behavior. In present-day rural Taiwan the rate of family division has not actually changed significantly, but the villagers' attitude toward it certainly has. Today, the individual small family is becoming the most significant unit in terms of actual behavior and values.

In Hsin Hsing, internal family conflict remains a primary cause of family division, but new forces place an added strain between conjugal units. The increased pressure of population on an insufficient land base leads sons to migrate to the city to work, and the increased economic value this gives the sons weakens the father-son tie and generally speeds up the undermining of the father's authority. Women have greater economic importance now; this frequently leads to delayed marriage. A girl upon marriage is thus older and more mature, which tends to weaken her mother-in-law's authority over her. And as the authority of the elders weakens, the tie between husband and wife is strengthened. Add to this a growing demand for widely available material goods, and we can easily see the potential these factors contain for independence of the conjugal unit, a potential which has undoubtedly had an important bearing on family division.

At the same time, the increasingly greater impingement by the government on the local area has created forces which further family division. The conscription of men, land reform, and taxation, all noted in Chapters 4 and 5, have made it beneficial for families to divide. While it is true that family division has not increased significantly, it is noteworthy that all these new factors added to the balance already weighed down by internal conflict have tipped the scales so that family division now takes place openly. There is little attempt to disguise division, and where the pressures of government impingement make it seem advantageous, divsion is almost advertised. The openness with which division now takes place might in itself yet become a new force of strain within the joint family leading to division; a habitual example can become a weighty model on which to base a demand.

The significance of such demands by the small family unit for independence from the restraints of the larger joint family does not, however, imply an analogous call for independence from their more loosely organized and less demanding large kinship group or *tsu*. This has never been the case in Hsin Hsing nor, for that matter, in mainland China generally, according to most of the ethnographies. The villagers continue to lean on their *tsu* or other smaller and less organized patrilineal kin groups for many activities and functions, since they are the only basic groupings with which villagers maintain continuous, uniform, stable relations. This larger group is the sociopolitical organization most likely to work in their and their entire family's behalf over the years.

However, the villagers also feel a certain amount of socioeconomic need and desire for relations with non-kin villagers and outsiders, since most often neither their own *tsu* nor family groupings are large enough in numbers to offer sufficient possibilities for relationships. As I have indicated throughout the book, although *tsu* and kinship is the most important single basis for relationships with others, Hsin Hsing villagers are far from being tied to one another exclusively on the basis of kinship or *tsu* relationship.

Hsin Hsing has many formal and informal "social associations," activities and relationship groupings whose membership roles cross kinship lines. We have seen this in groups of villagers based on membership in a particular irrigation system or pumping station association, exchange labor groups, cooperating groups in vegetable marketing, loan associations, father-mother burial associations, sworn-brother age groups, and so on. Each non-kinship based formal or informal activity and association that a villager participates in and depends on performs an important function and fulfills a need. By doing this, such diversified non-kin relationships also tend somewhat to interfere with and weaken *tsu* organization by impairing its solidarity and therefore its ability to achieve security for its members. By doing what the kinship organizations cannot do, such associations expose the inherent weakness of the kinship-based organizations.

At the same time, the non-kinship based organizations have inherent weaknesses of which the villagers are aware. Each has a different composition of members, and the villager does not share membership in all the different associations with a single uniform grouping of fellow villagers. The *tsu* or smaller patrilineal kin group thus remains the primary basis for the most continuous and stable long-term relationships; such relationships are institutionalized and, unlike relationships with fellow villagers or outsiders, do not change from time to time. The villager therefore appreciates the importance of his kinship group and is desirous of maintaining his close relationship to it. But he also appreciates the necessity of establishing supportive socioeconomic relationships beyond the *tsu* and village, and it is these kinds of relationships which appear to be increasing in both frequency and importance and to be fostering a decline in identification with the village as a community.

Such a decline means that villagers today find it increasingly difficult to cooperate for mutual aid, even when it is still necessary. It is even questioned whether aid should be offered to a non-*tsu* fellow villager in times of emergency, such as when problems arise with other villages. The case of Li Fan discussed in Chapter 6 shows that the villagers now often have little basis for cooperation and mutual aid and, in addition, are today faced with a conflict of loyalties—a waning loyalty to their fellow villagers and, at the same time, at least a continuing and perhaps even growing loyalty to people in other vil-

lages with whom they have developed strong relationships on the basis
of being *ch'in ch'i* or friends.

The apparently recent relative importance of these latter connections stems from the individual family's increased need to solidify
matrilateral and affinal relationships as well as friendship ties outside the village for purposes of status and socioeconomic security. The
intensity of these relationships beyond the village in many cases sur-
passes those with non-kin fellow villagers. These relationships, however, must not and do not supercede loyalty to *ch'in tsu*.

Villagers today, therefore, continue to prefer marriage with nonrelatives or strangers with whom they can establish outside *ch'in ch'i* relationships which will lead to added security. Such connections better fit
the present socioeconomic and political needs of villagers who no
longer necessarily find it advantageous to focus their relationships
within the village or even to continue to live in the village. In turn
extra-village contacts, once developed, tend to reinforce the growing
socioeconomic self-reliance of the economic family unit already heightened by mobility and nonvillage-based relationships.

We have already seen how these factors have weakened the villagers'
traditional ties to their home village and *tsu*. But at the same time, the
impingement of the government, through its Land Reform Program,
has played a part in this process. In Chapter 4 we saw how the land
reform, by placing limitations on the accumulation of land, affected
the traditional means by which social status and leadership can be
achieved. Thus, stimulated by such a complex of developments, we
find that more and more villagers are far from averse to the sale of
their land for immediate financial advantage.

Often the family, *tsu*, or village cannot exert the necessary pressure
to keep the land in the hands of the family or at least among members
of the larger kinship group. This is partly because of the relatively
small and weakened state of *tsu* organization in the Hsin Hsing village
area and partly because of the weakening of the organization of the
village itself. Where either *tsu* or village organization was strong, the
situation could be quite different. Fei and Chang (1948:126) noted in
their 1939–1943 study in Yunnan province that it was a duty of "clans-
men" to retain land inherited from ancestors and that custom decreed
that such land be sold only to "clan" members. Only if "clan" members
were unable to buy the land or to assist their kinsman in "extricating
himself from his financial difficulties" could the land be sold to an
outsider. In such case, all the "near members of the seller's clan"
would have to consent to the sale in writing, and if this were not done
the sale was "both customarily and legally invalid."

However, for many village families in the Hsin Hsing village area,
whatever feeling of intimacy or even reverence they may retain for the

native soil, it usually becomes unimportant in the face of better economic opportunities off the land. As we saw in Chapter 4 especially, it
is not only peasants who will willingly sell their land once other forms
of economic security are firmly established elsewhere, but even the
wealthy landlord of long-standing tradition on the land in the area.
Such a man who, if anyone, is well indoctrinated with the concept of
the Great (Confucian) Tradition and the value placed on ancestral
land has willingly sold off not only sections of land since the land
reform but even his total family landholdings when outside commercial investment seemed more feasible. When a peasant family establishes itself in Taipei or another urban center and retains its land, it
apparently does so for economic security only, not for the land's "symbolic value." Also, migration to a city by Hsin Hsing area villagers if
economically successful, is very frequently conceived as a permanent
rather than a temporary family move. This seems to be quite different
from numerous observations in various areas of the mainland by Kulp
(1925:42–45), M. Yang (1945:229), and C. K. Yang (1959:71–75),
where migration was almost always undertaken as a temporary
measure.

Families who remain in the village regardless of their inability to
reap an adequate living from insufficient landholdings do so because
they consider village life a more desirable way to live. Since there is
little industry and few steady work opportunities in the local area,
some find low paying and seasonal jobs as local laborers or establish
some kind of itinerant business operation to supplement their meager
income. Others are switching from the traditional rice crops to cash
crops such as vegetables for market. This development has occurred
despite the obstacles which the government, perhaps inadvertently,
places in the way of farmers who wish to grow almost anything other
than rice as their main crop.

Apparently, these people care more for the continued enjoyment of
a rural mode of life than for the land itself. Many, having tried city
life and work, come back to live and work in the village primarily
because they did not like the urban conditions. These people do not
remain in the village and on the land for conservative reasons or as a
reaction to change. In Hsin Hsing, it is this group of people which is
most active in the community. They bring about internal economic
and social changes in the village through their attempt to improve
agricultural methods, which brings them into contact with government and JCRR agriculture agents as well as with farmers in the
surrounding rural area. This group stands in contrast to a larger
group of conservative villagers who have continued to cultivate their
diminishing land base in the traditional manner.

It becomes evident then that there has been significant change in the traditional Chinese value toward the land held earlier. Were it not for fellow villagers and *ch'in tsu* who still are critical of those who sell off their land in the indiscriminate manner in which it is so often done today, and for those villagers who still prefer the village and the agricultural way of life, it would be tempting to deny almost completely any residue of the feeling of "reverence or intimacy" toward the land which the peasant may have held in the past.

The villagers' attitude toward education is another evidence of the lack of real attachment to the land and village. Education to them means a way to rise above the life of a farmer or farm worker, although they do not necessarily expect it to raise them to civil service or elite status. Their primary interest in education is the attainment of an easier life, financial betterment, and power for the individual family. Thus, typically, village farmers want their daughters to marry businessmen. Education has far less inherent value of its own per se than it had in the Confucian tradition, and the materialistic ambitions are against the tradition as well.

Today there are few well-educated villagers who remain active in village affairs in the Hsin Hsing area. Usually, they go into business outside the village or accept employment in local government, such as in the district Public Office. When a man establishes a business outside the village area, as we saw happening after the land reform, he usually shifts his social as well as his economic interests. Once he accepts a position in local government, the educated villager tends to become cliquish and spend most of his time with high-status fellow government employees. Because of his position, he may be called upon by his village to help in certain problem situations, but generally, he takes little interest in most of his village's affairs and does little to furnish leadership. To a great degree nowadays in rural Taiwan, as a result of the new paths to status, education has come to have consequences contrary to the traditional function of education in the society. It now tends to foster greater individualism and detachment from the village and the local larger kinship group, and at times even from one's family.

This attitude held toward the village by the educated man who, usually, is financially well off, begins during earlier student days. Almost immediately upon entering middle school, the bond between the student and his fellow villagers weakens—that is except for those who happen to be school chums. Thus, only in a limited number of cases do middle school graduates serve as leaders or innovators in their village. The relatively better educated village members rarely enrich any of the village community functions, nor do they by their own example bolster the declining role of the village as a source of security and identification. Considering their potential, such men contribute relatively little to their villages.

Coupled with this has been the more recent decline of the traditional landlord leadership as an effect of the Land Reform Program and an ever-increasing vacuum of qualified leadership which has developed in the village. When leadership was sorely needed, as in the Li Fan case for example, the villagers actually turned to me, the alien anthropologist, as a potential source of leadership and help. Many former leaders, now prefer not to become too involved in other people's problems or those of the village. In fact, it is now often difficult for villages to find qualified and respected men even to run for the office of mayor or to assume the responsibilities of a leadership role.

The ever-increasing vacuum of qualified leadership affects not only the operation of the village but that of the *tsu* organizations. One important area of village life adversely affected by the lack of leadership is the apparently increasing inability to resolve local conflict by the traditional method of mediation which was usually carried on by respected *tsu*, village, or area leaders. A particular mediator was selected according to the relationship of the disputants and the nature of the conflict, which might involve intravillage or intervillage disputes over water for irrigation; disputes over landownership and property boundaries; or power struggles between families, especially between *tsu* organizations, over such questions as village administration or the expenditure of funds by village or *tsu* for religious or festive activities; and so on.

Almost always, regardless of the nature of the dispute or the level on which it occurred, mediation had been sought and applied with these aims: first, that the scope and resolution of the conflict be kept localized so as not to invite possible government interference into village affairs, and, second, that the resolution permit the diputants to continue to live harmoniously together. Villagers felt a great degree of permanency since most, tied as they were to the land and to their village, were likewise tied by the particular kinds of relationships developed over the years with local people, both kin and non-kin. There were few opportunities to leave the area, land, or kinship group and go elsewhere so as to avoid the repercussions of an ill-settled dispute.

In recent years, however, it has been becoming increasingly difficult to resolve conflict through mediation and to achieve these aims. In part this is a result of the deterioration of the accepted hierarchal relationship system on both the kin and non-kin levels. On the non-kin level the concept or code of *kan-ch'ing* (as discussed in Chapter 6) and the quality of interpersonal relations governed by it have been weakened. The situation developed largely when the traditional land

tenure system was modified by Taiwan's Land Reform Program between 1949–1953. An important aspect of the reform was the initiation
of a rent reduction and limitation law, but even more important was
the introduction of an official contract between landlord and tenant
which secured the tenant's rights on the land whatever the relationship, good or bad *kan-ch'ing*, he had with the landlord. The contract
for the first time made it clear that the relationship between landlord
and tenant and their mutual responsibilities were economic. Once their
interaction was limited to an economic relationship as circumscribed
by an official contract, it was no longer as important whether either
party concerned himself with the traditional maintenance of good *kan-
ch'ing*.

Thus, in addition to the already discussed decline of some landlords'
socioeconomic and even political interests in the village as a result of
the land reform, the deterioration in the basis of *kan-ch'ing*, and with
it the prestige of many in the landlord class, has frequently meant that
unless landlords who remained in the village had other ways of maintaining their high positions in the community, they lost their useful-
ness as mediators, being no longer capable of exerting influence and
leadership in the community.

On the kinship level the code which regulated relationships between hierarchal unequals has likewise been affected by change, thus
worsening the community's ability to resolve local social conflict. This
has occurred on the levels of the *tsu* and even, to some degree, the
family. In conflict within the *tsu* or village, as well as beyond the
village, the *tsu* organizations through their leaders have always played
a role in settling all conflict by mediation. While the several Hsin
Hsing *tsu* have never been powerful organizations backed by extremely wealthy members and wealth in corporate land usually necessary to give them extensive local sociopolitical influence, *tsu* authority
has recently been further weakened, as we have seen above, by the
extension of the villagers' socioeconomic interests beyond the home
area. As a result, even the *tsu* have apparently lost much of their
ability to exert sanctions against their own members or their op-
ponents. Thus, as a result of the weakening of the social hierarchy,
there has developed a more general inability to use the former traditional respect for particular leaders of the landlord class or *tsu* as a
force with which to settle disagreements.

It is not purely a matter of the weakening of the traditional hier-
archical relationships between people, however, which has diminished
the respect for traditional mediators. This has been intensified by the
tendency toward a growing equalitarianism on both the social and
economic levels of life among the villagers. The tendency was born of
greater educational opportunities, increased election of officials, land

redistribution, and land contracts, all of which have helped to equalize economic means and social relations. While this has not stopped the peasants from recognizing the former landlords' higher status and power, their willingness to accept them as mediators has clearly diminished, as has this formerly powerful group's interests in such community service.

The loss of prestige and authority of the traditional mediators, and thus the decline of success of mediation, has also been accompanied by a questioning of a principle aim of mediation—that the goal of the conflict resolution is to enable the people concerned to continue to live harmoniously together.

Many local villagers are no longer so strongly wedded to the village as a result of their newly developing relations with the greater market economy and the increased economic opportunities for migration to cities. For example, one consequence is that they are no longer concerned with settling disputes with the idea of solely preserving harmonious relations locally. While this is still very important for many people, it is no longer practically universal.

Thus, as a result of the greater society's impingement on village life and, at the same time, the villagers' economic need for involvement beyond the village area, the village and even the kinship groups now have difficulty in maintaining themselves as the villagers' source of solidarity and identification. The villagers' response is actively and consciously to reach out beyond the village and even the *tsu*, not particularly for political power as the gentry always did, but primarily for the socioeconomic reinforcement of their security. As the villager is more and more forced to reach beyond the village, the effect is to further weaken his identification with his village and to a lesser extent with his local kinship group, thus necessitating his even further dependency on and need of the outside.

It appears that such a breakdown of traditional village and kinship relationships has long been going on in much of rural China as a result of some form of urban contacts. Such social change has been accelerated even more markedly in mainland China under the Communists during this last decade and a half. The more extreme breakdown of such traditional village, kinship, and family relationships now apparently taking place on the mainland of China has been attributed to the introduction of communism and its ideological attack on such traditional Chinese concepts as the large family and kinship group. However, taking the situation in Taiwan as an analogy it appears likely that such developments are equally attributable to the urbanization and socioeconomic changes of the twentieth century, speeded up through the methods employed by the Chinese Communists rather than merely a consequence of the applications of the communist ideology to Chinese culture.

A similar although less drastic breakdown has been taking place in recent decades in Taiwan, where the process of culture change has not been under the influence of a communist or other new ideology. Here it appears to be a result of such developments as socioeconomic factors and improved communications which increasingly draw the rural areas into closer contact and relationship with the changing urban and industrial forms of life. Therefore, it appears that the Japanese and Nationalist Chinese rule in Taiwan and Chinese Communist rule on the mainland have acted only as catalysts in the process of accelerated change. With or without these particular governments, the village social organization and the whole socioeconomic systems of these two areas today would still be far different from the traditional and idealized Chinese system.

APPENDIXES

APPENDIX 1

Translation Methods and the Interpreter in the Field

Before my work in Hsin Hsing village, I had been trained in Mandarin. This enabled me to converse freely and conduct interviews with Mandarin speakers. However, the majority of villagers and other people of the area spoke little or no Mandarin. At that time Taiwanese (Min-nan *Hua* or Amoy), which is one of the Fukinese languages, was their native tongue and Japanese in many instances their second language.

After a short time in the field, I was able to handle the common courtesies of the Taiwanese language of the village. And after a time I understood a great deal more of Taiwanese than I could actually speak. But this lack of a working knowledge of Taiwanese and Japanese meant that if the research was to be carried on in any depth, an interpreter who could speak both languages was necessary.

The individual employed for this purpose was a twenty-five-year-old Taiwanese man. Although brought up in Taichung—then a city of 225,000 about twenty-five miles from the village—the interpreter had secured much of his formal education in an agricultural high school. Moreover, his father operated a small farm outside the city limits. He had a great deal of familiarity with rural life and farming techniques, and throughout the course of the research his familiarity proved to be of great value. He helped facilitate good relations with the villagers, since he shared the same cultural and linguistic background as the inhabitants of Hsin Hsing.

The age and sex of the interpreter was an important consideration. His sex made it possible to interview the majority of the villagers. This even included most women, except young girls in their teens, young women not yet married, and some newlywed girls. At the age of twenty-five, he was young enough to have good rapport with teen-age boys and with boys of marriageable age. At the same time, he was old enough—mostly by virtue of his education and his recognized experience—to have good rapport with the older men and local officials.

The interpreter was fluent in four languages—Taiwanese, Japanese, Mandarin, and English. Soon after beginning the research, he could rapidly and accurately translate Taiwanese, Japanese, and Mandarin into English and easily reverse the process. In addition to his language facility, the interpreter was especially well suited for the job because of his pleasant personality and lack of condescension toward the village people. Just as my wife and I came to

285

be genuinely fond of many of the villagers as people, so did the interpreter. His warm attitude toward the villagers was extremely important. The villagers' impression of the interpreter—at least at the beginning—is likely to be transferred to the researcher. What the researcher says to the informant or hears from the informant must pass through the interpreter, who merely by tone of voice and facial expressions can either hinder or help in creating a warm and friendly relationship. Under such circumstances the researcher has little control over the situation. Although a single poor translation may produce some inaccurate data, a slight conflict in personality between interpreter and informant may cause the alienation of one and perhaps more of the informants.

On those occasions when the interpreter translated from Mandarin to English, I had the opportunity to check on the accuracy of his translations. Especially at the beginning of the fieldwork, I specifically requested that the interpreter translate from Mandarin. Since I knew Mandarin, I could make any necessary corrections in the translation or could at least discuss his translation technique. It was hoped that any necessary improvements would then be carried into the translation of Japanese to Mandarin or English.

Throughout the research period the interpreter lived in the village as a member of our household. Through frequent discussions, he became quite familiar with the nature of the research and usually knew the objectives of each interview. Although the interviews were directed, they were of a free conversational type which permitted following up promising leads as they developed in the course of a conversation.

On frequent occasions it became necessary and feasible for the interpreter to carry on lengthy, uninterrupted discussions with an informant on some question raised during the course of the interview. Since the interpreter had proven himself to be accurate and reliable, such a situation was not detrimental. But regardless of how good the interpreter is, something must be lost to the researcher, who in this case, more than ever the third party, must wait patiently to hear what has taken place between the interpreter and the informant. The interpreter's familiarity with the nature of the research can be of great help in such an interview situation.

But a serious problem may be created by the situation which has just been described. The interpreter may not be aware of points raised by his discussion with the informant which may need further investigation. The researcher may lose the opportunity to delve more deeply into leads which might be pertinent for his study. Under such a system something must be lost, but this is only one of the many problems inherent in an interview technique which relies on the use of an interpreter (Phillips 1959–1960).

At the same time, there are many positive things to be said for the use of an interpreter. The interview situation, to say the least, is not an easy one. For the researcher it is often quite wearisome not only to ask the questions and listen to answers but to keep the conversation flowing, always watching for information or a lead on a totally different subject. Such an interview does not usually go according to any schedule. In addition to all this, the researcher must record all the pertinent data, either in writing or, in my case, by committing it to memory for later recording. A well-trained interpreter may relieve the interviewer of some of these burdens and so, in many ways, actually improve the quality of the interview and the data obtained. A good interpreter may enable the interviewer to mull things over and to concentrate on the possible implications of the data obtained while the interpreter discusses things with the informant.

Another initial problem was my original lack of familiarity with details of local etiquette. It is entirely too easy for an unsuspecting anthropologist to commit a *faux pas* which could permanently affect his relations with people. An interpreter who is native to the area and hence aware of local customs can be of great value here. He may be better equipped to interpret signs or hints of the end of an interview, or of what to do in certain situations.

I found that once the interpreter was familiar enough with the nature of the research and the interview technique, it was possible to have him carry on certain types of routine interviews while I was busy recording earlier joint interviews. The interpreter was able in this way to help collect kinship data as well as detailed descriptions of the agricultural cycle and techniques.

As already noted, during the greater part of the village study, I usually recorded interviews well after the interview was concluded. Therefore, to provide a possible check on my understanding of the translation and also on my memory, the interpreter read over the interview for possible inaccuracies before it was considered acceptable. Entire interviews were then recorded on unisort cards and carbon duplicates. The use of the unisort card system later facilitated the cross-categorizing of the field data.

Whenever possible, I conducted interviews in Mandarin by myself. This, of course, could only be done with Mandarin speakers such as local policemen, teachers, younger village people, and other villagers who had picked up Mandarin while working in the capital city of Taipei. Speaking Mandarin, especially with local officials, greatly aided me in establishing better rapport and in obtaining access to important official documents and statistics. Occasionally, when the interpreter was not available for translation of Taiwanese, a Mandarin-speaking villager—such as a young boy—could be used for this purpose.

My wife, who had an adequate command of Mandarin and knew the Taiwanese language somewhat better than I, helped with the research. She interviewed women and girls of the village, often using young people as translators from the Taiwanese to Mandarin. Since she was allowed to go where a man was not admitted, such as the room of a prospective bride about to leave her parents' home, she could advantageously observe events closed to all men.

APPENDIX 2

Kinship Terminology for Cousins in Hsin Hsing

In the accompanying lists of kinship terminology for first cousins used in the Hsin Hsing area, it can be seen that the terms of reference for all first cousins have three Chinese characters. The character in the third position is in actuality a sibling term and is used for all types of cousins as well as for siblings; it varies only on the basis of sex and age. For example, *hsiung*, older brother (under kinship chart and list numbers 9, 14, 38) or *mei*, younger sister (under chart and list numbers 13, 17, 44) would be used in this position. These characters, however, are not very important in distinguishing relationships since they are also used rather indiscriminately by the villagers (and Chinese generally) as courtesy terms for many people with whom no kinship relationship exists. However, the other two terms or characters are significant, since they do indicate important distinctions beyond that of sex and age, between the four types of first cousins.

The most significant distinction between types of first cousins is that of bifurcation between patrilateral parallel cousins (father's brother's children) and the other three types of first cousins: patrilateral cross-cousins, matrilateral cross-cousins, and matrilateral parallel cousins. This distinction is indicated in the kinship terminology by the first two characters used. *Only* patrilateral parallel cousins have as their first two characters *shu pe* (meaning paternal uncle and noted under kinship chart and list numbers 18 and 21).

The other three types of cousins are designated by two different characters which sharply distinguish them from patrilateral parallel cousins. The second of these two different characters is always *"piao"* (loosely translated as "outside" relatives and found under kinship chart and list numbers 14, 17, 41, 44, 45, 47, and so on). This term is applied to descendants of female relatives on the father's side and to descendants of mother's brothers as well as mother's sisters.

In the latter three types of cousins (all of which have the middle character *"piao"*), we again find bifurcation indicated. This time, according to informants, it is the first character which distinguishes patrilateral and matrilateral cross-cousins from matrilateral parallel-cousins, at least in the Hsin Hsing area and also generally in the west-central coastal area of Taiwan. The first character for both types of cross-cousins is *"ku"* (meaning girl or parental aunt and found under kinship chart and list numbers 14, 17, 45, 47, and so on). Only the matrilateral parallel cousins (mother's sister's children) have

288

as a first character *"I"* (meaning wife's sister and mother's sister and found under the kinship chart and list numbers 41, 44, and so on).

Therefore, in order to categorize the Chinese system of kinship terminology for first cousins, we must consider the following: (1) the initial and most significant bifurcation between patrilateral parallel cousins and the other three types of cousins (the patrilateral parallel cousin is also the only one with whom marriage is, of course, strictly forbidden), and (2) the secondary bifurcation between the patrilateral and matrilateral cross-cousins and the matrilateral parallel cousins (a distinction apparently not found universally throughout China or even throughout Taiwan). This secondary bifurcation, which, terminologically, actually tends to separate matrilateral parallel cousins from both types of cross-cousins as well as from the patrilateral parallel cousins, is also indicated in the fact (as seen in the body of Chapter 5 and in an accompanying note) that while the villagers have these kinship terms for matrilateral parallel cousins, in actuality many of them do not apply the terms to their matrilateral parallel cousins. Rather, they think of them merely as *ch'in ch'i* (relatives), so that Hsin Hsing villagers say that marriage to a matrilateral parallel cousin is the closest one can come to marrying a stranger. Such is clearly not the case for any of the other three types of cousins.

Diagramatically, the distinctions between reference terms for the four types of cousins can be briefly shown as follows:

Bifurcation $\begin{cases} \text{A–Patrilateral parallel cousins} \\ \overline{\text{Patrilateral cross-cousins}} \\ \text{B–Matrilateral cross-cousins} \\ \text{Matrilateral parallel cousins} \end{cases}$

Bifurcation $\begin{cases} 1-\dfrac{\text{Patrilateral cross-cousins}}{\text{Matrilateral cross-cousins}} \\ 2-\text{Matrilateral parallel cousins} \end{cases}$

Examples

Patrilateral parallel cousins	FaBrSo	*Shu pe hsiung*
	FaBrDa	*Shu pe mei*
Patrilateral cross-cousins	FaSiSo	*Ku piao hsiung*
	FaSiDa	*Ku piao mei*
Matrilateral cross-cousins	MoBrSo	*Ku piao hsiung*
	MoBrDa	*Ku piao mei*
Matrilateral parallel cousins	MoSiSo	*I piao hsiung*
	MoSiDa	*I piao mei*

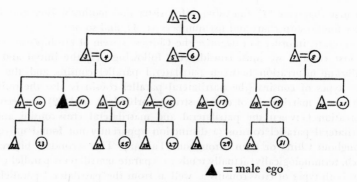

FIG. 4. Kinship terminology in Hsin Hsing village: male
ego's patrilineal and patrilateral kin.

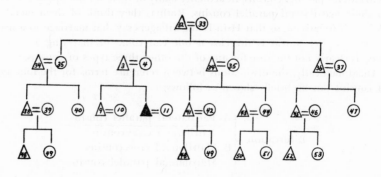

FIG. 5. Male ego's matrilateral kin.

a) Terms of reference
b) Terms of address   used by ego for his relatives *

1. a) *Tsu fu*   祖 父

   b) *A kung*   阿 公

2. a) *Tsu mu*   祖 母

   b) *A ma*   阿 媽

* Whenever the term of address is omitted, it usually means that ego ad-
dresses that particular person by his first name or else some other personal
name.

3. a) *Fu*　　　　　　　　　　　　　父

   b) *A pa*　　　　　　　　　　　阿　爸

4. a) *Mu*　　　　　　　　　　　　母

   b) *A ma*　　　　　　　　　　阿　媽

5. a) *Ku chang*　　　　　　　　姑　丈

   b) *Ku chang*　　　　　　　　姑　丈

6. a) *Ku mu*　　　　　　　　　　姑　母

   b) *A ku*　　　　　　　　　　阿　姑

7. a) *Shu fu*　　　　　　　　　叔　父

   b) *A shu*　　　　　　　　　阿　叔

8. a) *Shen mu*　　　　　　　嬸　母

   b) *A shen*　　　　　　　阿　嬸

9. a) *Hsiung*　　　　　　　　兄

   b) *A hsiung*　　　　　　阿　兄

10. a) *Hsiung sao*　　　　兄　嫂

    b) *A sao*　　　　　　　阿　嫂

11. a) *Chi* 妻

b) —

12. a) *Mei fu (hsu)* 妹夫 (婿)

b) —

13. a) *Mei* 妹

b) —

14. a) *Ku piao hsiung* 姑表兄

b) *A hsiung* 阿兄

15. a) *Ku piao hsiung sao* 姑表兄嫂

b) *A sao* 阿嫂

16. a) *Ku piao mei fu (hsu)* 姑表妹夫 (婿)

b) —

17. a) *Ku piao mei* 姑表妹

b) —

18. a) *Shu pe ti* 叔伯弟

b) —

19. a) *Shu pe ti fu* 叔 伯 弟 婦 (小 嬸)
    (*hsiao shen*)

    b) —

20. a) *Shu pe mei fu (hsu)* 叔 伯 妹 夫 (婿)

    b) —

21. a) *Shu pe mei* 叔 伯 妹

    b) —

22. a) *Chih tzu* 姪 子

    b) —

23. a) *Chih nu* 姪 女

    b) —

24. a) *Sheng tzu (wai sheng)* 甥 子 (外 甥)

    b) —

25. a) *Sheng nu* 甥 女

    b) —

26. a) *Ku piao chih tzu* 姑 表 姪 子

    b) —

27. a) *Ku piao chih nu*   姑 表 姪 女

    b) —

28. a) *Ku piao sheng tzu*   姑 表 甥 子

    b) —

29. a) *Ku piao sheng nu*   姑 表 甥 女

    b) —

30. a) *Shu pe chih tzu*   叔 伯 姪 子

    b) —

31. a) *Shu pe chih nu*   叔 伯 姪 女

    b) —

32. a) *Wai tsu fu*   外 祖 父

    b) *A kung*   阿 公

33. a) *Wai tsu mu*   外 祖 母

    b) *A ma*   阿 媽

34. a) *I chang*   姨 丈

    b) *I chang*   姨 丈

35. a) *I mu* 　　姨母

　　b) *A i* 　　阿姨

36. a) *Chiu fu* 　　舅父

　　b) *A chiu* 　　阿舅

37. a) *Chiu mu* 　　舅母

　　b) *A chin* 　　阿妗

38. a) *I piao hsiung* 　　姨表兄

　　b) *A hsiung* 　　阿兄

39. a) *I piao hsiung sao* 　　姨表兄嫂

　　b) *A sao* 　　阿嫂

40. a) *I piao chieh* 　　姨表姊

　　b) *A chieh* 　　阿姊

41. a) *I piao ti* 　　姨表弟

　　b) —

42. a) *I piao ti fu* 　　姨表弟婦

　　b) —

43. a) *I piao mei fu (hsu)*   姨表妹夫 (婿)

    b) —

44. a) *I piao mei*   姨表妹

    b) —

45. a) *Ku piao ti*   姑表弟

    b) —

46. a) *Ku piao ti fu*   姑表弟婦

    b) —

47. a) *Ku piao mei*   姑表妹

    b) —

48. a) *I piao chih tzu*   姨表姪子

    b) —

49. a) *I piao chih nu*   姨表姪女

    b) —

50. a) *I piao sheng tzu*   姨表甥子

    b) —

51. a) *I piao sheng nu* 姨表甥女

    b) —

52. a) *Ku piao chih tzu* 姑表姪子

    b) —

53. a) *Ku piao chih nu* 姑表姪女

    b) —

GLOSSARY OF CHINESE KINSHIP TERMS

A	阿	Prefix to names of people; used to show respect
Chang	丈	An elder
Ch'i	妻	Wife
Chieh	姊	Elder sister
Chih	姪	Nephew or niece; child of a brother
Chin	妗	Wife of a mother's brother
Chiu	舅	Maternal uncle
Fu	父	Father

Fu	婦	Woman; wife
Hsiung	兄	Brother; elder brother; a senior
Hsu	婿	Son-in-law
I	姨	Wife's sister; mother's sister
Ku	姑	Girl; paternal aunt
Ku chang	姑丈	Husband of father's sister
Ku mu	姑母	Father's sisters; paternal aunts
Ma	媽	Mother; mama
Mei	妹	Younger sister
Mu	母	Mother
Pa	爸	Father
Pe	伯	Father's elder brothers; uncle
Piao	表	Applied to descendants of female relatives on the father's side and to descendants of the mother's brothers; "outside" (relative)

Sao	嫂	Elder brother's wife
Shen	嬸	Aunt; father's younger brother's wife
Sheng	甥	Children of a sister
Shu	叔	Father's younger brother
Tsu	祖	Ancestor; founder
Tzu	子	Son; a child
Wai	外	Outside; beyond

NOTES

Chapter 1: Introduction

[1] During the last six or seven years of their regime, the Japanese government attempted to strengthen support of the war effort amongst the Taiwanese population. To do this, they expanded the compulsory school system and put in force many new regulations, i.e., only the Japanese language was used in the schools, Shinto religious symbols such as the Shinto God's shelf (*kamidana*) and Japanese patriotic scrolls replaced the traditional Taoist gods' statues and scrolls, Japanese festivals were observed, and many Taiwanese had to take Japanese names. However, immediately after war's end, the Taiwanese reverted to their traditional Taiwanese (Chinese) customs.

Chapter 2: The Setting

[1] The amount and distribution of rainfall in the Hsin Hsing area is: January .79–1.97 inches, April 3.93–5.90 inches, July 7.86–11.80 inches, October .79 inches. The average annual rainfall in the Chang-hua Hsien area is 39.37–59.05 inches.

[2] A great many of the overseas Chinese living in the Southeast Asian countries also came from the Ch'uan Chou and Chang Chou areas near Amoy.

[3] The historical information gathered from older residents of the area was based mainly on their own experiences as children and on stories told to them by their elders.

Some of the numerous gazetteers available are listed in the section of the bibliography on Chinese and Japanese Language Sources. Chen Shao-hsing, Professor of Sociology and Demography at National Taiwan University, first warned me in 1957 that some problems exist in using these and other such materials in attempting to gain detailed information about Taiwan generally, or about local areas particularly. Although Chen notes in his recent book (1964:196–197) that some earlier Ch'ing dynasty chroniclers, e.g., Chen Meng-lin, author of *Chu Lo Hsien Chih* (1716), and Chen Wen-ta, compiler of the *Taiwan Hsien Chih* (1720), were reliable, he also points out that some later ones such as Yu Wen-i (1758), Wang Ying-ts'eng (1764), Hsieh Chin-luan (1807), and Chen Shu-chün (1852) were unreliable. Chen (1964:196–197) points out that these latter authors cited what was mentioned in the Chen Wen-ta (1720) book regardless of the actual change in customs through time. Apparently, then, they employed the practice of compiling at least some of their data from previously written gazetteers rather than going out into the countryside to obtain the necessary information. But even the reliable gazetteers usually still presented a composite picture of life rather than ethnographic-type studies of any one area.

During the Japanese period in Taiwan (1895–1945), Japanese police, administrators, and academic researchers also made extensive detailed studies in Taiwan. These works, such as the *Taiwan Szu Fa* (1910–1911), also were usually composite studies. But these more often dealt with specific aspects of Taiwanese (Chinese) life, such as: family, civil law, economics and agricultural processes, religion and magic (frequently viewing the local people as superstitious and backward), and general customs and habits of the Taiwanese. In these studies, the researchers frequently used scattered illustrative material drawn from either the cities and/or the rural areas of Taiwan.

Thus, a number of the Chinese and Japanese studies are generally valuable for providing a picture of early conditions for some general areas and on many specific subjects in Taiwan. They are, of course, also valuable for comparative purposes. Unfortunately, rarely, if ever, do any of them furnish any ethnographic or contextual picture of Taiwanese life for any particular area in Taiwan, and especially not for the area of Hsin Hsing village. This has meant, therefore, that the available material has been of only limited value in the historical reconstruction of life in the immediate area of Hsin Hsing. It is also unfortunate that either during or after World War II, the historical records for Hsin Hsing and its immediate area which, during Japanese times, were usually kept in the district police station were apparently destroyed or lost.

[4] *Pu Yen Chuang Yen Ke Chih,* no author, Ta Chen 15 or 1925, handwritten in Japanese with additions made in Chinese after the war. Found in the Pu Yen Hsiang Public Office. This source notes that in the Pu Yen area only about 600 *chia* of land were irrigated in the early 1900's. But by 1922 there were 2,100 *chia* of land irrigated, and in 1923 another irrigation system, the Er Pao Chen, was added.

[5] Barclay discussed how Taiwan was built up economically as a colonial area of Japan.

[6] Demographic figures for the whole island of Taiwan are based on local statistics from district public offices such as the Pu Yen Hsiang office.

The 1958 village population figures, the most recent ones cited in this section, differ from those 1959 figures used in the material in Chapter 5 on social organization. Figures from the earlier date are used in this section because they are the ones most comparable with the census figures available for the *hsiang* and all of Taiwan. On the other hand, the 1959 figures were the only ones specific and complete enough to be useful for the breakdown in social organization and family.

[7] These population growth rate figures are for Taiwanese only; aboriginals are not included.

[8] This population growth rate figure is only for Taiwanese and mainlanders in Taiwan; aboriginals are not included.

[9] Based on a discussion in May, 1959, with Professor Chen Shao-hsing, sociologist and demographer at the National Taiwan University. Some of the social factors affecting the birthrate and the trends in population growth will be examined in the chapters on social organization and especially on life cycle.

10 All population figures for Hsin Hsing village and Pu Yen Hsiang are based upon records found in the Pu Yen Hsiang Public Office. Unfortunately, the demographic statistics available for Hsin Hsing and Pu Yen Hsiang were limited to only certain years and then only beginning in 1953. Data for Taiwan as a whole are only readily available for specific years such as census years. For Hsin Hsing itself it will be noted that all population data for 1955 have been omitted. This is because of some radical errors in the official records—not explainable by the Public Office officials.

11 The reason for comparing figures of different years in Table 4 is entirely determined by the availability of data. But it is felt that the differences in the years considered do not detract from the validity of the comparison.

12 The figures in Tables 9 and 10 are again compared for different years entirely because data for only the years cited were available. Nevertheless, I feel that the sets of data are comparable.

13 All land tenure figures for Hsin Hsing village and Pu Yen Hsiang are based upon the official records of the government Land Office in Lukang and the Pu Yen Hsiang Public Office.

14 However, in order to compare the average cultivated landholding, by household, in Hsin Hsing village with that of Pu Yen Hsiang as a whole, it is necessary to use the average landholding figure for the total number of households in Hsin Hsing, i.e., 115 farming and nonfarming households in 1958, since the only readily available figure for the twenty-two villages of the *hsiang* was the total number of households, farming and nonfarming. On this basis then, the average amount of land operated in Hsin Hsing was 0.53 *chia* (1.3 acres) per household, as compared to an average of close to 0.8 *chia* (less than 2 acres) per household for the entire *hsiang*. These figures indicate that, although the average landholding in Hsin Hsing is below the all-*hsiang* average, there is a general, serious land scarcity in the whole area. (A complete breakdown of village land tenure figures appears in Chapter 4.)

15 A good deal of mint (used for distilling menthol oil) is grown in the area.

16 In 1958 officially NT $36 = US $1, but the actual equation on the open market was about NT $45 = US $1. All figures quoted will be at the equivalence of the official NT $36 = US $1.

Chapter 3: The Land and the Agricultural Process

1 There are twenty-four solar terms (*er shih sze chieh ch'i*) for the twenty-four periods of fifteen days each which make up a year. For a more complete explanation of the calendrical system, see Fei Hsiao-tung (1939:144–153).

2 *Kan-ch'ing* is the good or bad sentiment, feeling, or relationship existing between individuals (and, in Hsin Hsing, between relatives as well). Fried (1953:226) observes that *"Kan-ch'ing* differs from friendship in that it presumes a much more specific common interest, much less warmth and more formality of contact, and includes a recognized degree of exploitation." In effect, it is basically a matter of structured obligation. The feeling or sentiment results from satisfied or disappointed expectations of appropriate behavior, and the expected behavior is behavior appropriate to the formal relationship of the two individuals within the social structure.

[3] For a detailed description of the operation of such clubs and how some participants profit financially from them, see Fei (1939) and Embree (1939). Although the actual details are here somewhat different, the general idea and method are similar.

Chapter 4: Changing Land Tenure and Its Effect on Community Organization

[1] Land tenure records for the Hsin Hsing area are kept in the Lukang Land Office, the local branch of the Taiwan Provincial Land Bureau in Taipei. The Lukang office maintains sets of maps and many different forms on which are recorded all land tenure operations, including those of the land reform. However, only two types of land tenure record forms are kept fully up to date for each village.

Of these two, one type is the landownership card for privately owned land holdings. Files of these cards are maintained under three separate categories: "individual," "joint," and "corporate" ownership. There is a card in the name of each primary owner. The other type, which records all land operations by the villagers, is maintained in loose-leaf notebooks, one for each village. Each village family which owns and/or rents any land has a few pages in the book. The book is apparently kept for the purpose of observing annual variations in kind and amount of land cultivated as they relate to and affect the standard of living. Towards this end, it also indicates changes in the amount of livestock and farm equipment and the make-up of family population, but these items are not usually kept up to date.

The Pu Yen Hsiang Public Office also keeps records which can be of help in determining the total village land tenure situation. These records, which are used by the Public Office for assessment purposes, include listings of landlord-tenant contracts, villagers who received land under the 1953 Land-to-the-Tiller Act, and general totals of land cultivated by the people in each village.

[2] During the post-land reform period (1953–1957), these figures remained almost constant, so that the above figures and those used from now on will be from the 1957 records, since that year's data are the most detailed.

[3] Some landlords sold their land before the act of expropriation.

[4] The 0.5 *chia* of K'ang *tsu* land was not expropriated under the Land-to-the-Tiller Act of 1953. Article 8, category 5, of this act stipulates in section 1 that tenant-cultivated land owned by private individuals or family "clans" for purposes of ancestor worship be expropriated. However, as Wang (1964: 79) points out, sections 2 and 3 of Article 8 alter this part of the law. These sections stipulate that the landowning group, e.g., a *tsu*, may retain an amount of land sufficient to provide for the expenditures of ancestor sacrifices. The two sections also stipulate that all such land, if used for other purposes, be expropriated, noting that in the past such land and income derived from it were the source of a great deal of conflict and litigation. As a result of the ambiguity in the basic law and the added sections, implementation of it has varied from place to place according to the particular situation and idiosyncratic interpretation.

5 For a more detailed discussion of attitudes towards the land, see my "Chinese Peasant Values Toward the Land."

Chapter 5: Family and Kinship

1 Freedman's (1958:2) "inflated families" would apparently be a group of related families oriented around their kinship relationship and in which the activities of the group are aimed primarily at the maintenance of their kinship ties. For such a group, kinship is both the basis of the relationships and also an end in itself. On the other hand, a lineage (*tsu*) uses its kinship relationships as a means to an end: to tie the group members together into an organization so that they might better exert sociopolitical influence to insure their own welfare and security.

2 These 99 had a population of 609 persons and included members of village households who were working in Taipei. The figures, from October, 1959, will be used throughout the chapter because they are the most complete tabulations which can be used for a detailed breakdown of the village *tsu* groups and families. The figures used in the demographic section of Chapter 2 for 1958 made it possible to compare Hsin Hsing with the *hsiang* and Taiwan as a whole, since the 1959 figures for Pu Yen Hsiang and Taiwan were not available.

The decline in the general population and the number of families in Hsin Hsing which is reflected in the difference between the 1958 and 1959 figures (657 persons living in 115 households in 1958) represents the village's losses through urban migration. As noted in Chapter 4, whole families and members of families had gradually been moving to Taipei; the movement had increased somewhat in the previous two years. Further, many families which had only partially made the move now made it complete, thus changing their residence registration from Hsin Hsing to Taipei.

3 It is difficult from this distance to ascertain just how such arrangements were worked out among the village *tsu* organizations. Like so many other ethnographic field studies, much of what is written in this book was analyzed from data only after leaving the field. Since my field research did not focus specifically on such questions as lineage cleavages, my data often are not detailed enough to carry either the description or analyses to their logical conclusions. Therefore, all I can do in such instances is to present and analyze the data as best I can and hope that it may have some value to others.

4 Included in the registration of each household unit are such data as the number of people, ages, schooling, occupations, and temporary residences. However, little of this information is kept up-to-date by the local official appointed by the Public Office to act as village secretary. In addition, much of the information recorded is simply not accurate. For example, although many village women and girls engage in full-time local outside employment or perhaps are responsible for tending the family's fields, nevertheless, almost all women are officially recorded as housewives, with no indication of what they actually do.

5 These definitions by Lang (1946:14) of nuclear (conjugal) and joint family forms approximate Murdock's definitions (1949:2). The Lang definitions for

these two forms (plus that for the stem family form) have been cited here mainly because they are more detailed, and since they are based on actual Chinese data, they are more descriptive of the Taiwanese situation.

[6] Kulp (1925:145–148) used the term "religious-family" as the best functional name for the "ancestral-group." Hu Hsien-chin (1948:17) used the term "circle of mourning relatives" for a group which is actually identical with Kulp's religious-family.

[7] For a more detailed discussion of cousin marriage in mainland China and Taiwan see my "Cousin Marriage in China."

[8] Using Cantonese and Shantung samples, Murdock (1957:664–687) reports that "cross-cousin marriage is allowed symmetrically, i.e., with either Mo-BrDa or FaSiDa." However, the data gathered for mainland China by Hsu (1945:84), Fried (1953:64n), and so on, and my own data from Taiwan, do not bear out Murdock's point. Again, for further discussion see my "Cousin Marriage in China."

[9] This use of *ku piao* as part of the reference terminology used by a male ego for his mother's brother's daughter or son in the general area of Hsin Hsing village may not be as common in other parts of China, including some areas of Taiwan. In other places, especially on the mainland of China, the term used for mother's brother's children may be *chiu piao;* several scholars have insisted it is the only logical kinship term for such a relationship, rather than *ku piao* (which in these other places is supposed to be a term reserved for father's sister's children). All Hsin Hsing village informants questioned on this issue insist that in this area they "have *never* heard *chiu piao* used to refer to mother's brother's children. In fact, *ku piao* is used in most of the central area of Taiwan; this is more convenient than when these cousins refer to each other by different terms." When asked for an explanation of this form in terminology, some villagers noted that "logically mother's brother's children should be *chiu piao.*" But they then immediately insisted that "there is no such term as *chiu piao* in actual practice." However, one or two of all the informants did note that sometimes a distinction is made between father's sister's children and mother's brother's children by referring to the former as *ku piao* and the latter as just *piao* (followed, of course, by the standard term used for an older or younger brother or sister).

Interestingly enough, the differences in patterns and preferences for marriage with the two kinds of cross-cousins (discussed in some detail in the remaining part of the chapter), although explained by "a feeling of greater closeness in blood with father's sister's daughter," is nevertheless not reflected in the kinship terms used for these two kinds of cousins. It is clear then, that in the Hsin Hsing area, the kinship terms used for cross-cousins have little functional value with regard to marriage pattern differentiation.

[10] Exact figures were not easily available, but on the basis of observations and interviews the figures given seem at least close enough to approximate the situation.

[11] According to the law, either a husband or wife can initiate divorce proceedings. Each district now has a semiofficial special office set up by the Kuomintang (K.M.T.) as an arbitration service for marital troubles; if necessary, it will help either or both parties to arrange a divorce settlement. The dis-

trict police office as well as the local officials in the district Public Office will
also assume this function on an unofficial basis.

Chapter 6: Personal Relationships and Cooperation Within and Beyond the Village

1 Some villagers even approached me with the hope that I might act as their
leader. Because of their insistence, I did participate in a very minor way.
The minimal participation, however, yielded extremely valuable insights
into village interpersonal relationships. Also, after this occasion, I found
most villagers much more willing to aid me in my research. For a more detailed discussion of my involvement in this case and the consequences to
my field work, see my "A Case for Intervention in the Field."
2 Several villagers also insisted that I be part of Hsin Hsing village's delega-
tion. This turned out to be my only opportunity to attend any kind of mediation session.

Chapter 7: Life History of the Villager

1 A woman's menstrual blood is also considered unclean, and a wash amah
employed in a Chinese household is not expected to wash the mistress's
undergarments if they have been stained with menstrual blood.
2 This figure is based on the Chinese calculation of age. A child is said to be
one year old at the time of his birth and two years old on the first Chinese
New Year after his birth. This boy is therefore fourteen or fifteen by Western calculations.
3 A somewhat similar kind of arrangement is reported by Robert J. Smith
(1956:77–78) for Japan.
4 If a woman dies before she bears a child or before a child is adopted into
the family, her name is not recorded on the family ancestral tablet because
she lacks descendants to worship her.
5 In some instances when a family does not have daughters of their own they
may take a "recognized daughter" (or a "recognized son") who in a sense
is temporarily adopted and who will then come to mourn and worship at
the funeral of her "recognized parents." The girl is usually the daughter
of close family friends, and she will still worship her own parents. Sometimes a family may also give their girl as a recognized daughter if she is a
sickly child and a fortune-teller recommends such action to avoid further
illness.

Chapter 8: Religion and Magic in Hsin Hsing Village

1 During 1957–1958 government troops were billeted in the temple and at
the same time were renovating it.
2 The belief in the ubiquity of Matsu's powers, however, is not universal
among the Taiwanese. Norma Diamond, an anthropologist working in
southern Taiwan in 1960–1961, has told me that Matsu is not considered

at all important by the residents of the fishing village she is studying. This is interesting, since the villagers spend so much time on the sea.

3 Some villagers say that people with such an illness could be sent to a hospital in the city, but "people don't come back from there."

4 Most of the villagers at least do not disbelieve in the possibility of witchcraft. Although it is not considered to be a common practice any more, on occasion a person may employ a powerful *fa shih* to cast a spell on someone whom he wishes to harm. In addition, some villagers feel that the same effect can be achieved if the nail cuttings of the intended victim are burned. Thus, when the villagers cut their finger nails, they may spread them about so that they will not be noticed by others.

GLOSSARY OF CHINESE NAMES AND WORDS*

Chao fu	招 夫	Adopted-in husband
Chao ti	招 弟	To invite in a younger brother
Chen	鎮	A market-township area
Ch'eng szu	承 嗣	A term referring to a person adopted for the purpose of "continuing the family line"
Chia	甲	A measure of land equal to about 2.39 acres
Chia chang	家 長	Head of an economic family
Chieh	節	A festival
Chieh pai hsiung ti	結 拜 兄 弟	Sworn brothers
Ch'in ch'i	親 戚	Matrilateral and affinal relatives, or relatives through adoption
Ch'in t'ang	親 堂	People bearing same surname, but not part of same *tsu* (lineage)
Ch'in tsu	親 族	Members of the same *tsu* (lineage) or patrilineal kinship group
Ching	驚	A scare (a fright)
Ch'ing Ming Chieh	清 明 節	A festival for worshipping at graves
Chui hsü	贅 婿	Adopted son-in-law

* For additional Chinese kinship terms, see Appendix 2.

Chu Wang Yeh	朱 王 爺	A minor Hsin Hsing village private god
Chung Yuan	中 元	Seventh month, fifteenth day (lunar); festival for *hao hsiung-ti*
Ch'ung	冲	Hit into a bad thing (as a demon)
Er Shih Kung	二 使 公	A private god worshipped in Hsin Hsing village
Fa shih	法 師	A powerful shaman who exorcises demons or negative spirits
Hao hsiung-ti	好 兄 弟	Unworshipped ancestors ("good brothers")
Hsiang	鄉	A district or sub-unit of a *hsien* (county)
Hsiang chang	鄉 長	A *hsiang* (district) mayor
Hsien	縣	A county, several of which make up a *sheng* (province)
Hsien chang	縣 長	County magistrate
Hsiu ching	修 驚	To fix a "scare" (a fright)
Hu	戶	A household registered as the administrative or tax unit
Je nao	熱 鬧	Interesting; bustling; noisy; exciting
Kan-ch'ing	感 情	The emotional feeling or relationship (good or bad) between people
Kuan Yin	觀 音	Buddhist Goddess of Mercy
Kuei	鬼	Demon or evil spirit
Kung t'ing	公 庭	Central room in a house; used for an-

		cestral worship and other festive functions; often a kind of family room
Kuo-Yu	國語	Mandarin; the "national language"
Lin	鄰	A neighborhood; a village is divided into several lin
Lu chu	爐主	Pot master
Matsu	媽祖	A goddess in the Taoist hierarchy
Min-nan *hua*	閩南話	Taiwanese language; one of the Fukienese languages from the Amoy area
Pai-pai	拜拜	A ritual in which food and other sacrifices are offered to gods and spirits; to worship
Shang Yuan	上元	First month, fifteenth day (lunar); first full moon of year
Shen	神	A spirit, a god
Ta Shih Kung	大使公	Hsin Hsing village's main ambassador god
Tao shih	道士	A Taoist priest
T'iao t'ung	跳童	A shaman (in Taiwanese, called a *dang-ki*); one who is possessed by a god; a medium
T'ien Kung	天公	God of Heaven; highest of all gods; equivalent to Yu ti, the Jade God
Tso p'ing-an	做平安	A festival held sometime after the autumn harvest in thanksgiving

Tsu	族	A patrilineal, patri-local lineage organization with a demonstrated common ancestor
Ts'un	村	A village
Ts'un chang	村長	A village mayor
T'u Ti Kung Miao	土地公廟	The Earth God temple
Tung Chieh (chih)	冬節(至)	Winter solstice festival
Wei Ya	尾芽	Twelfth month, sixteenth day (lunar); last day of year for worshipping *hao hsiung-ti*
Yu Ying Kung Miao	有應公廟	Considered a "devil temple" but euphemistically referred to as "temple of responding gods"

BIBLIOGRAPHY

ENGLISH LANGUAGE SOURCES

Barclay, George W.
  1954a *A Report on Taiwan's Population.* Taipei: Joint Commission on Rural Reconstruction (JCRR).
  1954b *Colonial Development and Population in Taiwan.* Princeton: Princeton University Press.

Buck, J. Lossing
  1930 *Chinese Farm Economy: A Study of 2866 Farms in Seventeen Localities and Seven Provinces in China.* Chicago: University of Chicago Press.
  1937 *Land Utilization in China,* vol. I. Nanking: University of Nanking Press.

Chang Yen-t'ien
  1954 *Land Reform in Taiwan.* Taichung: Department of Agricultural Economics, Taiwan Provincial College of Agriculture.

Chen Cheng-siang
  1950 *Atlas of Land Utilization in Taiwan.* Taipei: Taiwan National University.

Chen Han-sheng
  1936 *Landlord and Peasant in China.* New York: International Publishers.

DeGroot, J. J. M.
  1892– *The Religious System of China.* 6 vols. Leyden: Brill.
  1910

Directorate-General of Budgets, Accounts and Statistics, Executive Yuan, Republic of China
  1955 *Statistical Abstract of Republic of China.* Taipei.

Embree, John F.
  1939 *Suye Mura, A Japanese Village.* Chicago: University of Chicago Press.

Fei Hsiao-tung
  1939 *Peasant Life in China.* London: Kegan Paul, Trench, Trubner & Co., Ltd.

Fei Hsiao-tung and Chang Chih-i
  1945 *Earthbound China.* Chicago: University of Chicago Press.

Feng Han-yi (Feng Han-chi)
  1948 *The Chinese Kinship System.* Cambridge, Mass.: Harvard-Yenching Institute, Harvard University Press (Reprinted from *Harvard Journal of Asiatic Studies,* vol. II, no. 2, July, 1937).

313

Freedman, Maurice
   1958   *Lineage Organization in Southeastern China.* London: University
           of London, Athlone Press.
Fried, Morton H.
   1953   *Fabric of Chinese Society, A Study of the Social Life of a Chinese
           County Seat.* New York: Praeger.
Gallin, Bernard
   1959   "A Case for Intervention in the Field," *Human Organization,* vol.
           XVIII, no. 3, pp. 140–144.
   1960   "Matrilateral and Affinal Relationships of a Taiwanese Village,"
           American Anthropologist, vol. LXII, no. 4, pp. 632–642.
   1963a   "Cousin Marriage in China," *Ethnology,* vol. II, no. 1, pp. 104–108.
   1963b   "Land Reform in Taiwan: Its Effect on Rural Social Organization
           and Leadership," *Human Organization,* vol. XXII, no. 2, pp. 109–
           112.
   1964a   "Chinese Peasant Values Toward the Land," *Proceedings of the
           1963 Annual Spring Meeting of the American Ethnological Society,*
           Seattle: American Ethnological Society, University of Washington
           Press, pp. 64–71.
   1964b   "Rural Development in Taiwan: The Role of the Government,"
           Rural Sociology, vol. XXIX, no. 3, pp. 313–323.
Geddes, W. R.
   1963   *Peasant Life in Communist China.* Ithaca, N.Y.: Society for Applied
           Anthropology.
Ginsburg, Norton S.
   1953   *Economic Resources and Development of Formosa.* New York: In-
           stitute of Pacific Relations.
Grajdanzev, Andrew J.
   1942   *Formosa Today.* New York: Institute of Pacific Relations.
Hsu, F. L. K.
   1945   "Observations on Cross-Cousin Marriage," *American Anthropologist,*
           vol. XXXXVII, no. 1, January–March.
   1949   *Under the Ancestors' Shadow, Chinese Culture and Personality.*
           London: Routledge & Kegan Paul Ltd.
Hu Hsien-chin
   1948   *The Common Descent Group in China and Its Functions.* New
           York: Viking Fund Publications in Anthropology, no. 10.
Klein, Sidney
   1958   *The Pattern of Land Tenure Reform in East Asia After World
           War II.* New York: Bookman Associates.
Kulp, Daniel H.
   1925   *Country Life in South China, The Sociology of Familism, Volume I,
           Phenix Village, Kwangtung, China.* New York: Teachers College,
           Columbia University.
Lang, Olga
   1946   *Chinese Family and Society.* New Haven: Yale University Press.
Lin Yueh-hwa
   1947   *The Golden Wing, A Sociological Study of Chinese Familism.* Lon-
           don: Kegan Paul, Trench, Trubner & Co., Ltd.

Malinowski, Bronislaw
1948   *Magic, Science and Religion and Other Essays.* Glencoe: Free Press.
Murdock, George P.
1949   *Social Structure.* New York: Macmillan Company.
1957   "World Ethnographic Survey," *American Anthropologist,* vol. LIX, no. 4, August, pp. 664–687.
Phillips, Herbert P.
1959–   "Problems of Translation and the Meaning of Field Work," *Human*
1960   *Organization,* vol. XVIII, no. 4, Winter, pp. 184–192.
Riggs, Fred W.
1952   *Formosa Under Chinese Nationalist Rule.* New York: Macmillan Company.
Smith, Robert J., and Cornell, John B.
1956   *Two Japanese Villages: Kurusu, A Japanese Agricultural Community; Matsunagi, A Japanese Mountain Community.* Ann Arbor: University of Michigan Press, Center for Japanese Studies, Occasional Papers No. 5.
Stanford University China Project
1956   *Taiwan (Formosa).* 2 vols. New Haven: Human Relations Area Files (HRAF).
T'ang Hui-sun
1954   *Land Reform in Free China.* Taipei: Chinese American Joint Commission on Rural Reconstruction.
United Nations, Statistical Office
1945   *Statistical Yearbook.* New York.
United Nations, Statistical Office, Department of Economic and Social Affairs
1957   *Demographic Yearbook.* New York.
Yang, C. K.
1959   *A Chinese Village in Early Communist Transition.* Cambridge. Mass.: Technology Press.
1961   *Religion in Chinese Society.* Berkeley and Los Angeles: University of California Press.
Yang, Martin C.
1945   *A Chinese Village, Taitou, Shantung Province.* New York: Columbia University Press.

CHINESE AND JAPANESE LANGUAGE SOURCES *

Chen Meng-lin (陳 夢 林)
1716   *Chu Lo Hsien Chih,* 諸 羅 縣 志 (Chu Lo Hsien Gazetteer), Taipei.

Chen Shao-hsing (陳 紹 馨)
1964   *Taiwan Sheng Tung Chih Kao; Chuan Erh: Jen Min Chih, Jen K'ou Pen,* 臺灣省通志稿卷二人民志人口篇

* All are in Chinese except those asterisked, which are in Japanese.

(General Gazetteer of Taiwan Province; vol. II. Population
History of Taiwan), Taipei: Taiwan Sheng Wen Hsien Wei
Yuan Hui,(臺灣省文獻委員會)(Historical Re-
search Commission of Taiwan Province).

Chen Shu-chun （陳淑均）
1852   *Ko Ma Lan T'ing Chih,* 噶瑪蘭廳志 (Ko Man Lan
            T'ing Gazetteer), Taipei: Republ. by Bank of Taiwan, 1963.

Chen Wen-ta （陳文達）
1720   *Taiwan Hsien Chih,* 臺灣縣志 (Taiwan Hsien Gazet-
            teer), Taipei: Republ. by Taiwan Sheng Wen Hsien Wei Yuan
            Hui (Historical Research Commission of Taiwan Province),
            1958; also Republ. by Bank of Taiwan, 1961.

Chou Hsi （周　璽）
1830   *Chang-hua Hsien Chih,* 彰化縣誌 (Chang-hua Hsien
            Annals), Taipei: Republ. by Bank of Taiwan, 1957, No. 48 of
            Taiwan Yen Chiu Ts'ung K'ang, 臺灣研究叢刊 (Tai-
            wan Study Series).

Hsieh Chin-lüan （謝金鑾）
1807   *Hsu Hsiu Taiwan Hsien Chih,* 續修臺灣縣志(Tai-
            wan Hsien Gazetteer Cont.), Taipei: Republ. by Bank of
            Taiwan, 1962.

Ko Kuo-chi （郭國基）
1958   *Tzu Chih,* 自治 (Self-Government Magazine), Taipei, Jan-
            uary 1.

Liu K'e-ming （劉克明）
1928   *Taiwan Chin Ku T'an* * (Old and New Taiwan), Taipei.

Wang I-t'ao （王益滔）
1964   *Taiwan Chih T'u Ti Chih Tu Yu T'u Ti Cheng Ts'e,*臺灣之
            土地制度與土地政策 (Taiwan's Land System and
            Land Policy), Taipei: Bank of Taiwan.

Wang Ying-ts'eng （王瑛曾）
1764   *Chung Hsiu Feng Shan Hsien Chih,* 重修鳳.山縣志

(Revised ed. of Feng Shan Hsien Gazetteer), Taipei: Republ. by Bank of Taiwan, 1962.

Yu Wen-i (余 文 儀)

1758   *Hsu Hsiu Taiwan Fu Chih,* 續 修 臺 灣 府 志 (Taiwan Fu Gazetteer Cont.), 2 vols.; Taipei: Republ. by Bank of Taiwan, 1962.

ANONYMOUS WORKS

1925   *Pu Yen Chuang Yen Ke Chih* * 埔 鹽 庄 沿 革 誌 (A History of Pu Yen Chuang), found in the Pu Yen Hsiang Public Office, Chang-hua Hsien, unpubl. (handwritten).

———

1910–1911   *Taiwan Szu Fa,** 臺 灣 私 法 (Taiwan's Customs and Laws), 6 vols.; and *Taiwan Szu Fa Fu Lu Ts'an K'ao Shih,** 臺 灣 私 法 附 錄 參 考 書 (Reference as Appendix to Taiwan's Customs and Laws), 7 vols. (partially in Japanese and partially in Chinese), Taipei: Lin Shih Taiwan Chiu Kuan Tiao Ch'a Hui, 臨 時 臺 灣 舊 慣 調 查 會 (Temporary Taiwan Old Customs Survey Association).

———

(1954 ?)   *Women te Lukang Chen,* 我 們 的 鹿 港 鎮 (Our Lukang Chen), found in Chang-hua Hsien Wen K'ai Primary School in Lukang.

INDEX

Administrative setting, 21–23
Adoption, 160–169, 179; girl, 161–163; *siaosiv,* 163–166; boy, 166–168
Adulthood, 214–215
Agriculture, 4, 15, 16, 270, 271; rice cultivation, 12, 13, 16–17, 38–39, 48–52, 55–56, 63–83 *passim,* 112, 176, 177, 200, 251–255 *passim,* 276; three-crop system, 13; sweet potato cultivation, 13, 15, 17, 38–39, 50–51, 61, 64, 65, 77, 112, 240; sorghum, 15; soybeans, 15, 51; marketing of produce, 17, 62–64; consumption of produce, 38–39; *hutze* (interplanting) system, 51; vegetable cultivation, 51–53; sugarcane, 53, 54, 64, 69, 77, 100; mint, 53, 54; cycle, 54–56, 254, 255; implements and machinery, 56–59, 57; animal husbandry, 59–62, 59; Farmers' Association, 69–79; 4-H movement, 71, 72; use of fertilizer, 75–78; agrarian image, 124–125; role of *tsu,* 128, 129; changing patterns of, 276
Ancestor worship, 169, 233–235; *kung t'ing,* 62, 145–148, 220, 239–241, 247; *tsu,* 134–135; ancestral group, 145–149; in event of matrilocal marriage, 157; by adopted sons, 161, 166; *ch'in t'ang,* 169; and funeral rites, 225, 228; as cyclic rite, 247; spirits of unknown dead, 248–249; celebration of Tung Chieh, 255–256
Ancestral halls. *See* Ancestor worship, *kung t'ing*

Barclay, George, 2; on *tsu* groups, 130
Birth, 190–192
Birthrate. *See* Demography
Brokerage: in marketing crops, 63; in contracting labor, 66; as source of extra income, 121

Buddhism, 39, 232, 235; funeral rites, 221
Burial. *See* Death

Calendar: lunar system, 54–55, 248–249; solar system, 55; cyclic rites, 247–256 *passim*
Chang Yen-t'ien, 90, 93, 106; on land ownership, 108–109; on inheritance, 257
Chang-hua, 11, 41, 197; market in, 63
Chang-hua Water Conservation Association, 81
Chi Hu, 12, 45, 154; water buffalo market, 62
Chia (family), 9, 24, 127; land ownership, 109, 111; and socioeconomic mobility, 123–125 *passim;* organization and role in multi-*tsu* villages, 129–133 *passim;* economic, 135, 137–142; stem, 137–142 *passim;* conjugal, 137–142 *passim,* 145–146; joint, 137–142 *passim,* 272; structure, 139; division, 142–145, 272, 273; ancestral group, 145–149; and marriage, 149–160; and adoption, 163–168; interfamily relations, 169–173; size, 188; role of daughter-in-law, 214; need for matrilateral and affinal relations, 275
Chia chang (family head), 138, 162; role, 139, 143; role of wife of, 140; in old age, 216
Chiang Kai-shek, 198
Children, 188; care and training of, 193–195; primary and secondary education, 195–199; adolescence, 199–202
China (mainland), 3, 4, 75, 93, 138, 155, 163, 172, 270, 273, 277, 280, 281
Civil Administration, Department of, 79
Climate, 11–13 *passim*
Clothing, 41–43 *passim*

319